# The Expedition to Borneo of H. M. S. Dido

H.M.S. Dido at Sarawak

# The Expedition to Borneo of H. M. S. Dido

The Royal Navy, Rajah Brooke and
the Malay Pirates & Dyak Headhunters 1843

Henry Keppel

Two volumes in
1 special edition

LEONAUR

*The Expedition to Borneo of H. M. S. Dido*
*The Royal Navy, Rajah Brooke and*
*the Malay Pirates & Dyak Headhunters 1843*
by Henry Keppel
Two volumes in 1 special edition

First published under the title
*The Expedition to Borneo of H. M. S. Dido*


Leonaur is an imprint
of Oakpast Ltd


Copyright in this form © 2010 Oakpast Ltd


ISBN: 978-0-85706-280-2(hardcover)
ISBN: 978-0-85706-279-6 (softcover)


**http://www.leonaur.com**

# Contents

My dear Father,

You could scarcely have anticipated from my profession, the dedication of a book in testimony of my gratitude and affection; but, having had the good fortune to acquire the friendship of Mr. James Brooke, and to be intrusted by him with a narrative of his extraordinary career in that part of the world where the services of the ship I commanded were required, I am not without a hope that the accompanying pages may be found worthy of your approval, and not altogether uninteresting to my country.

I am, my dear father,

Your affectionate son,

Henry Keppel.

Droxford, January, 1846.

# Preface

The visit of Her Majesty's ship *Dido* to Borneo, and her services against the pirates, occupy comparatively so small a portion of this volume, that some excuse may be necessary for its leading title.

It was only by undertaking to make the account of them part of the narrative, that I could prevail upon my friend Mr. Brooke to intrust me with his *Journal* for any public object; and when I looked at his novel and important position as a ruler in Borneo, and was aware how much of European curiosity was attached to it, I felt it impossible not to consent to an arrangement which should enable me to trace the remarkable career through which he had reached that elevation. I hope, therefore, to be considered as having conquered my own disinclination to be the relater of events in which I was concerned, in order to overcome the scruples which he entertained against being the author of the autobiographical sketch, embracing so singular a portion of his life, which I have extracted from the rough notes confided to me.

That his diffidence in this respect was groundless will, I trust, be apparent from these pages, however indifferently I may have executed my unusual task, during a long homeward sea-voyage; and, from the growing interest which has arisen throughout the country for intelligence on the subject of Borneo and the adjacent *archipelago*, I venture also to indulge the belief that the general information will be deemed no unfit adjunct to the story of personal adventure.

H. K.

Droxford, January, 1846.

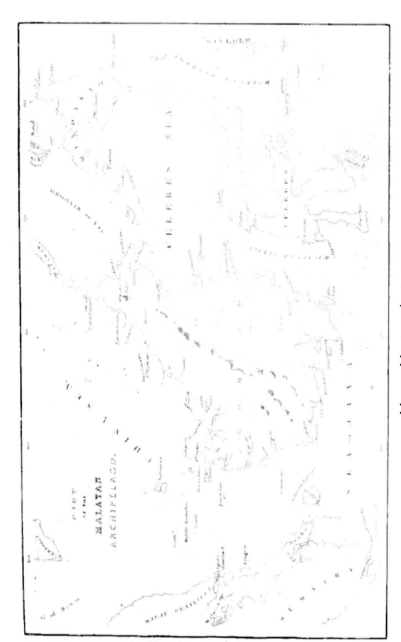

Map of Malayan Arcipelago

# CHAPTER 1

# Arrival off the Coast of Borneo

At the conclusion of the Chinese war, the commander-in-chief, Vice-Admiral Sir William Parker, ordered the *Dido* to the Malacca Straits, a station in which was included the island of Borneo; our principal duties being the protection of trade, and suppression of piracy.

In the month of March, 1843, while at Pinang, I received intimation from the governor of various daring acts of piracy having been committed near the Borneon coast on some vessels trading to Singapore. I proceeded to that port; and, while undergoing a partial refit, made the acquaintance of Mr. Brooke, who accepted my invitation to return to Sarawak in the *Dido*; and I could not have visited Borneo with a more agreeable or intelligent companion.

The objects of Mr. Brooke in leaving England, the reasons which induced him to settle at Sarawak, and the circumstances which have led him to take so deep an interest in promoting the civilization and improving the condition of the singular people whom he has adopted, form indeed a story very unlike the common course of events in modern times.

But before illustrating these circumstances from his own journals, it may be acceptable to say a few words respecting the individual himself, and his extraordinary career. I am indebted to a mutual friend, acquainted with him from early years, for the following brief but interesting outline of his life; and have only to premise, that Mr. Brooke is the lineal representative of Sir Robert Vyner, baronet, and lord mayor of London in the reign of Charles II.; Sir Robert had but one child, a son, Sir George Vyner, who died childless, and his estate passed to his heir-at-law, Edith, his father's eldest sister, whose lineal descendant is our friend. Sir Robert was renowned for his loyalty to his sovereign, to whom he devoted his wealth, and to whose memory he raised a monument.

"Mr. Brooke was the second, and is now the only surviving son of the late Thomas Brooke, Esq., of the civil service of the East India Company; was born on the 29th April, 1803; went out to India as a cadet, where he held advantageous situations, and distinguished himself by his gallantry in the Burmese war. He was shot through the body in an action with the Burmese, received the thanks of the government, and returned to England for the recovery of his prostrated strength. He resumed his station, but shortly afterward relinquished the service, and in search of health and amusement left Calcutta for China in 1830. In this voyage, while going up the China seas, he saw for the first time the islands of the Asiatic Archipelago—islands of vast importance and unparalleled beauty—lying neglected, and almost unknown. He inquired and read, and became convinced that Borneo and the Eastern Isles afforded an open field for enterprise and research.

"To carry to the Malay races, so long the terror of the European merchant-vessels, the blessings of civilization, to suppress piracy, and extirpate the slave-trade, became his humane and generous objects; and from that hour the energies of his powerful mind were devoted to this one pursuit. Often foiled, often disappointed, but animated with a perseverance and enthusiasm which defied all obstacle, he was not until 1838 enabled to set sail from England on his darling project.

"The intervening years had been devoted to preparation and inquiry; a year spent in the Mediterranean had tested his vessel, the *Royalist*, and his crew; and so completely had he studied his subject and calculated on contingencies, that the least sanguine of his friends felt as he left the shore, hazardous and unusual as the enterprise appeared to be, that he had omitted nothing to insure a successful issue. 'I go,' said he, 'to awake the spirit of slumbering philanthropy with regard to these islands; to carry Sir Stamford Raffles' views in Java over the whole archipelago. Fortune and life I give freely; and if I fail in the attempt, I shall not have lived wholly in vain.'

"In the admiration I feel for him, I may farther be permitted to add, that if any man ever possessed in himself the resources and means by which such noble designs were to be achieved, that man was James Brooke! Of the most enlarged views; truthful and generous; quick to acquire and appreciate; excelling in every manly sport and exercise; elegant and accomplished; ever accessible; and above all, prompt and determined to redress injury and relieve misfortune, he was of all others the best qualified to impress the native mind with the highest opinion of the English character. How he has succeeded, the influence he has acquired, and the benefits he has conferred, his own uncoloured narrative, contained in the following pages, best declares, and impresses on the world a lasting lesson of the good that attends individual enterprise, when well directed, of which every Englishman may feel justly proud."

Such is the sketch of Mr. Brooke by one well competent to judge of that to which he bears witness. In pursuance of the mission thus eloquently and truly described, that gentleman left his native shores in the year 1838, in his yacht the *Royalist* schooner, of 142 tons, belonging to the Royal Yacht Squadron, with a crew of upward of twenty men. His general views were distinct and certain; but the details into which they shaped themselves have been so entirely guided by unforeseen occurrences, that it is necessary to look to his first visit to Borneo for their explanation; and in order to do so, I must refer to his private journal, which he kindly confided to me, after I had in vain tried to persuade him to take upon himself the publication of its contents, so rich in new and interesting intelligence

### EXTRACTS FROM MR. BROOKE'S JOURNAL

"I had for some years turned my mind to the geography of the Indian Archipelago, and cherished an ardent desire to become better acquainted with a country combining the richest natural productions with an unrivalled degree of luxuriant beauty. Circumstances for a time prevented my entering on this field for enterprise and research; and when the barriers were removed, I had many preparations to make and some difficulties to overcome.

"In an expedition conducted by government, the line of discipline is so distinctly understood, and its infringement so strictly punished, that small hazard is incurred of any inconvenience arising from such a source. With an individual, however, there is no such assurance, for he cannot appeal to the articles of war; and the ordinary legal enactments for the protection of the mariner will not enable him to effect objects so far removed beyond the scope of the laws. I was fully aware that many would go, but that few might stay; for while a voyage of discovery *in prospectu* possesses great attractions for the imagination, the hardship, danger, and thousand other rude realities, soon dissipate the illusion, and leave the aspirant longing for that home he should never have quitted. In like manner, seamen can be procured in abundance, but cannot be kept from desertion whenever any matter goes wrong;

and the total previous ignorance of their characters and dispositions renders this more likely, as the admission of one 'black sheep' goes far to taint the entire crew.

"These considerations fully convinced me that it was necessary to form *men* to my purpose, and, by a line of steady and kind conduct, to raise up a personal regard for myself and attachment for the vessel, which could not be expected in ordinary cases. In pursuance of this object, I was nearly three years in preparing a crew to my mind, and gradually moulding them to consider the hardest fate or misfortune under my command as better than the ordinary service in a merchant-vessel. How far I have succeeded remains yet to be proved; but I cannot help hoping that I have raised the character of many, and have rendered all happy and contented since they have been with me; and certain am I that no men can do their duty more cheerfully or willingly than the crew of the *Royalist*.

"I may pass over in silence my motives for undertaking so long and arduous a voyage; and it will be sufficient to say, that I have been firmly convinced of its beneficial tendency in adding to knowledge, increasing trade, and spreading Christianity. The prospectus of the undertaking was published in the *Geographical Journal*, vol. 8 part 3, of 1838, when my preparations for sea were nearly complete. I had previously avoided making any public mention of my intentions, for praise before performance is disgusting; and I knew I should be exposed to prying curiosity, desirous of knowing what I did not know myself.

"On the 27th October, 1838, the *Royalist* left the river; and, after a succession of heavy gales, finally quitted the land on the 16th December. I may here state some farther particulars, to enable my readers to become better acquainted with her and her equipment. The *Royalist*, as already noticed, belonged to the Royal Yacht Squadron, which in foreign ports admits her to the same privileges as a man-of-war, and enables her to carry a white ensign. She sails fast, is conveniently fitted up, is armed with six six-pounders, a number of swivels, and small arms of all sorts, carries four boats, and provisions for four months. Her principal defect is being too sharp in the floor, which, in case of taking the ground, greatly increases the risk; but I comfort myself with the reflection that a knowledge of this will lead to redoubled precaution to prevent such a disaster. She is withal a good sea-boat, and as well calculated for the service as could be desired.

"Most of her hands had been with me for three years or upward, and the rest were highly recommended. They are, almost without exception, young, able-bodied, and active—fit in all respects for enduring hardship and privation, or the more dangerous reverse of self-indulgence, and willing to follow the fortunes of the *Royalist* and her commander through all the various shades of good or evil fortune which may betide. A fine, though slow passage took us to Rio Janeiro, which presents features of natural beauty rarely equalled. The weather during our stay was hot in the extreme, and very wet, which marred, in some degree, the satisfaction I should otherwise have enjoyed in wandering about this picturesque country. I passed ten days, however, very agreeably, and departed with some regret from this brief visit to America and from my friends (if they will so allow me to call them) on board H.M.S. *Calliope.*

"I must not omit to mention that, during my stay, I visited a slaver, three of which (prizes to our men-of-war) lay in the harbour. It is a most loathsome and disgusting sight. Men, women, and children—the aged and the infant—crowded into a space as confined as the pens in Smithfield, not, however, to be released by death at the close of the day, but to linger, diseased and festering, for weeks or months, and then to be discharged into perpetual and hopeless slavery. I wish I could say that our measures tended toward the abolition of this detestable traffic; but from all that I could learn and observe, I am forced to confess that the exertions made to abolish slavery are of no avail in this country, and never will be till harsher means are resorted to.

"There are points of view in which this traffic wears a more cheering aspect; for any one comparing the puny Portuguese or the bastard Brazilian with the athletic negro, cannot but allow that the ordinary changes and chances of time will place this fine country in the hands of the latter race. The negro will be fit to cultivate the soil, and will thrive beneath the tropical sun of the Brazils. The enfeebled white man grows more enfeebled and more degenerate with each succeeding generation, and languishes in a clime which nature never designed him to inhabit. The time will come when the debased and suffering negroes shall possess this fertile land, and when some share of justice shall be awarded to their cheerful tempers and ardent minds.

"Quitting Rio on the 9th, we cruised for a day or two with H.M.S. *Calliope* and *Grecian*; and on the 11th, parting company, prosecuted our voyage for the Cape of Good Hope."

The next notice runs thus:—

"The aspect of Tristan d'Acunha is bold even to grandeur. The

15

peak, towering upward of eight thousand feet above the sea, is inferior only to Teneriffe, and the precipitous cliffs overhanging the beach are a fitting base for such a mountain. I regretted not being able to examine this island for many reasons, but principally, perhaps, on account of the birds of the South Atlantic I had hoped to collect there, many of which are so often seen by voyagers, yet so little known and so vaguely described.

"On the 29th March, after being detained a fortnight [at the Cape of Good Hope] by such weather as no one could regret, we sailed again in a southeaster, and after a passage of six weeks reached Java Head.

"I had been suffering for some time under a severe indisposition, and consequently hailed the termination of our voyage with double satisfaction, for I greatly required rest and quiet—two things impossible to be had on ship-board. From Java Head we glided slowly through Prince's Strait, and coasting along the island, dropped our anchor in Anjer Roads. The scenery of this coast is extremely lovely, and comprises every feature which can heighten the picturesque; noble mountains, a lake-like sea, and deeply indented coast-line, rocks, islets, and, above all, a vegetation so luxuriant that the eye never wearies with gazing on its matchless tints. Anjer combines all these beauties, and possesses the incalculable advantage of being within a moderate ride of the refreshing coolness of the hills.

"We here procured water and provisions in abundance, being daily visited by crowds of canoes filled with necessaries or curiosities. Fowls, eggs, yams, cocoa-nuts, and sweet potatoes, were mixed with monkeys of various sorts, paroquets, squirrels, shells, and similar temptations on the stranger's purse or wardrobe. Great was the bartering for old clothes, handkerchiefs, and hats; and great the number of useless and noisy animals we received in exchange. Great, too, was the merriment aboard, and the excitement when the canoes first came. The transition from the monotony of a sea-life to the loquacious bustle of barter with a half-civilized people is so sudden, that the mind at once feels in a strange land, and the commonest productions proclaim the luxuriant climes of the tropics. Until this impression is made, we hardly know why we have been sailing onward for four months past, so quiet and unvarying is the daily tenor of a life aboard ship.

"*1st June, Singapore.*—On reaching Singapore I was most hospitably received by the kind inhabitants, and took up my abode with Mr. Scott. The quiet and repose of my present life, the gentle ride in

16

the cool of the morning and evening drive after an early dinner, are already restoring my shattered strength, and I trust soon to be enabled to prosecute my farther undertaking. In the mean time the *Royalist* is undergoing a refit after her passage, and, like her owner, is daily improving in good looks.

"I could say much of Singapore, for it is the pivot of the liberal system in the Archipelago, and owes its prosperity to the enlightened measures of Sir Stamford Raffles. The situation is happily chosen, the climate healthy, the commerce unshackled, and taxation light; and these advantages have attracted the vessels of all the neighbouring nations to bring their produce to this market in order to exchange it for the manufactures of England.

"The extent of the island is about 27 miles by 11 broad. The town of Singapore stands on the south side, facing the shores of Battam, and is intersected by a salt-water stream, which separates the native town from the pleasant residences of the European inhabitants; the latter stretch along the beach, and cover a space which extends to the foot of a slight eminence, on which stands the governor's house. Off the town lie the shipping of various countries, presenting a most picturesque and striking appearance. The man-of-war, the steamer, and the merchant-vessels of the civilized world, contrast with the huge, misshapen, and bedizened arks of China! The awkward *prahus* of the Bugis are surrounded by the light boats of the island. The semi-civilized Cochin-Chinese, with their vessels of antiquated European construction, deserve attention from this important step toward improvement; and the rude *prahus* of some parts of Borneo claim it from their exhibiting the early dawn of maritime adventure.

"*27th July.*—After various causes of delay I sailed on this day from Singapore. When I contrast my state of health at my arrival with what it now is, I may well be thankful for the improvement. Every kindness and hospitality has been shown me.

"On Saturday at noon we got under weigh with a light breeze, and stood down the Strait on our way to Borneo.

"*28th.*—In the morning we were well out in the China Sea, running six knots per hour, N. ¾ E. Lines of discoloured water were seen about us, and about 11 a.m. we entered a field some two miles long and 400 yards wide. The consistence of this dirty mass was that of peasoup, which it likewise resembled in colour; and I doubt not the white water of the China Sea (*vide Nautical Magazine*) is referable to this appearance seen in the night, as may the report of rocks, &c. The Malays on board called it '*sara,*' and declared it to come from the rivers. On examination it appeared, when magnified, somewhat like a grain of barley or corn. The particles were extremely minute, soft, and, when rubbed between the fingers, emitted a strong smell like paint-oil; a potent odour arose while passing through the thick patch.

"It may not be superfluous to recount here the preparations I have made for this trip to Borneo, or my intentions when I get there. Borneo Proper, once the seat of piracy, which few vessels could approach with safety, is now under the sway of the Rajah Muda Hassim. The character given this *rajah* by many persons who know and have traded with him is good, and he is spoken of as generous and humane, and greatly inclined to the English. These reasons have induced me to abandon my intention of proceeding direct to Malludu Bay, and during the season of the southwest monsoon to confine myself principally to the northwest coast. Muda Hassim being at present reported to be at Sarawak, I propose, after taking a running sketch of the coast from Tanjong Api, to enter the river of that name, and proceed as far as the town.

"I believe I have availed myself of every means within my reach to render my visit agreeable to the *rajah*. I carry with me many presents which are reported to be to his liking; gaudy silks of Surat, scarlet cloth, stamped velvet, gunpowder, &c., beside a large quantity of confectionery and sweets, such as preserved ginger, jams, dates, syrups, and to wind up all, a huge box of China toys for his children! I have likewise taken coarse nankeen to the amount of 100*l.* value, as the best circulating medium in the country. Beside the above mentioned preparations, I carry letters from the government of Singapore, to state, as far as can be done, the objects of my voyage, and to caution the *rajah* to take every care of my safety and that of my men. The Board of Commerce have at the same time entrusted me with a letter and present to him, to thank him for his humanity to the crew of an English vessel wrecked on this coast.

"The story, as I had it from the parties shipwrecked, is highly creditable to his humanity. The vessel, called the *Napoleon*, was wrecked on the bar of Sarawak River in the northeast monsoon. The people were saved with difficulty, and remained in the jungle, where they were after a time discovered by some Malays. Muda Hassim, on receiving intelligence of this, sent down and brought them to his town, collected all that he could recover from the wreck, clothed them handsomely, and fed them well for several months, and, on an opportunity arriving, sent them back to Singapore free of expense.

"At the same time, however, that I have prepared to meet the natives as friends, I have not neglected to strengthen my crew, in case I should find them hostile. Eight stout men of the Ourang Laut, or men of the sea (Malays), have been added to the force. They are an athletic race, cheerful and willing; and though not seaman in our sense of the term, yet well calculated for this expedition. They pull a good oar, and are invaluable in saving the Europeans the exposure consequent to wooding and watering. They possess, likewise, the knowledge of the jungle and its resources, and two of them have before been to Sarawak and along the coast.

"Beside these, a young gentleman named Williamson accompanies me as interpreter; and I have fortunately met with a medical gentleman, Mr. Westermann, a Dane, who is surgeon for this voyage, Mr. Williams having left me at Singapore. With these arrangements I look without apprehension to the power of the Malays; and without relaxing in measures of the strictest vigilance, I shall never sleep less soundly when it comes to my turn so to do.

"*August 1st.*—I am, then, at length, anchored off the coast of Borneo! not under very pleasant circumstances, for the night is pitchy dark, with thunder, lightning, rain, and squalls of wind.

"*2nd.*—Squally bad night. This morning, the clouds clearing away, was delightful, and offered for our view the majestic scenery of Borneo. At nine got under weigh, and ran in on an east-by-south course 4½ or 5 miles toward Tanjong Api. Came to an anchor about five miles from the land, and dispatched the boat to take sights ashore, in order to form a base-line for triangulation. The scenery may really be called majestic. The low and wooded coast about Tanjong Api is backed by a mountain called Gunong[1] Palo, some 2000 feet in height, which slopes down behind the point and terminates in a number of hummocks, showing from a distance like islands.

"The coast, unknown, and represented to abound in shoals and reefs, is the harbour for pirates of every description. Here, every man's hand is raised against his brother man; and here sometimes the climate wars upon the excitable European, and lays many a white face and gallant heart low on the distant strand.

"*3rd.*—Beating between Points Api and Datu. The bay, as far as we

---

1. Gunong, a mountain, part of a chain.

19

have seen, is free from danger; the beach is lined by a feathery row of beautiful casuarinas, and behind is a tangled jungle, without fine timber; game is plentiful, from the traces we saw on the sand; hogs in great numbers, troops of monkeys, and the print of an animal with cleft hoofs, either a large deer, tapir, or cow. We saw no game save a tribe of monkeys, one of which, a female, I shot, and another quite young, which we managed to capture alive. The captive, though the young of the black monkey, is grayish, with the exception of his extremities, and a stripe of black down his back and tail. Though very young, he has already taken food, and we have some hope of preserving his life.

"We witnessed, at the same time, an extraordinary and fatal leap made by one of these monkeys. Alarmed by our approach, he sprang from the summit of a high tree at the branch of one lower, and at some distance. He leaped short, and came clattering down some sixty or seventy feet amid the jungle. We were unable to penetrate to the spot on account of a deep swamp to ascertain his fate.

"A rivulet flows into the sea not far from where we landed; the water is sweet, and of that clear brown colour so common in Ireland. This coast is evidently the haunt of native *prahus*, whether piratical or other. Prints of men's feet were numerous and fresh, and traces of huts, fires, and parts of boats, some of them ornamented after their rude fashion. A long pull of five miles closed the day.

"*Sunday, 4th.*—Performed divine service myself! manfully overcoming that horror which I have to the sound of my own voice before an audience. In the evening landed again more to the westward. Shore skirted by rocks; timber noble, and the forest clear of brushwood, enabling us to penetrate with ease as far as caution permitted. Traces of wild beasts numerous and recent, but none discovered. Fresh-water streams, coloured as yesterday, and the trail of an alligator from one of them to the sea. This dark forest, where the trees shoot up straight and tall, and are succeeded by generation after generation varying in stature, but struggling upward, strikes the imagination with pictures trite yet true. Here the hoary sage of a hundred years lies mouldering beneath your foot, and there the young sapling shoots beneath the parent shade, and grows in form and fashion like the parent stem.

"The towering few, with heads raised above the general mass, can scarce be seen through the foliage of those beneath; but here and there the touch of time has cast his withering hand upon their leafy brow, and decay has begun his work upon the gigantic and unbending trunk. How trite and yet how true! It was thus I meditated in my walk.

The foot of European, I said, has never touched where my foot now presses—seldom the native wanders here. Here I indeed behold nature fresh from the bosom of creation, unchanged by man, and stamped with the same impress she originally bore! Here I behold God's design when He formed this tropical land, and left its culture and improvement to the agency of man. The Creator's gift as yet neglected by the creature; and yet the time may be confidently looked for when the axe shall level the forest, and the plow turn the ground.

"*6th.*—Made sail this morning, and stood in for an island called Talang Talang, anchoring about eight miles distant, and sending a boat to take correct observations for a base-line.

"Our party found Malays of Sarawak on the island, who were civil to them, and offered to conduct us up tomorrow, if we wanted their assistance. The pirates, both Illanuns and Dyaks, have been gone from the bay but a few days; the former seaward, the latter up the rivers.

"*7th.*—Morning calm. In the afternoon got under weigh, and anchored again near the island of Talang Talang; the smaller one a conical hill bearing south. The *bandar*² of the place came off in his canoe to make us welcome. He is a young man sent by Rajah Muda Hassim to collect turtles' eggs, which abound in this vicinity, especially on the larger island. The turtles are never molested, for fear of their deserting the spot; and their eggs, to the amount of five or six thousand, are collected every morning and forwarded at intervals to Sarawak as articles of food.

"Our visitor was extremely polite, and, in common with other Asiatics, possessed the most pleasing and easy manners. He assured us of a welcome from his *rajah*, and, in their usual phrase, expressed himself that the *rajah's* heart would dilate in his bosom at the sight of us. His dress consisted of trowsers of green cloth, a dark green velvet jacket, and his sarong round his waist, thrown gracefully over two *krisses*, which he wore at his girdle. His attendants were poorly attired, and mostly unarmed—a proof of confidence in us, and a desire to assure us of his own friendly intentions. I treated him with sweetmeats and syrup, and of his own accord he took a glass of sherry, as did his chief attendant. On his departure he was presented with three yards of red cloth, and subsequently with a little tea and gunpowder."

---

2. Pronounced short, for (properly) *bandhara*; a treasurer, chief steward.

# CHAPTER 2

# Excursion to Dyak Tribes

I Resume Mr. Brooke's *Journal*, which requires no introductory remark.

"*Aug. 8th.*—A cloudy day, preventing us from taking our wished-for observations. I made a boat-excursion round the two islands. The north one is somewhat the larger; the southern one, running north and south, consists of two hills joined by a low and narrow neck of land. The water between these islands is deep, varying from seven to six fathoms; but between the smaller one and the main there are rocks and reefs; and though a passage may exist, it would not be advisable for a vessel to try it. These two small islands possess all the characteristic beauties of the clime. Formed of brown granite, with a speck of white sandy beach, and rising into hills covered with the noblest timber, wreathed with gigantic creepers.

"Cream-coloured pigeons flit from tree to tree, and an eagle or two soared aloft watching their motions. Frigate-birds are numerous; and several sorts of smaller birds in the bush, difficult to get at. A small species of crocodile, or alligator, was likewise seen: but we were not fortunate enough to shoot one. The natives, when asked whether they were alligators, answered in the negative, calling them crocodiles. The tides appear to be as irregular as tides usually are in a deep bay. The rise and fall of the tide is about fifteen feet.

"*9th.*—After breakfast this morning took our sights, and at twelve o'clock the latitude of the smaller Talang Talang and the ship for a base-line. We yesterday took the same base-line by sound, firing alternately three guns from the vessel and three from the shore.

"*10th.*—A squall from the northward brought in a chopping sea in the morning. We were favored with a visit from another native party, but the chief was in every respect inferior to our first acquaintance, Bandar Dowat.

"*11th Sunday.*—Got under weigh early, after a night of torrents of rain. The breeze being directly out of Lundu River, I stood as near it as I could, and then bore away for Santobong, in order to reach Sarawak. From Gunong Gading the coast gradually declines, and forms two points. The first of these is Tanjong Bloungei, near which, on the right hand, runs a small river, of the same name. The next point is Tanjong Datu, which shows prominently from most parts of the bay. From Tanjong Datu the coast recedes into a bay, and again forms a low point, which I have christened Tanjong Lundu. The River Lundu disembogues itself into the bay just beyond the point of the same name; and the land on its far bank forms a bight of considerable depth. The Lundu is a barred river with but little water; though, judging from the opening, it is by no means small. Our pilots inform me at the same time, however, that within the bar there is considerable depth of water.

"From the Sungei Lundu the land rises behind a wooded beach. The first hill, which may be said to form the larboard entrance of the river, is peaked, and called Sumpudin, and near it is a barred river of the same name. This range of high land runs some distance; and near its termination is the river Tamburgan. The low coast runs into another bight; and the first opening after the termination of the high land is the mouth of the river Seboo. Then comes another river; after which the land rises into hills, gradually larger, till they terminate in a round-topped hill, which forms the starboard entrance (going in) of the Sarawak River.

"This river discharges itself at the east corner of the bay; and its locality is easily recognized by the highest peak of Santobong, which towers over its left bank, close to the entrance. A ship rounding Datu will readily perceive the high land of Santobong, showing like a large island, with another smaller island at its northern extremity. Both these, however, are attached to the main: and the northernmost point, called Tanjong Sipang, is distinguished by two peaks, like horns, one small, the other larger. Steer from Datu a direct course toward this high land, and when within a mile and a half or two miles of the shore, haul in along the land, as there is a sand nearly dry at low water on the starboard hand, stretching from the shore to the Saddle island, or Pulo Satang.

"The leading mark to clear this sand is to bring the hollow formed

23

between the round hill at the right entrance of the Sarawak River and the next hill a-head, and as you approach the river's mouth, steer for a small island close to the shore, called Pulo Karra, or Monkey Island. These marks will conduct you over a shoal with ¼ three, the least depth at high water; you will then deepen your water, and keep away for the low green point on the far side of the river, edging gradually in; and when you are some distance from the opposite low point on the port hand, cross the bar in three fathom (high water) nearly in the centre of the river.

"You must not, however, encroach on the larboard side. The bar is narrow, and just within is 7 and 7½ fathom, where we are at present anchored. The scenery is noble. On our left hand is the peak of Santobong, clothed in verdure nearly to the top; at his foot a luxuriant vegetation, fringed with the *casuarina*, and terminating in a beach of white sand. The right bank of the river is low, covered with pale green mangroves, with the round hill above mentioned just behind it. Santobong peak is 2050 feet, or thereabouts, by a rough trigonometrical measurement.

"*12th.*—Lay at anchor; took angles and observations, and shot in the evening without any success. There is a fine species of large pigeon of a gray colour I was desirous of getting, but they were too cunning. Plenty of wild hogs were seen, but as shy as though they had been fired at all their lives. When the flood made, dispatched my gig for Sarawak, in order to acquaint the *rajah* of my arrival.

"*13th.*—Got under weigh, and in the second reach met our gig returning, followed by a large canoe, with a *pangeran* of note to welcome us. We gave him a salute of five guns; while he, on his part, assured us of his *rajah's* pleasure at our arrival, and his own desire to be of service. With the Pangeran Oula Deen (or Illudeen, *anglicè* Aladdin), came the *rajah's* chief writer, his *shroff*, a renegade Parsee, a war-captain, and some others, beside a score of followers. They made themselves much at home, ate and drank (the less scrupulous took wine), and conversed with ease and liveliness. No difference can be more marked than between the Hindoostani and the Malay. The former, though more self-possessed and polished, shows a constraint in manners and conversation, and you feel that his training has made him an artificial character. The Malay, on the contrary, concealing as well the feelings upper-most in his mind, is lively and intelligent, and his conversation is not confined to a dull routine of unmeaning compliments.

24

JUNGLE NEAR SANTOBONG

"*August 13th.*—The *pangeran* spoke to me of some ship-captain who was notoriously cruel to his lascars, and insolent in his language to the Malays. He was murdered by his crew, and the circumstance was related to me as though I was to approve the act! 'No Malay of Borneo (added the *pangeran*) would injure a European, were he well treated, and in a manner suitable to his rank.' And I am sure such a declaration, in a limited sense, is consonant with all known principles of human nature, and the action of the passions and feelings.

"Our *pangeran* was quite the gentleman, and a manly gentleman too. His dress was a black velvet jacket, trimmed with gold lace, and trowsers of green cloth, with a red *sarong* and *kris*. He was the only one of the party armed while aboard. The rest were good, quiet men, and one or two of them very intelligent. They took their leave of us to get back to the town at sunset; but the ebb making, returned and stayed until twelve at night, when the tide turned in their favor. We had some difficulty in providing beds. The *pangeran* slept in my cabin, and the rest were distributed about on couches or carpets.

"*August 14th.*—Got under weigh with the flood, and, favoured by a light breeze, proceeded up the river nearly as far as the town. From the ignorance of the pilots, however, we grounded on a rock in the middle of the river in 1½ fathom water, and it took us an hour to heave the vessel off by the stern. Had the tide been falling, we should have been in a critical situation, as the rock is dry at low water; but as it was, we received no damage. Shortly after getting off, several boats with assistance came from the place, dispatched in haste by the *rajah*. The intention was kind, though we needed not the aid. Being dark, we dropped anchor in 5½ fathom, about 1½ mile from the town.

"*15th.*—Anchored abreast of Sarawak at seven, and saluted the *rajah* with twenty-one guns, which were returned with eighteen from his residence. The *rajah's* own brother, Pangeran Mahammed, then saluted the vessel with seven guns, which were returned. Having breakfasted, and previously intimated our intention, we pulled ashore to visit the great man. He received us in state, seated in his hall of audience, which outside is nothing but a large shed, erected on piles, but within decorated with taste. Chairs were placed on each side of the ruler, who occupied the head seat. Our party were placed on one hand; on the other sat his brother Mahammed, and Macota and some others of his principal chiefs, while immediately behind him his twelve younger brothers were seated.

"The dress of Muda Hassim was simple, but of rich material; and most of the principal men were well, and even superbly, dressed. His countenance is plain, but intelligent and highly pleasing, and his manners perfectly elegant and easy. His reception was kind, and, I am given to understand, highly flattering. We sat, however, trammelled with the formality of state, and our conversation did not extend beyond kind inquiries and professions of friendship. We were presented with tobacco rolled up in a leaf, each about a foot long, and tea was served by attendants on their knees. A band played wild and not unmusical airs during the interview, and the crowd of attendants who surrounded us were seated in respectful silence. After a visit of half an hour, we rose and took our leave.

"Sarawak is but an occasional residence of the Rajah Muda Hassim, and he is now detained here by a rebellion in the interior. On my inquiring whether *the war* proceeded favourably, he replied that there was *no war*, but merely *some child's play among his subjects*. From what I hear, however, from other quarters, it is more serious than he represents it; and hints have been thrown out that the *rajah* wishes me to stay here *as a demonstration* to intimidate the rebels. We shall see.

"The town consists of a collection of mud huts erected on piles, and may contain about 1500 persons. The residences of the *rajah* and his fourteen brothers occupy the greater part, and their followers are the great majority of the population. When they depart for Borneo (or Bruni), the remainder must be a very small population, and apparently very poor. The river affords a few fish; but there is little sign of cultivation either of rice or other grain. Fowls and goats seem the only other means of subsistence of these people. The geological features of the country are easily described. Vast masses of granite rock are scattered along the coast; for instance, Gunong Poe, Gading, Santobong, &c. &c., which have evidently at some former period been detached islands.

"The spaces between these granite masses is now filled in with alluvial soil, intersected in every direction with rivers and streams, and on the low alluvial bank of the Sarawak River stands this little town. The distance from the sea is about twenty-five miles, through banks of mangrove and the Nepa palm, until approaching the town, where some jungle-trees first appear. The breadth is about 100 yards, and the depth six fathoms at low water spring-tides in mid river opposite the *rajah's* residence. In some places below, the river is narrower, and the depths considerable, varying from three to seven fathoms. The

The Rajah Muda Hassim

prominent points, however, are shallow, and the rocks below the town lie on the starboard hand coming up just as the first houses appear in sight. The larboard hand should then be kept close aboard. Some other rocks are likewise reported; and in ascending the stream, though it be generally clear, a vessel *with* or without a pilot should have a boat a-head sounding. In the evening I went ashore suddenly to pay a visit to the *rajah*, in order, if possible, to break through the bonds of formality.

"The great man soon made his appearance, and received us very well. We talked much of the state of his country and of ours; but he was very guarded when I spoke of the Dutch. 'He had no dealings whatever (he said) with them, and never allowed their vessels to come here, and therefore could not say what they were like.' We sat in easy and unreserved converse, out of hearing of the rest of the circle. He expressed great kindness to the English nation; and begged me to tell him *really* which was the most powerful nation, England or Holland, or, as he significantly expressed it, which is the 'cat, and which the rat?' I assured him that England was the mouser, though in this country Holland had most territory. We took our leave after he had intimated his intention of visiting us tomorrow morning.

"*16th.*—We were ready to receive the *rajah* after breakfast; but these affairs of state are not so easily managed. There came two diplomatists on board to know, in the first place, how many guns we intended to salute with, and, in the second, whether I would go ashore in my gig, in order to fetch the chief and his brother off. The latter request I might have refused, and in a diplomatic light it was inadmissible; but I readily conceded it, because, in the first place, it was less troublesome than a refusal; and, in the next, I cared not to bandy paltry etiquettes with a semi-savage; and whatever pride might whisper, I could not, as an individual traveller, refuse an acknowledgment of the supremacy of a native prince. I went accordingly.

"The great man came on board, and we treated him with every distinction and respect. Much barbaric state was maintained as he quitted his own residence. His sword of state with a gold scabbard, his war-shield, jewel-hilted *kris*, and flowing *horse*-tails, were separately carried by the grand officers of state. Bursts of wild music announced his exit. His fourteen brothers and principal *pangeran*s surrounded him, and a number (formidable on the deck of a vessel) covered the rear. He stayed two hours and a half; ate and drank, and talked with great familiarity; till the oppressive heat of the crowded cabin caused me to wish them all to another place. However, he departed at last, under a salute of twenty-one guns; and the fatigues of the day were satisfactorily brought to a close. I afterward sent the *rajah* the presents I had brought for him, consisting of a silk sarong, some yards of red cloth and velvet, a pocket-pistol, scissors and knives, with tea, biscuits, sweetmeats, China playthings, &c. &c.

"A person coming here should be provided with a few articles of small importance to satisfy the crowd of inferior chiefs. Soap, small parcels of tea, lucifers, writing-paper, a large stock of cigars, biscuits, and knives, are the best; for, without being great beggars, they seem greatly to value these trifles, even in the smallest quantity. The higher class inquired frequently for scents; and for the great men I know no present which would be more acceptable than a small pier-glass. All ranks seemed greatly pleased with those aboard; and some of the lower orders, quite ignorant of the reflection, were continually laughing, moving, sitting, and rising, to observe the corresponding effect.

"*18th.*—In the morning I intimated my intention of paying a visit to the Pangeran Muda Mahammed; and being apprised of his readiness to see us, I went ashore to his house. He was not, however, in the room to receive us; nor, indeed, was I much surprised at this slight, for he is a sulky-looking, ill-favoured savage, with a debauched appearance, and wanting in the intelligence of his brother the *rajah*. I seated myself, however, and remained some time; but the delay exceeding what I considered the utmost limit of due forbearance, I expressed to the Pangeran Macota my regret that his compeer was not ready to receive me, adding that, as I was not accustomed to be kept waiting, I would return to my vessel. I spoke in the quietest tone imaginable, rose from my seat, and moved away; but the assembled *pangerans*, rising likewise, assured me it was a mistake; that he was not yet dressed, and would greatly regret it himself. I repeated that when I visited the *rajah*, he received me in the hall.

"While this brief discussion passed, the culprit Muda Mahammed appeared and apologized for his remissness, assuring me that the error was his attendants', who told him I was not coming for an hour. The excuse of course passed current, though false, as excuses generally are. I vindicated my independence, not until it was necessary; and I am well aware that any endeavour of a native to commit an indirect rudeness, if met with firmness and gentleness, always recoils on his own head. The routine of the visit resembled our last—tea, cigars, complimentary conversation and departure. The *pangeran* afterward sent me a present of fowls and goats, and I was right glad to have it over. Muda Mahammed is the 'own' brother to Muda Hassim, and next in rank here. As yet I had not made any request to the *rajah* to allow me to visit various parts of his country; but thinking the time to do so was come (the ceremonial of arrival being past), I sent Mr. Williamson, my interpreter, to express my wish to travel to some of the Malay towns and into the country of the Dyaks.

"The latter request I fully expected, would be evaded, and was therefore the more pleased when an answer came giving a cheerful consent to my going among the Dyaks of Lundu, and visiting the towns of Sadung, Samarahan, &c. At the same time the *rajah* informed me, that if I went up the river, he could not be answerable for my safety, as the rebels were not far distant, and constantly on the watch. Sarebus, another large Dyak town, he advised me not to visit, as they were inimical to his government, and a skirmish had lately taken place between them and some of his subjects.

"*18th, Sunday.*—Performed service. In the evening walked ashore, but the jungle was wet after rain. Every day or night since arriving it has rained, sometimes in torrents, at others in showers, and the sky has been so obscured that no observations can be obtained. The thermometer never ranges above 81°, and sometimes stands at 59°.

"At twelve at night we were surprised by a boat sent from the *rajah*, to say he was taken ill, and wanted some physic. We dispatched our surgeon, but it was found impossible to admit him into the sacred precincts of the *seraglio*, and he returned with the information that the *rajah* was asleep.

"*21st.*—Our fleet were in readiness before daylight, and by five o'clock we left Kuching,[1] and dropped down the river. The Pangeran Illudeen and the *panglima*, both in *prahus*, accompanied us, and with our long-boat (the *Skimalong*) formed quite a gay procession. The *prahu* of the *pangeran* pulled twelve paddles, mounted two brass swivels, and in all had a crew of about twenty men. The *panglima's* boat likewise carried a gun, and had about ten men; while the *skimalong* mounted an iron swivel, and carried six Englishmen and one of our Singapore Malays. With this equipment we might be pronounced far superior to any force of the *rajah's* enemies we were likely to meet.

"We passed from the Sarawak River into the Morotaba. At the junction of the two streams the Morotaba is narrow; but at no great

---

1. The old name for the town of Sarawak.

distance, where it meets the Quop, it becomes wider, and in some places more than half a mile across.

"The River Quop is a fine stream, fully, as far as I could see, as broad as the Morotaba or Sarawak. Beyond the junction of the Quop and Morotaba the latter river divides into two branches—the left-hand one, running to the sea, retains the name of Morotaba, while the right is called Riam.

"The Riam is a fine stream; at its junction with the Morotaba it takes that name, as the Morotaba does that of Sarawak where they join. Low mangrove or Nepa palm banks characterize these streams; and occasionally slight eminences, with timber, are to be seen. The highest hill is about 3000 feet high, called Matang, and is at the point of junction between the Morotaba and Riam.

"The next river on the starboard hand is the Tanjan, a small stream; and some distance from it, the Kulluong, or Parwheet river, more properly the continuation of the Riam. On the port hand is a smaller river, running N. 35° E. We pursued this stream, called Ugong Passer; and after a hard pull against a strong tide, emerged into the larger river of Samarahan. The tide was so strong against us that we brought up for a couple of hours till it slacked, and between four and five got under weigh again, with the expectation of shortly arriving at our place of destination. Hour after hour passed, however; the sun set; the glorious moon rose upon our progress as we toiled slowly but cheerfully onward. Silence was around, save when broken by the wild song of the Malay boatmen, responded to by the song of our tars to the tune of 'Bonnie laddie, Highland laddie.'

"It was such a situation as an excitable mind might envy. The reflection that we were proceeding up a Borneon River hitherto unknown, sailing where no European ever sailed before; the deep solitude, the brilliant night, the dark fringe of retired jungle, the lighter foliage of the river bank, with here and there a tree flashing and shining with fireflies, nature's tiny lamps glancing and flitting in countless numbers and incredible brilliancy! At eleven at night we reached Samarahan, having been eighteen hours in the boat, and fifteen at the oars, chiefly against tide. The men were tired, but cheerful. Indeed, I can give them no praise beyond their merits for conduct spirited, enduring, and yet so orderly as never to offend the native inhabitants, or infringe upon their prejudices. A glass of grog with our supper, and we all soon closed our eyes in comfortable sleep, such as fatigue alone can bring.

"*22nd.*—The village of Samarahan consists of a few houses, built, as usual, upon posts, and standing close to the brink of the river. It contains from sixty to eighty inhabitants in all, and there is nothing in its site different from the rest of the country. While here, a boat, with a Dyak family, came alongside, consisting of a father, his son, and two daughters. They belonged to the Sibnowan tribe, and had a 'ladang,' or farm, on the Samarahan, toward the sea. The women were good-looking; one, indeed, handsome, plump, and intelligent. They were naked to the waist, and ornamented with several cinctures of brass and coloured rattans scraped very thin.

"About ten we quitted Samarahan and proceeded up the river, stopping only to take a set of sights, and about seven in the evening reached Sibnow, having previously passed the villages of Rembas and Siniawan. Siniawan and Sibnow are not above half a mile from each other, and Rembas not far distant. They are all about the same size, consisting each of eight or ten houses, and containing sixty or eighty inhabitants. The river, during its course so far, is characterized by the same clay-mud bank, evidently an alluvial deposit, without one rock to be seen. The banks are low, and for the most part cleared a quarter of a mile or more on either side, but the jungle is rarely disturbed beyond that distance.

"Occasionally, however, the scene is varied by the rich foliage of this jungle, which here and there kisses the tide as it flows by, and in some spots on the cleared ground arise clumps of trees that would be the pride of any park in Europe. Monkeys in great numbers frisked among the branches; and though unable to shoot them, they amused us often by their grotesque attitudes and the tremendous leaps they made. On one occasion we saw as many as twenty throw themselves, one after the other, from the branch of a high tree into a thick bush full forty feet below, and not one missed his distance or hold! On our way to Sibnow the *pangeran* had collected a number of men for a deer-hunt.

"The nets used for this purpose are formed of rattans strongly wove together, which, being stretched along the jungle, have nooses of the same material, at three feet apart, attached to this ridge-rope. Beaters and dogs then hunt from the opposite quarter, and the deer, in escaping them, is caught in this trap. A length of several hundred fathoms is stretched at once, each separate part of thirty or forty fathoms being joined on as required; and I was told that in this way many deer were taken.

"A heavy rain came on directly after we had brought up, and

33

quickly dispelled all our preparations for supper, by putting out our fire, cooling our hot water, and soaking our half-broiled fowls. To a hungry man such an event is very disastrous; but nothing could exceed the kindness of our Malay friends. They took us to the best house in the village, prepared our supper, and provided us with comfortable mats and pillows to sleep on. Some of our party preferred a bad supper and wet bed to these accommodations; and, to consummate their discomfort, they were kept awake a great part of the night by sandflies. Our lot in the house was more fortunate. We heard the rattling of the pitiless rain, and commiserated those whose choice or distrust kept them in the boat.

"I obtained by this means an excellent opportunity of seeing a Malay *ménage* in its primitive simplicity. Women, children, and all their domestic arrangements, were exposed to view. Nothing appeared to be concealed, nor could anything exceed the simple, kind-hearted hospitality of the inhabitants. The women gazed upon us freely; and their children, with the shyness natural to their age, yet took a glance at the strangers. Never having seen a white man, their curiosity was naturally excited; but it was never offensive. Our supper consisted of an excellent curry, and cold venison broiled on a stick, flavoured with a glass of sherry, and concluded by a cigar. We retired to a dry bed, laying our head on the pillow with as entire a feeling of security as though reposing in England.

"A description of this Malay dwelling, situated so far up this hitherto unknown river, may be interesting. Built, like other Malay houses, on posts, floored with split bamboo, and covered with the leaf of the Nepa palm, it presents the very *beau ideal* of fragility, but affords, at the same time, many advantages, and with a little improvement might be rendered admirably calculated for a new settler in any warm country. It is built at very small expense, is remarkably roomy, free from damp, and weather-proof. The interior of the house consists of four rooms, the centre one large and commodious, the front narrower, but thirty-six feet in length, a family sleeping-apartment on one side, and a kitchen at the back.

"These apartments are divided one from the other by partitions made of the Nepa; the floors were nicely spread with strong mats of Dyak manufacture, and on our arrival finer white mats were laid over there. The entrance of the house is approached by a steep ladder, which in case of attack is easily removed. The River Samarahan is admirably calculated for trade, and, indeed, the same may be said of the whole country, from the great facility it offers of inland communication. There is no impediment for small vessels of 200 or 300 tons navigating as far as Sibnow, the stream being deep and clear of danger. The tides in the river are strong, but not dangerously so; and, sounding occasionally in every reach, we never found less water than three fathoms. The distant mountains, called Bukar (and some other name), are inhabited by Dyaks, and are said to offer many valuable articles of trade; and we may presume this true from the riches of the region whence the Sarawak River takes its rise.

"It is highly probable, indeed, that both these rivers, as well as the Quop and others, have their source in the same range, and will be found to afford the same mineral productions. Tin, the natives confidently assert, can be procured, and birds' nests in very considerable quantities. The latter article, I have heretofore understood, was found only in the vicinity of the sea, whence the material of which they are composed is gathered; but both here and at Sarawak the best informed and most intelligent Malays assure me it is likewise found in the interior, and brought by the Dyaks from the mountains.

"The alluvial soil is a rich clay loam. The principal production at present is rice, of which considerable quantities are grown on the banks of the river, which accounts for the clearing of so many miles of the jungle. The mode of cultivation is similar to what is pursued in Sumatra, and so well described by Marsden. A small spot is cleared of jungle, and when the soil is exhausted of its primeval richness, is deserted for another, which again in turn is neglected, and returns to its wild state. The rice produced is of excellent quality, and of a smaller grain than the Java rice we have with us. It is very white and of excellent flavour, and I am inclined to think is the '*Padi ladang*,' or rice grown on dry ground. (For rice, cultivation of, &c., &c., *vide* Marsden's *Sumatra*, p. 65.)

"Beside rice, rattans are found in great quantities, and likewise Malacca canes, but whether of good quality I am not able to say. On my expressing a wish to see one, a man was dispatched into the jungle, and returned with one in a few minutes. Bees-wax is another article to be procured here *at present* to the amount of thirty or forty *peculs* per year from Sibnow, Malacca canes a small ship-load, rattans in abundance, and any quantity of Garu wood.[2] When we consider the antimony of Sarawak, beside the other things previously mentioned (to say nothing of gold and diamonds), we cannot doubt of the richness of the

2. Aloes wood, *Lignum aloes.*

35

country: but allowance must be made for the exaggeration of native statements.

"It must likewise be borne in mind, that these articles are collected in small quantities in a country thinly populated; and for the purposes of trade it would be necessary to have a resident European on the spot to gather the produce of the country ready for exportation. I have no doubt that permission might be obtained for an English merchant to reside in the country, and that during the lifetime of the Rajah Muda Hassim he would be secure from outrage. The produce of the country might likewise be obtained (at first) at a low rate in exchange for European goods suited to native tastes. In addition to the articles I have already mentioned, I must here add pins, needles, and thread, both gold and white, showy cheap velvets, yellow, green, and red cloth, Surat silks, cottons, coloured beads (for the Dyaks), *nankeens* in small quantities, gold-lace of various qualities, gunpowder, muskets, pistols, flints, &c., &c. The head man of Sibnow (Orang Kaya), when I asked him why he did not collect the produce of the country, replied, that the inhabitants were few, and unless an English merchant was settled at Kuching to buy the things, it was no use collecting them.

"The uncertainty of sale, as well as the very small prices to be obtained from trading Malays, prevents these people using the advantages of their country, and as yet they seemed to consider it impossible that vessels would come for them. That they will one day or other be convinced to the contrary, I am sure; that it will be soon, I sincerely hope; for I can see no reason, with a population and rulers so pacific, why a trade highly advantageous to Singapore should not be opened. I considered our reception as an additional proof how much better the natives are disposed where they have had no intercourse with Europeans; how perfectly willing they are to extend a friendly hospitality when never previously injured or aggravated; and as the first white men who ever visited their country, we can bear the most cordial testimony to their unaffected kindness.

"It is true that we were under the protection of the *rajah* and accompanied by a *pangeran*, and could have insisted on obtaining what was readily granted. But in case the natives had shown any aversion or antipathy toward us, it would easily have been observed.

"*23rd.*—Heavy rain all the morning. Our salt provisions being exhausted, we procured a goat, which was cooked to last during our upward passage.

"At 12, the flood making, we quitted Sibnow, and passing through

36

the same description of country, reached the village of Guntong, consisting of eight houses, and about sixty or seventy inhabitants. The scattered population on the banks of the river amounts, however, to an equal, or probably greater number than in the villages. Beyond Guntong the country becomes wild, but beautiful, and the river gradually narrows until not above twenty-five yards wide. The depth, however, was three fathoms at high water, where we brought up for the night, about five hours' pull from Guntong. The course of the river is so tortuous, that in one place two reaches are only divided by a neck of land five yards across!

"We were now fairly in the bush, and beyond the range of our *pangeran's* knowledge; and I was not therefore surprised (though disappointed) when he intimated the necessity of returning. 'There was nothing to see; the river was narrow, rapid, and obstructed by trees; the Dyaks hostile; the *rajah's* enemies in ambush.'

"I had nothing to answer, save my desire to proceed; but I felt, at the same time, bound in honour to return; for to abuse the indulgence of a native prince on our first excursion would have been a poor way to obtain his future permission to visit other places.

"I did everything man could do to shake the *pangeran's* resolution; and I believe I should have been successful, had his stock of tobacco and *sirih*[3] not been expended. My last resource was resorting to the means found efficient with most men to induce them to alter their opinion. I was content to gain a consent to our proceeding some miles farther up the stream in the morning, and then returning with the ebb. Nothing during this contention could be more polite than the *pangeran's* manner; for he not only expressed but looked his regret, and urged on me his responsibility to the *rajah*. The plea was unanswerable, though I could not help suspecting the want of tobacco and betel as the leading motive.

"*24th.*—We proceeded, as previously agreed, up the river some ten or twelve miles farther, during which distance it narrows to an inconsiderable but deep stream. In many places it was not above eighteen feet wide, with trees overhanging the water. The depth was 2½ fathoms high water; but being the rainy season, it would not be deeper than necessary for boats all the year round. In the early morning the jungle presented a charming scene. Long *vistas* of noble trees with a diversity of richest foliage were before us—in some places overarch-

---

3. The Malay name for the betel, the aromatic leaves of which are chewed along with the *pinang* or *area* nut, a little pure lime, and various spices.

ing the water, and forming a verdant canopy above our heads. Birds were numerous, and woke the woods with their notes, but rarely approached within shot. Pigeons in numbers and of several varieties were seen, but very shy and wild.

"We pushed on ahead of our attendant *pangeran*, and pulled up long after the ebb had made. He had a long chase, and exhausted his lungs in shouting to us to return; and at last, from pity and according to promise, I did so. Poor fellow, he was very glad, fired his swivel-gun, and then brought up for breakfast. I believe a few hours' progress would have brought us to the vicinity of the hills and into the country of the Dyaks; and although disappointed at not being allowed to proceed thither, I nevertheless comfort myself that we have penetrated a hundred miles up a Bornean river hitherto unknown—a river likewise (as far as we have yet examined it) admirably calculated for the purposes of navigation and trade, and which may at some future period become of importance not only to the trade of our settlement of Singapore, but even to the commercial interests of Great Britain.

"The general character of the Samarahan is similar to that of other rivers flowing through alluvial soils; the stream is deep, with muddy banks and bottom, and apparently free from danger or obstruction. Of course these remarks are not meant to prevent the necessity of caution in any vessel proceeding up, as our survey was necessarily very brief; and, like other rivers, one bank will usually be found deep, the other shallow; which must be attended to.

"It now remains for us to proceed up the river from its mouth to its junction with the Ugong Passer; and should it prove to have sufficient water for vessels on the bar, nothing more will be desired.

"Returning, it took us five hours with a fair tide to Sibnow; the next ebb we reached Samarahan in three hours, where we stopped for the night. A heavy rain set in after we brought to, and continued till morning.

"*25th.*—The morning was cold and raw; but cleared up as the sun rose. At 7 we started, and at a quarter past 10 reached the mouth of the Ugong Passer and thence into the Riam. Thus it took us 11¼ hours, with a strong ebb tide, to pull the distance. We had ascended the river from the junction of the Ugong Passer. Mr. Murray's plan of the river will show the distance as taken of each reach, together with its bearing. The ebb tide lasted us some distance up the Riam; but the flood making, we entered a small creek, called Tarusongong, scarce wide enough for the boat to get through, and entirely overarched with the Nepa palm. The general direction of the creek was N.W., and we emerged from it into the Boyur River; and pulling through several reaches, got into the Quop,[4] and thence, after a while, into the Morotaba; from the Morotaba into the Sarawak River, reaching the schooner at sunset, all well and happy. Thus ended our first cruise into the interior of Borneo."

---

4. The banks of the Boyur and Quop are Nepa palm.

# CHAPTER 3

# Excursion Continued

"*Aug. 30th.*—Our flotilla, constituted as before, quitted Sarawak with the ebb tide, and reached Santobong, at the mouth of the river, soon after the flood had made. We waited for the turn of the tide; and in wandering along the sand, I had a shot at a wild hog, but unluckily missed. I likewise saw a deer, very like a red deer, and nearly as large. The hog I fired at was a dirty white, with a black head, very unlike in this particular to any wild hogs I have hitherto seen either in India or Europe; but several young pigs, likewise seen, were black.

"With the flood we weighed anchor, intending to bring up at the mouth of the Seboo River; but the *skimalong* outsailing the *prahus*, foolishly parted company, causing me much uneasiness, and keeping the *prahus* under weigh all night. I was at this time aboard the *pangeran's* boat, where I usually slept. About 10 on the 31st we reached Lobrek Bay, and rejoined our boat.

"With the flood tide we proceeded up Lundu River, which has Gunong Gading on the right hand. The course of the river is very tortuous, but it appears everywhere of more than sufficient depth. The Dyak village of Tungong is situated about eighteen miles from the mouth, and takes its name from a small stream which joins the Lundu just below, on the left hand. It was dark when we arrived, and we ran against a boom formed of large trees run across the river as a defence against adverse Dyak tribes. We could see nothing of the town, save that it appeared longer than any we had yet visited.

"*September 1st.*—The River Lundu is of considerable breadth, about half a mile at the mouth, and 150 or 200 yards off Tungong. Tungong stands on the left hand (going up) close to the margin of the stream, and is inclosed by a slight stockade. Within this defence there is *one* enormous house for the whole population, and three or four small huts. The exterior of the defence between it and the river is occupied by sheds for *prahus*, and at each extremity are one or two houses belonging to Malay residents.

"The common habitation, as rude as it is enormous, measures 594 feet in length, and the front room, or *street*, is the entire length of the building, and 21 feet broad. The back part is divided by mat partitions into the private apartments of the various families, and of these there are forty-five separate doors leading from the public apartment. The widowers and young unmarried men occupy the public room, as only those with wives are entitled to the advantage of separate rooms. The floor of this edifice is raised twelve feet from the ground, and the means of ascent is by the trunk of a tree with notches cut in it—a most difficult, steep, and awkward ladder. In front is a terrace fifty feet broad, running partially along the front of the building, formed, like the floors, of split bamboo. This platform, as well as the front room, besides the regular inhabitants, is the resort of pigs, dogs, birds, monkeys, and fowls, and presents a glorious scene of confusion and bustle.

"Here the ordinary occupations of domestic labour are carried on—*padi* ground, mats made, &c., &c. There were 200 men, women, and children counted in the room and in front while we were there in the middle of the day; and, allowing for those abroad and those in their own rooms, the whole community cannot be reckoned at less than 400 souls. Overhead, about seven feet high, is a second crazy story, on which they stow their stores of food and their implements of labour and war. Along the large room are hung many cots, four feet long, formed of the hollowed trunks of trees cut in half, which answer the purpose of seats by day and beds by night.

"The Sibnowan Dyaks are a wild-looking but apparently quiet and inoffensive race. The apartment of their chief, by name Sejugah, is situated nearly in the centre of the building, and is larger than any other. In front of it nice mats were spread on the occasion of our visit, while over our heads dangled about thirty ghastly skulls, according to the custom of these people. The chief was a man of middle age, with a mild and pleasing countenance and gentle manners. He had around him several sons and relations, and one or two of the leading men of his tribe, but the rest seemed by no means to be restrained by his presence, or to show him any particular marks of respect: certainly nothing of the servile obsequiousness observed by the Malays before their prince. Their dress consists of a single strip of cloth round the loins, with the ends hanging down before and behind, and a light turban, composed of the bark of trees, twined round the head, and so arranged that the front is stuck up somewhat resembling a short plume of feathers.

"Their figures are almost universally well made, showing great activity without great muscular development; but their stature is diminutive, as will be seen by the following measurements, taken at random among them, and confirmed by general observation:

Sejugah, the chief, height, 5 ft. 1¾ in. Head round, 1 ft. 9 in. Anterior portion, from ear to ear, 1 foot; posterior, 9 in.; across the top, 1¼ ft.

Kalong, the chief's eldest son, height, 5 ft. 2¼ in. Anterior portion of head, 1 ft.; posterior, 8¾ in.; across the top, 1 ft., wanting a few lines.

|                      | Height |        |
| -------------------- | ------ | ------ |
| Man from the crowd   | 5 ft.  | 1¾ in. |
| Another              | 5      | 1½     |
| Another              | 5      | 4      |
| Another              | 4      | 10     |
| Another              | 5      | 3      |
| Another              | 5      | 4      |

"The following is a specimen of their names, and some few words of their dialect, the only ones I could get not Malayan. The fact, indeed, appears to be that, from constant intercourse, their Dyak language is fast fading away; and, while retaining their separate religion and customs, they have substituted the soft and fluent Malay for their own harsher jargon. The names are, Jugah or Sejugah, Kalong, Bunshie, Kontong, Lang, Rantie.

The vocabulary:

hairs, *bok* (similar to the Lundu Dyaks).
woman, *indo*.
father, *api*.
sea, *tasiek*.
slave, *ulon*.
spear, *sancho*.
black, *chelum*.
good, *badass*.
bad, *jaie*.

that, *kneah* (nasal, like *kgneah*).
thigh, *pah*. this, *to*.
to go, *bajali*.
there, *kein*.
come, *jali*
here, *keto*.
come here, *jali keto*.
to give, *bri*.
give all, *bri samonia* (M).
to bring, *bii*.

| quick, *pantass.* | bring that, *bii kneah.* |
| slow, *bagadie.* | bring here, *bii keto.* |

"The corruptions of the Malay are *langan* for *tangon,* arm; *ai* for *ayer,* water; *menua* for *benua,* country; *komah* for *rumah,* house; *besi* for *besar,* great.

"Like the rest of the Dyaks, the Sibnowans adorn their houses with the heads of their enemies; but with them this custom exists in a modified form; and I am led to hope that the statements already made public of their reckless search after human beings, *merely* for the purpose of obtaining their heads, will be found to be exaggerated, if not untrue; and that the custom elsewhere, as here and at Lundu, will be found to be more accordant with our knowledge of other wild tribes, and to be regarded merely as a triumphant token of valour in the fight or ambush; similar, indeed, to the scalps of the North American Indian.

"Some thirty skulls were hanging from the roof of the apartment; and I was informed that they had many more in their possession; all, however, the heads of enemies, chiefly of the tribe of Sarebus. On inquiring, I was told that it is indispensably necessary a young man should procure a skull before he gets married. When I urged on them that the custom would be more honoured in the breach than the observance, they replied that it was established from time immemorial, and could not be dispensed with. Subsequently, however, Sejugah allowed that heads were very difficult to obtain now, and a young man might sometimes get married by giving presents to his lady-love's parents. At all times they warmly denied ever obtaining any heads but those of their enemies; adding, they were bad people, and deserved to die.

"I asked a young unmarried man whether he would be obliged to get a head before he could obtain a wife. He replied, 'Yes.' 'When would he get one?' 'Soon.' 'Where would he go to get one?' 'To the Sarebus River.' I mention these particulars in detail, as I think, had their practice extended to taking the head of any defenceless traveller, or any Malay surprised in his dwelling or boat, I should have wormed the secret out of them.

"The men of this tribe marry but one wife, and that not until they have attained the age of seventeen or eighteen. Their wedding ceremony is curious; and, as related, is performed by the bride and bridegroom being brought in procession along the large room, where a brace of fowls is placed over the bridegroom's neck, which he whirls

43

seven times round his head. The fowls are then killed, and their blood sprinkled on the foreheads of the pair, which done, they are cooked, and eaten by the new-married couple *alone*, while the rest feast and drink during the whole night.

"Their dead are put in a coffin, and buried; but Sejugah informed me that the different tribes vary in this particular; and it would appear they differ from their near neighbours the Dyaks of Lundu.

"Like these neighbours, too, the Sibnowans seem to have little or no idea of a God. They offer prayers to Biedum, the great Dyak chief of former days. Priests and ceremonies they have none; the thickest mist of darkness is over them: but how much easier is it to dispel darkness with light than to overcome the false blaze with the rays of truth!

"The manners of the men of this tribe are somewhat reserved, but frank; while the women appeared more cheerful, and more inclined to laugh and joke at our peculiarities. Although the first Europeans they had ever seen, we were by no means annoyed by their curiosity: and their honesty is to be praised; for, though opportunities were not wanting, they never on any occasion attempted to pilfer anything. Their colour resembles the Malay, and is fully as dark; and the cast of their countenance does not favour the notion that they are sprung from a distinct origin. They never intermarry with the Malays, so as to intermingle the two people, and the chastity of their women gives no presumption of its otherwise occurring. Their stature, as I have before remarked, is diminutive, their eyes are small and quick, their noses usually flattened, and their figures clean and well formed, but not athletic. Both sexes generally wear the hair long and turned up, but the elder men often cut it short.

As is natural, they are fond of the water, and constantly bathe; and their canoes are numerous. I counted fifty, besides ten or twelve small *prahus*, which they often build for sale to the Malays, at a very moderate price indeed. The men wear a number of fine cane rings, neatly worked (which we at first mistook for hair), below the knee or on the arm, and sometimes a brass ring or two; but they have no other ornaments. The ears of a few were pierced, but I saw nothing worn in them except a roll of thin palm-leaf, to prevent the hole closing. The women are decidedly good-looking, and far fairer than the men; their figures are well shaped, and remarkable for their *embonpoint*.

"The expression of their countenance is very good-humoured, and their condition seems a happy one. Their dress consists of a coarse stuff, very scanty (manufactured by the Sakarran Dyaks), reaching from the waist to the knee; around the waist they have rings of rattan, either black or red, and the loins are hung round with a number of brass ornaments made by their husbands. Above the waist they are entirely naked, nor do they wear any covering or ornament on the head. They have a few bracelets of brass, but neither ear-rings nor nose-rings; and some, more lucky than the rest, wear a necklace of beads. They prefer the smallest Venetian beads to the larger and more gaudy ones of England.

"The labour of the house, and all the drudgery, falls on the females. They grind the rice, carry burdens, fetch water, fish, and work in the fields; but though on a par with other savages in this respect, they have many advantages. They are not immured; they eat in company with the males; and, in most points, hold the same position toward their husbands and children as European women. The children are entirely naked; and the only peculiarity I observed is filing their teeth to a sharp point, like those of a shark. The men marry but one wife, as I have before observed. Concubinage is unknown; and cases of seduction or adultery very seldom arise. Even the Malays speak highly of the chastity of the Dyak women; yet they are by no means shy under the gaze of strangers, and used to bathe before us in a state of nudity.

"That these Dyaks are in a low condition there is no doubt; but, comparatively, theirs is an innocent state, and I consider them capable of being easily raised in the scale of society. The absence of all prejudice regarding diet, the simplicity of their characters, the purity of their morals, and their present ignorance of all forms of worship and all idea of future responsibility, render them open to conviction of truth and religious impression. Yet, when I say this, I mean, of course, only when their minds shall have been raised by education; for without previous culture I reckon the labours of the missionary as useless as endeavouring to read off a blank paper. I doubt not but the Sibnowan Dyaks would readily receive missionary families among them, provided the consent of the Rajah Muda Hassim was previously obtained.

"That the *rajah* would consent I much doubt; but if any person chose to reside at Tungong, for the charitable purpose of leading the tribe gradually, by means of education, to the threshold of Christianity, it would be worth the asking, and I would exert what influence I possess with him on the occasion. I feel sure a missionary would be safe among them, as long as he strictly confined himself to the gentle precepts and practice of his faith; he would live abundantly and cheaply, and be exposed to no danger except from the incursion of hostile tribes, which must always be looked for by a sojourner amid a Dyak community.

"I must add, that this day, when so many of my friends are destroying partridges, I have had my gun in my hand, to procure a few specimens.

"*2nd.*—To continue my account of the Sibnowan Dyaks. I made particular inquiry about the superstition stated to exist regarding birds, and the omens said to be drawn from their flight; but I could trace no vestige of such a belief, nor did they seem at all acquainted with its existence. The government of the Sibnowans may be called patriarchal. The authority of the chief appears limited within very narrow bounds; he is the leader in war, and the dispenser of the laws; but possesses no power of arbitrary punishment, and no authority for despotic rule. The distinction between Sejugah and the lowest of his tribe is not great, and rather a difference of riches than of power. A few ornamented spears, presented by the Malays, seem his only insignia of office; and these were never displayed in our presence, save in the dance.

"The chiefship would appear to be elective, and not hereditary; but I could not distinctly understand whether the appointment rested with the *rajah* or the tribe. The former claims it; but the latter did not speak as though his right were a matter of necessity or certainty. On asking Kalong, the eldest son of Sejugah (a young man of twenty years of age, active, clever, and intelligent), whether he would succeed his father, he replied, he feared he was not *rich* enough; but two or three of the tribe, who were present, asserted that he would be made chief. The Rajah Muda Hassim told me that the only hold he had on the Dyaks was through the chief and his family, who were attached to him; but that the tribe at large cared nothing for the Malays. I can easily believe this, as any ill treatment or cruelty directed against a Dyak community would soon drive them beyond the power and the territory of the prince. This is the best safeguard of the Dyaks; and the Malays are well aware that a Dyak alliance must be maintained by good treatment. They are called subjects and slaves; but they are subjects at pleasure, more independent and better used than any Malay under his native prince.

"The laws of this Dyak tribe are administered by the chief and the two principal men. They have no fixed code, nor any standard of punishment, each case of crime being judged according to its enormity. In the event of murder in their own tribe, the murderer suffers death by decapitation, *provided he be in fault*. Theft is punished by fine, and adultery (stated as a heinous offense) by severe beating and heavy *mulct*[1]. Other crimes are, in like manner, punished by fine and beating—one or both, according to their various shades of evil. The latter varies greatly in degree, sometimes being inflicted on the head or arm, with a severity which stops short only of death. The arm is often broken under this infliction; so, according to their representation, it is a risk to be dreaded and avoided.

"Slavery holds among them; and, as among the Malays, a debtor is reduced to this state until his debt be discharged. Children are likewise bought, and must be considered as slaves.

"In the evening I requested Sejugah to collect his tribe, and to show me their dances and musical instruments. They readily consented, and about nine at night we went to witness the exhibition. The musical instruments were, the *tomtom*, or drum, and the Malayan gong; which were beat either slow or fast, according to the measure of the dance. The dances are highly interesting, more especially from their close resemblance, if not identity, with those of the South Sea Islanders. Two swords were placed on the mat, and two men commenced slowly, from the opposite extremities, turning the body, extending the arms, and lifting the legs, in grotesque but not ungraceful attitudes.

"Approaching thus leisurely round and round about, they at length seize the swords, the music plays a brisker measure, and the dancers pass and repass each other, now cutting, now crossing swords, retiring and advancing, one kneeling as though to defend himself from the assaults of his adversary; at times stealthily waiting for an advantage, and quickly availing himself of it. The measure throughout was admirably kept, and the frequent turns were simultaneously made by both dancers, accompanied by the same eccentric gestures. The effect of all this far surpasses the impression to be made by a meagre description.

"The room partially lighted by *damar* torches; the clang of the noisy instruments; the crowd of wild spectators; their screams of encouragement to the performers; the flowing hair and rapid evolutions of the dancers, formed a scene I wish could have been reduced to painting by such a master as Rembrandt or Caravaggio. The next dance was performed by a single person, with a spear, turning like the last; now advancing, retiring, poising, brandishing, or pretending to

---

1. Fines—J.H.

47

hurl his weapon. Subsequently we had an exhibition with the sword and shield, very similar to the others, and only differing in the use of the weapons; and the performance was closed by a long and animated dance like the first, by two of the best performers.

"The dance with the spear is called *Talambong*; that with the sword, *Mancha*. The resemblance of these dances to those of the South Seas is, as I have observed, a remarkable and interesting fact, and one of many others which may, in course of time, elucidate the probable theory that the two people are sprung from a common source. The Malays of Sarawak, and other places in the neighbourhood of the Dyak tribes, dance these dances; but they are unknown to Borneo Proper, and the other Malay islands; and although the names may be given by the Malays, I think there is no doubt that the dances themselves belong to the Dyaks: a correcter judgment can be formed by a better acquaintance with other Dyak tribes.

"The household utensils in use here are few and simple. The mode of grinding *padi* clear of the husk is through the trunk of a tree cut into two parts, the upper portion being hollow, the lower solid; small notches are cut where the two pieces fit, and handles attached to the upper part, which being filled with *padi* and kept turning round, the husk is detached and escapes by the notches.

"The Dyaks, as is well known, are famous for the manufacture of iron. The forge here is of the simplest construction, and formed by two hollow trees, each about seven feet high, placed upright, side by side, in the ground; from the lower extremity of these, two pipes of bamboo are led through a clay-bank, three inches thick, into a charcoal fire; a man is perched at the top of the trees, and pumps with two pistons (the suckers of which are made of cocks' feathers), which being raised and depressed alternately, blow a regular stream of air into the fire. Drawings were taken of these and other utensils and instruments. The canoes are not peculiar, but the largest *prahus* (some forty feet long, with a good beam) are constructed, in the first place, exactly like a small canoe: a single tree is hollowed out, which forms the keel and kelson, and on this foundation the rest of the *prahu* is built with planks, and her few timbers fastened with rattans.

"A *prahu* of fifty feet long, fitted for service, with oars, mast, attops, &c., was ordered by the Panglima Rajah while we were with him, which, completed, was to cost thirty *reals*, or sixty Java *rupees*, or £6 English. During the course of the day we ascended the river to visit the settlement of Chinese lately established here. It is situated about two and a half miles up the river, on the same side as Tungong, and consists of thirty men (real Chinese), and five women of the mixed breed of Sambas. Nothing can be more flourishing than this infant settlement, and I could hardly credit their statement that it had only been formed between four and five months. The soil they represented as most excellent, and none are better judges; many acres were cleared and under cultivation; rice, *sirih*, sweet potatoes (convolvulus), Indian corn, &c., &c., were growing abundantly; and they were able to supply us with seven *pecul*, or 933 pounds of sweet potatoes, without sensibly diminishing their crop.

"They showed me samples of birds' nests, bees' wax, *garu* wood (lignum aloes), and ebony, collected in the vicinity, chiefly from Gunong Gading. Several *peculs* of birds-nests and bees-wax, and the wood in large quantity, could *now* be brought to market; and no doubt, when demand stimulates industry, the quantities would greatly increase. The Dyaks, they told me, collected rattans, and likewise canes, which are plentiful. The mixed breed of the Chinese with the Malay or Dyak are a good-looking and industrious race, partaking much more of the Chinese character than that of the natives of this country. This mainly arises from education and early-formed habits, which are altogether Chinese; and in religion and customs they likewise follow, in a great measure, the paternal stock. The race are worthy of attention, as the future possessors of Borneo. The numbers of this people cannot be stated, but it must amount to many thousand persons: 3000 were said to be on their way to the Borneon territory.

"The head man of this settlement, a Chinese of Quantung, or Canton, but long resident in the vicinity of Sambas, gave me some valuable information respecting the Sarawak mountains. He had, with a considerable party of his countrymen, been employed there at the gold-mines, and he spoke of them as abundant, and of the ore as good. Tin they had not found, but thought it existed. Antimony ore was to be had in any quantities, and diamonds were likewise discovered. I mention these facts as coming from an intelligent Chinese, well able from experience to judge of the precious metals, and the probability of their being found.

"*3rd.*—Night, as usual, set in with torrents of rain, which lasted until the morning: the days, however, are fine, though cloudy. Got sights in the afternoon; and, leaving our Dyak friends, we dropped down to the mouth of the river, where we slept.

"*4th.*—At 2 a.m. got under weigh for the Samatan River, which we reached at 8 a.m. I had been given to understand that the Lundu and Sibnowan Dyaks were to be found on this river; but on arriving, I was informed we must proceed to Seru, where we should see plenty of Dyaks. I accordingly started immediately after breakfast, and reached Seru after midday. Here we found a small Malay fishing village, with two or three stray Dyaks of the Sibnowan tribe; and, on inquiring, we were told by them that their country was far away. Being convinced that the *pangeran* had dragged me all this distance to answer some purpose of his own, I re-embarked on the instant, and set off on my return to Lundu, indignant enough. However, I had the poor satisfaction of dragging them after me, and making them repent their trick, which I believe was nothing else than to visit the island of Talang Talang for turtles' eggs. We were pretty well knocked up by the time we reached Samatan, having been pulling thirteen hours, the greater part of the time under a burning sun.

"The Samatan River, like the others, is inclosed in a bay choked with sand: the boat-passage is on the right-hand side, going in near Point Samatan. The sands are mostly dry at low water, and stretch out a considerable distance. There is a fishing station here, though not so large as at Seru, and the fish at both places are very plentiful, and are salted for exportation to Sambas, and along their own coast. Seru is a shallow creek; the village may consist of 50 or 60 inhabitants, and the sands stretch a long way out. We thus lost two days, through the cunning of our Malay attendant; and the only advantage gained is being enabled to fill up the details of our survey of this bay.

"*5th.*—The day consumed returning along the coast to the Lundu, and we did not reach Tungong till late.

"*6th.*—Remained at Tungong. Every impediment was thrown in my way to prevent my reaching the Lundu Dyaks; the distance was great, the tribe small and unsettled, there was little probability of finding them, &c. I would, however, have gone; but another cause had arisen of a more serious nature. My feet, from the heat of the sun, mosquito-bites, and cuts (for I foolishly went without shoes that unlucky day to Seru), had become so painful and inflamed that I felt great doubt whether, if I walked in pain to Lundu, I could come back again. With the best grace I could, I yielded the point; with a vow, however, never to have the same *pangeran* again. I did *manage* to be civil to him, from policy alone. He was superfluously kind and obliging.

"*7th.*—Left Tungong on our return to the vessel, and brought-to for the night at Tanjong Siri. In the evening I walked along the fine sandy beach as far as the entrance of the Sumpudin River. We saw many wild hogs; and on one occasion I was able to get within twenty yards of some ten of them together, among some large drift-wood. Just as I was crawling over a tree and balancing, I found myself confronted by these animals; but they were out of sight almost before I could cock my gun and fire. They were of a large size, and most of them we saw during the evening either dirty white, or white and black. At night, after we had retired to our quarters in the *pangeran's* boat, she filled with water, and was near going down. The first intimation we had of it was the water wetting our mats on which we were sleeping. She was beached and baled out, and a hand kept baling all night, as they had laden her so deep that she leaked considerably.

"*8th.*—In the morning we got our anchor at daylight, and breakfasted on the island of Sumpudin. There are deer, hogs, and pigeons on Sumpudin Island; but what was more interesting to me was, the discovery of the wild nutmeg-tree in full flower, and growing to the height of twenty or thirty feet. The nutmegs lay in plenty under the trees, and are of considerable size, though elongated in shape, and tasteless, as usual in the wild sorts. While the East India Company were sending Captain Forest from their settlement of Balambangan as far as New Guinea in search of this plant, how little they dreamed of its flourishing so near them on the island of Borneo!

"The soil on which they grow is a yellowish clay, mixed with vegetable mould. I brought some of the fruit away with me. After breakfast, a breeze springing up, we sailed to the mouth of the Sarawak River, waited for the tide, and pushed on for the vessel, getting aboard about half past three in the morning. Our Malay attendants were left far, far behind, and there is little chance of their being here tomorrow, for their boats sail wretchedly."

# CHAPTER 4

# Attack by Pirates

Having returned to Sarawak, Mr. Brooke renewed his intercourse with the *rajah*; and his *Journal* proceeds:

"*Sept. 9th.*—Visited the *rajah*; civil and polite—I ought indeed to say friendly and kind. Der Macota was on board, speaking on the trade, and very anxious for me to arrange the subject with the *rajah*. I could only say, that I would do so if the *rajah* wished, as I believed it would be greatly for the benefit of their country and Singapore.

"*10th.*—Laid up with my bad legs, and hardly able to crawl. Muda Hassim presented us with another bullock, which we salted. At Lundu we bought eight pigs, which arrived today in charge of Kalong, the young Dyak. He is a fine fellow. I gave him a gun, powder-flask, powder, &c. He was truly delighted. Our *pangerans* arrived at the same time.

"*11th.*—Very bad; got a novel, and read all day. Went ashore to see Muda Hassim in the evening. He gave us a private audience: and we finished our discussion respecting the trade, and I think successfully.

"I began by saying, that I as a private gentleman, unconnected with commerce, could have no personal interest in what I was about to speak; that the *rajah* must clearly understand that I was in no way connected with the government of Singapore, and no way authorized to act for them: that he must, therefore, look upon it merely as my private opinion, and act afterward as his wisdom thought fit. I represented to him that the kingdom of Borneo was the last Malay state possessing any power, and that this might be in a great measure attributed to the little intercourse they had had with European powers.

"I thought it highly advisable to call into play the resources of his country, by opening a trade with individual European merchants.

Sarawak, I stated, was a rich place, and the territory around produced many valuable articles for a commercial intercourse—bees-wax, birds-nests, rattans, beside large quantities of antimony ore and sago, which might be considered the staple produce of the country. In return for these, the merchants of Singapore could send goods from Europe or China which his people required, such as gunpowder, muskets, cloths, &c.; and both parties would thus be benefited by their commercial interchange of commodities. I conceived that Singapore was well fitted for trade with this place. The *rajah* must not suppose I was desirous of excluding other nations from trading here, or that I wished he should trade with the English alone; on the contrary, I thought that the Americans, the French, or any other nation, should be admitted on the same terms as the English.

"Of course, I was not allowed to proceed without much questioning and discussion; many of the views were urged and re-urged, to remove their false notions. That Mr. Bonham had the supreme command of the trade of Singapore was the prominent one; and when he died, or was removed, would not the next governor alter all kind intentions and acts? 'What friend should they have at Singapore then?'

"Again they thought that a few ships might come at first; but then they would deceive them, and not come again. It was very difficult to explain, that if they procured cargoes at an advantageous rate, they would come here for their own benefit; if not, of course it would not be worth their while to come at all. The entire discussion proceeded with the utmost good-will and politeness.

"That the political ascendency of the English is paramount here is apparent. They might if they pleased, by means of an offensive and defensive alliance between the two powers, gain the entire trade of the northwest coast of Borneo, from Tanjong Datu to Malludu Bay.

"I obtained subsequently from Macota the following list of imports and exports; which I here commit to paper, for the information of those whom it may concern.

*From Singapore.*—Iron; salt, Siam; nankeen; Madras, Europe, and China cotton cloth, coarse and fine; Bugis and Pulicat *sarongs*; gold and other threads, of sorts and colours; brass wire, of sizes; iron pans from Siam, called *qualis*; chintzes, of colours and sorts; coarse red broadcloth, and other sorts of different colours; China crockery; gunpowder; muskets; flints; handkerchiefs (Pulicat and European); *gambir*; dates; Java tobacco; soft sugar; sugar-candy; biscuits; *baharri*; common decanters; glasses, &c. &c.; China silk, of colours; ginghams; white cottons; nails; beside other little things, such as Venetian beads; ginger; curry-powder; onions; ghee; &c. &c.

The returns from Sarawak are now: antimony ore, sago, timber (*lackah, garu*), rattans, Malacca canes, bees-wax, birds-nests, rice, &c. Other articles, such as gold, tin, &c. &c., Macota said, would be procured after the war, but at present he need say nothing of them; the articles above mentioned might subsequently be greatly increased by demand; and, in short, as every person of experience knows, in a wild country a trade must be fostered at first.

To the foregoing list I must add, pipeclay, vegetable tallow, which might be useful in commerce, being of fine quality; and the ore, found in abundance round here, of which I can make nothing, but which I believe to be copper.

"*12th.*—I received from the *rajah* a present of an ourang-outang, young, and like others I have seen, but better clothed, with fine long hair of a bright chestnut colour. The same melancholy which characterizes her race is apparent in Betsy's face; and though but just caught, she is quite quiet unless teased.

"From the man who brought Betsy I procured a *Lemur tardigradus*, called by the Malays *Cucan*, not *Poucan*, as written in Cuvier—Marsden has the name right in his dictionary—and at the same time the mutilated hand of an ourang-outang of *enormous* size. This hand far exceeds in length, breadth, and power, the hand of any man in the ship; and though smoked and shrunk, the circumference of the fingers is half as big again as an ordinary human finger. The natives of Borneo call the ourang-outang the *mias*, of which they say there are two distinct sorts; one called the *Mias rombi* (similar to the specimen aboard and the two in the Zoological Gardens), and the *Mias pappan*, a creature far larger, and more difficult to procure. To the latter kind the hand belongs. The *mias pappan* is represented to be as tall or taller than a man, and possessing vast strength: the face is fuller and larger than that of the *mias rombi*, and the hair reddish, but sometimes approaching to black. The *mias rombi* never exceeds four or four and a half feet; his face, unlike the *pappan*, is long, and his hair redder. I must own myself inclined to this opinion from various reasons:—1st. The natives appear so well agreed on the point, and so well acquainted with the distinction and the different names, that it is impossible to suppose it a fabrication for our peculiar use. Of the many whom I asked respecting them, at different times and in different places, the greater part of their own accord mentioned the difference between the *mias pappan* and the *mias rombi*. The animal when brought aboard was stated to be the *mias rombi*, or small sort. In short, the natives, whether right or wrong, make the distinction. 2nd. The immense size of the hand in my possession, the height of the animal killed on the coast of Sumatra, and the skull in the Paris Museum, can scarcely be referred to an animal such as we know at home; though by specious analogical reasoning, the great disparity of the skulls has been pronounced the result merely of age.

"However, facts are wanting, and these facts I doubt not I can soon procure, if not actual proof; and whichever way it goes, in favour of Buffon's Pongo or not, I shall be contented, so that I bring truth to light.

"*19th.*—From the 12th to the 19th of September we lay, anxious to be off, but delayed by some trifling occurrence or other, particularly for the letters which I was to receive for the merchants of Singapore. Our intercourse the whole time was most friendly and frequent; almost daily I was ashore, and the *rajah* often visited the vessel. How tedious and *ennuyant* to me can only be known by those who know me well, and how repugnant these trammels of society and ceremony are to nature. Nevertheless, I suffered this martyrdom with exemplary outward patience, though the spirit flagged, and the thoughts wandered, and the head often grew confused, with sitting and talking trifling nonsense, through a poor interpreter.

"I here bid *adieu* to these kind friends, fully impressed with their kindness, and the goodness of their dispositions. To me they are far different from anything I was at all prepared to meet, and devoid of the vices with which their countrymen are usually stigmatized by modern writers. I expected to find an indolent and somewhat insolent people, devoted to sensual enjoyments, addicted to smoking opium, and eternally cock-fighting or gambling: let me speak it to the honour of the Borneons, that they neither cock-fight nor smoke opium; and in the military train of their *rajah* they find at Kuching few conveniences and fewer luxuries.

"Like all the followers of Islam, they sanction polygamy; and the number of their women, and, probably, the ease and cheerfulness of the seraglio, contrasted with the ceremonial of the exterior, induce them to pass a number of their hours amid their women, and excite habits of effeminacy and indolence. I should pronounce them indolent and unwarlike; but kind and unreserved to foreigners, particularly to Englishmen. They are volatile, generally speaking very ignorant, but by no means deficient in acuteness of understanding; and, indeed, their chief defects may be traced entirely to their total want of education, and the nature of their government. The lower orders of people are poor and wretched, and the freemen are certainly poorer and more wretched than the slaves.

"They are not greatly addicted to theft, and yet, unlike the scrupulous honesty of the Sibnowans, they pilfered some trifling articles occasionally when left in their way. The retainers of the court showed much the same mean intriguing spirit which is too often found in courts, and always in Eastern ones; and the *rajah* himself seldom requested any favour from me directly, but employed some intermediate person to sound me—to get whatever was required for himself if possible, if not for the *rajah*. I took the hint, and always expressed my wishes through the interpreter when not present myself. In this way we were enabled to grant or refuse without the chance of insult or offence. The suite of the *rajah* consists principally of slaves, either purchased or debtors: they are well treated, and rise to offices of some note.

"The *panglima rajah* was a slave-debtor, though we did not know it for some time after our arrival. I never saw either cruelty or undue harshness exercised by the great men during my stay, and in general their manners were affable and kind to those about them. The Rajah Muda Hassim is a remarkably short man, and slightly built; about 45 years of age; active and intelligent, but apparently little inclined to business. His disposition I formed the highest estimate of, not only from his kindness to myself, but from the testimony of many witnesses, all of whom spoke of him with affection, and gave him the character of a mild and gentle master. Muda Hassim's own brother, Muda Mahammed, is a reserved and sulky man, but they spoke well of him; and the *rajah* said he was a good man, but given to fits of sulkiness.

"Der Macota, unlike other Malays, neither smokes tobacco nor chews *sirih*. He sought our society, and was the first person who spoke to me on the subject of the trade. His education has been more attended to than that of others of his rank. He both reads and writes his own language, and is well acquainted with the government, laws, and customs of Borneo. From him I derived much information on the subject of the Dyaks, and the geography of the interior; and if I have failed to put it down, it is because I have not departed from my general rule of never giving any native statements unless they go far to verify my own actual observations. I parted from the *rajah* with regret, some six or seven miles down the river. Never was such a blazing as when we left Sarawak; twenty-one guns I fired to the *rajah*, and he fired forty-two to me—at least we counted twenty-four, and they went on firing afterward, as long as ever we were in sight. The last words the Rajah Muda Hassim said, as I took my leave, were—'Tuan Brooke, do not forget me.'

"Among the curiosities in my possession are spears, swords, and shields, from various tribes; a coat of mail, made to the northward of Borneo, and worn by the pirates; specimens of Sakarran Dyak manufacture of cloth, and Sarebus *ditto*; ornaments and implements of the Sibnowans; and, last not least, a gold-handled *kris*, presented me by the *rajah*, which formerly belonged to his father, and which he constantly wore himself. I likewise presented him with a small English dagger, with a mother-of-pearl handle; and my favour was so high with him, that he used always to wear my gift, and I, to return the compliment, wore his.

"The climate of Sarawak is good, and is seldom hot: the last eight or ten days were oppressive, but until then we could sleep with a blanket, and seldom found it too warm in the day. Rain at this season falls in great quantities; and from imprudence, our crew suffered on their first arrival from colds and rheumatism; but getting more careful, we had latterly no sick-list.

"Farewell to Sarawak! I hope to see it again; and have obtained a promise from the *rajah* that he will go with me to Borneo, and show me every part of the country by the way.

"I may here state the result of some inquiries I have made respecting the government of Borneo. The form of government may be considered aristocratic rather than oligarchical: it is ruled by the *sultan*, but his power is kept in check by four great officers of government. These are, the Rajah Muda Hassim, the *bandar*, in whose hands is the government of the country; *Pangeran* Mumin, the Degadon, the treasurer, or, as Mr. Hunt says, controller of the household of the *sultan*; Pangeran Tizudeen, *tumangong*, or commander-in-chief; and Pangeran Kurmaindar, the Pen-damei, or mediator and interceder. This officer is the means of communication or mediation between the sultan and his *pangerans*; and in case of condemnation, he sues for the pardon or mercy of his sovereign.

"Mr. Hunt, in his short but excellent paper on Borneo, mentions some other officers of state: I will not follow him, but in the names, as well as duties of these officers, his account agrees with my information. Further than this, I have not yet learned, therefore state not; for I am not *manufacturing* a book, but gaining information. I may add, however, that these offices are elective, and not hereditary: as far as I yet know, I am inclined to believe the election rests with the chief *Pangerans* of the state; not only those in office, but others. When I reach Borneo I can procure more ample details.

"*23rd.*—Quitted the *Royalist* at the entrance of the Morotaba, and accompanied by Pangerans Subtu and Illudeen, set sail for the river Sadung.

"The town called Songi is of considerable size, and the entire population along the river may certainty be reckoned at from 2000 to 3000 persons, independent of Dyaks. The country has a flourishing aspect, but the soil is represented as bad, being soft and muddy. There is a good deal of trade from this river, and it annually sends several large prahus to Singapore: two were lying off the town when we arrived, and two others had sailed for that place twenty days before. The produce of the country is bees-wax, birds-nests, rice, &c. &c., but they seem to be procured in less abundance than in the other contiguous rivers.

"There is nothing peculiar about the Malay population, except that, generally speaking, it struck me, they appeared better off than the people of Sarawak, or others I have visited hereabouts. We ascended the river by night, anchored a short distance from the Songi, in a tideway like a sluice, and entered the smaller river shortly after daylight. Having sent the *pangerans* ahead to advise Seriff Sahib of our arrival, we pulled slowly up to the campong of the Data Jembrong, where we brought up to breakfast. Data Jembrong is a native of Mindanao, an Illanun and a pirate; he is slightly advanced in years, but stout and resolute-looking, and of a most polite demeanour—as oily-tongued a cut-throat as a gentleman would wish to associate with. He spoke of his former life without hesitation, and confessed himself rather apprehensive of going to Singapore. He was remarkably civil, and sent us a breakfast of some fruit, salt fish, stale turtles' eggs, and coffee sweetened with syrup; but spite of all this, his blood-thirsty education and habits prejudiced me against him.

"Breakfast finished, we went forward to visit Seriff Sahib, who received us in an open hall; promised to get us as many animals as he could now; regretted our short stay, and assured me he would collect more by the time I returned. Among these is to be a *mias pappan*, living or dead. I at the same time offered ten dollars for the skeleton belonging to the hand already in my possession, and a less sum for the parts. Being the first Europeans Seriff Sahib had ever met, he was rather puzzled to know what we were like; but we had every reason to be satisfied with his kindness and the civility of his people: the inhabitants, though crowding to see us, are by no means intrusive, and their curiosity is too natural to be harshly repressed. I need hardly remark here how very erroneously the position of the Sadung River is laid down in the charts, it being placed in the bay, to the westward of Santobong, and nearly in the position of the Samatan River.

"*25th.*—The last night was passed off Datu Jembrong's house, and I left him with a firm impression that he is still a pirate, or at any rate connected with them. He resides generally at Tawarron, to the northward of Borneo Proper, where his wives and children now are, and he has come here to superintend the building of a *prahu*. The people about him speak of his pursuits without disguise, and many informed us the *prahu* near his house is intended for a piratical vessel. Nothing could exceed the polite kindness of our rascally host, and I spent the rainy evening in his house with some satisfaction, acquiring information of the coast to the northward, which he is well able to give.

"In the morning we dropped down with the last of the ebb to the mouth of the Songi, and took the young flood to proceed up the Sadung. Beyond the point of junction with the Songi the Sadung retains an average breadth of from three-quarters of a mile to a mile. The banks continue to be partially cleared, with here and there a few Dyaks residing in single families or small communities on their *ladangs* or farms. The Dyak *campong*, which terminated our progress up the stream, consists of three moderately long houses inhabited by Sibnowans. The manners, customs, and language of the Sibnowans of the Sadung are the same as those of their Lundu brethren; they are, however, a wilder people, and appear poor. Like other Dyaks, they had a collection of heads hanging before the entrance of their chief's private apartments.

"Some of these heads were fresh, and, with the utmost *sang-froid*, they told us they were women's. They declared, however, they never took any heads but those of their enemies, and these women (unhappy creatures) had belonged to a distant tribe. The fresh heads were ornamented with fowl's feathers, and suspended rather conspicuously in separate rattan frames of open work. They professed themselves willing to go with me up the river to the mountains; and on the way, they informed me, were some large Malay towns, beside some more *campongs* of their own countrymen. Farther up they enumerated some twenty tribes of Dyaks, whose names I thought it useless to preserve. Late in the evening we set off on our return, and anchored once again near Datu Jembrong's house.

"*26th.*—Again visited Seriff Sahib. His name and descent are Arabic; his father, an Arab, having married a daughter of the Borneo Rajah. The Malays evidently honour this descent, and consider his birth very high. His power, they say, equals his family; as he is, in some measure, independent; and were he to instigate the Sadung country to take arms against Borneo, it is very probable he would overthrow the government, and make himself Sultan of Borneo. In person, this noble partakes much of his father's race, both in height and features, being tall and large, with a fine nose and contour of face. His manners are reserved but kind; and he looks as if too indolent to care much about acquiring power; too fat for an active traitor, though a dangerous man to oppress.

"We were the first Europeans he had ever seen; but, on our second visit, he lost much of his previous reserve, and was curious in examining our arms and accoutrements. We, as usual, *exchanged* presents; mine consisting of some nankeen, red cloth, knife, scissors, and handkerchief; while he gave me the shield of a great Kayan warrior, a Bukar spear, a goat, fowls, and our dinner and breakfast daily. He promised me specimens of the arms of all the Dyak tribes, and plenty of animals, particularly my much-desired *mias pappan*; and I, in return, agreed to bring him two small tables, six chairs, and a gun. Subsequently to our interview he sent me a tattooed Dyak, the first I had seen. The lines, correctly and even elegantly laid in, of a blue colour, extended from the throat to his feet. I gained but little information; yet the history of the poor man is curious, and similar to that of many other unfortunates. He represented himself as a chief among his own people in the country of Buyat, five days' journey up the Cotringen River (*vulgo* Coti River).

"Going in his canoe from the latter place to Banjamassim, he was captured by Illanun pirates, with whom he was in bondage for some time, but ultimately sold as a slave to a resident of Sadung. It was now five years since he became first captive; but having lately got money enough to buy his liberty, he is again a freeman; and having married, and turned to the religion of Islam, desires no longer to revisit his native country. The language of the tribe of Buyat he represents as entirely Malay. I made him a small present for the trouble I had given him, and he departed well content.

"About three o'clock in the afternoon we had a heavy thunderstorm, with lightning as vivid as the tropics produce. Torrents of rain descended, and continued a great part of the night; but, sheltered by our *kajangs* or mats, we managed to keep tolerably dry. Indeed, the voyager on this coast must be prepared for exposure to heavy rains, and considerable detention from thick and cloudy weather. The latter obstruction, of little moment or even agreeable to those making a passage, is a cause of much vexation in surveying the coast, as for days together no observations are to be had.

"*27th.*—About 7 a. m. we quitted Songi, and dropped down as far as Tanjong Balaban, a low point forming the larboard entrance into the Sadung River, and bounding the bay, which lies between it and Tanjong Sipang. Coming to this point gave us a good offing for our return, and enabled me to take a round of angles to finish the survey as far as this point and Pulo Burong, which lies off it. We crossed over the sand flats with a light breeze, and reached the *Royalist* at 4 p.m. In the evening the Datu Jembrong, who had preceded us from Sadung, spent the evening aboard. He expressed his willingness to accompany me next season: whether I shall take him is another question; but, could he be trusted, his services might be highly useful.

"Our *pangerans* arrived early this morning from Sadung; and tomorrow was fixed for our departure, when an unforeseen occurrence caused a farther detention. The day passed quietly: in the evening I was ashore, and took leave of the Pangerans Subtu and Illudeen, who returned to Sarawak, leaving the *panglima rajah* to pilot us out. The first part of the night was dark; and the *panglima* in his *prahu*, with twelve men, lay close to the shore, and under the dark shadow of the hill. About nine, the attention of the watch on deck was attracted by some bustle ashore, and it soon swelled to the wildest cries; the only word we could distinguish, however, being 'Dyak! Dyak!'

"All hands were instantly on deck. I gave the order to charge and fire a gun with a blank cartridge, and in the mean time lit a blue light. The gig was lowered, a few muskets and cutlasses thrown into her, and I started in the hope of rescuing our poor Malay friends. The vessel meanwhile was prepared for defence; guns loaded, boarding-nettings ready for running up, and the people at quarters; for we were ignorant of the number, the strength, or even the description of the assailants.

I met the *panglima's* boat pulling toward the vessel, and returned with her, considering it useless and rash to pursue the foe. The story is soon told. A fire had been lit on the shore; and after the people had eaten, they anchored their boat, and, according to their custom, went to sleep. The fire had probably attracted the roving Sarebus Dyaks, who stole upon them, took them by surprise, and would inevitably have cut them off but for our presence.

"They attacked the *prahu* fiercely with their spears; five out of twelve jumped into the water, and swam ashore; and the *panglima rajah* was wounded severely. When our blue light was seen they desisted; and directly the gun fired, paddled away fast. We never saw them. The poor *panglima* walked aboard with a spear fixed in his breast, the barb being buried, and a second rusty spear-wound close to the first; the head of the weapon was cut out, his wounds dressed, and he was put to bed. Another man had a wound from a wooden-headed spear; and most had been struck more or less by these rude and, luckily, innocuous weapons. A dozen or two of Dyak spears were left in the Malay boat, which I got. Some were well-shaped, with iron heads; but the mass simply pieces of hard wood sharp-pointed, which they hurl in great numbers.

"Firearms the Dyaks had none, and during the attack made no noise whatever; while the Malays, on the contrary, shouted lustily, some perhaps from bravery, most from terror. The force that attacked them was differently stated; some said the boat contained eighty or a hundred men, others rated the number as low as fifty; and, allowing for an exaggeration, perhaps there might have been thirty-five—not fewer, from the number of spears thrown. Being fully prepared, we set our watch, and retired as usual to our beds; the stealthy and daring attack, right under the guns of the schooner, having given me a lesson to keep the guns charged in future. The plan was well devised; for we could not fire without the chance of hitting our friends as well as foes, and the deep shadow of the hill entirely prevented our seeing the assailants.

"*29th.*—I considered it necessary to dispatch a boat to Sarawak to acquaint the *rajah* with the circumstance of the attack made on his boat. The wound of the *panglima* was so severe, that in common humanity I was obliged to wait until all danger for him was past. He was soon well; and, as with natives in general, his wound promises favourably; to a European constitution a similar wound would be imminently dangerous.

NIGHT ATTACK ON THE PANGLIMA'S PRAHU

"*30th.*—Took the long boat, and sounded along the edge of the sand; soundings very regular. In the evening Mr. Williamson returned in the gig, and a host of *pangerans*; the Pangeran Macota at the head. He urged me much to go and see Muda Hassim. The *rajah*, he said, desired it so much, and would think it so kind, that I consented to go up tomorrow. I am very desirous to fix their good feelings toward us: and I was prompted by curiosity to see the *rajah's ménage* as his guest.

"*October 1st.*—We had a heavy pull against tide, and arrived at Sarawak about 4 p.m. We had eaten nothing since breakfast at 8; and we had to sit and talk, and drink tea and smoke, till 8 in the evening; then dinner was announced, and we retired to the private apartments—my poor men came willingly too! The table was laid *à la Anglaise*, a good curry and rice, grilled fowls, and a bottle of wine. We did justice to our cheer; and the *rajah*, throwing away all reserve, bustled about with the proud and pleasing consciousness of having given us an English dinner in proper style; now drawing the wine; now changing our plates; pressing us to eat; saying, 'You are at home.'

"Dinner over, we sat, and drank, and smoked, and talked cheerfully, till, tired and weary, we expressed a wish to retire, and were shown to a private room. A crimson silk mattress, embroidered with gold, was my couch: it was covered with white gold-embroidered mats and pillows. Our men fared equally well, and enjoyed their wine, a luxury to us; our stock of wine and spirits having been expended some time.

"*2nd.*—Once more bade *adieu* to our kind friends; reached the vessel at 4 p.m., and got under weigh directly. At dusk anchored in the passage between the sands.

"*3rd.*—Five a.m. under weigh. Clear of the sands about midday, and shaped our course for Singapore.

"*4th.*—Strong breeze from w.s.w. Beating from leeward of Datu to Pulo Murrundum, in a nasty chop of a head sea."

CHAPTER 5

# Sail from Singapore

Mr. Brooke's *journal* continues his observations on the people and country he had just left; and, I need hardly say, communicates much of novelty and interest in his own plain and simple manner.

"*Oct. 5th.*—Just laying our course. I may here briefly recapitulate the information acquired during the last two months and a half. Beginning from Tanjong Api, we have delineated the coast as far as Tanjong Balaban, fixing the principal points by chronometer and observation, and filling in the details by personal inspection. The distance, on a line drawn along the headlands, may be from 120 to 130 miles, the entire coast being previously quite unknown.

"Within this space are many fine rivers, and some navigable for vessels of considerable burden, and well calculated for the extension of commerce, such as Sarawak, Morotaba, and Sadung. The others, equally fine streams, are barred, but offer admirable means for an easy inland communication; these are the Quop, Boyur, Riam, Samarahan, Lundu, Samatan, &c. In our excursions into the interior of the island, most of these streams have been ascended to a distance of 25 or 30 miles, and some further. We traced the Samarahan River for 70 or 80 miles from its mouth, and passed through portions of the intermediate streams of the Riam, Quop, and Boyur.

"The Morotaba, which is but another mouth of the Sarawak, we passed through several times from the sea to its junction with that river. The Lundu and Sadung rivers were likewise ascended to the distance of near 30 miles; and plans of all these rivers have been taken as accurately as circumstances would permit, by observations of the latitude and longitude, and various points, and an eye-sketch of the distance of each reach and the compass bearing. The entrances into the Sarawak and Morotaba were carefully examined, and the former accurately laid down. The productions of the country attracted our attention, and the articles best fitted for commerce have been already enumerated. Among these are, first, minerals; say gold, tin, probably copper, antimony-ore, and fine white clay for pipes. Secondly, woods of the finest descriptions, for ship-building, and other purposes; besides aloes wood (*lignum aloes*), and *arang* or ebony wood, canes, and rattans. To these may be added, among vegetable productions, sago, compon, rice, &c., &c.

"The wild nutmeg was found growing on the islands of Sadung and Sumpudin in abundance and perfection, proving that by cultivation it might be brought into the market as cheap, and probably as good, as those produced in the Moluccas. We have various specimens of ores and stones, which, on being tested, may prove valuable commodities. Among these is decomposed granite rock (I believe), containing minute particles of what we conceive to be gold, and an ore believed to be copper. Besides the articles above enumerated, are birds-nests and bees-wax in considerable quantities, and others not worth detailing here.

"We have been able, during our residence with the Borneons, to continue on the most friendly terms with them, and to open a field of research for our subsequent inquiries in the proper season. My attention has been anxiously directed to acquiring a knowledge of the Dyak tribes; and for this purpose I passed ten days among them at Lundu. I have made such vocabularies of the language of the Sibnowans and Lundus as my means allowed; and a further addition of their various dialects will furnish, I conceive, matters of high importance to those interested in tracing the emigration of nations. I may here briefly notice, that the nation of Kayans, included under the common denomination of Dyak, are a tattooed race, who use the *sumpitan*, or blow-pipe; while the other Dyak tribes (which are very numerous) are not tattooed, and never use the blow-pipe.

"The arms and instruments of many tribes are in my possession; and among the Sibnowans I had the opportunity of becoming acquainted with their habits, customs, and modes of living.

"The appellation of the Dyak tribes near the coast is usually the same as the rivers from which they originally came. The Dyaks of Sibnow come from the river of that name, just beyond Balaban Point, though large communities are dispersed on the Lundu and the Sadung. The same may be said of the Sarebus tribe (the most predaceous and wild on the coast), which has powerful branches of the original stock on the Skarran River. Beyond Point Balaban is a bay—between that point and Point Samaludum; the first river is the Sibnow; the next the Balonlupon, which branches into the rivers of Sakarran and Linga; passing Tanjong Samaludum you come to the two islands of Talison; and between it and the next point, or Banting Marron, lies the Sarebus River.

"Between Banting Marron and Tanjong Siri are the Kaleka River, a high mountain called Maban, and then Rejong, the chief river of the Kayans. I may here likewise correct some of the statements and names usually current in England. The Idaan, represented as a Dyak tribe, are a hill people, and probably not Dyaks; and the name Marat is applied by the natives of Borneo to the various wild tribes, Dyaks and others, without any specific meaning.

"In natural history the expedition has done as much as was in its power, by forming collections of birds, animals, and reptiles; but these collections are as small as our means. Specimens of woods and seeds have been preserved; but the season was not the proper one for flowers, as very few indeed were seen. The specimen of the hand of the *mias pappan* and the head of an adult *mias rombi* will, I believe, go far to establish the existence of an animal similar to the Pongo of the Count Buffon. I have little doubt that I shall be able in the ensuing season to establish the fact, or set it at rest forever; though I confess myself greatly inclined to think that the former will be the case. I here leave the coast with an excellent prospect for the coming year; and I would not now have quitted it so soon, but for the want of provisions, added to which, the change of the monsoon, bringing squally and dark weather, greatly interferes with our further progress in surveying.

"*Nov. 22nd, 1839.*—The Malayan language has been compared to the *lingua franca* of Europe. They are both, indeed, used by various nations in their commercial transactions; but, beyond this, nothing can be more unjust or absurd than the comparison. The *lingua franca* is a jargon compounded at random, devoid of grammar or elegance; the Malayan, on the contrary, is musical, simple in its construction, and well calculated for the expression of poetry. It boasts many dialects, like the Italian, of superior softness, and, like the Italian, it is derived from many sources, refining all to the most liquid sounds by the addition of a final vowel.

"I fully concur with Mr. Marsden in his opinion that the Malayan tongue, though derived from the Sanscrit, the Arabic, the Hindoostani, &c., &c., is based on the language which he calls the Polynesian; a language which may be considered original (as far as we know), and which embraces so vast an extent of geographical surface. The proof of this rests mainly on the fact that the simple wants of man, as well as the most striking features of nature, are expressed in the Polynesian; while the secondary class of ideas is derived from the Sanscrit, or some other language, and usually grafted in a felicitous manner on the original stem. By an original language, I must be understood, however, to mean only a language which cannot be derived from any other known tongue.

"I seek not to trace the language of Noah, or to raise a theory which shall derive the finished and grammatical Sanscrit, the pure and elegant Greek, from some barbarous stock, whether Celtic or Teutonic. Such inquiries are fitted for those with leisure and patience to undertake a hopeless task, and learning enough to achieve better things. When we look for the origin of languages we are lost, for those existing afford us no help. They present some affinities, as might be expected; but their discrepancies are irreconcilable; and, amid many equally good claims, who shall be able to demonstrate the only one which is right?

"Supposing even that all languages agreed as to primary ideas, it would be difficult to determine the original; but when this primary class of ideas is expressed by sounds entirely and totally different, the task becomes utterly hopeless, and the labour as vain as that of Sisyphus. Indeed, it would be very difficult to show how languages, derived from one stock, could possibly differ so far in their expression of the simplest ideas and wants as not to be mutually traceable: and truly, until this is done (which I conceive impossible), I am content to rest in the belief that there are more original languages *than one*—a conclusion agreeable to common sense, and consonant with the early history of the Hebrews.

"To trace the original identity of distant races, and their early migrations, through the affinity of language, is indeed a limited task compared with the other, but one both feasible and useful. To further this labour, the smallest additional information is valuable; and the dialects of the rude people inhabiting the interior of the islands of Borneo and Celebes would be highly important. Previously, however, to instituting such a comparison, as far as in my power, I propose taking a brief glance at the different races whose languages may be included under the common name of Polynesian.

"In the first place, the Malayan. Issuing from the interior of Sumatra, there is reason to conjecture, and even facts to prove, that originally the dialect of Menangkabau resembled the other dialects of its birthplace. The gradual extension of a warlike race gave a polish to the language; additional wants, increasing luxury, extended knowledge, and contact with the merchants of many Eastern nations, all combined to produce the Malayan in its present form. But, during the progress of this change, the radical Polynesian stock remained; and we find, consequently, that the words necessary to mankind in their earliest stage bear a striking and convincing resemblance to the dialects of Rejong and Lampung, in Sumatra.

"Subsequent improvements were largely adopted from the Sanscrit and the Arabic; but the fact of the primary ideas being expressed in the Polynesian must preclude the conclusion of either of these being the source whence the Malayan is derived, its improvement and extension being alone referable to them. Marsden positively states his inability to trace the Polynesian to any other Eastern language; and, at the same time, he has demonstrated, in what he considers a convincing manner, the identity of this language from Madagascar and the islands of the Pacific to the Philippines and Sumatra.

"It may here be incidentally remarked, that while so many authors are endeavouring to prove that the Asiatic archipelago was peopled from the Western Continent,[1] they overlook the fact of the radical difference of language. Unless the roots of the language can be traced either to India, Cambodia, or other parts, it must follow, as a matter of course, that the islands were peopled at a time previous to the introduction of the language now spoken on the Continent; else how are we to account for the simple dialects of a rude people being radically distinct from the language of the mother country? If the Dyaks of Borneo and the Arafuras of Celebes and New Guinea speak a dialect of the Polynesian, it will go far to prove an original people as well as an original language, that is, as original as the Celtic, the Teutonic, the South American; original because not derived from any known source.

"These brief remarks on the Malayan will, I believe, apply to the language of the island of Java, which, equally improved and enlarged by the addition of Sanscrit and Arabic words, and differently modified, retains, nevertheless, its radical Polynesian stock and its distinct written

---

1. Western as regards Polynesia.

character, as do likewise the dialects of the islands of Bally and Lombock. The districts of Rejong, Lampung, &c., in Sumatra, retain the original language in a much higher degree, possess distinctive written characters, and have little intermixture of Sanscrit or Arabic. Celebes, or Bugis-land, with a distinct language and character, will probably be found to follow the same rule; and the Philippines, including Mindanao, according to Marsden, possess the same language, though altered and modified into the Tagala tongue.

"Madagascar, so far removed, exhibits in its language a dialect of Tagala, or, strictly speaking, of Polynesian; and the South Sea islands present striking and almost convincing proofs of the same origin.

"The inquiry ought to be pushed to the languages of the Mexicans and Peruvians of South America; and, as far as our knowledge permits, their identity established or disproved; for the language of this bygone people would go far toward tracing the course of emigration, it being evident that a strong argument would be raised in favour of the migration proceeding from east to west, if the language is common to South America and Sumatra, and not traceable to any country of the Continent of India.

"It remains, however, to inquire into the language of the interior tribes of Borneo, Celebes, and New Guinea; and, on such inquiry, should they be found to possess the same primary roots as the rest, I believe the conclusion must ultimately be arrived at of the existence of a Polynesian language common to this vast geographical extent, and distinct from the languages of Asia. In tracing this identity, we can only, of course, find it in few instances in the cultivated Javanese and Malayan languages. Discrepancies must naturally be great from the intermixture, from early recorded times, of all languages in the archipelago; but, nevertheless, if the radical affinities be striking, they will be conclusive in establishing the original identity of all the races before mentioned; for, without this original identity, how can we account for these affinities of language?

"It may, indeed, be urged that this language has gradually crept into the dialects of Java and Menangkabau. But, in the first place, the affinities will be found in the very roots of the language—in the expressions for the primary and necessary ideas, which seldom alter in any people; in the next, there is a high degree of improbability in supposing a rude dialect to supplant a substantial portion of a more polished one; and, thirdly, we must not overlook the collateral evidence of the similarity of conformation pervading the entire race from Polynesia to the archipelago—distinct alike from the Caucasian and the Mongolian.

"In tracing the identity of this language, we may reckon the dialects of the Dyaks of Borneo, &c., as the lowest step of the ladder; those of the Pacific islands next; and so through the dialects of Sumatra and Tagala, up to the Malayan and Javanese. For this purpose, a comparative view of all must be attained; and Eastern scholars should point out, when possible, the words taken from Sanscrit and other languages. For my own part, these remarks are made as a sketch to be enlarged on, and to assist in obtaining the vocabularies of the Dyaks and Arafuras.

"*Dec. 6th.*—In looking over Marsden's admirable Introduction to his Malayan Grammar, I find I have taken many of his views in the foregoing remarks; but I consider that his opinions may be pushed to conclusions more extended than he has ventured upon. Having described the 'exterior circumstance' of the Malayan language, he proceeds to point out those more original languages from whence we may presume it to be derived.

"'The words of which it consists may be divided into three classes, and that two of these are Hindoo and Arabic has been generally admitted. The doubts that have arisen respect only the third, or that original and essential part which, to the Malayan, stands in the same relation as the Saxon to the English, and which I have asserted to be one of the numerous dialects of the widely-extended language found to prevail, with strong features of similarity, throughout the archipelago on the hither side of New Guinea, and, with a less marked resemblance, among the islands of the Pacific Ocean.

"To show the general identity, or radical connection of its dialects, and, at the same time, their individual differences, I beg leave to refer the reader[2] to the tables annexed to a paper on the subject which I presented, so long ago as the year 1780, to the Society of Antiquaries, and is printed in vol. 6 of the *Archæologia*; also, a table of comparative numerals, in the appendix to vol. 3 of Captain Cook's last voyage; and likewise to the chart of ten numerals, in two hundred languages, by the Rev. R. Patrick, recently published in Valpy's *Classical, Biblical and Oriental Journal.*'

"Again, Marsden states:

But whatever pretensions any particular spot may have to precedence in this respect, the so wide dissemination of a language

---

2. Also, vol. 4 of the *Bengal Asiatic Researches*.

common to all bespeaks a high degree of antiquity, and gives a claim to originality, as far as we can venture to apply that term, which signifies no more than the state beyond which we have not the means, either historically or by fair inference, of tracing the origin. In this restricted sense it is that we are justified in considering the main portion of the Malayan as original, or indigenous, *its affinity to any Continental tongue not having yet been shown*; and least of all can we suppose it connected with the monosyllabic, or Indo-Chinese, with which it has been classed.

"When we find an original language bearing no traces of being derived from any Continental tongue, we must conclude the people likewise to be original, in the restricted sense, or to have emigrated with their language from some source hitherto unknown. The Sanscrit and Arabic additions to the original stock are well marked, though the period of the introduction of the former is hidden in darkness. It may be inferred, however, that it came with the Hindoo religion, the remains of which are yet in existence. It is evident that the question resolves itself into two distinct branches: first, the original language, its extent, the coincidence of its dialects, its source, &c.; secondly, its discrepancies, whence arising, &c.; together with the inquiry into the probable time and mode of the introduction of the Sanscrit. With the latter of these inquiries I have nothing to do; on the former subject I may collect some valuable information by adding the dialects of the savage tribes in the interior of Borneo and Celebes.

"The alphabets of the island of Java, of the Tagala, and the Bugis of Celebes, are given by Corneille, Le Brun, Thevenot, and Forrest."

Of Mr. Brooke's sojourn at Singapore it is unnecessary to speak; and I accordingly resume my extracts with his ensuing voyage from that port, and again for the Indian *archipelago*, but contenting myself, for reasons which need not be entered into at length, with only that portion of his excursion to Celebes and among the Bugis which particularly bears upon his Bornean sequel.

"*Dec. 7th, 1839.*—Off Great Solombo. Never was there a more tedious passage than ours has been from Singapore. Sailing from that place on the 20th of November, we have encountered a succession of calms and light winds—creeping some days a few miles, and often lying becalmed for forty-eight hours without a breath to fill the sails. Passing through the straits of Rhio and Banca, and watering at the islands of Nanka, we stood thence for Pulo Babian, or Lubeck, lay a night becalmed close to the Arrogants Shoal, of which, however, we saw nothing, owing, probably, to the smoothness of the water. The depths are greater than laid down on Horsburgh's chart, varying from thirty-six to thirty-eight fathoms. A calm now keeps us off the greater Solombo, which it is my intention to visit when in my power.

"*8th.*—Drifted past Solombo in the calm, and, reluctant to return, I continued on my voyage with a light breeze from the eastward. This island is well laid down: from the sea we made its longitude 113° 31'; Horsburgh gives it 113° 28', which, considering that both observations were made afloat, is a near enough approximation. The land is low, with a single hill, showing round from the westward, flat or wedge-shaped from the eastward. The smaller Solombo is low: both wooded.

"*10th.*—In sight of Laurots Islands.

"*11th.*—In the evening stood within four miles of the southern island of Laurots. These islands are high and steep, covered with wood, and uninhabited. The easternmost island seems, by bearings, badly laid down, being not far enough to the southward and eastward. The southern island is called by the Bugis, Mata Siri; the eastern, Kadapan-gan; the northern one, Kalambow. A few rocks and islets lay off them; water deep, and apparently clear of all danger.

"*15th.*—Turatte Bay. After experiencing continued calms and light winds, and falling short of water, we at length reached this bay, and anchored in 7½ fathoms. The first impression of Celebes is highly fa-vourable. The mountains present a bold outline, and rise in confused masses, until crowned by what is commonly called *Bonthian Hill.* The sides of the mountains slope gradually to the sea, and present an in-viting and diversified aspect of wood and cleared land. I dispatched a boat for water to a small village; and the crew were well received by the natives, after they became assured that they were not pirates.

"The outline of this bay, in Norie's chart, is not badly laid down; but on either side there is great room for improvement and survey. Turatte Bay may be fairly so called, as the district (or *negri*) generally bears that name. The larboard point of Turatte Bay (approaching) is called Malasaro, which comes next to Tanjong Layken in the charts. The starboard point is Tanjong Uju Loke, and from Uju Loke the land runs low to the point of Galumpang, the entrance of a river marked in the charts. From Uju Loke (named Bolo Bolo in Norie's chart) the coast-line runs for 12 or 15 miles to Bolo Bolo, which space is entirely omitted. Bolo Bolo forms the entrance of Bonthian Bay.

"*16th.*—Bonthian Bay. Called Banthi by the natives: is in lat. 5° 37' S.; long. 119° 33' E.

"The bay is pretty well laid down by Dalrymple. The small Dutch fort, or intrenchment, stands rather on the eastern bight of the bay, and is composed of a few huts, surrounded by a ditch and green bank. Two guns at each corner compose its strength, and the garrison consists of about thirty Dutchmen and a few Javanese soldiers. We were cordially and hospitably received by the officers, and, after a great deal of trouble and many excuses, here procured horses to carry us to the waterfall. Bonthian Hill is immediately over this place; a flat space of rice-ground, some miles in extent, only intervening. The hill (so called) may with more propriety be designated as a range of mountains, which here attain their utmost height and sink down gradually almost across the peninsula.

"The view is most attractive; the green and refreshing rice-grounds in the front and behind, the slopes of the mountain and its various peaks, verdant grass, wooded chasms, and all the inequalities which mark a mountain region. I am very anxious to mount to the summit; but so many difficulties are thrown in the way, that I almost despair— horses and guides are not to be procured. The Dutch say the natives are lazy: the natives say they dare not go without authority—either way we are the losers; but the officers certainly exert themselves in our favour. Coming into this bay, there is some difficulty in distinguishing the fort; but coming from the westward, its position may readily be known by steering for two lumps on the S.E. declivity of the mountain.

"*18th.*—Got ashore by seven o'clock to start for the waterfall; till nine we were detained by want of horses, but after much trouble the animals were procured, and off we started. Our party consisted of three doctors (him of the fortification, a German gentleman, Treacher, and Theylingen) and myself, with native guides. The road lay for a short way along the beach, then struck into the thicket, and we commenced a gradual ascent. The scenery was most striking and lovely; glades and glens, grassy knolls and slopes, with scattered trees, and the voice of a hidden river which reached our ears from a deep valley on the left hand. Proceeding thus for some distance, we at length plunged into the wood, and descending a short space, found ourselves by the sides of the stream below the waterfall. Here, breakfast being finished, we all stripped to our trowsers, entered the water, and advanced along the bed of the river to the fall. The banks on either hand, steep and woody, prevented any other mode of approach, and the stream, rushing down and falling over huge rocks, rendered the only available one anything but easy.

"At times we were up to the arms, then crawling out and stealing with care over wet and slippery stones, now taking advantage of a few yards of dry ground, and ever and anon swimming a pool to shorten an unpleasant climb. In this manner we advanced about half a mile, when the fall became visible; thick trees and hanging creepers intervened; between and through the foliage we first saw the water glancing and shining in its descent. The effect was perfect. After some little further and more difficult progress, we stood beneath the fall, of about 150 feet sheer descent. The wind whirled in eddies, and carried the sleet over us, chilling our bodies, but unable to damp our admiration.

"The basin of the fall is part of a circle, with the outlet forming a funnel; bare cliffs, perpendicular on all sides, form the upper portion of the vale, and above and below is all the luxuriant vegetation of the East; trees, arched and interlaced, and throwing down long fantastic roots and creepers, shade the scene, and form one of the richest sylvan prospects I have ever beheld. The water, foaming and flashing, and then escaping amid huge gray stones on its troubled course—clear and transparent, expanding into tranquil pools, with the flickering sunshine through the dense foliage—all combine to form at scene such as Tasso has described.[3]

"Inferior in body of water to many falls in Switzerland, it is superior to any in sylvan beauty; its deep seclusion, its undisturbed solitude, and the difficulty of access, combine to heighten its charms to the imagination. Our descent was like our upward progress. Having again dressed ourselves, we rested for a time, and then started for Bonthian—wearing away the rest of the day shooting amid the hills. Theylingen and myself procured many specimens, and returned laden with our spoil, and charmed with our day's excursion. The waterfall is called Sapo, from the neighbouring green peak of that name. The height of our resting-place (not the highest point of the day's ascent) was 750.5 feet, by Newman's two barometers; yet this is the bottom of the mountain on its western slope. The officers dined with us; they are very polite and kind; and we retired early to rest, all the better for

3. *Canto* 15, *stanza* 55, 56.

our excursion.

"*19th.*—At 6 a.m. went with the Dutch officers shooting, and reached the same stream which forms the waterfall. The scenery delightful; water cool, and pleasant for bathing, a luxury I enjoyed in high perfection. Aboard again to a late breakfast."

## CHAPTER 6

# Dispute With the Rajah's Son-in-law

"I may here, indulge in a brief episode to introduce my Bugis companion, Dain Matara,—which properly I should have done long since,—a man well born, and, for his country, affluent and educated: he offered at Singapore, to accompany me on this expedition, refusing all pay or remuneration, and stating that the good name to be acquired, and the pleasure of seeing different places, would recompense, him. At first, I must own this disinterestedness rendered me suspicious; but conceiving that the greatest utility might accrue from his assistance, I agreed to take him with his servant. Our long passage seemed to make us well acquainted, and, I believe, raised a mutual confidence. Dain, cheerful, good-tempered, and intelligent, gained daily on my esteem; and, by the time we reached Bonthian, I was rejoiced that he accompanied me.

"On this day we succeeded in procuring horses and guides for the *hill*, as it is called.

"*20th.*—By 8 a.m. our preparations were complete, and we mounted our horses; a motley group we formed, composed of Treacher, Theylingen, and myself, two seamen (Spence and Balls), Dain Matara, a son-in-law of the Bonthian Rajah, and six footmen. Provisions for four days were on one of the horses, and a goodly stock of fowling-pieces, beside my mountain barometer. The plain was soon cleared; and three hours' ride by a good horse-path brought us to the village of Senua, consisting of a dozen houses. We found the inhabitants hospitable, and took refuge from a heavy squall of wind and rain in the best house the place afforded. During the rain the thermometer sunk to 76°, but rose directly afterward.

"At half-past one the rain cleared away, but we were detained until three by the Bugis getting their dinner. During this time I strayed along the sparkling stream which runs by the village, and after enjoying a bathe, called to horse, in order to proceed. Great was my surprise, however, to be told by the *rajah's* son-in-law that he supposed we were going back. A discussion arose,—he declaring there was no road for the horses, and that we could not go farther; while I insisted, if he would not advance, I should continue my journey on foot. After much time had been lost, our guide set off slowly and reluctantly, and we proceeded for two or three miles, when, finding our head turned to the southward, and the road descending, I again called a halt, and was once more told it was not possible to mount farther.

"A scheme had been formed to lead us round about, and take us gradually down, until too late to mount again. A long parley ensued; both parties seemed resolute; and it finished by our unloading the baggage-horse, and making a small parcel of necessaries to carry on foot. Our guide, however, never intended matters to go so far, and we finished at last by taking half the horses, and allowing him (the *rajah's* son-in-law) to descend with the rest. This being done, we had to retrace our road nearly to Senua; and a little before sunset our party crossed an awkward stream, and struck into the path up the mountains.

"A short walk brought us to Lengan Lengang about dusk, where we put up for the night. For the first time, this day I saw the cockatoo in his wild state; I was within easy shot of two of them, but the stream lay between us, and I felt some compunction at shooting these favourite birds.

"*Lourikeets* were in great plenty, and many varieties of pigeons and doves, beside other birds. Near Lengan Lengang we encountered a community of dusky baboons, many of them very large and powerful: after a hard scramble I got within shot of them; on my firing the first barrel, the young ones and females made off, but the leaders of the band disdained to retreat, and, with threatening gestures and grimaces, covered the retreat of their party. The consequence was, I sacrificed one of these heroes, of a large size: he fell from the branch on which he was seated into a deep valley, and his fall completed the rout of the rest. Spence, in the mean time, having arrived, I dispatched him to secure the prize; but at the bottom of the valley the baboons again showed themselves, and manifested every inclination to fall on him; another barrel put them to flight, and between us we dragged the fallen hero to the horses.

"The village of Lengan Lengang consists of about a dozen houses, is situated in a nook of the hills, and surrounded by cocoanut-trees. We were accommodated in the principal house, and treated with every hospitality. The people of the hills are poor, though their land is fertile, and produces abundance of rice and Indian corn. Theft is said to be common, especially of horses, and the care of the horses belonging to travellers devolves on the villagers; for, in case a horse is stolen, a fine is imposed on the population in general. To prevent this misfortune, our hosts kept playing, as long as we could bear it, on an instrument like a clarinet; but at twelve o'clock, after trying in vain to sleep, we were obliged to stop the noise and risk the horses.

"This instrument is about three feet long, with five or six holes, and a flat mouthpiece on the cane-tube; the sound is musical when gently breathed into, but in their usual mode of playing, it emits frightful shrieks. During the night the thermometer sunk to 69°, and we were glad of our blankets.

"*21st.*—Rose between five and six. Took some barometrical observations, and at half-past six continued our upward way. As far as Lengan Lengang the country presents beautiful woodland and mountain scenery, with luxuriant vegetation, thickly wooded valleys, and sparkling streams. The flats and valleys are occupied by rice-grounds, and the pasturage is of the very finest description for all sorts of cattle: the grass short and rich. Lengan Lengang is the last point where the cocoanut or other palms is seen; but there it grows remarkably well, and attains a great height. Above this point the wood, generally speaking, becomes smaller, and the vegetation more coarse, the hills being covered with a rank high grass, and ferns, similar to those in England. Three hours' slow travelling brought us to the village of Lokar, situated at the foot of the peak of that name. I mounted, while breakfast was preparing, nearly to the top, and up to the belt of thick wood which surrounds the last 100 or 150 feet.

"Observations were repeated here, showing a great fall of the mercury, and afterward taken at the village. Lokar consists of a few scattered huts, situated amid gardens of fruit and vegetables: the mango, the guava, the jack, and the plantain, with cabbages and Indian corn, compose the stock of the inhabitants; the latter constitutes their principal food, and is granaried for use in large quantities, not only in the house, but on frameworks of bamboo without, on which it is thickly hung in rows, with the head downward, to protect it from the weather. The highest summit, called Lumpu Balong, was visible when we first arrived, some miles in advance: at breakfast-time the clouds entirely covered it, and rolled down upon Lokar in heavy rain, driving us into a miserable hut for shelter.

"During the rain the thermometer fell to 70°. At 3 p.m. started for some huts we saw at the foot of Lumpu Balong, having first sent our horses back to Lengan Lengang, being assured their farther progress was impracticable. When, however, our guide from Lokar understood our intention of reaching Lumpu Balong, he objected to proceed, on the plea that the village in advance was inhabited by people from Turatte. We managed to coax him on, and, after two and a half hours' walk, reached Parontalas. The country, ascending gradually, becomes more and more wild; the wood stunted; and the streams, finding their way through masses of rock, leave strong traces of their occasional violence.

"Parontalas stands on the edge of the forest which skirts Lumpu Balong, from which it has not long been retrieved. It consists of a few scattered huts, far apart. Potatoes, tobacco, and coffee are grown here, the former in great abundance. Like the rest of the people, their food consists of Indian corn; and, as in the other villages, they breed horses. Our host of Parontalas was very polite, and gave us some fowls and the accommodation of his house; the latter, indeed, was needful, for we were all badly provided with covering, and the mountain air was raw and cold. To our request for guides to ascend the mountain he replied, that it was necessary to consult the head man of the district, who lived some little distance off. In the interim we made ourselves very happy, determined to ascend with or without a guide or guides. We lay down at nine, in order to be ready for the morning's work, the thermometer standing at 59° in the house.

"*22nd.*—At five, when we rose, the thermometer stood at 56° in the air. The head man had arrived, and willingly gave us guides, warning us only of the difficulty of the ascent. Nothing could exceed the kindness and attention of this simple old man. He remembered the time the English had the country, and spoke of his people's respect for our nation, and their regret that we had left the country. At 6 a.m. we started, and, after walking about a mile, plunged into the belt of forest which environs Lumpu Balong. From six till half-past two, we were alternately ascending and descending, scrambling over rocks or fallen timber, or cutting a path through the most tangled thicket that ever tore the wayfarer. To add to our difficulty, during the latter half of the ascent, we could procure no water, which caused us considerable suffering.

"At length, however, we stood at the summit of Lumpu Balong, and looked, on either side, over a vast sea of fleecy clouds which rolled beneath. The top is a narrow ridge, covered with stunted trees and luxuriant moss; and a second peak to the westward, of rather less elevation, is separated from it by a declivity. I climbed to the top of a tree to look along the mountain, and make certain that we were at the highest point; and having convinced myself of this, I proceeded with the barometric observations, which were concluded by 3 p.m.; for it was highly necessary to get down before night overtook us in the dreary and inhospitable forest. Our thirst, too, was tormenting, and increased by hearing the fall of a torrent deep in the valley to the northward.

"As far as I could observe, the northern face of the mountain was perpendicular, and the ascent on that side would have been attended with greater difficulty than from the point we chose. Our way down was easier, and the descent was made as expeditiously as the nature of the ground would allow. Having fairly worn our shoes off our feet, we were pierced by brambles and thorns in a cruel manner. Our guide, in going down, discovered a tree with a bee-hive in it containing great store of honey. The Bugis instantly attacked the tree, on seeing which my first impression was, that it would be prudent to retreat to a distance; but their composure induced me to remain; and, to my surprise, when the tree was laid open, the honey was taken out in large quantities, and the bees brushed off the comb without offering to sting.

"Though flying round about us, and on the hands of all the people, they were quite innocent of harm; and I conclude, therefore, they were different from the common honey-bee. The honey was excellent, and refreshed us for a few minutes, but ultimately only added to our thirst. At length, about five, we reached a stream of water, and quenched our thirst with draughts of the coolest and most limpid mountain stream. The Bugis, though, like ourselves, they had been, without any water from nine o'clock in the morning till five in the evening, refused to drink, alleging that it was highly injurious after eating honey! Glad were we, just at dark, to get clear of the forest; and a short walk farther brought us to our temporary dwelling. We were much knocked up, and very much torn with the thorns. A brief dinner and a delicious cigar, and we lay down to sleep—not even incommoded by the cold, which kept us awake the last night.

"*23rd.*—Having, through mistake, forgotten to bring up any money, I had no means of repaying the obligations received from these simple hill-people except *by promises*. My old friend ordered the guide of yesterday to accompany us to the plains, to receive his own payment, and to bring some things, for others, up there.

"At ten we hobbled forth, very foot-sore, and lacking proper covering for our feet. The prospect of four or five hours' walk to Lengan Lengang was very unpleasant; and in proportion to our expected pain was our gratification on meeting *all* our horses within three miles of Parontalas—*all* the horses, which all the men swore could not, by any possibility, ascend, were there; and though without saddles and bridles, or the Bugis, we were too glad to mount. We went down by another road. Four hours brought us to Lengan Lengang, where we rested for two hours, and, remounting, reached Bonthian at about seven o'clock in the evening. Thus concluded this interesting excursion into a hill-region, where we attained the summit of Lumpu Balong, never before reached by European. The Dutch officers informed me that three successive residents of Bonthian had attempted it and failed.

"Before I conclude, I may take a brief survey of the country. The hills are generally rounded or flat at top, and not offering any rugged or broken peaks. The scenery about Senua and Lengan Lengang is the perfection of woodland, with the picturesque characteristics of a mountain region; the climate admirably suited, thence to the summit, for Europeans, and capable of producing most European and tropical plants to perfection. Coffee plantations on these hills might be undertaken with certainty of success, and there is much in the character of the natives which would facilitate the operation. To the westward of Lokar, and somewhat lower, is a fine extensive plain, which we just skirted coming down; it was cultivated in every part, apparently with rice. The vegetable productions of the hills I have briefly mentioned; but I may add that the wild raspberry was found, and that wild guavas grow in the greatest abundance, as well as oranges and grapes.

"The animal kingdom, of course, we had no time to examine; but the *babi rupa* is said to be found in the higher regions; and in the forest, toward the summit of Lumpu Balong, we saw the dung of wild cattle, which, I am told, are a species of *urus*. The birds we saw were, paroquets of two sorts, *viz.*, the *lourikeet* and a small green paroquet; a large green pigeon, specimens of which we got; the cream-coloured pigeon of Borneo, beside many others.

"The geological formation of the region I must leave to others. I brought down some specimens of the rocks and loose stones, which are, I believe, pumice; if so, I presume the formation volcanic, similar to Java.

"*24th.*—Called on the resident, and saw the *rajah*.

"*25th.*—Christmas, with his jolly nose and icy hands. Here it is hot enough! Were I to live in this country, I should retire for the season up in the mountains. Dined with the Resident of Bonthian; by no means surprised that he and his congeners had failed in their attempt to climb the mountain: the resident is a native! In the evening, celebrated the day with all sorts of sports.

"*26th.*—Midday, quitted Bonthian, and ran to Boele Comba or Compa.

"*27th.*—I have little to say of Boele Comba. It is situated in the bight of the bay, eastward of Bonthian. There appears to be much, confusion in *Horsburgh's Directory* about the latitude and longitude, and the hill called after the place. This hill is the last of the mountain-range, somewhat detached, covered with wood, of moderate elevation, and peaked. From our anchorage, two miles from the fort, it bore N.N.W. The fort is similar to the one at Bonthian, the country pretty, and nearly level. The Bonthian mountains (*i. e.* Lumpu Balong and the range) show steep and well in the background. Game abounds, by report. Europeans are subject to complaints of the eyes, and occasionally to fever. Any vessel running in should be very careful, for the charts are defective, and Boele Comba reef is said to project farther to the westward of the fort than laid down.

"I here subjoin a list of our barometric observations, the upper barometer reduced to the rate of the lower and standard one:—

*Senua, 20th December, 1839.*

|   | Bar. | A. | D. |   |
|---|------|-----|-----|---|
| 1. | 30.054 | 86 | 87 | 3h. 15m. p.m. |
| 2. | 28.385 | 79 | 80 | 3h. 15m. p.m |

*Lengan Lengang, 21st December.*

|   | Bar. | A. | D. |   |
|---|------|-----|------|---|
| 1. | 30.119 | 79 | 78.5 | 6h. 30m. a.m. |
| 2. | 27.988 | 70 | 69.5 | 6h. 0m. a.m. |

*Lokar Peak, 21st December, 100 feet below summit.*

|   | Bar. | A. | D. |   |
|---|------|-----|------|---|
| 1. | 30.095 | 90 | 90 1 | 0h. 30m. a.m. |
| 2. | 25.795 | 79 | 79 | 0h. 30m. a.m. |

*Hill on the way to Lumpu Balong, 22nd December.*

| | Bar. | A. | D. | |
|---|---|---|---|---|
| 1. | 30.144 | 90 | 90 | Mean bet. 8h. And noon. |
| 2. | 23.612 | 66 | 65.5 | 10h. 40m. a.m. |

*Lumpu Balong Peak, 22nd December.*

| | Bar. | A. | D. | |
|---|---|---|---|---|
| 1. | 30.146 | 89.5 | 90.5 | 2h. 0m. p.m. |
| 2. | 23.718 | 64 | 63.5 | 2h. 30m. p.m. |

*28th.*—Leaving Boele Comba after breakfast, we shaped our course for Point Berak.

"With the richest country, the natives of these places are poor, and they bear no goodwill to their rulers. It is likewise certain that few active measures are resorted to for forwarding the development of the native character and local resources. The resident is a Macassar-born native, and this fact alone speaks volumes for the mode and manner of government. The people of the country I found a kind and simple race; and though they are accused of pride and laziness by their masters, I could not, circumstances taken into consideration, discover any trace, of the latter vice, and the former I can readily forgive them. That the Bugis are not an indolent race is well proved by their whole conduct, wherever circumstances offer any inducement to exertion.

"Even here, the cleared country and the neat cultivation prove them far otherwise; and traces are visible everywhere on the mountains of their having been more highly cultivated than at present. Coffee plantations once flourished, and being destroyed during a war, years ago, have never been renewed. Inclosures and partition walls in decay are very frequent, marking the former boundary of cultivation. That they are independent enough to be proud, I honour them for! The officers allowed they were courageous, and one designated them as '*fier comme un Espagnol*;' and, on the whole, no doubt exists in my mind that they are people easily to be roused to exertion, either agricultural or commercial; their sullen and repulsive manners toward their masters rather indicating a dislike to their sway, and the idleness complained of only proving that the profits of labor are lower than they ought to be.

"Nothing so strongly marks the degradation of a race or nation as a cheerful acquiescence under a foreign rule. The more virtuous, the more civilized, the more educated a people, the more turbulent, indolent, and sullen, when reduced to a state of subjection; the fewer qualities will they have to please their masters, when foreign rule is oppressive, or looks solely to the advantage of the country of the conquerors, and not of the conquered. There is no race will willingly submit: the bayonet and the sword, the gallows and the whip, imprisonment and confiscation, must be constantly at work to keep them under.

"Leaving Boele Comba, as I before said, we shaped our course for Tanjong Berak, passing between that point and the north island. The passage is excellent, clear of all danger, as far as we could see, with deep water. The rocks reported to exist by Horsburgh, and put down on Norie's chart, have no existence. The Bugis *prahus* always use this channel, and know them not; and the captain of a Dutch cruiser informed me that he had often run through the passage at night, and that it was clear of all danger or obstruction.

"My own observation went to verify the fact, for every part of the passage appears deep and clear, and we passed over the spots where these rocks are marked. Approaching Tanjong Berak, there is a sandy beach, where a vessel may get anchorage in case the wind dies away. The tides in the channel are strong; here, and along the south coast, the ebb runs from the eastward, the flood from the west. Having cleared the channel, we hauled into the Bay of Boni, which, although running in a north and south direction, has some headlands extending to the eastward. There are two places marked on the chart, viz. Berak and Tiero; but these, instead of being towns or villages, are names of districts; the first, reaching from Tanjong Berak, about 15 miles, till it joins Tiero; Tiero, extending from the northern confine of Berak to Tanjong Labu, 15 miles in all.

"To the northward and eastward is a high island called Balunrueh. From Tanjong Berak the water along the coast is very deep; no soundings with 50 fathoms. Toward evening we went into Tiero Bay, a pretty secluded spot. The southern part of the bay is foul, having a reef visible at low water, The northern headland has a spit running from it, with 14 fathom half a mile (or little more) off. Within the bay there is no bottom with 50 fathom till near its northern extremity, where the water shoals suddenly. Running in, in a squall, we got into 3¼ fathom, where we anchored. This country belongs to the Dutch as far as Point Labu.

"*29th.*—Calm all day. Sounded the bay: the southern point has a steep coral reef nearly a quarter of a mile off. The southern part of the bay is inclosed by a reef, part of which seems to me artificial, for the purpose of catching fish, and is shallow: outside the reef the water is deep dose to. The western shore is lined by a reef close to it, and the water is deep. The centre part of the bay is very deep; and within 100 yards of where we lay we got no bottom at 17 fathoms. The next cast was six, and the next three fathoms—hard clay bottom. A small river discharges itself, in the northern part, inside the anchorage: there is a considerable depth within, but the bar is shallow. The scenery on the river is beautiful; wild at first, and gradually becoming undulating and cultivated. Birds are plenty: cockatoos abound, of which I shot two. This part of the country possesses considerable geological interest: the hills round the bay are of slight elevation; and 80 or 100 feet from the sea level are large masses of coral rock, upheaved by some convulsion.

"*30th.*—Under weigh. Brought up in 23 fathoms, amid the coral shoals.

"*31st.*—Visited the island of Balunrueh for sights.

"Tanjong Labu is bluff and bold, and of moderate elevation. The land from thence trends away westward, forming a long bay, which, for distinction, may be called Labu Bay, at the N.W. part of which is the town of Songi, the principal place about here. Between Labu and Songi are the following countries: Kupi Kajang, Pakah, Buah, Kalaku, Baringan, and Magnarabunbang; each with a separate petty *rajah*. The country is moderately well cleared; about an average height, near the shore, of 300 feet; with few habitations about, but no towns or villages. The mountain range throws a spur downward to the sea in the vicinity of Songi and the fine peaks of Lumpu Balong; and Wawa Karang, with the *confusion* of mountains, form a magnificent background to the prospect.

"From Magnarabunbang the land runs away to the eastward toward Tanjong Salanketo, which must be described on a future occasion. In the offing are several islands and numerous reefs. The principal island is Balunrueh, 400 or 500 feet high; bold, steep, and covered with trees, except at its northern extremity; where it is low, with a sandy point. Off this north point runs a coral reef; direction 354°, and extent about two miles. At the S.W. angle of the island there is likewise a reef stretching half a mile; and the shores all round, for a short distance, are lined with coral, outside of which the water is apparently very deep. We could get no soundings with a hand lead, half a mile to the westward.

"Off Balunrueh, to the S.E., is the islet of Liang Liang; next to

86

Liang Liang, Tanbunoh, which is larger; then Cadingareh Batantampeh (the largest), Cotingduan Lariahriah, and two islands to the northward called Canallo. Balunrueh and Batantampeh have both indifferent fresh water; the former near the low point at the north end. From the S.W. end of Liang Liang a reef runs out. The bearing, from the small hill, over the watering place of Balunrueh, was 77°. The reef extends to 104°, and stretches to the southward beside: near Liang Liang it is narrow. Its limits I could not define.

"Between Liang Liang and Tanbunoh a narrow reef, and spits from most of the islands. Two patches lay off Balunrueh about two miles and a half: the first, bearing 319°, is narrow, and about half a mile long; the other smaller, and bearing 287°. Part of the day we passed on Balunrueh was very hot; but we got satisfactory sights, and sailed round the island, returning to the vessel about six in the evening.

"I must now return to Labu, to give some account of the channel between the reefs; as, from the appearance of the charts, it would seem impossible to navigate the western side of the bay. Having passed Tanjong Labu at a distance of 3½ or 4 miles, get the flat-topped hill called Bulu Tanna ahead. Close to the Bulu Tanna, in the foreground, is another smaller hill, with two remarkable tufts on the top: this hill, just open to the eastward of Bulu Tanna, is the leading mark for Songi, which stands to the westward. This mark will lead clear, or very nearly so, of all the reefs; but as there is uncertainty in the distance from Tanjong Labu, it may be necessary to diverge from the straight course in order to avoid some of the patches.

"In the daytime the coral is seen with the greatest ease; and a vessel with a lookout aloft, and a breeze, may proceed with safely. The first reef is on the starboard hand; part was dry, and shoal-water about. This first patch is in the proximity of the great reef called Melompereh, which runs to the eastward. Beside these, the channel is occasionally lined by patches on either hand; but is nowhere narrower than a mile and a half, and is anything but difficult navigation, so far, in clear weather.

"*Jan. 4th, 1840.*—Arrived off Songi on the 1st, and dispatched a boat to the old *rajah*, or *rana*, of Lamatte. Our answer was, that not, having been to Boni, she feared receiving us, as she felt inclined; but if we would come to her house, she should be glad to see us. On the following day, accordingly, we paid our visit at her residence, which is situated about four miles up the river Tanca.

"The old lady is about sixty-five years of age, and (as she herself informed us) very poor. Her house, indeed, bears every mark of great poverty; having a leaky roof, and not sufficient matting to cover the bamboo floors. She was kind, and seemed pleased to see us; said I should henceforward be her son, and that nothing but her fear of the Boni Rajah prevented her receiving me in the best way in her power; but pointing to the roof and to the floor, she repeated, 'I have nothing.' I presented her with such articles as I thought would be acceptable to her; and, in return, she gave me a sarong.

"The population of the country is considerable. The last district I mentioned was Magnarabunbang. The town of that name, on the sea-side, consists of forty-five houses, beside a roving population of Bad-jows. Along the coast to the eastward, and close to Magnarabunbang, is the river of Songi. Proceeding up this shallow river, the first village is Tacolompeh, situated on the right bank, and consisting of twenty houses; nearly opposite the village of Pangassa, of thirteen houses; and farther up, about four miles from the river's mouth, stands Songi, con-sisting of 164 houses on the right bank, and 60 on the left. These plac-es are all on the low ground, and surrounded with cocoanut-trees.

"Joining the district of Magnarabunbang, on the coast, is Lamatte, the rajanate of our old friend. The river, like the Songi, is shallow, and running through very low ground. On the left bank is Luppa, consist-ing of twenty-five houses; then, on the right, Ulo, twenty-two houses; and above Ulo comes Ullue, of twelve houses. Nearly opposite Ullue is Balammepa, with thirty houses, superior to the others, and inhab-ited by merchants who have made money in trading voyages. This village sends yearly two *prahus* to Singapore. Just above Ullue stand seven houses; and above Balammepa is Tanca, the residence of the Rajah of Lamatte, consisting of ten houses. The streams, as I have said, are shallow, and the ground low, neatly cultivated with Indian corn, and abounding in cocoanut-trees. Behind Magnarabunbang there is a narrow strip of low ground, which becomes wider as it advances to the eastward, with here and there moderate elevations.

"The chief product of the country is coffee, which is grown in great quantities on the hills, but brought down as it ripens, when it is collected by the Bugis merchants for their yearly shipments. The yearly produce is stated to be 2000 *coyans* or 80,000 *peculs*. The price is from fifteen to sixteen Java rupees the *pecul*; to which must be added the trouble and expense of storing and clearing from the inner skin. Tortoise-shell is brought in by the Badjows; and mother-of-pearl shells in any quantity there is demand for. Taking the number of houses in this small space, above described, the total will be 308 houses, which reckoned at the low estimate of eight persons for each house, will give 2464 inhabitants; this, however, is far below the proper estimate, as there are villages scattered between the rivers, and numbers of detached houses; in all, therefore, safely computed at 5000 persons.

"The villages, with the exception of Balammepa, have an aspect of poverty, and the country is ravaged by that frightful scourge the smallpox, and likewise some cases apparently of cholera, from the account given of the complaint. Near the hill of Bulu Tanna there is a hot spring, and likewise, by the report of the natives, some slight remains of an old building. I regretted much not seeing these; but the natives, with much politeness, begged me not to go previous to my visit to Boni, as they would be answerable for allowing strangers to see the country without orders from the chief *rajah*. All I see and hear convinces me that the Rajah of Boni has great power over the entire country. On a friendly communication with him, therefore, depends our chance of seeing something of the interior.

"The inhabitants here are polite, but shy and reserved: and the death of the Rana of Songi and the absence of the Rajah Mooda, her reported successor, have been against us.

"*5th.*—Sailing from Songi about 4 p.m., we directed our course for Tanjong Salanketo. The breeze was stiff, which caused us to use considerable precaution in sailing among the shoals. Assisted by a native Nacòdah, by name Dain Pativi, we were enabled to keep the tortuous channel, of which otherwise we should have been ignorant. A little farther than the Tanca River is a shoal stretching from the shore, to avoid which we kept Canallo on our lee bow: this being cleared, we gradually luffed up, ran between two shoals, and passed several others."

# CHAPTER 7

# Conduct of the War

Mr. Brooke continued his cruise for some time, and made very interesting collections of natural history, beside acquiring much insight into the native history, language, and customs, his detailed remarks on which it is to be hoped he will at a future day give to the public. He then returned to Singapore, where he was detained for several months by ill health; but availed himself of the opportunity to recopper and refit the *Royalist*, and set everything else in order for his next visit to Sarawak, the remarkable results of which are related in the following pages. Still sick and languid though he was, the very air of Borneo, and the prospect of activity, seemed to restore him to life, after the listless rest at Singapore, with "nothing to observe;" and only cheered by the kindest attentions and hospitalities of the inhabitants of that interesting and important settlement.

On the second visit of Mr. Brooke to Sarawak, about the end of August, 1840, he found the inhabitants in nearly the same state as at first, although there was much talk of reinforcements, and decisive measures for bringing the war to a close. The two parties lay within thirty miles of each other, the rebels holding the upper part of the river, and communication with the interior. The *sultan*, however, had sent down the Orang Kaya de Gadong to take more active measures, and his arrival stimulated Muda Hassim to something like exertion. This occurred on the fourth September, 1840, as appears by Mr. Brooke's journal, from which I shall give various extracts indicative not only of the character of my friend, whose ideas were written down at the time the impressions were made, but also supplying a distinct picture of the progress of this novel and amusing civil warfare, and demonstrating the unwarlike character of the Sarawak Borneons.

"An army of mixed Malays and Dyaks was raised to attack the Dyak tribes in rebellion, and this service was successfully performed; the rebel Dyaks were defeated, and most of them have since come over to the *rajah*. Their forces being weakened by desertion, were reported not to amount to more than 400 or 500 men, in four or five forts situated on the river; and it now remained to drive them from their last stronghold of resistance. It was confidently asserted by the *rajah* and Macota, that, were it not for the underhand assistance of the Sultan of Sambas, who had constantly supplied them with food and ammunition, the insurgents would long since have been dispersed.

"At the period in question they were said to be in great distress for want of provisions; and as a force was collecting to attack them from various quarters, it was greatly to be hoped that the war was verging to a termination. During my week's stay I have frequently visited Muda Hassim, and he has likewise been on board: our good understanding knows no interruption; and these savage, treacherous, bloodthirsty Borneons are our good friends, with whom we chat and laugh every evening in familiar converse. I find no cause to alter my last year's opinion, that they have few active vices; but indolence is the root of their evils.

"*Sept. 7th.*—Last night I received a strange and embarrassing present, in the shape of a young Dyak boy of five years old—a miserable little prisoner, made during this war, from the tribe of Brong. The gift caused me vexation, because I knew not what to do with the poor innocent; and yet I shrink from the responsibility of adopting him. My first wish is to return him to his parents and his tribe; and if I find I cannot do this, I believe it will be better to carry him with me than leave him to become the slave of a slave: for should I send him back, such will probably be his fate. I wish the present had been a calf instead of a child.

"*9th.*—Situ, my Dyak boy, seems content and happy; and judging by his ways, and his fondness for tobacco, he must be older than I at first supposed. In pursuance of my desire to restore him to his parents I made every inquiry as to their probable fate; but have learned nothing that leaves me any hope that I shall be able to do so. The Brong tribe having taken part with the rebels, were attacked by the *rajah's* people; and many were killed and the rest scattered. Pino, the Brong, knows not whether Situ's parents are alive or dead; nor, if the former, whither they have fled. Supposing my endeavours to restore the child fail, I have resolved to keep him with me, for many reasons. The first is that his future prospects will be better, and his fate as a freeman at Singapore happier, than as a slave in Borneo; the second, that he can be made a Christian. I can easily provide for him in some respectable household, or take him to England, as may hereafter be most advantageous for him; and at the former place he can always be made a comfortable servant with good training.

"Yet with all this, I cannot disguise from myself that there is responsibility—a heavy moral responsibility—attached to this course, that might be avoided: but then, *should* it be avoided? Looking to the boy's interests—temporal, perhaps, eternal—I think it ought not; and so, provided always I cannot place him where humanity and nature dictate, I will take the responsibility, and serve this wretched and destitute child as far as lies in my power. He is cast on my compassion; I solemnly accept the charge; and I trust his future life may bear good fruit and cause me to rejoice at my present decision.

"*Oct. 2nd.*—Lying at Sarawak, losing valuable time, but pending the war difficult to get away; for whenever the subject is mentioned, Muda Hassim begs me not to desert him just as it is coming to a close; and daily holds out prospects of the arrival of various Dyak tribes. The *rajah* urged upon me that he was deceived and betrayed by the intrigues of *pangerans*, who aimed at alienating his country; and that if I left him, he should probably have to remain here for the rest of his life, being resolved to die rather than yield to the unjust influence which others were seeking to acquire over him; and he appealed to me that after our friendly communication I could not, as an Engliah gentleman, desert him under such circumstances. I felt that honourably I could not do so; and though reluctantly enough, I resolved to give him the aid he asked;—small indeed, but of consequence in such a petty warfare.

"*3rd.*—I started to join Macota at Leda Tanah. At 4h. 30m. p.m. a pouring rain delayed us some time: and darkness setting in, rendered our pull a long and very disagreeable one. We did not reach Leda Tanah until eleven, when we found *the army* in their boats, and a small fort they had built on the bank of the river. I moved into Macota's large boat, and slept there; while he, as commander-in-chief, went backward and forward from one post to another during the night.

"*4th.*—At Leda Tanah the river divided into two branches; one part running past Siniawan, and the other to the left—likewise to another point of the mountain-range. Above Siniawan is Sarambo, a high detached mountain, perhaps 3000 feet in height, with a notch in the centre. Off Leda Tanah is a sand and pebble bank formed by the junction of the two streams, and the country around is well cleared for this part; while the graves on the right bank bear witness to the population of former days. It is represented to have been a flourishing place, and the neighbourhood well inhabited, until the breaking out of this unhappy war. The situation is delightful, and advantageously chosen at the confluence of the two streams.

"5th.—Ascended that to the left for a short distance. On the left hand, just above Leda Tanah, is the small creek of Sarawak, the original settlement, and from which the larger river now takes its name. I intended to have returned today; but as the weather threatened another deluge, I stopped till the following morning. It was a curious sight to see the whole army bathe, with the commander-in-chief at their head, and his *pangerans*. The fare of these people is anything but luxurious, for they get nothing but rice and salt; and they were thankful in proportion for the small supplies of tea, sugar, and biscuit I was able to spare them.

"6th.—Quitted Leda Tanah, and reached the *Royalist* in five hours, one of which we were delayed by the way. The river is remarkably pretty; banks cleared of jungle, with fine trees, and a view of the mountains. Many parts are exceedingly shallow; but the natives state there is a channel for a moderate-sized vessel as far as Leda Tanah."

On Mr. Brooke's return on board the *Royalist*, he found his steward Rankin, who had been lingering some time, still alive; and a seaman named Daniel, whom he had left with a slight fever, suddenly expired at ten at night in a fainting fit. He writes in his journal:

"It is difficult to allege the immediate cause of his death, which probably arose from some organic complaint of the heart or the brain, quite independent of fever. Five minutes before his decease the man's pulse was high and full. The steward will follow in a few days; and death, which has never before entered on board, will thus strike two blows. To me it is a satisfaction that neither is in any way attributable to climate.

"7th.—Muda Hassim rendered me every assistance. A grave was prepared, and wood for a coffin, so that by two o'clock we proceeded to inter the dead. His last resting-place was situated on a gently rising ground behind the Chinamen's houses. The ensign was placed over his simple bier, and he was carried by his shipmates to the grave. All who could be spared attended, and I performed the service—that impressive and beautiful service of the Church of England.

"*8th.*—Having the melancholy duty of yesterday over was a relief, only alloyed by the sad prospect of a near recurrence. I now turned my mind seriously to departure, having well weighed the pros and cons of the subject.

"In the first place, the greatest advantage would result from my accompanying the *rajah* along the coast of Borneo; and if I could hope a reasonable time would leave him free to go there, I would wait spite of the season: for it is evident that by myself I should have to form fresh connections among the chiefs, and without that I reckon it next to impossible to penetrate even a moderate distance from the coast in a strange place. The next reason is, that it has been intimated to me that a rival faction, headed by Pangeran Usop, exists in Borneo Proper, and that that *pangeran*, from my known friendship to Muda Hassim, might endeavour to injure me, *i. e.* kill me. At any rate, during Muda Hassim's absence, I should be obstructed in all my proceedings, and could not do more than sketch the bare coast-line. These are strong and cogent reasons for remaining *for a time*, if the ultimate object be attainable; and to these may be added my own feelings—my reluctance to quit the *rajah* in the midst of difficulty and distress, and his *very very sad face* whenever I mention the topic.

"On the other hand must be weighed the approach of the adverse monsoon, the loss of time, and the failure of provisions, which, though but luxuries to gentlemen which they can readily dispense with, are nevertheless necessaries to seamen, without which they get discontented, perhaps mutinous. There are good reasons on both sides.

"*9th.*—I sent Williamson to intimate my approaching departure; and when I went in the evening the little man had such a sorrowful countenance that my heart smote me. When I told him I would remain if there were the slightest chance of a close to the war, his countenance cleared, and he gaily repeated that my fortune and his would bring this struggle to an end, though others forsook him. I then consented to await the issue a few days longer, and to revisit Leda Tanah to ascertain if the news were true. It ran to the effect that the rebels, under the Patingi and Tumangong, are fortified at the foot of the mountain of Sarambo, on which hill are three Dyak tribes below that of Sarambo; over them Bombak; and on the summit the Paninjow.

The Bombak and Paninjow have already, in part, joined Macota, and the Sarambo are to come in as today.

"These three last Dyak tribes deserting the rebels will leave them surrounded in their forts, which are commanded by the rest of the hill; and everything promises well, if the opportunity be vigorously used. The Sow and the Singè are in part at Leda Tanah, and more Dyaks daily joining. I must push the *rajah* on to action, for help from without is not likely to come. Yet I wish still more to accommodate matters; and if he would spare the leaders' lives, I believe they would lay down their arms on my guaranty. But though he does not say that he will kill them, he will listen to no terms of compromise; and when I reflect that a European monarch, in the same circumstances, would act in the same way—that the laws of my own country would condemn the men for the same offence—I cannot urge the subject into a personal matter.

"*16th.*—Rankin's (my steward's) death having been some time inevitable, it was a relief when the event occurred. He was cut off in the flower of manhood, from the effects of hard drinking, which even his fine constitution could not resist. I buried him near the other man, and had a neat inscription, with the name of the individual, his ship and age, placed over each.

"Days passed on, but not quite unrelieved by events. And now I may positively state, that the war will be over in a few days, or not over at all. The first of these events was the desertion of the Dyaks, and the arrival of their chiefs with Macota. Next arrived 200 Chinese from Sambas, under a very intelligent *capitan*. Rajah Ali came next, bringing some ourang-outangs' heads; then Datu Naraja; and lastly, *Pangeran Jedut* from Sarebus, with the information that the Dyaks of that name, in consequence of a war with Linga, would not come here. Thus they not only refused to come themselves, but obliged the Linga people to stay at home to defend their country. To quiet this coast the Sarebus should receive a severe lesson.

"*17th.*—I had a large party of Dyaks on board in the evening, viz. the Singè, Sow, Bombak, and Paninjow, in all about fifteen men and two old chiefs. They ate and drank, and asked for everything, but stole nothing. One man wore a necklace of beads set with human teeth, taken of course in war, which I got from him for two yards of red cloth. Another was ornamented with a necklace of bears' teeth; and several had such a profusion of small white beads about their necks as to resemble the voluminous foldings of the old fashioned cravat. As far as I could observe, they all seemed in earnest about attacking Siniawan; and their allegiance to the *rajah* was as warm now (in words) as it had been heretofore defective in action.

"*18th.*—Proceeded in the long-boat to Leda Tanah, which we reached in three and a half hours' pulling, and just in time to witness the start of 150 Malays and 100 Dyaks of Lundu for the mountain of Sarambo, at the foot of which Siniawan and the enemies' forts are situated.

"*19th.*—Did everything in my power to urge Macota to advance and divert the attention of the rebels from the party going up the mountain, but in vain: Malay-like, he would wait.

"*20th.*—I have before remarked that two rivers formed a junction at Leda Tanah; and this day I ascended the left hand stream, or, as they call it, the Songi besar (*i. e.* great Songi). The scenery is picturesque; the banks adorned with a light and variegated foliage of fruit-trees; and everywhere bearing traces of former clearing and cultivation. In the background is the range of mountains, among which Stat is conspicuous from his noble and irregular shape. On our return, the white flag (a *hadji's* turban) was descried on the mountain, being the prearranged signal that all was well. No news, however, came from the party; and in spite of the white banner Macota took fright at the idea that the rebels had surrounded them.

"*21st.*—Detachments of Dyaks are coming in. Ten of the tribe of Sutor were dispatched as scouts; and in a few hours returned with the welcome intelligence that the detachment was safe on the top of the mountain, and that the three tribes of Paninjow, Bombak, and Sarambo, had finally decided on joining the *rajah*, and surrendering their fortified houses. Soon after this news the chiefs of the tribes arrived with about 100 men, and were of course well received; for if chargeable with deserting their cause, it is done with the utmost simplicity, and perfect confidence in their new associates. From their looks it was apparent they had suffered greatly from want of food; and they frankly confessed that starvation was their principal motive for coming over.

"I did all in my power to fix their new faith by presents of provisions, &c. &c.: and I think they are trustworthy; for there is a straightforwardness about the Dyak character far different from the doublefaced dealings of the Malay. Their stipulations were, forgiveness for the past, and an assurance that none of the Dyaks from the sea (*i. e.* Sarebus and Sakarran) should be employed; for they were, they said, hateful to their eyes. These terms being readily conceded—the first from interest, the second from necessity—they became open and communicative on the best means of attacking the forts. A grand council of war was held, at which were present Macota, Subtu, Abong Mia, and Datu Naraja, two Chinese leaders, and myself—certainly a most incongruous mixture, and one rarely to be met with. After much discussion, a move close to the enemy was determined on for tomorrow, and on the following day to take up a position near their defences.

"To judge by the sample of the council, I should form very unfavourable expectations of the conduct in action. Macota is lively and active; but whether from indisposition or want of authority, undecided. The Capitan China is lazy and silent; Subtu indolent and self-indulgent; Abong Mia and Datu Naraja stupid. However, the event must settle the question; and, in the mean time, it was resolved that the small stockade at this place was to be picked up, and removed to our new position, and there erected for the protection of the fleet. I may here state my motives for being a spectator of, or participator (as may turn out), in this scene. In the first place I must confess that curiosity strongly prompted me; since to witness the Malays, Chinese, and Dyaks in warfare was so new, that the novelty alone might plead an excuse for this desire. But it was not the only motive; for my presence is a stimulus to our own party, and will probably depress the other in proportion.

"I look upon the cause of the *rajah* as most just and righteous: and the speedy close of the war would be rendering a service to humanity, especially if brought about by treaty. At any rate much might be done to ameliorate the condition of the rebels in case of their defeat; for though I cannot, perhaps ought not to, save the lives of the three leaders, yet all the others, I believe, will be forgiven on a slight intercession. At our arrival, too, I had stated that if they wished me to remain, no barbarities must be committed; and especially that the women and children must not be fired upon. To counterbalance these motives was the danger, whatever it might amount to, and which did not weigh heavily on my mind. So much for reasons, which, after all, are poor and weak when we determine on doing anything, be it right or be it wrong. *If* evil befall, I trust the penalty may be on me rather than on my followers.

"*22nd.*—At daylight the fleet was astir; and in an hour the defences were cut down, the timber, bamboos, &c., formed into rafts ready for transportation, and the stockade, by breakfast-time, had as completely vanished as though it had been bodily lifted away by some genius of the Wonderful Lamp. Everything was ready for a start, and we waited lazily for the flood-tide; but when it did make, the usual procrastination ensued, and there was no move till it was near done. Then, indeed, we proceeded up about two-thirds of the way, and brought up with two good hours' daylight, in spite of my remonstrances. No place could be better calculated than where we rested for an attack upon boats: high banks covered with grass and trees offered a safe shelter for musketry, against which no return could be made. The night, however, passed away quietly.

"*24th.*—Dawn found us on the advance to our proper position. A thick fog concealed us, and in half an hour the people were on shore busy re-erecting our fort, less than a mile from two forts of the enemy, but concealed from them by a point of the river. No opposition was offered to us; and in a few hours a neat defence was completed from the *débris* of the former. The ground was cleared of jungle; piles driven in a square, about fifteen yards to each face; and the earth from the centre, scooped out and intermixed with layers of reeds, was heaped up about five feet high inside the piles. At the four corners were small watch-towers, and along the parapet of earth a narrow walk connecting them. In the centre space was a house crowded by the Chinese garrison, a few of whose harmless *gingalls* were stuck up at the angles to intimidate rather than to wound.

"While they laboured at the body of the defence, the Dyaks surrounded it by an outer work, made of slight sticks run into the ground with cross binding of split bamboo, and bristling with a *chevaux de frise* (if it may be so styled) of sharpened bamboos about breast-high. The fastenings of the entire work were of rattan, which is found in plenty. It was commenced at 7 a.m. and finished about 3 p.m., showing how the fellows can get through business when they choose. This stockade, varying in strength according to circumstances, is the usual defence of the Sambas Chinese. The Malays erect a simple and quicker-constructed protection by a few double uprights, filled in between with timber laid lengthwise and supported by the uprights. Directly they are under cover, they begin to form the *ranjows* or *sudas*, which are formidable to naked feet, and stick them about their position.

"Above our station was a hill which entirely commanded both it and the river; to the top of which I mounted, and obtained an excellent view of the country around, including the enemies' forts and the town of Siniawan. A company of military might finish the war in a few hours, as these defences are most paltry, the strongest being the fort of Balidah, against which our *formidable* assault was to be levelled. It was situated at the water's edge, on a slight eminence on the right bank of the river; and a large house with a thatched roof and a lookout house on the summit; a few swivels and a gun or two were in it, and around it a breastwork of wood—judging from a distance, about six or seven feet high. The other defences were more insignificant even than this; and the enemies' artillery amounted, by account, to three six-pounders and numerous swivels; from 350 to 500 men, about half of whom were armed with muskets, while the rest carried swords and spears. They were scattered in many forts, and had a town to defend, all of which increased their weakness.

"Their principal arm, however, consisted in the *ranjows*, which were stated to be stuck in every direction. These *ranjows* are made of bamboo, pointed fine and stuck in the ground; and there are beside, holes about three feet deep, filled with these spikes, and afterward lightly covered, which are called *patobong*. Another obstacle consists of a spring formed by bending back a stiff cane with a sharp bamboo attached to it, which, fastened by a slight twine, flies forcibly against any object passing through the bush and brushing against it: they resemble the mole-traps of England. The Borneons have a great dread of these various snares; and the way they deal with them is by sending out parties of Dyaks during the night to clear the paths from such dangers.

"Though I have stated the insignificant nature of the enemies' lines, it must not be supposed I imagined them at all inferior to our own resources. Our grand army consisted of 200 Chinese, excellent workmen, but of whose qualities as soldiers I can say nothing. They were, however, a stout, muscular set of men, though wretchedly armed, having no guns and scarcely any muskets; but swords, spears, and shields, together with forty long thin iron tubes with the bore of a musket and carrying a slug.

"These primitive weapons were each managed by two men, one being the carrier of the ordnance, the other the gunnery for while one holds the tube over his shoulder, the other takes aim, turns away his head, applies his match, and is pleased with the sound. Their mode of loading is as curious as the piece and its mode of discharge. Powder is poured in, the end knocked on the ground, and the slug with another knock sent on the powder, without either ramming or cartridge. Indeed, it is difficult to imagine any weapon more rude, awkward, or inefficient.

"Of Malays we had 250, of whom 150 were on the Sarambo mountain, occupied in defending the Dyak houses. Of the hundred remaining with the grand army, about half were armed with muskets. A few brass guns composed our artillery; and in the boats were a good many swivels. The Dyaks amounted to about 200, of various tribes, *viz.*, Sibnowans, Paninjows, Bombak, Sarambo, Kampit, Tabah, Sanpro, Suntah; but these were merely pioneers, and would not face the report of fire-arms. The Borneons, in fighting, wear a quilted jacket or spencer, which reaches over the hips, and from its size has a most unservicelike appearance: the bare legs and arms sticking out from under this puffed-out coat, like the sticks which support the garments of a scarecrow.

"Such was our incongruous and most inefficient array; yet with 300 men who would fight, nothing would have been easier than to take the detached defences of the enemy, none of which could contain above thirty or forty men. But our allies seemed to have little idea of fighting except behind a wall; and my proposal to attack the adversary was immediately treated as an extreme of rashness amounting to insanity. At a council of war it was consequently decided that advances should be made from the hill behind our fort to Balidah by a chain of posts, the distance being a short mile, in which space they would probably erect four or five forts; and then would come a bombardment, noisy but harmless.

"During the day we were not left quiet. The beating of gongs, shouts, and an occasional shot, gave life to the scene. With my glass I could espy our forces at the top of the hill, pleased no doubt to see us coming to their support. At night loud shouts and firing from the rebels caused us to prepare for an attack; but it proved to be nothing but lights moving about the hill-side, with what intent we were ignorant. The jungle on the left bank having been cleared, we did not much expect any skirmishers; but some spies were heard near our boats. With this exception the night passed away unbroken on our part, though the rebels kept up an incessant beating of gongs, and from time to time fired a few stray shots, whether against an enemy or not was doubtful.

"*25th.*—The grand army was lazy, and did not take the field when they possessed themselves of two eminences, and commenced forts on each. About 11 a.m. we got intelligence that the enemy was collecting on the right bank, as they had been heard by our scouts shouting one to another to gather together in order to attack the stockades in the course of building. Even with a knowledge of their usual want of caution, I could not believe this, but walked nevertheless to one of the forts, and had scarcely reached it when a universal rebel shout, and a simultaneous beating of the silver-tongued gongs, announced, as I thought, a general action. But though the shouts continued loud and furious from both sides, and a gun or two was discharged in the air to refresh their courage, the enemy did not attack, and a heavy shower damped the ardour of the approaching armies, and reduced all to inaction.

"Like the heroes of old, however, the adverse parties spoke to each other: 'We are coming, we are coming,' exclaimed the rebels; 'lay aside your muskets and fight us with swords.'

"'Come on,' was the reply; 'we are building a stockade, and want to fight you.' And so the heroes ceased not to talk, but forgot to fight, except that the rebels opened a fire from Balidah from swivels, all of which went over the tops of the trees. Peace, or rather rest, being restored, our party succeeded in entrenching themselves, and thus gained a field which had been obstinately assaulted by big words and loud cries. The distance of one fort from Balidah was about 800 yards, and manned with sixty Malays; while a party of Chinese garrisoned the other.

"Evening fell upon this innocent warfare. The Borneons, in this manner, contend with vociferous shouts; and, preceding each shout, the leader of the party offers up a prayer aloud to the Almighty, the chorus (or properly response) being the acclamation of the soldiery. We, on our side, kept up a firing and hallooing till midnight, to disguise the advance of a party who were to seize and build a stockade within a shorter distance of Balidah. When they reached the spot, however, the night being dark, the troops sleepy, and the leaders of different opinions, they returned without effecting anything."

# CHAPTER 8

# Renewed Treachery of the Malays

"*26th.*—I must here pause in my account of this extraordinary and novel contest, briefly to describe the general appearance of the country.

"It is one delightful to look upon, combining all the requisites of the picturesque, *viz.* wood, water, mountain, cliff, and a foreground gently undulating, partially cultivated, and of the richest soil. The mountain of Sarambo, about 3000 feet in height, is the principal feature in the scene, situated at a short distance from the left bank of the river. The remainder of the ground slopes gradually; and the town of Siniawan, likewise on the left bank, is close to the water, and at the foot of the eminence called Gunga Kumiel.

"The advance of the party last night was, as I have said, disguised by firing, drumming, and shouting from the fleet and forts; and, in the deep stillness of the fine night, the booming of the guns, the clamour of the gongs, and the outcries raised from time to time, came on our ears like the spirit of discord breaking loose on a fair and peaceful paradise. About one o'clock the noises died away, and I enjoyed as quiet a slumber till daylight as though pillowed on a bed of down in the heart of Old England. About six I visited the three forts. The Chinese, Malays, and Dyaks were taking their morning meal, consisting of half a cocoanut-shell full of boiled rice with salt. The Dyaks were served in tribes; for as many of them are at war, it is necessary to keep them separate; and though they will not fight the enemy, they would have no objection to fall out with one another, and the slightest cause might give rise to an instant renewal of hostilities.

"About 9 a.m. a party proceeded to the elevation previously marked, within 300 yards of Balidah, and worked quietly till 2 p.m., by which time they had made considerable progress; and being then reinforced, they soon finished this new stockade, with a strong face toward their adversaries, and an outer fence. This erection, however, being below the brow of the hill, is useless as a post whence to assault Balidah; and tomorrow another stockade is to be made close to it on the summit, the present being intended to cover the working party at the next. The enemy, about 4 p.m., having discovered the stockade, opened a fire for half an hour; but finding it ineffectual, they sank into their usual apathy. It is difficult to attribute this quietude to any other cause than weakness; and they are doubtless harassed by the want of Dyak light troops, as they are unable to oppose stockade to stockade.

"Our party, by these successful advances, seem to gain confidence; and it must soon come to an issue one way or other. To make it favourable, I have sent for two six-pounder carronades, guns of vast calibre here, together with a small addition to our force. I had the curiosity to inquire of Macota the progress of his former campaign, when he had 1000 Malays with only a few Dyaks. He represented the enemy as active and daring then, and very different from their want of spirit now. They had, he declared, combats by sea and by land; stockade was opposed to stockade, and the fighting was constant and severe; but he never lost a man killed during the two months, and only boasted of killing five of the enemy! The principal danger in Malay warfare is the '*Mengamuk*' (*Anglicè*, running a-muck), which is the last resource of a desperate man.

"*27th.*—The night passed quietly as usual. About 6 a.m. I started for the hills, and inspected each post in turn. They are about commencing another fort. I visited the spot to reconnoitre it; and the enemy opened a fire directly they perceived me, which we returned. They shot wretchedly ill; and the position is good, but exposed. About 10 a.m. they again began to fire from their fort, and detached thirty or forty men, who crept out between our forts in order to interrupt the work. The Malays, however, received them steadily; while the Chinese placed them between two fires, and, by a discharge from a tube, knocked down *one* man. The rebels showed anxiety to possess themselves of their fallen comrade, while the opposite party shouted, 'Cut off his head;' but he was carried off; and the enemy, when they had saved his body, fled in all directions, dropping a number of their small bamboo powder flasks on the way.

"Some fierce alarms were given of an attack by water, and I went up the river to ascertain really whether there was any mischief to be expected; but there was no appearance of any adversary. A slack fire from the hill proclaimed that our work was going on there; and toward evening all was in repose.

"28th.—The stockade was completed in the evening, with *ranjows* stuck round the outer defence. It was excellently situated for battering Balidah; but Balidah, I fear, is too loosely constructed to be battered to the best advantage. During the day the Sow and Singè Dyaks joined, to the amount of about 150 men, and other tribes have been gradually dropping in; so that altogether there are not fewer than 500 of these men joined to our equipment. Most of them show all the characteristics of a wild people; never openly resisting their masters, but so obstinate that they can always get their own way in everything; to all threats and entreaties opposing a determined and immovable silence. Many of them depend upon us for their food and salt, and their applications are endless.

"Three women of Singè are our regular pensioners; for their sex excludes them from the rations granted to the men. By these means we had many excellent opportunities of judging of their habits and temper. Among all these tribes the language differs but slightly—so slightly, indeed, that it is needless to note the variations in detail. They have the same superstition about particular birds, and I often heard this omen alluded to in conversation; but their birds are not the same as those of the sea Dyaks. . . . The chief of the Sarambo, explaining his reasons for leaving the rebels, urged the constant unfavourable omen of the birds as one. Often, very often, he said, when he went out, the bird cried, and flew in the direction of Siniawan, which will be explained by what I have before stated; for if they hear the bird to the right, they go to the left, and *vice versâ*; so that the bird may be considered as warning them from evil.

"The Sow Dyaks brought in the head of an unfortunate Malay whom they had decapitated in the jungle. This species of warfare is extremely barbarous, and in its train probably brings more evil than the regular campaigns of civilized nations. Not that it is by any means so fatal to human life directly; but it is the slow poison which wastes the strongest frame, the smouldering fire which does its work of destruction slowly but surely. Year after year it is protracted; few fall in open fight, but stragglers and prisoners are murdered; and while both weak parties, gradually growing weaker, hold their own ground, the country becomes a desert.

"First, trade stagnates, agriculture withers, food becomes scarce, all are ruined in finances, all half-starved and most miserable—and yet the war drags on, and the worst passions are aroused, effectually preventing the slightest concession, even if concession would avail. But each combatant knows the implacable spirit—the deep desperation—of the other too well to trust them; and if at length the fortunes of famine decide against them, they die rather than yield; for a Dyak can die bravely, I believe, though he will not fight as long as life has any prospect. This is also the case here: for the rebel chiefs know there is no pardon, and the *bandar* is disgraced if he fails. It is indeed a slow process, but one of extermination.

"*29th.*—Our guns arrived with a welcome reinforcement. In the evening I dropped up the river to reconnoitre; but the adversary discovered us, as we were dressed in white clothes.

"*30th.*—Fort not finished. All quiet.

"*31st.*—Got the guns and ammunition up, and while fixing them opened a fire from one of our swivels to overbear the fire of the enemy. The little piece was well served; and, in a quarter of an hour, we silenced their fire entirely, and knocked about the timber considerably, making a breach which several men could enter together. Seeing the effect, I proposed to Macota to storm the place with 150 Chinese and Malays. The way from one fort to the other was protected. The enemy dared not show themselves for the fire of the grape and canister, and nothing could have been easier; but my proposition caused a commotion which it is difficult to forget, and more difficult to describe. The Chinese consented, and Macota, the commander-in-chief, was willing; but his inferiors were backward, and there arose a scene which showed me the full violence of the Malay passions, and their infuriated madness when once roused.

"Pangeran Houseman urged with energy the advantage of the proposal, and in the course of a speech lashed himself to a state of fury; he jumped to his feet, and with demoniac gestures stamped round and round, dancing a war-dance after the most approved fashion; his countenance grew livid, his eyes glared, his features inflamed; and, for my part, not being able to interpret the torrent of his oratory, I thought the man possessed of a devil, or about to 'run a-muck.' But after a minute or two of this dance, he resumed his seat, furious and panting, but silent. In reply, Subtu urged some objections to my plan, which was warmly supported by Illudeen, who apparently hurt Subtu's feelings; for the indolent, the placid Subtu leapt from his seat, seized his spear, and rushed to the entrance of the stockade, with his passions and his pride desperately aroused.

"I never saw finer action than when, with spear in hand, pointing to the enemy's fort, he challenged any one to rush on with him. Houseman and Surradeen (the bravest of the brave) like madmen seized their swords to inflame the courage of the rest—it was a scene of fiends—but in vain; for though they appeared ready enough to quarrel and fight among themselves, there was no move to attack the enemy. All was confusion; the demon of discord and madness was among them, and I was glad to see them cool down, when the dissentients to the assault proposed making a round tonight and attacking tomorrow. In the mean time our six-pounders were ready in battery, and it is certain the assailants might walk nearly to the fort without any of the rebels daring to show themselves in opposition to our fire.

"*Nov. 1st.*—The guns were ready to open their fiery mouths, and their masters ready to attend on them; but both had to wait till midday, when the chiefs of the grand army, having sufficiently slept, breakfasted, and bathed, lounged up with their straggling followers. Shortly after daylight the forts are nearly deserted of their garrisons, who go down at the time to the water more like a flock of geese than warriors. The instant the main division and head-quarters of the army arrived at the battery, I renewed my proposal for an assault, Which was variously received. If the Malays would go, the Chinese agreed; but the Malays had grown colder and colder. In order to encourage them, I opened a fire to show the effect of our guns; and having got a good range, every ball, as well as grape and canister, rattled against and through the wood. I then urged them again and again, but in vain; that coward *panglima rajah* displayed that dogged resolution which is invincible—an invincible resolution to do nothing; and the cold damp looks of the others at once told the amount of their bravery!

"A council of war was called—grave faces covered timid hearts and fainting spirits. The Chinese contended with justice, that in fairness they could not be expected to assault without the Malays did the same; Abong Mia was not brave enough. The *datu* agreed, and *panglima* delivered himself of a wise harangue, to the effect that, 'the last campaign, when they had a fort, how had the enemy fired then?—stabbed them, speared them, &c. &c.; and without a fort, assaulting!—how could it be expected they should succeed? how unreasonable they should go at all!' But even his stolid head seemed to comprehend the sarcasm when I asked him how many men had been killed during all this severe fighting.

"However, it was clear that it was no battle. We were all very savage, and I intimated how useless my being with them was, if they intended to play instead of fight. 'What,' I asked, 'if you will not attack, are you going to do?' Oh, the wise councils of these wise heads! Abong Mia proposed erecting a fort in a tree, and thence going 'puff, puff,' down into Balidah, accompanying the words 'puff, puff,' with expressive gestures of firing; but it was objected, that trees were scarce, and the enemy might cut down the tree, fort and all.[1]

"*2nd.*—Till two o'clock last night, or thereabouts, I sat on our rampart and gazed upon the prospect around, shaded with gloom. The doctor was with me, and we ran over every subject—the past, present, and the future. Such a scene—a rude fort in the interior of Borneo; such a night, dark but starlight—leaves an indelible impression on the mind, which recurs to move it even after long years. The morning, however, found us ready, and no one else. The fort was left to ourselves; we waited and waited until 2 p.m., when I was made aware that all thoughts of attack were at an end. Macota, for very shame, staid below; and I must say there was not a countenance that met mine but had that bashful and hang-dog look which expresses cowardice and obstinacy predominant, yet shame battling within.

"They were now resolved not to make the attempt; and I asked them casually whether they would fly a white flag, and hold a conference with the enemy. They caught at the alternatives; the flag was hoisted; the rebels were ready to *meet me*, and it was agreed that we should assemble on the morrow. But no sooner was the arrangement made than a thousand objections were started, and anything, even at-

---

1. The following is an extract from an equally sapient proposition, published in the Chinese state-papers on the 14th January, 1840; it is headed, Memorial of Toang Wangyen to the emperor, recommending plans for the extermination of barbarians: "Your minister's opinion is this: that we, being upon shore and they in their ships, it is not at all requisite to order our naval forces to proceed out a great distance to contend with them in battle. When the commercial intercourse of the said barbarians shall have been entirely put an end to, and their supplies grow scanty, it will be impossible for them to remain a long time anchored in the outer seas, and they will necessarily, as formerly, enter the inner waters in order to ramble and spy about them. We can then, by means of our naval vessels, tempt them and cause them to enter far in; and a previous arrangement having been made, we can summon the people who live along the coasts, such as are expert and able swimmers, and those who possess bravery and strength, to the amount of several hundreds of men: we can then cause them, during the night, to divide themselves into companies, and silently proceeding through the water, straightway board the foreign ships; and overcoming the crews in their unprepared state, make an entire massacre of the whole of them."

tack itself (though that was out of the question), was held to be preferable. I need not dwell on this mixture of deceit and fear; in short, as they would do nothing themselves, they expected us to do nothing: and without the courage to carry on the war, they had not either wisdom or sorcery to bring it to a conclusion.

"*3rd.*—Dispatched an express during last night to the *rajah*, and received an answer that he was coming up in person; but my resolve was taken, and I quitted the grand army, much to their evident surprise and vexation. Nevertheless, they were still friendly and polite, and very very lazy about bringing down our guns. This was, however, done at last, and we were ready for a start.

"*4th.*—Reached the ship at two p.m., saw *rajah*, &c. &c.

"From the 4th to the 10th of November I may condense into the shape of a narrative. I explained to the *rajah* how useless it was my remaining, and intimated to him my intention of departing; but his deep regret was so visible, that even all the self-command of the native could not disguise it. He begged, he entreated me to stay, and offered me the country of Siniawan and Sarawak, and its government and trade, if I would only stop, and not desert him. I could at once have obtained this grant, but I preferred interposing a delay; because to accept such a boon when imposed by necessity, or from a feeling of gratitude for recent assistance, would have rendered it both suspicious and useless; and I was by no means eager to enter on the task (the full difficulties of which I clearly foresaw) without the undoubted and spontaneous support of the *rajah*.

"*Jan. 8th, 1841.*—The following narrative, extracted from my journal, includes a period from the 10th of December to the 4th of January, and it is put into its present shape to avoid the tedium of detailing each day's proceedings. On the 10th of December we reached the fleet and disembarked our guns, taking up our residence in a house, or rather shed, close to the water. The *rajah's* brother, Pangeran Budrudeen, was with the army, and I found him ready and willing to urge upon the other indolent *pangerans* the proposals I made for vigorous hostilities. We found the grand army in a state of torpor, eating, drinking, and walking up to the forts and back again daily; but having built these imposing structures, and their appearance not driving the enemy away, they were at a loss what next to do, or how to proceed.

"On my arrival, I once more insisted on mounting the guns in our old forts, and assaulting Balidah under their fire. Macota's timidity and vacillation were too apparent; but in consequence of Budrudeen's overawing presence, he was obliged, from shame, to yield his assent. The order for the attack was fixed as follows:—Our party of ten (leaving six to serve the guns) were to be headed by myself. Budrudeen, Macota, Subtu, and all the lesser chiefs, were to lead their followers, from 60 to 80 in number, by the same route, while 50 or more Chinese, under their captain, were to assault by another path to the left. Macota was to make the paths as near as possible to Balidah, with his Dyaks, who were to extract the *sudas* and fill up the holes.

"The guns having been mounted and their range well ascertained the previous evening, we ascended to the fort at about eight a.m., and at ten opened our fire, and kept it up for an hour. The effect was severe: every shot told upon their thin defences of wood, which fell in many places so as to leave storming breaches. Part of the roof was cut away and tumbled down, and the shower of grape and canister rattled so as to prevent their returning our fire, except from a stray rifle.

"At midday the forces reached the fort, and it was then discovered that Macota had neglected to make any road because it rained the night before! It was evident that the rebels had gained information of our intention, as they had erected a frieze of bamboo along their defences on the very spot which we had agreed to mount. Macota fancied the want of a road would delay the attack; but I well knew that delay was equivalent to failure, and so it was at once agreed that we should advance without any path. The poor man's cunning and resources were now nearly at an end. He could not refuse to accompany us; but his courage could not be brought to the point, and, pale and embarrassed, he retired. Everything was ready—Budrudeen, the Capitan China, and myself, at the head of our men—when he once more appeared, and raised a subtle point of etiquette which answered his purpose.

"He represented to Budrudeen that the Malays were unanimously of opinion that the *rajah's* brother could not expose himself in an assault; that their dread of the *rajah's* indignation far exceeded the dread of death; and in case any accident happened to him, his brother's fury would fall on them. They stated their readiness to assault the place; but in case Budrudeen insisted on leading in person, they must decline accompanying him. Budrudeen was angry, I was angry too, and the doctor most angry of all; but anger was unavailing: it was clear they did not intend to do anything in earnest; and after much discussion, in which Budrudeen insisted that if I went he should likewise go, and the

Malays insisted that if he went they would not go, it was resolved we should serve the guns, while Abong Mia and the Chinese (not under the captain) should proceed to the assault.

"But its fate was sealed, and Macota had gained his object; for neither he nor Subtu thought of exposing themselves to a single shot. Our artillery opened and was beautifully served. The adverse troops advanced; but our fire completely subdued them, as only three rifles answered us, by one of which a seaman (Williams) was wounded in the hand, but not seriously. Two-thirds of the way the storming-party proceeded without the enemy being aware of their advance; and they might have reached the very foot of the hill without being discovered, had not Abong Mia, from excess of piety and rashness, begun most loudly to say his prayers.

"The three rifles then began to play on them; one Chinaman was killed, the whole halted, the prayers were more vehement than ever, and, after squatting under cover of the jungle for some time, they all returned. It was only what I expected; but I was greatly annoyed at their cowardice and treachery—treachery to their own cause. One lesson, however, I learned, and that was, that, had I assaulted with our small party, we should assuredly have been victimized! The very evening of the failure the *rajah* came up the river. I would not see him, and only heard that the chiefs got severely reprimanded; but the effects of reprimand are lost where cowardice is stronger than shame. Inactivity followed; two or three useless forts were built, and Budrudeen, much to my regret and the detriment of the cause, was recalled.

"Among the straggling arrivals I may mention Panglima Dallam, with a number of men, consisting of the Orang Bentulu, Meri Muka, and Kayan, Dyaks from the interior. Our house—or, as it originally stood, shed—deserves a brief record. It was about twenty feet long, with a loose floor of reeds, and an attop roof. It served us for some time; but the attempts at theft obliged us to fence it in and divide it into apartments: one at the end served Middleton, Williamson, and myself; adjoining it was the store-room and hospital; and the other extreme belonged to the seamen. Our improvements kept pace with our necessities.

"Theft induced us to shut in our house at the sides, and the unevenness of the reeds suggested the advantage of laying a floor of the bark of trees over them, which, with mats over all, rendered our domicile far from uncomfortable. Our forts gradually extended at the back of the enemy's town, on a ridge of swelling ground; while they kept pace with us on the same side of the river on the low ground. The inactivity of our troops had long become a by-word among us. It was indeed truly vexatious, but it was in vain to urge them on, in vain to offer assistance, in vain to propose a joint attack, or even to seek support at their hands; promises were to be had in plenty, but performances never!

"At length the leaders resolved on building a fort at Sekundis, thus outflanking the enemy and gaining the command of the river. The post was certainly an important one, and in consequence they set about it with the happy indifference which characterizes their proceedings. Pangeran Illudeen (the most active among them) had the building of the fort, assisted by the Orang Kaya Tumangong of Lundu. Macota, Subtu, &c. were at the next fort, and by chance I was there likewise; for it seemed to be little apprehended that any interruption would take place, as the Chinese and the greater number of Malays had not left the boats. When the fort commenced, however, the enemy crossed the river and divided into two bodies, the one keeping in check the party at Pangeran Gapoor's fort, while the other made an attack on the works.

"The ground was not unfavourable for their purpose; for Pangeran Gapoor's fort was separated from Sekundis by a belt of thick wood which reached down to the river's edge. Sekundis itself, however, stood on clear ground, as did Gapoor's fort. I was with Macota at the latter when the enemy approached through the jungle. The two parties were within easy speaking distances, challenging and threatening each other; but the thickness of the jungle prevented our seeing or penetrating to them. When this body had advanced, the real attack commenced on Sekundis with a fire of musketry, and I was about proceeding to the scene, but was detained by Macota, who assured me there were plenty of men, and that it was nothing at all.

"As the musketry became thicker, I had my doubts, when a Dyak came running through the jungle, and with gestures of impatience and anxiety begged me to assist the party attacked. He had been sent by my old friend the Tumangong of Lundu, to say they could not hold the post unless supported. In spite of Macota's remonstrances, I struck into the jungle, winded through the narrow path, and after crossing an ugly stream, emerged on the clear ground. The sight was a pretty one: to the right was the unfinished stockade, defended by the Tumangong; to the left, at the edge of the forest, about twelve or fifteen of our party, commanded by Illudeen, while the enemy were stretched along between the points and kept up a sharp shooting from the hollow ground on the bank of the river. They fired, and loaded, and fired, and had gradually advanced on the stockade as the ammunition of our party failed; and as we emerged from the jungle, they were within twenty or five and twenty yards of the defence.

"A glance immediately showed me the advantage of our position, and I charged with my Europeans across the *padi*-field; and the instant we appeared on the ridge above the river, in the hollows of which the rebels were seeking protection, their rout was complete. They scampered off in every direction, while the Dyaks and Malays pushed them into the river. Our victory was decisive and bloodless: the scene was changed in an instant, and the defeated foe lost arms, ammunition, &c. &c., whether on the field of battle or in the river, and our exulting conquerors set no bounds to their triumph.

"I cannot omit to mention the name of Si Tundo, the only native who charged with us. His appearance and dress were most striking, the latter being entirely of red, bound round the waist, arms, forehead, &c. with gold ornaments; and in his hand bearing his formidable Bajuck sword, he danced or rather galloped across the field close to me, and mixing with the enemy was about to dispatch a *hadji* or priest who was prostrate before him, when one of our people interposed and saved him by stating that he was a companion of our own. The Lundu Dyaks were very thankful for our support, our praises were loudly sung, and the stockade was concluded.

"After the rout, Macota, Subtu, and Abong Mia arrived on the field; the latter with forty followers had ventured half way before the firing ceased, but the detachment, under a paltry subterfuge, halted, so as not to be in time. The enemy might have had fifty men at the attack; the defending party consisted of about the same number; but the Dyaks had very few muskets. I had a dozen Englishmen, Seboo, one of our boatmen, and Si Tundo. Sekundis was a great point gained, as it hindered the enemy from ascending the river and seeking any supplies.

"Macota, Subtu, and the whole tribe arrived as soon as their safety from danger allowed, and none were louder in their own praise; but nevertheless their countenances evinced some sense of shame, which they endeavoured to disguise by the use of their tongues. The Chinese came really to afford assistance, but too late. We remained until the stockade of Sekundis was finished, while the enemy kept up a wasteful fire from the opposite side of the river, which did no harm.

"The next great object was to follow up the advantage by crossing the stream; but day after day some fresh excuse brought on fresh delay, and Macota built a new fort and made a new road within a hundred yards of our old position. I cannot detail further our proceedings for many days, which consisted on my part of efforts to get something done, and on the others a close adherence to the old system of promising everything and doing nothing. The Chinese, like the Malays, refused to act; but on their part, it was not fear, but disinclination.

"By degrees, however, the preparations for the new fort were complete, and I had gradually gained over a party of the natives to my views; and, indeed, among the Malays, the bravest of them had joined themselves to us, and what was better, we had *datu pangeran*, thirteen Illanuns, and the Capitan China allowed me to take his men whenever I wanted them. My weight and consequence were increased, and I rarely moved now without a long train of followers. The next step (while crossing the river was uncertain) was to take my guns up to Gapoor's fort, which was about 600 or 700 yards from the town, and half the distance from a rebel fort on the river's bank.

"*Panglima rajah*, the day after our guns were in battery, took it into his head to build a fort on the river's side close to the town, in front and between two of the enemy's forts. It was a bold undertaking for the old man, after six weeks of uninterrupted repose. At night, the wood being prepared, the party moved down, and worked so silently that they were not discovered till their defence was nearly finished, when the enemy commenced a general firing from all their forts, returned by a similar firing from all ours, none of the parties being quite clear what they were firing at or about, and the hottest from either party being equally harmless. We were at the time about going to bed in our habitation; but expecting some reverse, I set off (to scale the hills) to the stockade where our guns were placed, and opened a fire upon the town and the stockade near us, till the enemy's fire gradually slackened and died away.

"We then returned, and in the morning were greeted with the pleasing news that they had burned and deserted five of their forts, and left us sole occupants of the right bank of the river. The same day, going through the jungle to see one of these deserted forts, we came upon a party of the enemy, and had a brief skirmish with them before they took to flight. Nothing can be more unpleasant to a European than this bush-fighting, where he scarce sees a foe, while he is well aware that their eyesight is far superior to his own. To proceed with this narrative, I may say that four or five forts were built on the edge of the river opposite the enemy's town, and distant not above 50 or 60 yards; here our guns were removed, and a fresh battery formed ready for a bombardment, and fire-balls essayed to ignite the houses.

"At this time Seriff Jaffer, from Singè, arrived with about seventy men, Malays and Dyaks of Balow. The River Singè being situated close to Sarebus, and incessant hostilities being waged between the two places, he, with his followers, was both more active and more warlike than the Borneons, but their warfare consists of closing hand to hand with spear and sword. They scarcely understood the proper use of firearms, and were of little use in attacking stockades.

"As a negotiator, however, the *seriff* bore a distinguished part; and on his arrival a parley ensued, much against Macota's will, and some meetings took place between Jaffer and a brother *seriff* at Siniawan, named Moksain. After ten days' delay nothing came of it, though the enemy betrayed great desire to yield. This negotiation being at an end, we had a day's bombardment and a fresh treaty brought about thus; Macota being absent at Sarawak, I received a message from Seriff Jaffer and Pangeran Subtu to say that they wished to meet me; and on my consenting, they stated that Seriff Jaffer felt confident the war might be brought to an end, though alone he dared not treat with the rebels; but in case I felt inclined to join him, we could bring it to a favourable conclusion.

"I replied that our habits of treating were very unlike their own, as we allowed no delays to interpose; but that I would unite with him for one interview, and if that interview was favourable, we might meet the chiefs at once and settle it, or put an end to all farther treating. Pangeran Subtu was delighted with the proposition, urged its great advantages, and the meeting by my desire for that very night, the place Pangeran Illudeen's fort at Sekundis. The evening arrived, and at dark we were at the appointed place, and a message was dispatched for Seriff Moksain. In the mean time, however, came a man from Pangeran Subtu to beg us to hold no intercourse; that the rebels were false, meant to deceive us, and if any did come, we had better make them prisoners.

"Seriff Jaffer, after arguing the point some time, rose to depart, remarking that with such proceedings he would not consent to treat. I urged him to stay; but finding him bent on going, I ordered my gig (which had some time before been brought overland) to be put into the water, my intention being to proceed to the enemy's *campong*, and there hear what they had to say. I added that it was folly to leave undone what we had agreed to do in the morning because Pangeran Subtu changed his mind—that I had come to treat, and treat I would. I would not go away now without giving the enemy a fair hearing—for the good of all parties I would do it; and if the *seriff* liked to join me, as we proposed before, and wait for Seriff Moksain, good; if not, I would go in the boat to the *campong*.

"My Europeans, on being ordered, jumped up, ran out and brought the boat to the water's edge, and in a few minutes oars, rudder, and rowlocks were in her. My companions, seeing this, came to terms, and we waited for Seriff Moksain; during which, however, I overheard a whispering conversation from Subtu's messenger, proposing to seize him; and my temper was ruffled to such a degree that I drew out a pistol, and told him I would shoot him dead if he dared to seize, or talk of seizing, any man who trusted himself from the enemy to meet me! The scoundrel slunk off, and we were no more troubled with him. This past, Seriff Moksain arrived, and was introduced into our fortress alone—alone and unarmed in an enemy's stockade, manned with two hundred men! His bearing was firm; he advanced with ease and took his seat; and, during the interview, the only sign of uneasiness was the quick glance of his eye from side to side.

"The object he aimed at was to gain my guaranty that the lives of all the rebels should be spared; but this I had it not in my power to grant. He returned to his *campong*, and came again toward morning, when it was agreed that Seriff Jaffer and myself should meet the Patingis and the Tumangong, and arrange terms with them. By the time our conference was over, the day broke, and we descended to the boats to enjoy a little rest.

"On the 20th of December we met with the chiefs on the river; and they expressed themselves ready to yield, without conditions, to the *rajah*, if I would promise that they should not be put to death. My reply was, that I could give no such promise; that if they surrendered, it must be for life or death, according to the *rajah's* pleasure; and all I could do was to use my influence in order to save their lives. To this they assented after a while; but then there arose the more difficult question, how they were to be protected until the *rajah's* orders arrived. They dreaded both Chinese and Malays, especially the former, who had just cause for angry feelings, and who, it was feared, would make an attack on them directly their surrender had taken from them their means of defence.

"The Malays would not assail them in a body, but would individually plunder them, and give occasion for disputes and bloodshed. These apprehensions were almost sufficient to break off the hitherto favourable negotiations, had I not proposed to them myself to undertake their defence, and to become responsible for their safety until the orders of their sovereign arrived. On my pledging myself to this, they yielded up their strong fort of Balidah, the key of their position. I immediately made it known to our own party that no boats were to ascend or descend the river, and that any persons attacking or pillaging the rebels were my enemies, and that I should fire upon them without hesitation.

"Both Chinese and Malaya agreed to the propriety of the measure, and gave me the strongest assurances of restraining their respective followers, the former with good faith, the latter with the intention of involving matters, if possible, to the destruction of the rebels. By the evening we were in possession of Balidah, and certainly found it a formidable fortress, situated on a steep mound, with dense defences of wood, triple deep, and surrounded by two inclosures, thickly studded on the outside with *ranjows*. The effect of our fire had shaken it completely, now much to our discomfort; for the walls were tottering, and the roof as leaky as a sieve. On the 20th of December, then, the war closed. The very next day, contrary to stipulation, the Malay *Pangerans* tried to ascend the river, and when stopped began to expostulate.

"After preventing many, the attempt was made by Subtu and Pangeran Hassim, in three large boats, boldly pulling toward us. Three hails did not check them, and they came on in spite of a blank cartridge and a wide ball, to turn them back. But I was resolved; and when a dozen musket-balls whistled over and fell close around them, they took to an ignominious flight. I subsequently upbraided them for this breach of promise, and Macota loudly declared they had *been greatly to blame*; but I discovered that he himself had set them on.

"I may now briefly conclude this detail. I ordered the rebels to burn all their stockades, which they did at once, and delivered up the greater part of their arms; and I proceeded to the *rajah* to request from him their lives. Those who know the Malay character will appreciate the difficulty of the attempt to stand between the monarch and his victims; I only succeeded when, at the end of a long debate—I soliciting, he denying—I rose to bid him farewell, as it was my intention to sail directly, since, after all my exertions in his cause, if he would not grant me the lives of the people, I could only consider that his friendship for me was at an end.

"On this he yielded. I must own that during the discussion he had much the best of it; for he urged that they had forfeited their lives by the law, as a necessary sacrifice to the future peace of the country; and argued that in a similar case in my own native land no leniency would be shown. On the contrary, my reasoning, though personal, was, on the whole, the best for the *rajah* and the people. I stated my extreme reluctance to have the blood of conquered foes shed; the shame I should experience in being a party, however involuntarily, to their execution; and the general advantage of a merciful line of policy.

"At the same time I told him their lives were forfeited, their crimes had been of a heinous and unpardonable nature, and it was only from so humane a man as himself, one with so kind a heart, that I could ask for their pardon; but I added, he well knew that it was only my previous knowledge of his benevolent disposition, and the great friendship I felt for him, which had induced me to take any part in this struggle. Other stronger reasons might have been brought forward, which I forbore to employ, as being repugnant to his princely pride, *viz.* that severity in this case would arm many against him, raise powerful enemies in Borneo Proper, as well as here, and greatly impede the future right government of the country. However, I gained my point, and was satisfied.

"Having fulfilled this engagement, and being moreover, together with many of my Europeans, attacked with an ague, I left the scene with all the dignity of complete success. Subsequently, the rebels were ordered to deliver up all their arms, ammunition, and property; and last, the wives and children of the principal people were demanded as hostages, and obtained. The women and children were treated with kindness, and preserved from injury or wrong. Siniawan thus dwindled away; the poorer men stole off in canoes and were scattered about, most of them coming to Sarawak. The better class pulled down the houses, abandoned the town, and lived in boats for a month; when, alarmed by the delay and impelled by hunger, they also fled—Patingi Gapoor, it was said, to Sambas; and Patingi Ali and the *tumangong* among the Dyaks.

"After a time it was supposed they would return and receive their wives and children. The army gradually dispersed to seek food, and the Chinese were left in possession of the once-renowned Siniawan, the ruin of which they completed by burning all that remained, and erecting a village for themselves in the immediate neighbourhood.

Seriff Jaffer and many others departed to their respective homes, and the pinching of famine succeeded to the horrors of war. Fruit being in season, helped to support the wretched people, and the near approach of the rice-harvest kept up their spirits."

## CHAPTER 9

# Conditions of the Cession of Sarawak

I have gone into the details of this curious rebellion, and selected from my friend's memoranda more, perhaps, than the actual and
present importance of the circumstances might seem to require; but
I have done so under the impression that in developing the traits and
lineaments of the native character, I am laying the foundation for a
more accurate estimate of them and their bearing upon futurity. The
difference between the Malay and the Chinese, between the sea and
the land Dyak, and even between one tribe and another, presents a
variety of elements out of which a consistent whole has to be compounded, and a new state of things to be established in Borneo.

It is, therefore, of considerable interest to view these elements in
their earliest contact with European mind and civilization, and thence
endeavour to shape out the course which is best calculated to insure
the welfare of all in the closer ties and more extended connection
which is springing out of this new intercourse. To enlarge the beneficial effects of trade and commerce, it is not enough to ascertain the
products of a strange country, nor even the chief wants of its population; but to inform ourselves of their habits, feelings, and disposition,
and so devise the wisest measures for supplying what is immediate,
removing obstacles, and increasing demand by a continually growing
improvement in government and general condition.

Following the war, and receiving the investiture of the government
of Sarawak, Mr. Brooke was enabled, from the insight he had obtained
into the diversified relations and habits, motives and ways of thinking
of these people, to address himself clearly and at once to reform the
evils which oppressed, and the abuses which destroyed them. Had he

not mixed with them and shared in this protracted contest, he must have begun rather as an experimentalist with a theory which might be right or might be wrong. But he had acquired the necessary experience, and could proceed to put his finger where it was required to repress or to foster, without danger of mistake. It was extraordinary what his energy produced within a small compass of time.

Security succeeded the utmost uncertainty, equal justice superseded tyrannical caprice, order arose out of confusion, and peace was gradually spread over the fruitful soil so lately polluted by the murderous warfare of heads-taking and imperishable feud. It is to be hoped that such an example will not be lost in the further prosecution of international and commercial policy in this interesting and important quarter of the eastern world. Piracy must be put down, slavery must be effaced, industry must be cherished and protected; and these objects, we shall see, from the model afforded by our truly illustrious countryman, may be accomplished; and we may further learn from his example, that from the experience even of "a little war," an enlightened observer may deduce the most sound data on which to commence a mighty change, leading, probably, to the happiness of millions, and the foundation of colonial empire.

With these few retrospective remarks, I resume the sequel of my friend's Bornean *Journal*.

"Our subsequent adventures," he notes, "may be easily related. We lay for some days, after winding up our affairs, in order to have an agreement drawn out between the *rajah* and myself, and during this time heard the *bruit* of a pirate fleet being on the coast. In a day or two after, certain news arrived of their having taken two Sadung boats, bound from Singapore, and Datu *Pangeran* was, in consequence, dispatched to communicate with them. He returned from Tanjong Datu, bringing the fleet with him to the mouth of the river, whence they requested permission to visit Sarawak, and pay their respects to the *rajah*. I was consulted on the subject whether I would meet them; and as I preferred a pacific to a hostile rencounter, and had, moreover, a considerable curiosity to see these roving gentry, I consented without hesitation.

"Reports—a greater curse in Malay countries than elsewhere—stated their object to be the capture of the Royalist, as they had, it was averred, received positive accounts of her having fifty lacks of dollars on board, and that her figure-head was of solid gold. As, however, we had no such treasure, and the meeting was unavoidable, and might be hostile, I put myself into a complete posture of defence, with a determination neither to show backwardness nor suspicion. The day arrived, and the pirates swept up the river; eighteen *prahus*, one following the other, decorated with flags and streamers, and firing both cannon and musketry; the sight was interesting and curious, and heightened by the conviction that these friends of the moment might be enemies the next.

"Having taken their stations, the chief men proceeded to an interview with the *rajah*, which I attended to witness. Some distrust and much ceremony marked the meeting; and both parties had numerous followers, who filled the hall of audience and the avenues leading to it; and as few of the Illanuns spoke Malay, the communication was rendered difficult and troublesome. The pirates consisted of Illanuns and Malukus from Gillolo. The Illanuns are fine athletic men, with a strong resemblance in appearance to the Bugis; their bearing was haughty and reserved, and they seemed quite ready to be friends or foes, as best suited their purpose. The Malukus are from a bay in Gillolo, and their country is now in possession of the Dutch; they are a darker and an uglier race, but their manners more supple and pliant. They were the principal talkers, while the Illanuns maintained a dignified silence.

"These Malukus, from their own account, since the capture of their *rajah*, and the subjugation of their country, have led a wandering, piratical life; they represent their force at about twenty-five boats, of which three are now joined by the Illanuns, as a matter of mere convenience. Beyond the usual formalities, this meeting had nothing to distinguish it; one party retired to their boats, while the other went to their respective houses, and everything betokened quiet. In the evening I pulled through the fleet, and inspected several of the largest *prahus*. The entire force consisted of eighteen boats, *viz.*, three Malukus and fifteen Illanuns; the smallest of these boats carried thirty men, the largest (they are mostly large) upward of a hundred; so that, at a moderate computation, the number of fighting men might be reckoned at from five to six hundred.

"The Illanun expedition had been absent from Magindano upward of three years, during which time they had cruised among the Moluccas and islands to the eastward, had haunted Boni Bay and Celebes, and beat up the Straits of Makassar. Many of their boats, however, being worn out, they had fitted out Bugis prize *prahus*, and were now on their return home. They had recently attacked one of the Tambelan islands, and had been repulsed; and report said they intended a descent upon Sirhassan, one of the Southern Natunas group.

"These large *prahus* are too heavy to pull well, though they carry thirty, forty, and even fifty oars: their armament is one or two six-pounders in the bow, one four-pounder stern-chaser, and a number of swivels, besides musketry, spears, and swords. The boat is divided into three sections, and fortified with strong planks, one behind the bow, one amidships, and one astern, to protect the steersman. The women and children are crammed down below, where the unhappy prisoners are likewise stowed away during an action. Their principal plan is boarding a vessel, if possible, and carrying her by numbers; and certainly if a merchantman fired ill, she would inevitably be taken; but with grape and canister fairly directed, the slaughter would be so great that they would be glad to sheer off before they neared a vessel.

"This is, of course, supposing a calm, for in a breeze they would never have the hardihood to venture far from land with a ship in sight, and would be sorry to be caught at a distance. Their internal constitution is as follows: one chief, a man usually of rank, commands the whole fleet; each boat has her captain, and generally from five to ten of his relations, free men: the rest, amounting to above four fifths, are slaves, more or less forced to pursue this course of life. They have, however, the right of plunder, which is indiscriminate with certain exceptions; *viz.*, slaves, guns, money, or any other heavy articles, to-gether with the very finest description of silks and cloths, belonging to the chiefs and free men; and the rest obey the rule of 'First come, first served.'

"No doubt the slaves become attached to this predatory course of life; but it must always be remembered that they are slaves and have no option; and it appears to me that, in the operation of our laws, some distinction ought to be drawn on this account, to suit the circum-stances of the case. The *datus*, or chiefs, are incorrigible; for they are pirates by descent, robbers from pride as well as taste, and they look upon the occupation as the most honourable hereditary pursuit. They are indifferent to blood, fond of plunder, but fondest of slaves: they despise trade, though its profits be greater; and, as I have said, they look upon this as their 'calling,' and the noblest occupation of chiefs and free men.

"Their swords they show with boasts, as having belonged to their ancestors who were pirates, renowned and terrible in their day; and they always speak of their ancestral heirloom as decayed from its pristine vigour, but still deem the wielding of it as the highest of earthly existences. That it is in reality the most accursed, there can be no doubt, for its chief support is slaves they capture on the different coasts. If they attack an island, the women and children, and as many of the young men as they require, are carried off. Every boat they take furnishes its quota of slaves; and when they have a *full cargo*, they quit that coast or country and visit another, in order to dispose of their human spoil to the best advantage.

"Thus a cargo of slaves, captured on the east coast of Borneo, is sold on the west; and the slaves of the south find ready purchasers to the northward, and *vice versâ*. As the woolly-haired Papuas are generally prized by the natives, constant visits are made to New Guinea and the easternmost islands, where they are procured, and afterward sold at high prices among any Malay community. The great nests of piracy are Magindano, Sooloo, and the northern part of Borneo; and the devastation and misery they inflict on the rest of the Archipelago are well known; yet are no measures adopted for their suppression, as every European community, be it English, Dutch, or Spanish, seems quite satisfied to clear the vicinity of its own ports, and never considers the damage to the native trade which takes place at a distance.

"To be attacked with success, they must be attacked on their own coasts with two or three steamers. A little money would gain every intelligence as to where they were preparing; and while the steamers were so worthily engaged in suppressing piracy, they might at the same time be acquiring information respecting countries little known, and adding to our stock of geography and science. A few severe examples and constant harassing would soon cure this hereditary and personal mania for a rover's life; and while we conferred the greatest blessings on the rest of the Archipelago, Magindano itself would be improved by the change.

"The Illanun *datus* and the Gillolo chiefs visited the schooner constantly, and were always considerate enough to bring but few followers. We conversed much upon piracy in general, their mode of life, their successes, and their privations. They seemed to have but few fears of the Dutch or English men-of-war being able to take them, and during their three years' cruise had never been chased by any of them.

"After being three or four days in company with these worthies, *i. e.*, the fleet of Illanuns and Malukus, the *Royalist* dropped down the river to Santobong, while Williamson and myself stayed yet a few days with Muda Hassim in his house. We had a week's incessant torrent of rain. Nothing could exceed the kindness of the *rajah* during our stay, with his brothers, of all ages, as our constant companions. We had one day a dance of the Illanuns and Gillolos: they might both be called war-dances, but are very different. The performer with the Illanuns is decked out with a *fine helmet* (probably *borrowed* from our early voyagers), ornamented with bird-of-paradise feathers. Two gold belts, crossed, like our soldiers', over the breast, are bound at the waist with a fantastical garment reaching half way down the thigh, and composed of various-coloured silk and woollen threads one above another. The sword, or '*kempilan*,' is decorated at the handle with a yard or two of red cloth, and the long upright shield is covered with small rings, which clash as the performer goes through his evolutions.

"The dance itself consists of a variety of violent warlike gestures, stamping, striking, advancing, retreating, turning, falling, yelling, with here and there bold stops, and excellent as to *àplomb*, which might have elicited the applause of the opera-house; but, generally speaking, the performance was outrageously fierce, and so far natural as approaching to an actual combat; and in half an hour the dancer, a fine young man, was so exhausted that he fell, fainting, into the arms of his comrades. Several others succeeded, but not equal to the first; and we had hardly a fair opportunity of judging of the Maluku dance from its short continuance; but it is of a more gentle nature, advancing with the spear stealthily, easting it, then retreating with the sword and shield.

"The Maluku shield, it should be observed, is remarkably narrow, and is brandished somewhat in the same way as the single stick-player uses his stick, or the Irishman his *shillelah*, that is to say, it is held nearly in the centre, and whirled every way round. I procured some of the instruments, and found that the sword of the Malukus of Gillolo is similar to that of the Moskokas of Boni Bay, in Celebes. All these pirates are addicted to the *excessive* use of opium; but the effects of it are by no means so deleterious or so strongly marked as has been represented; and it must likewise be remembered that they are in other respects dissolute and debauched.

"Among the Chinese it would be difficult—nay, impossible—to detect the smokers of the drug. Here and there you may see an emaciated man; but, out of a body of five hundred, some are usually emaciated and unhealthy. I do not mean to deny the bad effects of opium; but the stories of its pernicious results are greatly exaggerated where the habit exists in moderation. The Chinese themselves, when I spoke to them of the bad consequences, always argued that, taken moderately, it was a stimulus to industry and activity; but they allowed, at the same time, that excess was highly injurious.

"The time at length came for my departure, but I was pressed to stay one day after another, for our society was a relief to the usual monotonous tenor of their lives. The papers were signed which made me Resident of Sarawak. I started to Santobong, and reached the vessel on the 13th of February; and after waiting two days, in the vain hope of a lull or change of wind, we beat out of the channel."

Mr. Brooke did not remain long at Singapore. His principal object was to procure a vessel to trade between that place and Sarawak. Trading, however, was not his forte; but he already felt the deepest interest in the welfare of those people. By accident—or, more properly, by Providence—he appears to have been sent to put a stop to an unnatural war, and to save the lives of the unfortunate rebels; and the benefit he had conferred on so many of his fellow-creatures, the good he had already done, and the infinity of good which he saw he still might do, made him anxious to return.

After some difficulty, he succeeded in purchasing a schooner of 90 tons, called the *Swift*, which I recollected in the Malacca Straits as the Zephyr, then a cruiser in the East India Company's service. Having put a suitable cargo into her, he sailed with his squadron (*Royalist* and *Swift*) for Sarawak early in April, 1841.

The *rajah*, already described as an indolent, weak-minded man, had promised Mr. Brooke the government of the country; but, among other obstacles with which he would have to contend in accepting it, I do not think my friend calculated on jealousy, low cunning, and treachery, or the dangerous enemy he had made in Pangeran Macota. He had been an eye-witness to his cowardice, and had more than once detected and exposed his cunning and trickery; sins not to be forgiven, especially by a Malay. Notwithstanding this, firmness, courage, and straightforward honesty gained the victory, as the sequel will show.

Among the characters with whom Mr. Brooke got acquainted during the rebel war was a young chief named Si Tundo, who was constantly by his side whenever there was danger. He was an Illanun, and had been sent from Sadung, with some thirteen of his countrymen, by Seriff Sahib, to offer his services to Macota, commander-in-chief of the *rajah's* forces; and I resume Mr. Brooke's memoranda, with the following interesting account of this poor fellow's fate:

"On my arrival at Sarawak, we were received with the usual honors; and the first thing I heard of was the decease of my poor companion, Si Tundo of Magindano, who had been put to death by the *rajah's* orders. The course of justice, or, rather, injustice, or perhaps, more justly, a mixture of both, is so characteristic of the people, that I am tempted to give the particulars. Si Tundo fell in love with a woman belonging to an adopted son of Macota, and the passion being mutual, the lady eloped from her master and went to her lover's house. This being discovered in a short time, he was ordered to surrender her to Macota, which he reluctantly did, on an understanding that he was to be allowed to marry her on giving a proper dowry. Either not being able to procure the money, or the terms not being kept, Si Tundo and a relation (who had left the pirate fleet and resided with him) mounted to Macota's hill, and threatened to take the woman and to burn the house.

"The village, however, being roused, they were unable to effect their purpose, and retired to their own residence. Here they remained for some days in a state of incessant watchfulness; and when they moved, they each carried their *kempilan*, and wore the *krisses* ready to the hand. The Rajah Muda Hassim, being well aware of the state of things, sent, at this crisis, to order Si Tundo and his friend to his presence; which order they obeyed forthwith, and entered the *balei*, or audience-hall, which was full of their enemies. According to Muda Hassim's account, he was anxious to save Si Tundo's life, and offered him another wife; but, his affections being fixed on the girl of his own choice, he rejected the offer, only praying he might have the woman he loved.

"On entering the presence of the *rajah*, surrounded by foes, and dreading treachery (which most probably was intended), these unfortunate men added to their previous fault by one which, however slight in European estimation, is here of an aggravated nature—they entered the presence with their *kempilans* in their hands, and their sarongs clear of the *kris*-handle; and instead of seating themselves cross-legged, they only squatted on their hams, ready for self-defence. From that hour their doom was resolved on: the crime of disrespect was deemed worthy of death, though their previous crime of abduction and violence might have obtained pardon.

"It was no easy matter, however, among an abject and timid population, to find executioners of the sentence against two brave and warlike men, well armed and watchful, and who, it was well known, would sell their lives dearly; and the subsequent proceeding is, as already observed, curiously characteristic of the people, and the deep disguise they can assume to attain their purposes. It was intimated to Si Tundo that, if he could raise a certain sum of money, the woman should be made over to him; and to render this the more probable, the affair was taken out of Macota's hands, and placed at the decision of the Orang Kaya de Gadong, who *was friendly* to the offenders, but who received his private orders how to act. Four men were appointed to watch their opportunity, in order to seize the culprits.

"It is not to be imagined, however, that a native would trust or believe the friendly assurances held out to him; nor was it so in the case of Si Tundo and his companion; they attended at the Orang Kaya de Gadong's house frequently for weeks, with the same precautions, and it was found impossible to overpower them; but the deceit of their enemies was equal to the occasion, and delay brought no change of purpose. They were to die, and opportunity alone was wanting to carry the sentence into effect. Time passed over, suspicion was lulled; and as suspicion was lulled the professions to serve them became more frequent. Poor Si Tundo brought *all* his little property to make good the price required for the woman, and his friend added his share; but it was still far short of the required amount.

"Hopes, however, were still held out; the Orang Kaya advanced a small sum to assist, and other *pretended* friends, slowly and reluctantly, at his request, lent a little money. The negotiation was nearly complete; forty or fifty *reals* only were wanting, and the opposite party were ready to deliver the lady whenever the sum was made good. A final conference was appointed for the conclusion of the bargain at the Orang Kaya's, at which numbers were present; and the devoted victims, lulled into fatal security, had ceased to bring their formidable *kempilans*. At the last interview, the forty *reals* being still deficient, the Orang Kaya proposed receiving their gold-mounted *krisses* in pledge for the amount. The *krisses* were given up, and the bargain was complete, when the four executioners threw themselves on the unarmed men, and, assisted by others, overpowered and secured them.

"Si Tundo, wounded in the scuffle, and bound, surrounded by enemies flourishing their *krisses*, remarked, 'You have taken me by treachery; openly you could not have seized me.' He spoke no more. They triumphed over and insulted him, as though some great feat had been achieved, and every *kris* was plunged into his body, which was afterward cast, without burial, into the river. Si Tundo's relation was spared on pleading for mercy; and after his whole property, even to his clothes, was confiscated, he was allowed to retire to Sadung. Thus perished poor Si Tundo, a Magindano pirate, with many, if not all, the vices of the native character, but with boldness, courage, and constancy, which retrieved his faults, and raised him in the estimation of brave men. In person he was tall, elegantly made, with small and handsome features, and quiet and graceful manners; but toward the Malays, even of rank, there was in his bearing a suppressed contempt, which they often felt, but could not well resent. Alas! my gallant comrade, I mourn your death, and could have better spared a better man; for as long as you lived, I had one faithful follower of tried courage among the natives. Peace be with you in the world to come, and may the great God pardon your sins and judge you mercifully!

"The case of poor Si Tundo proves that the feeling of love is not quite dead among Asiatics, though its power is obscured by their education and habits of polygamy; and that friendship and relationship may induce a man here, as elsewhere, to risk his life and sacrifice his property without any prospect of personal advantage. An old Magindano man, a sort of foster-father of Si Tundo's, when he saw me for the first time, clasped my arm, and repeatedly exclaimed, 'Si Tundo is dead; they have killed him;' adding, 'had you been here, he would not have been killed.' I was touched by the old man's sorrow, and his expression of feeling."

Datu Jembrong was likewise an Illanum, and retired to Sadung when the rebel war had closed, and died after a few days' illness. Mr. Brooke writes: "Thus I have lost the two bravest men—men whom I would rather trust for fair dealing than any score of Borneons; for the Magindanos, though pirates by descent and education, are a far superior people to any in the Archipelago, with the exception of the Bugis. Whatever may be their vices, they are retrieved by courage to a certain degree; and where we find a manly character, we may presume that the meaner arts of *finesse* and treachery are less prevalent. Dampier and Forrest both give them an excellent character; and it is a pity that of late years little is known of them, and so little pains taken to hold a friendly intercourse either with them or the Sooloos."

The important changes which ensued on the return of Mr. Brooke to Sarawak, in the spring of 1841, now demand attention; and, as heretofore, I proceed to describe them from the data intrusted to my charge.

"In a former part of my journal," says Mr. Brooke, "I have mentioned briefly the occasions which led to my invitation, and the reasons which induced me to accept the offer of the Rajah Muda Hassim; but I will repeat these, in order to bring the narrative at once more distinctly before the memory. When I returned here for the second time, in August of last year, it was with the determination of remaining for a few days only on my way to the northward; and nothing but my feeling for the miserable situation of Muda Hassim induced me to alter my intention.

"The rebellion, which he had come from Borneo to quell, had defied every effort for nearly four years; and the attacks he had made on the rebels had failed entirely and almost disgracefully. His immediate followers were few in number, and aid from the neighbouring countries was either denied, or withheld on trivial excuses; while the opposition of Pangeran Usop in Borneo paralyzed the efforts of his supporters in the capital, and, in case of non-success, threatened his own power. The pride, the petty pride of the Malay prince bent before these circumstances, and induced him to state his difficulties to me, and to request my assistance. His failure was strongly dwelt on, and his resolution to die here rather than abandon his undertaking—to die disgraced and deserted!

"Under these circumstances, could I, he urged upon me, forsake him? could I, 'a gentleman from England,' who had been his friend, and knew the goodness of his heart, could I leave him surrounded and begirt with enemies? It was possibly foolish, it was perhaps imprudent, but it accorded with my best feelings; and I resolved not to abandon him without at any rate seeing the probabilities of success; and it must always be remembered that, in doing so, I had no ulterior object, no prospect of any personal advantage. I joined his miserable army, which, in numbers, barely exceeded that of the rebels, strongly stockaded. I joined them at the outset of their campaign; and in a few days (ten days) witnessed such scenes of cowardice, treachery, intrigue, and lukewarmness among his followers, such a determination not to take advice or to pursue any active measures, that I left them and returned to my vessel.

"The Chinese I do not include in this representation; they were true and willing, but wretchedly armed, and very justly refused to be thrust forward into posts of danger, which the Malays in their own country would not share. On my return to the vessel, I frankly stated how useless my presence was among men who would not do anything I desired, yet would do nothing for themselves; and, under the circumstances, I intimated my intention of sailing. Here, again, I was pressed with the same entreaties; every topic was exhausted to excite my compassion, every aid was at my disposal; and lastly, if I would stay, and we were successful, the country was offered to me. The only inquiry was, whether the *rajah* had the right and authority to make over the country to me, and this I was assured he had.

"The government, the revenue (with slight deductions for the sultan), and one of his brothers to reside here in order to insure the obedience of the Malays, were all comprehended in this cession, freely and without condition. I might, at this point of the negotiation, have insured *the title* to the government as far as a written agreement could give it; but for two sufficient reasons I declined all treaty upon the subject until the war was over. The first of these reasons was, that it would have been highly ungenerous to take advantage of a man's distress to tie him down to any agreement which, in other circumstances, he might not be willing to adopt; and by acting thus ungenerously, it would be tempting the *rajah* to deceive me when the treaty came to be ratified.

"The second reason was equally cogent; for a mere barren bond, which I had no means to enforce, was worse than useless, and no man would be nearer possession by merely holding a written promise. I may add, likewise, that I saw so many difficulties in the way of the undertaking, that I was by no means over-anxious to close with it; and, previously to accepting and entering on so bold a project, I was desirous thoroughly to be assured of the good faith of the promiser. To the Rajah Muda Hassim's proposal I, therefore, replied, that I could not accept it while the war was pending, as I considered it wrong to take any advantage of his present situation; and that, if he conferred authority on me in the camp, I would once more go up the river and assist him to the utmost of my power. It is needless to repeat any details of the war, except to say that I found every support from him, and the highest consideration, both in personal attentions and the bestowal of influence.

"He conquered, I may say without self-praise, through my means; and on the close of hostilities our negotiation about the country was revived. In its progress I stated to him that Malay governments were so bad, that the high were allowed so much license, and the poor so oppressed, that any attempt to govern without a change of these abuses was impossible; and as a foundation of my acceptance was the proposition, that all his exertions must be employed to establish the principle that one man was not to take anything from another, and that all men were to enjoy the produce of their labour, save and except at such times as they were engaged in working for the revenue.

"That the amount of the revenue was to be fixed and certain for three years, at a stated quantity of rice per family; in lieu of which, should a man prefer it, he might pay in money or in labour: the relative price of rice to money or labour being previously fixed at as low a rate as possible. That the officers, *viz.*, Patingi, Bandar, and Tumangong, were to receive stated salaries out of this revenue, in order to prevent any extortion, either by themselves or in their name; and that they were to be answerable for the whole revenue under my superintendence. That the Dyaks were to be treated the same as the Malays, their property protected, their taxes fixed, and their labour free.

"At the same time, I represented to him the difficulty of doing this, and that nothing but his power could effect it; as any foreigner, without his unlimited support and confidence, would have no chance of finding obedience from the numerous inferior *pangerans* and their followers. This, with much more, was the theme of my conversation; to which was replied, *imprimis*, That their customs and religion must not be infringed. That with regard to the violence and rapacity of the higher classes, and the uncertainty of taxation, which led to so much oppression, they were by no means any part of the Ondong Ondong, *i. e.*, the written law of Borneo, but gross abuses which had arisen out of lax government. That it was the wish of his heart to see these things mended; and that nothing should be wanting on his part to assist me in accomplishing objects so desirable, particularly with respect to the Dyaks, who were so grossly abused.

"On this, a written agreement was made out, merely to the purport that I was to reside at Sarawak in order to 'seek for profit;' and on my remarking that this paper expressed nothing, he said I must not think that it was the one understood between us, but merely for him to show to the sultan at Borneo in the first place. I accepted this version of the story, though it looked suspicious; and on my part, over and above our written agreement, which expressed nothing, I consented to buy a vessel, and bring down trade to the place, in return for which I was assured of antimony ore in plenty; and though I knew that profit was not to be expected, I was desirous to comply, as, without a vessel regularly trading here, it would be impossible to develop the resources of the country.

"While I went to Singapore, the *rajah* promised to build me a house, in which I was to take up my residence. I sailed accordingly, and returned within three months, having performed all my engagements; but on reaching Sarawak, the first disappointment I experienced was, that the house was not commenced. I urged them to begin it, and after the most provoking delays at length got it finished. I mention this because it was the only instance in which good faith was kept.

"*August 3rd.*—The two schooners, *Royalist* and *Swift*, having arrived at Sarawak, I found myself with a heavy monthly expense, and was naturally anxious to dispatch them as speedily as possible. I was assured that 6000 *peculs* of antimony ore would be down immediately, and that whenever the people were set to work, any quantity might be procured without difficulty; which, indeed, I knew to be true, as Macotah had loaded a ship, a brig, and three native vessels in six weeks. The procrastination, therefore, was the more provoking; but as I had determined to arm myself with patience, and did not anticipate foul play, I was content to wait for a time. The *Swift* being leaky and requiring repairs, was another inducement to me to lie by and land her cargo, which, ever since my arrival, the *rajah* petitioned to have ashore, giving every pledge for a quick and good return.

"At length I consented to let him have the cargo into his own hands, on the assurance that the antimony ore" (*i. e.*, the 6000 *peculs* which were ready?) "should be brought down directly. Nothing could be more correct than the way they received the cargo, taking an account of each separate article, comparing it with the invoice, and noting down the deficiency; and the *rajah* himself superintended this interesting process from morning till dark. At this time, having agreed with him for the whole, as the easiest and best mode of dealing under the circumstances, I did not much trouble myself about the deposit; and my attention was first roused by the extreme apathy of the whole party directly the cargo was in their possession—overhauled, reckoned, and disposed of among them."

# CHAPTER 10

# Excursion up the River

During the succeeding pages of my friend's journal, one hardly knows which to admire most; his firmness, his cool courage, his determined perseverance, or his patience. On the other hand, it is difficult to decide whether the *rajah's* indolence and ingratitude, or Macota's low cunning and treachery are the more disgusting. But I continue the narrative, and readers will judge for themselves.

"Yet," says Mr. Brooke, "I had confidence, and was loath to allow any base suspicion to enter my mind against a man who had hitherto behaved well to me, and had not deceived me before. From the time the cargo had been disposed of, I found myself positively laid on the shelf. No return arrived; no steps were taken to work the antimony ore; no account appeared of the positive amount to be received: a promise was tendered; and all my propositions—nay, my very desire to speak of the state of the country—were evaded. I found myself clipped like Samson, while delay was heaped upon delay, excuse piled on excuse, and all covered with the utmost show of kindness and civility.

"It was provoking beyond sufferance; but with several strokes which I considered important, I bore it with saint-like patience. I remonstrated mildly but firmly on the waste of my money, and on the impossibility of any good to the country while the *rajah* conducted himself as he had done. I urged upon him to release the poor women whom he had kept confined for nearly five months; and I guaranteed the peaceful disposition of the people if it were done. I might as well have whistled to the winds, or have talked reason to stones. I was overwhelmed with professions of affection and kindness, but nothing ensued. I had trusted—my eyes gradually opened—I feared I was betrayed and robbed, and had at length determined to be observant and watchful, when an event occurred which finished the delusion, and woke me fully to the treachery, or at any rate the weakness, at work against me.

"My house was finished, and I had just taken possession of it, when I understood that an overwhelming body of Dyaks, accompanied by Malays, were proceeding up the river, with the avowed purpose of attacking a hostile tribe, but with the real design of slaughtering all the weak tribes in their way. Upward of 100 boats, with certainly not fewer than 2500 men, had been at Sarawak a week, asking permission for this expedition; and I was informed there was not the slightest chance of its being granted, when to my surprise I saw the expedition start.

"On being convinced that they really were going up the country, I instantly quitted the house and returned on board the *Royalist*, sending to know whether the *rajah* had granted leave for their entrance into the interior. By him the whole blame of the transaction was thrown upon Macota and the Orang Kaya de Gadong; and he himself was said to be so ill that he could not be seen; but it was added, as I disliked the measure so greatly, the same parties who had sent the Dyaks up could recall them down, which indeed I had insisted on being done. They accordingly retrograded and left; after which I continued sulky on board and the *rajah*, shamming sick, sulked in his *harem*.

"That any man beside the *rajah* himself would have been bold enough to grant the permission, I knew, from experience, was impossible. I accepted his denial as the groundwork of a reconciliation. In the mean time, as he continued indisposed, I intimated my intention of proceeding to Borneo in three days, and dispatching the *Swift* at the same time to proceed to Singapore; part of her cargo, 750 *peculs* of antimony ore, having been at length put on board.

"On this being made known to the *rajah*, he forgot his sickness, and came out and proffered me a meeting to discuss affairs, which I postponed until the following day. In the mean time I took a candid view of my position, and considered the best means of extricating myself from my difficulties with as little trouble and inconvenience as possible to either party.

"I had lost much valuable time, spent much money, and risked my life and the lives of my crew, in order to render assistance to Rajah Muda Hassim in his distress; in return for which he had voluntarily offered me the country. The conditions of my acceptance had been discussed and mutually understood, and I had, in fulfilment of my part, brought vessel and cargo. Profit I did not much care about; the development of the country was my chief, I may say my only, aim; and on my arrival I had been delayed and cheated by false promises, which showed too plainly that he neither meant to adhere to his former agreement, nor to pay for what he had on false pretences obtained. It may appear to many that no measures ought to be kept with one who had so behaved; but for the following reasons I resolved still to wait his pleasure.

"In the first place, it was barely possible that indolence, and not treachery, might have actuated him; and in the next place, if it was possible to arrange so as to get back the amount of the *Swift's* cargo, I was in duty and justice bound to use every endeavour before resorting to measures of force. As for the cession of the country, and all the good which must have resulted from it, I put these considerations altogether out of the question. I had been deceived and betrayed, and had met with the grossest ingratitude; but I had no claim, nor would any written agreement have given me one; and I was therefore constrained to submit without returning evil for evil. Every point weighed, I felt, from every motive, inclined, nay desirous, to avoid a rupture, or taking an equivalent for my property by force.

"The *Swift*, with the part of her cargo received on board, after three months' detention, and no more even talked of, I therefore resolved, as already stated, to dispatch to Singapore. My first intention on arriving here had been to send the *Royalist* back to that port and dispose of her; but a native rumour being afloat that the crew of a shipwrecked vessel were in Borneo Proper, I deemed it incumbent on me to visit that place and effect their release. I had used every means in my power since my arrival to induce the Rajah Muda Hassim to send one or two of his *pangeran*s and a letter from himself to the *sultan* by the *Royalist*, in order to insure that object; but although, day by day, I had received promises, they were never performed.

"Seeing now that this duty of humanity could no longer be delayed with propriety, I resolved to dispatch the *Royalist* to Borneo, and myself to remain here, to endeavour, if I could, to obtain *my own*. Each vessel was to return as quickly as possible from her place of destination; and I then resolved to give two additional months to the *rajah*, and to urge him in every way in my power to do what he was bound to do as an act of common honesty. Should these means fail, after making the strongest representations and giving amplest time, I considered myself free to extort by force what I could not gain by fair means.

"Having determined on these steps, I met the *rajah* by appoint-

135

ment, and repeated all my grievances, and set strongly before him the injury done in consequence; and lastly, plainly told him that I only came and now only stayed in his country at his request, but that the property he had taken must be repaid, and subsequently to that, if he had any proposition to make, I would endeavour to meet his wishes. To all this I received *no one satisfactory answer*, and, from the shuffling on every complaint, I formed the worst opinion of his intentions.

"My determination, however, having been previously made, the result of this conversation had no effect upon me; and at the end of three days, the time I had limited, no letter for the sultan being forthcoming, on the fourth morning the two schooners proceeded to sea, one for Borneo, the other for Singapore, while, with three companions, I remained in my new house.[1]

"I wish now to discuss a question which has often occupied my mind, and upon which I have been very desirous to arrive at a right conclusion. It is certain that a British subject cannot wrongfully attack or injure any prince or person in his own country without rendering himself liable to be punished by the laws of England. It is both right and just that it should be so, because in *demi*-civilized or savage countries the natives are often unable to protect themselves, and an attack upon them savours of piracy. On the other hand, if the native prince be the party to blame; if he fraudulently possess himself of property under false pretences, make promises which he breaks, and enter into agreements before witnesses which he never intends to fulfil; then, I ask, is a British subject to submit to the loss, when the party defrauding him is able to pay and will not? I answer decidedly, he is not bound to submit to be cheated, and, if he have the means, he has the right to enforce repayment.

"It may be urged that trust ought not to be reposed; but trust is the ordinary course of trade, and cannot alter the question. Again, it may be said, Apply to the government; but it is well known and acknowledged that the government will not interfere in any case of the

---

1. I need hardly remark on the singular courage and disregard of personal safety and life itself evinced by my friend on this occasion. At issue with the *rajah* on points of great temptation to him, beset by intrigues, and surrounded by a fierce and lawless people, Mr. Brooke did not hesitate to dispatch his vessels and protectors, the one on a mission of pure humanity, and the other in calm pursuance of the objects he had proposed to himself to accomplish; and with "three companions," place himself at the mercy of such circumstances, regardless of the danger, and relying on the overruling Providence in which he trusted, to bring him safely through all his difficulties and perils.—H. K.

sort. Seek redress by law! there is no law to meet the contingency. Bear the loss, *i. e.* be betrayed, deceived, and cheated, and submit! It cannot be; for although the law may properly inquire into the circumstances, yet as it will not protect me here, or give me any redress for *fraud* or *murder*, it cannot punish, if right be on my side.

"Am I quite sure that the right is on my side? It is, as far as I can judge; and having candidly stated every fact and circumstance, I am convinced there can be but one opinion on the subject. I am sure that if I seize property to the amount of that taken from me, I act justly, though perhaps not legally; yet I firmly believe legally likewise, although law and justice do not necessarily go always hand in hand. On the whole, there was the old sore rankling—the false promises, the gross deceit, the base ingratitude to a man who had done everything to relieve this equivocating *rajah* from disgrace, defeat, and perhaps death. But here I close this account for the present, to be resumed on the return of the *Royalist* from Borneo.

"*August 4th.*—Both retrospectively and prospectively the grounds for all these transactions were ever pressing on my mind and guiding my actions. The capabilities of the Sarawak country were very great. It could abundantly supply the richest produce of the vegetable kingdom; it abounded in mineral wealth, and especially in a vast staple commodity of antimony ore; with a considerable population of Dyaks, whose condition was decidedly improvable; a Malay population, by no means large, which was advantageous; and a Chinese population ready to immigrate with even a moderate prospect of protection.

"Beside these inducements, must be added its propinquity to the Pontiana River, and the trade which by that route might flow even from the centre of this little-known island. To crown all, there were the credit to myself in case of success, the amelioration of the native condition, however partial, and the benefit to commerce in general. These were the reasons that induced me to enter on this arduous task; and to these I may add a supplementary one, *viz.*, that when I had struggled for a time, I might rouse the zeal of others, and find efficient support either from government or the mercantile body.

"I have in a former part of my journal mentioned the Illanun pirates, and my meeting with them here. On our return we heard of their being still on the coast, and from that time to this they have been ravaging and plundering between Tanjong *datu*, Sirhassan, and Pontiana. Malays and Chinese have been carried off in great numbers; Borneo and Sambas *prahus* captured without end; and so much havoc committed, that the whole coast, as far as the natives are concerned, may be pronounced in a state of blockade.

"Beside the Illanuns, there are two other descriptions of pirates infesting these seas: one, the Dyaks of Sakarran and Sarebus, two predatory tribes already mentioned; the other called Balagnini, a wild people represented to come from the northward of Sooloo. I have not seen them; but their boats are said to be very long and swift, with sometimes outriggers; and one particular in their mode of attack is too curious to omit. In closing on their victims they use long poles, having a hook made fast at the extremity, with which, being expert, they hook their opponents at a distance and drag them overboard, while others are fighting with *saligis* and spears.

"I have before mentioned the arrival of one hundred Dyak boats at Sarawak, to request permission from the *rajah* to ascend the river and attack a tribe toward Sambas. What a tale of misgovernment, tyranny, and weakness, does this request tell! These Dyaks were chiefly from Sakarran, mixed with the Sarebus, and with them three boats of the Malo tribe, whose residence is toward the Pontiana River. The Sakarrans are the most powerful, the most predatory, and the most independent tribe on the N.W. coast, their dependence on Borneo being merely nominal. The latter are likewise predatory and numerous, but they are on good terms with all the coast tribes and with the Malays, while the Sarebus are against all, and all are against them.

"Speaking generally, they are a remarkably fine body of people, handsome, intelligent, powerful, well-made, beautifully-limbed, and clear-skinned. They are somewhat fairer than the Malays and the mountain Dyaks; but in manners, customs, and language, exactly resemble the Sibnowans, except that the last, from misfortune, have become a peaceful tribe. The Sarebus and Sakarrans are only distinguishable by the numerous rings they wear in their ears. On one man I counted fourteen of brass, various sizes, in one ear only. They are rather fond of ornament, and wear grotesque caps of various-coloured cloths (particularly red), some of them square, others peaked, and others like a cocked hat worn athwart-ships, and terminating in sharp points on the top of the head.

"These head-dresses are ornamented with tufts of red hair or black human hair, shreds of cloth, and sometimes feathers; but what renders them laughable to look at is, that the hair is cut close to match the shape of the cap; so that when a man displaces it, you find him bare of hair about the forehead and posterior part of the skull, that over the ears cut into points, and the rest of the skull showing a good crop of black bristles.

"The commanders of this party were yclept poetically by their own people, as *noms de guerre*, the Sun and the Moon, *i. e.*, *Bulan*, for moon, and *Matari* for sun. The Sun was as fine a young man as the eye would wish to rest upon; straight, elegantly yet strongly made, with a chest and neck, and head set on them, which might serve Apollo; legs far better than his of Belvidere; and a countenance mild and intelligent. I became very good friends with both Sun and Moon, and gave them a great deal of good advice about piracy, which, of course, was thrown away.

"Their boats are built very long, raised at the stern, and the largest pulling as many as sixty paddles; but I should not think them fast, and any boat with a swivel might cut them up. The least average I could give the hundred boats is twenty-five men per boat, making, as already observed, 2500 in all. We counted ninety, and there were others down the reach we could not see; and they themselves stated their force to be 140 boats and 4000 men. The manners of these Dyaks toward us were reserved, quiet, and independent. They stole nothing, and in trading for small quantities of rice, bees-wax, cotton, and their cloths, showed a full knowledge of the relative value of the articles, or rather they priced their own at far above their proper worth.

"I may indeed say of all the Dyaks I have seen, that they are anxious to receive, but very loath to give; and when they have obtained cloth, salt, copper, beads, &c. to the amount of two or three dollars as a present, will bring in a bunch of plantains or a little rice, and ask you *to buy*. The Sibnowans are the chief exceptions to this, and they are my pet tribe. The language of Sakarran and Sarebus is the same as the Sibnowan; and with all the word God, the *Allah Talla* of the Malays, is expressed by *Battara*, from which we may infer that their notion of the Deity, as probably was all the religion of these regions, was derived from the Hindoos.

"When this force of Dyaks was, contrary to the assurance given to me, sweeping up the river, I had just finished a late dinner. I was *angry enough*, and resolved instanter to leave the house, when who should come in, *as if by pure accident*, but Pangeran Budrudeen, the *rajah's* brother. I controlled myself, spoke strongly withal but civilly, and sent him away wishing he had not come near me; and the boat being ready, I retired from the house to the *Royalist*. Their immediate recall was the consequence; for the *rajah* having denied his permission, those who fathered the act dared not persist in it when I told them it was an act of disobedience. They tried to frighten me with the idea that the Dyaks would attack us; but as I felt sure we could blow them away in ten minutes, it had not the desired effect.

"They had in the meantime reached Leda Tanah, whence they were brought down again sulky enough, and did show a slight inclination to see whether the people on board the Swift were keeping watch; for several of their boats dropped close to her, and one directly under the bowsprit, as silently as death; but on being challenged, and a musket levelled near them, they sheered off, and the next day finally departed. The poor Dyaks in the interior, as well as the Chinese, were in the greatest state of alarm, and thence I gained some credit among them for my interference on their behalf. The very idea of letting 2500 wild devils loose in the interior of the country is horrible; for though they have one professed object, they combine many others with it, and being enemies of all the mountain tribes, they cut them up as much as they can.

"What object, it may be inquired, can the Malays have in destroying their own country and people so wantonly? I must endeavour to explain, to the best of my belief and knowledge. The Malays take part in these excursions, and thirty men joined the Sakarrans on the present occasion, and consequently they share in the plunder, and share largely. Probably Muda Hassim would have got twenty shares (women and children); and these twenty being reckoned at the low rate of twenty *reals* each, makes four hundred *reals*, beside other plunder, amounting to one or two hundred *reals* more. Inferior *Pangerans* would of course partake likewise. Muda Hassim *must* have given his consent, must have been a participator in this atrocity, nobody being desperate enough to do such a thing without his orders. In fact, they dare not move up the river themselves without leave, much less send up the Dyaks. It is a hateful feature in this government, newly developed since the close of the war.

"*August 5th.*—One excursion I made up the river over our old ground, staying a week, visiting various places. Where the village of Siniawan once stood is now a small Chinese settlement, and their garden bespeaks the fertility of the soil. From Siniawan I walked over to Tundong, now the principal Chinese station. The scenery was beautiful all the way from Siniawan to Tundong—gently undulating ground rising into respectable hills, and backed by noble mountains, and valleys so quiet and still, and looking so fertile, that I sighed to think man's cultivating hand was not here. We paused, and rested at a farm of the Paninjow. Their mode of cultivation is the same as described by Marsden—cutting, clearing, planting, and abandoning after one or two crops. They seem likewise to prefer the upland to the wet ground. Tundong is quite a new settlement, situated close on the banks of the river, which is here quite narrow and shallow. The distance may be ten miles by water, as it took our boat four hours and a half to pull against stream. We spent the same time walking, but diverged from the road.

"Wherever the Chinese are, the sound of the axe and the saw is to be heard in the woods as you approach, and all are industriously employed. They have their carpenters, sawyers, blacksmiths, and housebuilders, while the mass work the antimony ore, or are busy constructing the trench where they find and wash the gold. With such inhabitants a country must get on well, if they are allowed fair play. I was quite tired, and stayed all night at Tundong. On the following morning I started for the Singè mountain, which is the residence of the Dyak tribe of the same name. The walk, including a rest, occupied nearly three hours, the latter part uphill, and we reached the village a good deal knocked up from the heat of the sun and the badness of the way.

"Our entertainment was not of the best; yet the Singè were not inhospitable, but suspicious that we came to rob them. The rice and the fowls we required, although we paid for them at double their value, were reluctantly produced; while at the same time they showed themselves anxious enough to obtain the salt we had brought to exchange, without giving the equivalent.

"The village is built on the shoulder of a mountain, not half way up, and only accessible by a ladder-like path on either side. It consists of about 200 miserable huts, and is as dirty and filthy as any place I ever was in, with numerous half-starved pigs and dogs running about it. The houses are small and mean, and detached from each other, contrary to the usage of the other Dyaks, who inhabit one large house containing numerous partitions for families; here, however, they have one or two public halls or council-houses, which are built and thatched in a circular form, and in which their young men and bachelors sleep; here likewise are deposited the heads, of which they have more than enow, as above one hundred ghastly remnants of mortality ornamented the abode in which we slept.

"I could not on this occasion find out that they professed to take the heads of friends or strangers, though the latter may fall victims if on enemies' ground. They seem to have no idea of cannibalism or human sacrifice, nor did they accuse their enemies of these practices. They have a custom, that in case of sickness in a house, or child-bearing, the house is forbidden to the males and strangers, which is something similar to the taboo of the South-Sea Islands. This plea was urged as a reason why the head man or Orang Kaya Parembam could not receive us in his dwelling.

"The Dyaks are always decorous in their behavior, rarely give way to mirth, and never annoy by their curiosity. Toward the Malays they are extremely sulky and mulish; but they have good reasons, as the Malays are ever extorting from them, and threatening them with the anger of the *rajah* or the incursion of the Sakarrans. The women wear black bamboo stays, which are sewn on when they arrive at the age of puberty, and never removed save when *enceinte*. These Singè Dyaks, like the others, attend to the warning of birds of various sorts, some birds being in more repute than others. On starting for a hunting excursion we met one of them on the hill-side, who said, 'You will be fortunate: I heard the bird behind you.' Here, if a bird is before you, it is a sign that enemies are there too, and they turn back: if behind, they proceed in good spirits. They have a prejudice against the flesh of deer, which the men may not eat, but which is allowed to women and children. The reason given for this is, that if the warriors eat the flesh of deer, they become as faint-hearted as that animal. These may be called their superstitions, but religion they have none; and though they know a name for God, and entertain some faint notion of a future state, yet it is only in the abstract, for practically the belief seems to be a dead letter.

"At their marriage they kill fowls, as I have narrated; but this is a ceremony, not a sacrifice. They have no priests or idols, say no prayers, make no offerings to propitiate the Deity, and it is little likely therefore that human sacrifice should exist among them. In this respect they are different from any known people who have arrived at the same state of civilization. The New Zealanders, the inhabitants of the South Seas, &c. &c., for instance, all bow to their idols, toward which the same feelings of reverence and devotion, of awe and fear, obtain as with more civilized beings in regard to the invisible Deity; but here are the mere words, barren and without practice.

"The day following our arrival at Singè we descended into the plains, amid their former rice-fields, to shoot deer. The place is called *pasar* (bazaar or market), though it could scarcely ever have been one.

The rice-cultivation was formerly very extensive, and the low ground all about the mountain is well cleared of wood by the industry of these Dyaks. But the country becoming unsettled and troubled, and roving parties of strange Dyaks landing on the coast near Onetong, cut off the people employed in the fields, and they consequently were abandoned.

"We took up our quarters in a ruinous little deserted hovel, and in the evening walked over the neighbouring district, where the cocoanut and betel-trees mark its former state of prosperity. The sago is likewise planted in considerable quantity, and serves for food, when rice falls short. Deer, the large deer of Borneo, abound, and in a walk of a few miles we saw from fifteen to twenty, and from their tracks they must be very numerous indeed. The walking was difficult, for owing to the softness of the ground, we often sank in up to our thighs, and generally to our knees: and a short distance in this sort of wading in stiff mud serves to knock a man up. I was fortunate enough to kill one of the deer, and have no doubt that with more favourable light a man might get many.

"The night's repose in the hut was broken and uncomfortable, and our people were busy for several hours curing the flesh of the animal, which is done as follows: first it is slightly salted, and then burnt over a quick wood-fire in slices or lumps, and thus keeps for many days, and is very palatable. Seriff Hussein (formerly of Siniawan) was my companion on this excursion. He had three followers, while I had three Javanese with me, beside my Bugis boy Situ, who walks with the best of us. The morning after killing the deer we ascended the Singè again by a desperately steep path; and after resting an hour or two, walked to our boats, and descended the stream to Siniawan.

"The night was marked by torrents of rain, thunder, and lightning, which left the roads so bad that I resigned my intention of walking up to Sarambo, and in the evening dropped down to Leda Tanah, and tried unsuccessfully for another deer. We saw some, but could not get near them. Here likewise are plenty of rice-fields deserted, but which a little labour would bring again into cultivation. The day following we rejoined the schooner, and, as usual, found everything at a stand-still on shore.

"I may here mention our house, or, as I fondly styled it, our palace. It is an edifice fifty-four feet square, mounted upon numerous posts of the Nibong palm, with nine windows in each front. The roof (atap) is of Nipah leaves, and the floor and partitions are all of plank: furnished with couches, tables, chairs, books, &c. the whole is as comfortable as man would wish for in this out-of-the-way country; and we have, beside, a bathing-house, cook-house, and servants' apartments detached. The view from the house to the eastward comprises a reach of the river, and to the westward looks toward the blue mountains of Matang; the north fronts the river, and the south the jungle; and but for the uncertainty of our affairs, I would have had a garden ere this, and found amusement in clearing and improving.

"Farewell, I fear, to these aspirations; our abode, however, though spacious, cool, and comfortable, can only be considered a temporary residence, for the best of all reasons—that in the course of a year it will tumble down, from the weight of the superstructure being placed on weak posts. The original plan was to have had a lower story, but about this I am now indifferent. The time here passes monotonously, but not unpleasantly. Had we but the animation of hope, and the stimulus of improvement, time would pass rapidly, though without a companion to converse with.

"*August 6th.*—The *Royalist*, as I mentioned before I reverted to the subject of the pirate fleet, started for Borneo Proper, to inquire respecting the crew of an English vessel, reported to have been shipwrecked. Pangeran Sulieman brought the intelligence from Borneo, but he knew very few particulars; and having been here four months before my arrival, the chances were that with the change of the monsoon they had sailed for Manilla. As, however, he assured me he had seen European men and women, and a numerous Lascar crew, I thought it right, at all events, to ascertain the fact; and in case of their being there still, to endeavour to obtain their release.

"For this purpose I was very desirous of procuring a letter from Muda Hassim to the *sultan*, conveyed by a *pangeran* of rank; which, in addition to my own application, would most likely insure the object in view. This, however, though promised, I could not accomplish; delay coming upon delay, and the plague of my own affairs also intervening, postponed my intention till I could see the *Swift* fairly off for Singapore.

"The *Royalist* then went out with her on the Sunday, July 25th, proceeding to Borneo to demand the crew, if there: and the other to Singapore. On the 2nd of August I was surprised by the receipt of a letter brought from Sadong, and bearing date the 10th of July. The gentleman who writes it can best tell his own story.

144

Island Sirhassan, off Tan Datu,<br>July 10th, 1841.

A boat leaves this tomorrow for Sarawak; perhaps this may fall into the hands of Mr. Brooke, or some of my countrymen, which, should I not succeed in getting to Singapore, I trust will lose no time in letting the authorities know, so that steps may be taken for the release of the remaining thirty-six British subjects now at Borneo; which I fear nothing but one of H. M. ships will effect. The pirates are cruising in great force between Sambas and this, and have taken thirteen Borneo *prahus*, or more; they know that there are Europeans in the *prahu*, and have expressed a wish to take them. Our situation is not very enviable. The bearer of this has just escaped from them. I have been living ashore with Abduramon, a native of Pulo Pinang, who knows Mr. Brooke, and has been very kind to me. Trusting penmanship and paper will be excused,

I remain, &c. &c.

G. H. W. Gill.

"On the reverse was the following attestation, which threw more light on the circumstances:—

I, G. H. Willoughby Gill, late chief officer of the ship *Sultana*, of Bombay, do hereby certify that the said ship was totally destroyed by lightning, thirty miles N. E. of the Bombay shoal, coast of Palawan, on the 4th of January, 1841. Part of the crew, forty-one in number, succeeded in reaching Borneo on the 16th of January, in a state of starvation and misery not to be described; the remainder are reported to have landed on the coast of Borneo per long-boat:—Captain John Page; G. H. W. Gill, chief officer; Alexander Young, second officer; one gunner; five sea-cunnies; two carpenters; twenty-three natives and lascars; two Nakodas. Passengers:—Mrs. Page (of a daughter, 31st of March); Mr. and Miss de Souza; Mrs. Anderson, servant; one *ayah*; in all forty-two souls.

The *sultan* has permitted myself, Mr. and Miss de Souza, with three servants, to proceed to Singapore in one of his *prahus*, where I hope to succeed in procuring the release of the remainder of my companions from their present very uncomfortable situation. I dare not say more. Mr. de Souza and myself left on the 24th of May, and put in here dismasted on the 20th of June; since then have been detained by a fleet of piratical *prahus*, which arrived on the 24th, and left 9th of July. Should nothing prevent, we expect to be ready by the 15th; but am very doubtful of ever getting to Singapore, as I fear they are on the lookout for us outside.'

"This is the contents of the paper, which arriving after I had retired to rest, effectually banished sleep from my pillow. The 'uncomfortable situation,' coupled with 'I dare say no more,' gives the worst suspicions of their treatment in Borneo; while the chance of the party at Sirhassan falling into the hands of the pirates is extremely shocking. I instantly, on the receipt of the letter, sent to the *rajah* to request that he would dispatch a boat for Sirhassan, with a person competent to treat with the pirates; and on the morning of the 3rd I succeeded in dispatching a boat to Songi, in the Sadong, to get some of the *datu pangeran's* people, who are Illanuns; but up to this time they have not returned. I can only hope these poor people at Sirhassan will be wise enough to stay there, instead of risking a capture by the pirates.

"Should the *Royalist* return shortly, and have obtained the crew, we may fight our way to that place and release the party, who, I have little doubt, are still detained there. If the *Royalist* is long away, and the captain goes in search of the missing boat's crew, we may yet have the Illanuns from Sadong here in time to dispatch. As for myself, I am tied, and have not the means at present of locomotion; my situation is an anxious one. The *Swift* must have been liable to fall in with this great force of pirates on her way to Singapore, and will be again liable on her return. The doubt and uncertainty about the poor fellows in Borneo and Sirhassan, and the wretched condition of my own affairs, all cause unpleasant reflections to my mind; yet I yield not, but will fight it out.

"I have just brought up my history to the present time; and, like a log on the water, must wait for events to develop themselves.

"*7th.*—A report arrived this morning that the Sirhassan party sailed for Singapore on the 3rd of the moon; and as Mr. Gill says they would be ready for sea about the 15th of last month, I consider it likely to be true. I trust they may escape the pirates, and safely reach their destination."

# CHAPTER 11

# Malay Cunning and Treachery

While waiting events, Mr. Brooke amused himself by writing down such accounts of the interior as he was enabled to collect, from time to time, from the natives visiting Sarawak, as well as a brief description of the constitution and government, as enacted in Borneo Proper. But as my object now is to trace the progress of my friend up to the time when he embarked on board the *Dido*, I shall refer to these matters hereafter.

"*Tuesday, August 17th, 1841.*—Three weeks the *Royalist* has now been absent, and I begin, in spite of my determination to the contrary, to be somewhat uneasy about her. Suspense is certainly more difficult to bear than misfortune, for the certainty of an event arouses within us some of our best feelings to resist it; but suspense lets loose our imagination, and gives rise to that sickening feeling of 'hope deferred,' so truly characterized in the Scriptures.

"*18th.*—The *Royalist* arrived near Sarawak, having come into the river on the 16th, and in one tide from the Morotaba entrance as far as the Paduman[1] rocks. They reported that they had not effected the release of the prisoners, were very rudely treated, the boat detained at a fort near the entrance of the Borneo River, all communication denied with the Europeans, a letter for them seized from the native crew, and provisions and water refused. In addition to this, a letter from the *sultan*, addressed to me, stated to the effect, that the crew of the *Sultana* having entered into a treaty with him, the merchant and mate (Messrs. de Souza and Gill) had gone to Singapore to fulfil that agreement.

"The captain having a wife in the family way, preferred staying in Borneo, as the vessel was a small one, and therefore the *sultan* did not

---

1. Now called Samarang.

147

grant my request on this occasion; and further, having an agreement, he did not wish to be deceived regarding it. This was a falsehood from beginning to end, as will be clear by comparing it with Mr. Gill's statement, though I fear the poor men have been rash enough to enter into some arrangement to ransom themselves."

On the 19th of August the *Swift* arrived; but the journal was laid by until the 24th of October, when it thus recommences:

"I may now continue my narrative of events which have happened since I last used my pen, together with fresh details of my present intentions, and such additional knowledge as has been acquired. After the arrival of the *Swift*, I still adhered to my former resolution of waiting patiently for a settlement. I made several strong remonstrances, and urged for an answer to a letter I had addressed to Muda Hassim, in which was recapitulated our entire negotiation. This letter was acknowledged to be perfectly true and correct, and the *rajah*, in the conference which followed, again pledged himself to give me the country, saying he always intended to do so, but was involved in difficulties of the nature of which I could not be aware. Thus far things went well, and there appeared, indeed, a frankness in his manner which had formerly pleased me, but had long been in abeyance.

"On the return of the *Royalist* from Borneo, I had assured them that a government vessel would be sent to demand the captives; but, taking this assurance for a mere boast, they paid little attention to it, and were therefore excessively frightened when, a week after the *Swift*, the *Diana* steamer entered the river. I had the pleasure of calming their fears, and was too generous to push matters to a settlement during the two days the steamer remained.

"Muda Hassim now expressed himself desirous of sending some *pangerans* to Borneo, and I wished him likewise to do so on account of the reflective power of the steamer, which, in that case, would have shone upon him. With his usual delay, however, he failed to be ready, and these *pangerans* did not quit the river for two days afterward, when they proceeded in a native *prahu*. I accompanied the steamer to the mouth of the river, and wishing them success, pulled back to the capital of Sarawak.

"*Oct 30th.*—The *Swift* was slowly laden with antimony ore, worked by the Chinese; and I gradually robbed the *Royalist* of furniture for my house on shore. But I had no intention of allowing either vessel to sail until the time arrived which I had fixed on for the final adjustment of my affairs. By degrees, however, I learned many of the difficulties of poor Muda Hassim's situation, and much of the weakness of his character. The dissensions in Borneo; the intrigues of Macota; the rapacity of his own people, and their total want of fidelity; the bribes from the Sultan of Sambas; the false representations of numerous Borneo *pangerans* who asserted the immense profit to be derived from the country; the dilatory movements of the Chinese; some doubts of my good faith; and, above all, the natural tenacity of power, all conspired to involve the *rajah* in the utmost perplexity, and would, but for counterbalancing circumstances, have turned the scale against me.

"Muda Hassim knew Macota to be false and in league with the Sultan of Sambas; and he felt that he had no power, and that if he broke with me, it would be extremely difficult to support himself against the former rebels. He was fond of me, and trusted me more than he trusted anyone else; and pecuniary considerations had no doubt some weight, for with all Macota's promises he could not get sufficient ore to repay one quarter of his debt to me. However, all these conflicting considerations, instead of inducing Muda Hassim to take one course, only served to encourage his dilatory temper, and although puzzled, ashamed, and fearful, he could not decide.

"At this period a robbery was committed up the river by some of Macota's followers on a Chinese *hadji*, a converted Mohammedan. They beat the old man, threw him into the water, and robbed him of a *tael* of gold. The beating and attempt at drowning were certain, for the Chinese *hadji* was so ill for several days under my care, that he was in considerable danger. He complained to me loudly of Macota; and from other sources I gained a pretty accurate account of that gentleman's proceedings. By threats, by intrigue, by falsehood, and even by violence, he had prevented or driven all persons from daring to visit or come near me, whether abroad or ashore. He was taxing the poor Dyaks, harassing the Siniawans, and leagued with the Borneo *pangerans* to plunder and get all he possibly could.

"Every Dyak community was watched by his followers, and a spear raised opposite the chief's house, to intimate that no person was to trade or barter except the *pangeran*. The mode of plunder is thus perpetrated. Rice, clothes, gongs, and other articles are sent to a tribe at a fixed price, which the Dyaks dare not refuse, for it is at the risk of losing their children! The prices thus demanded by Macota were as follows: one *gantong* of rice for thirty birds-nests. Twenty-four *gantongs* here is equal to a *pecul* of rice—a *pecul* of rice costs one dollar and a half; whereas thirty birds-nests weigh one *catty*, and are valued at two *rupees*, so that the twenty-fourth part of one and a half dollars is sold for two *rupees*. Was it surprising that these people were poor and wretched? My astonishment was, that they continued to labour, and, indeed, nothing but their being a surprisingly industrious race can account for it, and they are only enabled to live at all by secreting a portion of their food. Yet war and bad government, or, rather, no government, have had the effect of driving more than half the Dyak tribes beyond the limits of Sarawak.

"The rapacity of these Malays is as unbounded as it is short-sighted; for one would think that the slightest degree of common sense would induce some of the chiefs to allow no one to plunder except themselves. But this is so far from being the case, that, when their demand has been enforced, dozens of inferior wretches extort and plunder in turn, each according to his ability; and though the Dyak is not wanting in obstinacy, he can seldom withstand these robberies, for each levy is made in the name of the *rajah*, or some principal *pangeran*; and the threat of bringing the powerful tribe of Sakarrans or Sarebus to deprive them of their heads and wives and families, generally reduces them to obedience. While on this subject, I may as well mention a fact that came later to my knowledge, when several of the Dyak chiefs, and one of particular intelligence, Si Meta by name, assured me that each family paid direct revenue from thirty to fifty *pasus* (tubs) of *padi*, besides all the other produces, which are extorted at merely nominal prices.

"To return to my relation: the Chinese *hadji* recovered, and I determined to punish the aggressors, for which purpose I seized an Illanun said to be concerned, but who was innocent. In the mean time the steamer returned from Borneo, and once more put in here for wood and water. She brought Captain and Mrs. Page, Mr. Young, the second officer, and all the rest of the crew, save only a few who had landed at the north part of Borneo, and there been seized and sold as slaves, and brought afterward as slaves to Borneo Proper. As the history of the shipwreck and detention is curious, I may here relate it as nearly as I can.

"The *Sultana*, a fine ship of 700 tons, the day previous to her being struck by lightning, found the French frigate *Magicienne* aground and deserted on the Bombay shoal; Captain Page boarded her, and discovered everything as it had been left by the crew—provisions, water, &c., in abundance. The day after, the *Sultana* met with a worse fate, being struck, and the cotton in the hold, fore and aft, fired by the electric fluid. They had scarcely time to hoist out the boat when the flames burst forth, and they quitted her very short of provisions, and saving only some money and jewels. Captain Page bore up for the wreck of the French frigate, intending to refit his long-boat aboard her, and take provisions and arms to last them to Singapore; but, on making her, there was so great a wash of the sea on the lee part of the reef, that it was totally impossible to reach the *Magicienne*.

"Under these unfortunate circumstances they bore up once more, still intending to prosecute the voyage to Singapore, and made the land to the southward of Palawan; and, being then short of water and provisions, landed on a small islet off Balabac, or Balambangan. Here they procured a few shell-fish and some very bad water; but seeing some natives in *prahus* on a neighbouring islet, and being-unarmed and apprehensive, they lighted large fires in the evening to mislead these people, and, as night advanced, silently put to sea, and made the best of their way along the coast.

"With a heavy sea, and often high wind, they reached as far as Labuan, off the entrance of the Borneo River; and here, being in the utmost want, and reduced to an allowance of half a biscuit and a cup of water per day, they were forced to put into Borneo Proper, not without hopes of being well used, and enabled to buy provisions and stores sufficient to carry them to Singapore or Sambas. I have omitted to mention that, on making the land the first time, they parted from the cutter, in consequence of the tow-rope breaking in the night; but as they were then within sight of Borneo, and the wind fair, there was no doubt of its making the land somewhere. This, indeed, it did at Malludu Bay, where the native crew were seized and sold as slaves.

"The arrival of Captain Page in his long-boat caused, as may well be imagined, considerable sensation in the *campong*; and they reached the *sultan's* house, thinking it the best place to seek shelter and protection. In this, however, they were soon undeceived; for neither the one nor the other was granted, but a message sent that they must deliver up all their property into the *sultan's* hands, as otherwise he was afraid they would be plundered by his people. Accordingly, having possessed himself of their money, some jewels, their boat, &c., he gave them a miserable shed to live in.

"Here they passed the time, and were gradually robbed of everything they had in the world, even to the baby-linen which Mrs. Page had prepared for an expected infant. Sometimes, indeed, when Captain Page refused to yield to the *sultan's* demands, their provisions were stopped till they could no longer hold out; and in this way they were compelled to sign bonds for considerable sums, with the understanding that, till these were procured and paid, they should be detained.

"In this sad situation Mrs. Page was confined of a daughter, on the 31st of March; and this miserable life continued from the 4th of January, 1841, to August of the same year. Their first ray of hope was the *Royalist* coming to fetch them: the steamer followed, and they were released.

"After a stay of two or three days, the steamer once more sailed; though I would fain have persuaded Captain Congleton to search for the piratical fleet, of which I had excellent information; but he considered himself not authorized, or, in other words, he declined the responsibility.

"As there was a chance that Mr. Gill and the De Souzas were either at Sirhassan or Tambelan, the steamer decided to touch at the latter place, and a native *chuliah* brig was directed to call at the former. I afterward learned that the pirates were then at Sirhassan; but as the brig knew nothing about Sirhassan, it is probable she never went there. In the evening the *Diana* sailed, and I reached Sarawak about two o'clock in the morning.

"I now return to my concerns. The Chinese *hadji*, whom I had protected, continued to reside with my servants, till one evening we were alarmed at an attempt to poison my interpreter, a native of the name of Mia. Arsenic had certainly been put into his rice; but as the servants endeavoured to point suspicion on this *hadji*, and as I learned, at the same time, that they did not agree with the old man, I cleared him in my own mind, and rather leaned to the opinion of Mia having placed the arsenic in the plate himself, for the express purpose of accusing the *hadji*. Connecting this event with all Macota's former intrigues, I determined to bring matters to a crisis, and test at once the strength of the respective parties.

"Accordingly, after complaining of the matter previously mentioned to the *rajah*, I landed a party of men, fully armed, and loaded the ship's guns with grape and canister; after which I once more proceeded to Muda Hassim, and, while I protested my kindness toward him, exposed Macota's machinations and crimes, his oppression and his deceit, and threatened him with an attack, as neither Muda Hassim nor myself were safe while he continued practicing these arts. Muda Hassim was frightened; but how Macota felt I cannot say, as he never moved out of his house, and it was long afterward before he was seen. From my knowledge, however, of his temperament, I can well conceive that he was reduced to a pitiable state of terror.

"The Siniawans took my part directly; and their chiefs came to me to say that 200 men were all ready whenever I pleased to call for them. The Chinese and the rest of the inhabitants took no side; and Macota did not get a single follower besides his immediate slaves, perhaps about twenty in number. After this demonstration affairs proceeded cheerily to a conclusion. The *rajah* was active in settling; the agreement was drawn out, sealed, and signed; guns fired, flags waved; and on the 24th of September, 1841, I became the Governor of Sarawak, with the fullest powers."

Being now regularly established in his government, Mr. Brooke, with his usual activity and circumspection, applied himself to the discharge of the onerous duties it imposed upon him; and his first acts were such as equally displayed his wisdom, firmness, and humanity. His journal runs thus:

"*Nov. 3rd.*—I have a country; but, oh! how beset with difficulties, how ravaged by war, torn by dissensions, and ruined by duplicity, weakness, and intrigue! Macota's underhand dealings, after the conclusion of my agreement with Muda Hassim had been ratified, soon brought letters from his Sambas friends, *i. e.*, one from the *sultan*, one from the *tumangong*, and one from another *pangeran*—an immense effort of conspiracy and correspondence! Of these letters the *sultan's* alone was curious; for the rest only dealt in professions of devoted attachment to the person and interests of Muda Hassim. But the *sultan*, for want of some better plea, made use of the following singular specimen of reasoning, *viz.*, that the Chinese Kunsi were indebted to him a sum of money, which they had agreed to pay him in antimony ore; the agreement was not to pay him in gold, or money, or other commodity—only in antimony ore; therefore he wanted antimony ore. To this it was properly replied, that an arrangement had been made with me, and that the Chinese could not agree to give antimony ore without his (Muda Hassim's) consent.

"My first object, on holding the reins of government, was to release the unfortunate women confined for a whole year by the *rajah*. This, indeed, was not only necessary to inspire confidence in my just intentions, but was dictated by humanity. I found Muda Hassim not averse to take the measure, *now* that he had really resolved to adhere to my advice, and consequently I had the sincere satisfaction, within a few days, of liberating upward of a hundred females and young children, and of restoring them to their husbands and fathers; this act being somewhat alloyed by Muda Hassim detaining twelve females, and among them *two wives*. I urged as strongly as I could, but without success, the advisability of releasing the whole; and I was obliged, at last, to content myself with the mass, and yield the few whom I could only have got *by force* or the utter abrogation of our infant treaty.

"When I pressed the affair, it was answered that, except for me, *none* would have regained their liberty; and that the release was an act of great kindness and unexampled confidence toward me; that what had been done was perfectly accordant with their customs; and that the women detained were for the *rajah's* brothers—so far, indeed, from being intended as an injury to the women, it was a great honour and advantage. I explained the circumstances to the *patingi* and *tumangong*, and they acquiesced in the decision—allowing the custom—and said they had gained so much more than they had ever hoped for, that they could submit to the rest.

"The next step was to assemble the Siniawans, who, since the close of the war, would run away, and whom it was found impossible to keep here. Some had retired to Sambas; some (among them Patingi Ali) had gone to Sariki; and others had built a village on the borders of the Sambas territory. The whole aim and object of Macota's government was to get these people back; and those who were already here were constantly plying backward and forward to recall their companions; but as soon as they succeeded in getting one family, another absconded. Confidence alone could restore them; and I therefore intimated to the *patingi* and *tumangong* that there was no occasion for their seeking them; that I by no means desired their return; and that any of their people who wished to leave the country were at liberty to do so whenever they felt inclined. This had the desired effect, in a short time, of bringing back the fugitives from Pankalon Nibong; and they continued daily to arrive from Sambas.

"My next measure was to inquire into the state of the Dyaks, to gain their confidence, and, as much as it was within my power, prevent the oppressions of the Malays. It was necessary, likewise, to fix a rate of tax to be levied yearly; and the prospect seemed fair, as the chief people of the following tribes had come in, and agreed that such a tax on rice, amounting to sixteen *gantongs*, would be required from each man, and that for the rest they would be obliged to labour; that they could trade at pleasure; that no man could demand anything from them; that their wives and children were safe; and that, in case any trouble arose, they were to let me know, and I would myself come to their assistance. The tribes were, Lundu, Sarambo, Bombak, Paninjow, and Sow. The only other tribe on the right-hand river were the Singè, a powerful and stiff-necked people, with good reason to be shy; but when once they are treated justly, their strength will be advantageous, and give them confidence to resist oppression.

"The story told me by the three heads of the Sow Dyaks brought tears into my eyes, as they each in turn related their grievances. One of them, a remarkably intelligent person, addressed me nearly in the following terms:

"'From former times we have been the subjects of the Patek of Borneo. The Borneons are the elder brothers, we the younger; and the custom of old was, that we should pay revenue and find protection. But they forgot what was right, and departed from the custom, and robbed the Dyaks, and oppressed them. We have done no wrong: we listened to the commands of the Patingi who was put over us by the Patek. If he did wrong, he should be punished; but we have suffered because we obeyed the commands of the officer legally appointed. You might, sir, a few years ago, have sought in this river, and not have found a happier tribe than ours.

"'Our children were collected around us; we had rice in plenty, and fruit-trees; our hogs and fowls were in abundance; we could afford to give what was demanded of us, and yet live happily. Now we have nothing left. The Sadong people and the Sakarran Dyaks attacked us: they burned our houses, destroyed our property, cut down our fruit-trees, killed many of our people, and led away our wives and young children into slavery. We could build another house; we could plant fruit-trees and cultivate rice; but where can we find wives? Can we forget our young children? We have asked the Patek to restore them; we have asked Pangeran Macota to restore them: they have told us they would, but have not; we cannot trust them; their words are fair, but in their hearts they do not mean to help us. We have now no one to trust but you—will you help us? Will you restore our wives and children? If we get our families, you will never repent it: you will find us true.'

"What could I answer? I could not deceive them, as I knew not how to obtain their object; I therefore told them I feared it was impossible; but I would try, and they themselves should go and try at the same time. Poor, unhappy people, who suffer for the crimes of others!

God knows, I will aid you to the utmost of my power.

"*Nov. 5th.*—Today the greatest, and I hope the final, struggle of the opposing faction was developed by the arrival of a brig from Sambas, with two of the *sultan's* sons on board; Macota in high spirits, and my party looking rather desponding; and, in fact, I cannot trust them against Sambas. For good or for bad, for success or for failure, for life or for death, I will act justly, and preserve the high hand over Macota.

"After the steps I have mentioned, I determined to open a court for the administration of justice, wherein I should preside, together with such of the *rajah's* brothers as liked to assist me. As for a jury, or any machinery of form or law, it was rejected, because it must be inefficient, if not corrupt; and the only object I aimed at was, keeping witnesses out of ear-shot of each other, hearing the evidence, deciding as appeared best, and in future punishing. This simple plan insured substantial redress; and it gave all the people confidence in me, and a notion of what was right.

"The first case was a follower of the *rajah's*, of the name of Sunudeen; and a greater villain could not exist either in this or any other land. It was as follows: A man from Samarahan, named Bujong, had undertaken to marry his daughter to a Sarawak man called Abdullah; but Abdullah proving a dissolute character, and greatly in debt, Bujong broke off the engagement before the proper authorities, and returned the presents which Abdullah, according to custom, had made. Abdullah, it appeared, was indebted a small sum to Matassim (Mohammed Orsin), and, between Sunudeen and Matassim, they resolved to lay the debt on Bujong's shoulders; in other words, to plunder Bujong under false pretences. Accordingly, Sunudeen, with his comrade, went to Samarahan; and, in his capacity of follower of the *rajah*, demanded the debt due by Abdullah to Matassim.

"Bujong having no money, Sunudeen proceeded and seized his nephew, a boy, and a slave-man belonging to him, as *his slaves*. Poor Bujong resisted, and recovered his nephew, but yielded his slave; he appealed, however, to the Orang Kaya de Gadong's sons, and they failing, a Nakodah stated the case secretly to me. I investigated it, and ordered the return of the slave in my presence, which was obeyed. This may give an idea of the state of the country, and the power of every petty scoundrel hanging about the *rajah* to rob and plunder at pleasure.

"*7th.*—I have before mentioned that the Dyaks of Sibnow bury their dead; but I always found a reluctance on their part to show me their place of sepulture. Once, indeed, chance led me to the burial-ground of part of that tribe settled at Simunjang; but, as they seemed restless to get away, I only took a hasty survey. The reason, I have lately learned, for this is, that in their graves they deposit the golden ornaments and other property of the person deceased, amounting frequently to a considerable value in the precious metals, brass swivels, gongs, &c.

"The tribe now at Lundu were formerly settled on the Samarahan river for many years; and their burial-place there contained the ashes of the parents and grandparents of the present chief, who, with his followers, were not long ago driven to Lundu; and their former settlement being deserted, it has been the employment of some of the rascals here to rob these graves of their contents, and to desecrate the repose of the dead. The Orang Kaya of Lundu complained to me sadly, but mournfully, on this account, and said that if he could not find redress from the *rajah*, he must obtain it himself by taking the heads of those who had disinterred the bones of his ancestors. His whole manner convinced me that they hold the burying-places in great respect; and my advice, to remove the wealth and bones to a place of security at Lundu, was rejected on the ground that they could not disturb the remains of those whom they had once deposited in the earth.

"While there is so much of right feeling and manly principle in the actions of these Dyaks, the miserable race who pretend to be their superiors have no single virtue or good intention. I do not, however, mean to confound the inhabitants of Sarawak, or the other rivers, with those of Borneo Proper. The latter are thoroughly corrupt and profligate. The former are Malays, but have their good qualities, and certainly are not possessed with the spirit of intrigue which seems the life, the only moving principle of the Borneons. It may truly be said of the latter, that they would tell a lie when the truth would serve them better.

"They will employ duplicity and treachery on every slight occasion; defeat their own purpose by their meanness, and yet continue in the same crooked paths. They will conspire without any object, or one too mysterious to arrive at; and, while they raise a cloud of doubts in the mind of the poor, their own equals look on and detect the game. Yet, after all, they gain but little individually; because so many are practicing the same arts at the same time with equal skill; and the country is so exhausted by their oppressions and rapacity, that in the end there is nothing to be got by their tricks and manoeuvres. It is a strange state of society, and it is only wonderful how it can exist; but they have their reward in being poor and ill-provided, though living in the midst of a marvellously fertile and luxurious country.

"*December 31st.*—The last day of the year, in which I must bring up the arrears of my account.

"The Sambas brig left only yesterday, after exhausting every effort of intrigue, and every artifice which Malays can invent, to compass their ends.

"With the Sambas brig came Seriff Hussein, a relation of the Sultan of Pontiana, and half Arab half Bugis by descent. He came with the avowed purpose of entering into the most friendly communication with me, and residing here, provided I gave him any encouragement. His real motive (if he has one) not being obvious, I, in the meantime, treated him with all kindness; and he is an intelligent and pleasing person, and, moreover, connected with the Siniawans, who have a good opinion of him."

# Chapter 12

# Wrongs and Sufferings
# of the Lundus

"*Jan. 1st, 1842.*—The past year is in the bosom of eternity, into which bourne we are all hurrying. Here we have no merry-making, no reunion of families, no bright fires or merry games, to mark the advent of 1842; but we have genial weather, and are not pinched by cold or frost. This is a year which to me must be eventful; for at its close I shall be able to judge whether I can maintain myself against all the circumstances and difficulties which beset me, or whether I must retreat, broken in fortune, to some retirement in my native land. I look with calmness on the alternative, and God knows no selfish motives weigh on me; and if I fail, my chief regret will be for the natives of this unhappy country. Let the year roll on, let the months pass; and whatever they bring—whether it be life or death, fortune or poverty—I am prepared; and in the deep solitude of my present existence I can safely say that I believe I could bear misfortune better than prosperity.

"In this, probably, I am not singular; for there is something in prosperity which, if it does not make us worse, makes us more foolish and more worldly—which decks passing time with wreaths of gay flowers, and gilds the things of this life with tinsel hopes and wishes, to the exclusion of the pure gold of reflection for the life to come. What are all these gewgaws, these artificial flowers, these momentary joys, these pleasures of the sense, before the war of time? Nothing!

"And yet, if exertion can benefit our race, or even our own country—if the sum of human misery can be alleviated—if these suffering people can be raised in the scale of civilization and happiness—it is a cause in which I could suffer, it is a cause in which I *have* suffered and *do suffer*, hemmed in, beset, anxious, perplexed, and the good intent marred by false agents—surrounded by weakness, treachery, falsehood, and folly, is suffering enough; and to feel myself on the threshold of success, and only withheld by the want of adequate means, increases this suffering. Hail, however, 1842! Come good, come ill, still hail! and many as are the light hearts which have already greeted thee, mine will be more ready to bow to the decrees of Providence which thy twelve months will develop.

"*Jan. 3rd.*—I have mentioned that the Sanpro had been attacked from Sadong; and I now learn that, at the time, the men were out of the village, and thus the women and children alone suffered; twenty-two have been carried away into slavery. The village was burned after being plundered, and the unfortunate people have since been living in the jungle, with only such food as they could get there. The head of the tribe and about six of his followers came down the river on a raft to ask assistance from me, and I had the story from them. They were relieved as far as my means admitted, and returned far happier than they came. The very same day arrived news that six men of the Sows were cut off by a wandering party of the Sakarrans.

"This leads me naturally to consider the means by which these atrocities may be prevented. I propose first to send letters to Seriff Sahib of Sadong, Seriff Muller of Sakarran, and Seriff Jaffer of Singè, stating that I wish to be on good terms with my neighbours, but am determined to attack any place which sends Dyaks to rob in my country; and that I call on them to restrain their subjects from making incursions here. In case this warning is neglected, I must strike one blow suddenly, as a farther warning, and keep a good lookout at sea to destroy any Dyak fleet that may be prowling outside.

"A good-sized boat, with a six-pounder and a swivel or two, will effect the latter object, backed by two or four light, fast-pulling boats, with musketry, which, when the Dyak *prahus* fly, may keep pace with them and thin their pullers, till the heavier boat can come up. To carry one of their *campongs*, I must have twenty-five Europeans, and from some thirty to fifty Bugis, who, coming from Singapore, may proceed at once to Sadong, or, rather, the Campong Tangi. Seriff Sahib is a great freebooter, and dispatches his retainers to attack the weak tribes here for the sake of the slaves, calculating, on the *rajah's* presumed weakness, that he can do so with impunity. He may find himself mistaken.

"Seriff Muller is a brother of Seriff Sahib, and lives at Sakarran, which powerful Dyak tribe are always willing to be sent by either brother on a forage for heads and slaves. It is certain, however, that they could never come from the Sadong side without Seriff Sahib's permission; and on the late attack on Sanpro they were accompanied by a party of Malays.

"Seriff Jaffer is by no means mixed up with these brothers, and there is no love lost between them; nor would he, I think, do anything to annoy me. This is the foreign policy.

"The domestic policy is as disturbed as the foreign. The *rajah* weak, Macota intriguing, and my ministers—*viz.*, the *patingi* (Abong Mia), the *bandar*, and *tumangong*—all false and foolish, and Macota's men; with me, however, are the Siniawans.

"*Jan. 6th.*—The Sambas brig returned, having been baffled and beat about, and nearly lost at sea, unable to weather Tanjong Datu. The crew say she was one hour under water. She now remains here to wait the change of the monsoon, and her intriguing *pangerans* return by land.

"*8th.*—Seriff Hussein returned from Sambas, having been nearly stabbed while there. The assassins, it was understood, were here, and I endeavoured to apprehend them; but, having heard of the *seriff's* arrival, they made off.

"*10th.*—This day the first laws and regulations are to be promulgated in Sarawak; and as the event is a rare one, I here inscribe a copy for the benefit of future legislators, observing that there is an absolute necessity for mildness and patience, and that an opposite course would raise such a host of enemies as to crush every good seed; for, as it is, the gentlest course of justice brings down much odium, and arouses intense dislike among a people who have had no law but their own vile intrigues to guide or control them.

"Two cases have lately come to notice, which will serve as examples of their singular crimes.

"One poor man owed another sixteen *reals*, and the debtor was away trading for a few days, when the creditor sold the daughter (a free woman) for thirty *reals*, to a person of influence.

"The second case, a respectable man, or a respectably born man, owed a *pangeran* fifty *peculs* of ore, and proposed to make over to him in payment, a slave woman and her four children. The woman *had been* a slave of his grandfather's, but was adopted as his daughter, and enfranchised publicly; yet by intimidation, they were near getting her and her offspring. Here the *pangerans* and *nakodas* bully a man into silence and acquiescence; and the people dare not, as yet, bring their complaints to me. But I hear these things, call the parties together, and often prevent the commission of a premeditated crime; by which means I save myself from the odium of punishing.

"There is great difficulty in acting at once with temper and firmness, so as to appear the benefactor rather than the tyrant. It is, indeed, an arduous and troublesome task; but *I think I see* a ray of light to encourage me.

"Here are the regulations, which I had printed at Singapore in the Malayan language:—

James Brooke, esquire, governor (*rajah*), of the country of Sarawak, makes known to all men the following regulations:—

1st. That murder, robbery, and other heinous crimes will be punished according to the *ondong-ondong* (*i.e.* the written law of Borneo); and no person committing such offences will escape, if, after fair inquiry, he be proved guilty.

2nd. In order to insure the good of the country, all men, whether Malays, Chinese, or Dyaks, are permitted to trade or labour according to their pleasure, and to enjoy their gains.

3rd. All roads will be open, that the inhabitants at large may seek profit both by sea or by land; and all boats coming from others are free to enter the river and depart, without let or hindrance.

4th. Trade, in all its branches, will be free, with the exception of antimony ore, which the governor holds in his own hands, but which no person is forced to work, and which will be paid for at a proper price when obtained. The people are encouraged to trade and labour, and to enjoy the profits which are to be made by fair and honest dealing.

5th. It is ordered that no person going among the Dyaks shall disturb them, or gain their goods under false pretences. It must be clearly explained to the different Dyak tribes, that the revenue will be collected by the three Datus, bearing the seal of the governor; and (except this yearly demand from the government) they are to give nothing to any person; nor are they obliged to sell their goods except they please and at their own prices.

6th. The governor will shortly inquire into the revenue, and fix it at a proper rate; so that everyone may know certainly how much he has to contribute yearly to support the government.

7th. It will be necessary, likewise, to settle the weights, measures, and money current in the country, and to introduce *doits*, that the poor may purchase food cheaply.

8th. The governor issues these commands, and will enforce obedience to them; and while he gives all protection and assistance to the persons who act rightly, he will not fail to punish those who seek to disturb the public peace or commit crimes; and he warns all such persons to seek their safety, and find some other country where they may be permitted to break the laws of God and man.'

"*Jan. 11th.*—I have frequently said that all law and custom have been long banished from this country; but I may here retrace the customs which once obtained, the best of which I wish to restore.

"The inhabitants were all considered the property of the *sultan*—serfs rather than slaves—and were divided into four classes. Imprimis, the Dyaks (the aborigines); the Bruni, or people of the soil, probably the descendants of the first Malay emigrants; the Awang-Awang, the meaning of which I am ignorant of; and the Hamba Rajah, or *rajah's* slaves. There is every reason to believe the Dyaks are an aboriginal people; but between the Bruni and Awang-Awang it is difficult to decide the priority. The Hamba Rajah speaks for itself.

"These three distinctions have been long confounded by intermarriage; and the names rather than the reality are retained. The governors of the country are the *patingi*, a *bandar*, and a *tumangong*, who are appointed from Borneo. Each of the classes was formerly ruled by its particular officer, and the Dyaks were appropriated likewise among them; the *patingi* holding the tribes on the right-hand river, the *bandar* to the left, and the *tumangong* on the sea-coast. The annual revenue paid to Borneo was 300 *reals*; but they were subject to extra demands, and to the extortions of the powerful chiefs.

"The government of the Dyaks I have already detailed; and though we might hope that in a more settled state of things they would have been more secure from foreign pillage, yet they were annually deprived of the proceeds of their labour, debarred from trade, and deprived of every motive to encourage industry. The character of their rulers for humanity alone fixed the measure of their suffering, and bad was the best; but it seems to be a maxim among all classes of Malays, that force alone can keep the Dyaks in proper subjection; which is

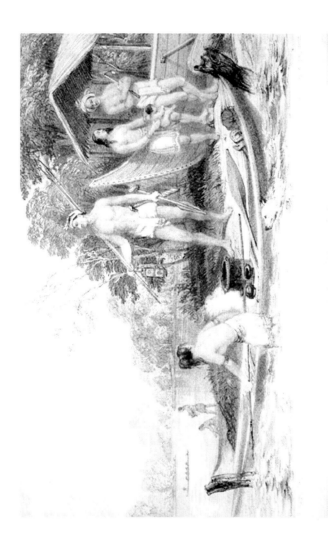

LUNDU DYAKS

so far true, that force alone, and the hopelessness of resistance, could induce a wild people to part with the food on which they depend for subsistence.

"At a distance I have heard of and pitied the sufferings of the negroes and the races of New Holland—yet it was the cold feeling dictated by reason and humanity; but now, having witnessed the miseries of a race superior to either, the feeling glows with the fervour of personal commiseration: so true is it that visible misery will raise us to exertion, which the picture, however powerfully delineated, can never produce. The thousands daily knelled out of the world, who lie in gorgeous sepulchres, or rot unburied on the surface of the earth, excite no emotion compared to that conjured up by the meanest dead at our feet. We read of tens of thousands killed and wounded in battle, and the glory of their deeds, or the sense of their defeat attracts our sympathy; but if a single mangled warrior, ghastly with wounds and writhing with pain, solicited our aid, we should deplore his fate with tenfold emotion, and curse the strife which led to such a result.

"Among the thousands starving for want of food we trouble not ourselves to seek one; but if the object is presented before our eyes, how certain a compassion is aroused! To assist is a duty; but in the performance of this duty, to be gentle and feeling is god-like; and probably between individuals, there is no greater distinction than in this tender sympathy toward distress. Poor, poor Dyaks! exposed to starvation, slavery, death! you may well raise the warmest feelings of compassion—enthusiasm awakes at witnessing your sufferings! To save men from death has its merit; but to alleviate suffering, to ameliorate all the ills of slavery, to protect these tribes from pillage and yearly scarcity, is far nobler; and if, in the endeavour to do so, one poor life is sacrificed, how little is it in the vast amount of human existence!

"*18th.*—A Chinese boat with four men was chased into the river by four Dyak *prahus*, and escaped with difficulty. On the intelligence reaching me, I, with some trouble, mustered three canoes, and we proceeded down, about one o'clock in the morning, in search of the enemy. After rowing in the dark for some hours, we discovered a light gliding up the river, and gave chase, but did not succeed; and at daybreak returned, wet and tired, without seeing anything more, when we learnt that the chase was a Sarawak boat, which, mistaking us for Dyaks, as we did them, pulled with all speed home, and gave the alarm of being nearly captured.

"In the evening I ordered a fine boat to be prepared for the war with Sarebus and Sakarran, which appears to me inevitable; as it is impossible, laying all motives of humanity aside, to allow these piratical tribes to continue their depredations, which are inconsistent with safety, and a bar to all trade along the coast. Eighty *prahus* of Sarebus and Sakarran are reported to be ready, and waiting for further reinforcements before putting to sea.

"*19th.*—Information of three more of my Dyaks being cut off in the interior by the predatory tribes.

"*20th.*—Opened the subject of restoring the old *patingi*, *bandar*, and *tumangong*, and found Muda Hassim quite willing, but wishing to wait till he hears from Borneo; at the same time telling me that I might employ them in their respective situations. This matter I consider, therefore, settled; and as these men are natives, and have the command of all the common people, and are, moreover, willing to serve under me, I conceive it a great advance in my government. Since my return here they have proved themselves faithful and ready; but though true in adversity, will they continue equally so in prosperity? I hope the best from them, especially as their circumstances will be easy; and I will endeavour to pay them as much as I can. Pay well, and men may be trusted. Either way, it is a great advance; for every change will not occur immediately; and, in the mean time, I shall be strengthened by in-comers, especially Chinese, so that the parties may be balanced, and each look to me as the link which holds them together.

"The government must be a patchwork between good and evil, abolishing only so much of the latter as is consistent with safety. But never must I appear in the light of a reformer, political or religious; for to the introduction of new customs, apparently trivial, and the institution of new forms, however beneficial, the disgust of the semi-barbarous races may be traced. People settled like myself too often try to create a Utopia, and end with a general confusion. The feeling of the native which binds him to his chief is destroyed, and no other principle is substituted in its stead; and as the human mind more easily learns ill than good, they pick up the vices of their governors without their virtues, and their own good qualities disappear, the bad of both races remaining without the good of either.

"We are in active preparation to fit out a fleet to meet the piratical Dyaks. The *rajah* has a fine *prahu*, which I have taken in hand to repair, and I have purchased a second; and the two, with three or four small canoes, will be able to cope with a hundred or a hundred and fifty

Dyak boats. The largest of these boats is worth a description. Fifty-six feet in length and eight in breadth; built with a great sheer, so as to raise the bow and stern out of the water, and pulling thirty paddles, she is a dangerous customer when mounting four swivels and carrying a crew of twenty men with small arms. She is called the *Snake*, or *Ular*. The second boat, somewhat shorter and less fast, is named the *Dragon*; her complement of paddles twenty, and her fighting-men twenty, make one hundred and forty in, two boats. The long canoes carry fifteen men each, which will bring the force up to one hundred and eighty-five; and one boat of the *rajah's* will complete two hundred men, of whom nearly one hundred are armed with muskets.

"To show the system of these people, I may mention that one of the principal men proposed to me to send to Sakarran and Sarebus, and intimate that I was about to attack Siquong (a large interior tribe), and invite them to assist. 'They will all come,' he said: 'nothing they will like so well; and when they are up the Samarahan River, we will sally forth, attack; and destroy them at one blow.' My answer was, that I could not deceive; but if they did come, I would attack them.

"*Feb. 1st.*—Matari, or 'the Sun,' the Sakarran chief I have already mentioned, arrived with two boats, and paid me several visits. He assured me he wanted to enter into an agreement, to the effect that neither should injure the other. To this treaty I was obliged to add the stipulation, that he was neither to pirate by sea nor by land, and not to go, under any pretence, into the interior of the country. His shrewdness and cunning were remarkably displayed. He began by inquiring, if a tribe, either Sakarran or Sarebus, pirated on my territory, what I intended to do. My answer was, 'To enter their country and lay it waste.' But he asked me again, 'You will give me, your friend, leave to steal a few heads occasionally?'

"'No,' I replied, 'you cannot take a single head; you cannot enter the country: and if you or your countrymen do, I will have a hundred Sakarran heads for every one you take here.' He recurred to this request several times: 'just to steal one or two!' as a schoolboy would ask for apples. There is no doubt that the two tribes of Sakarran and Sarebus are greatly addicted to head-hunting, and consider the possession as indispensable. The more a man has, the greater his honour and rank; nor is there anything without to check or ameliorate this barbarous habit; for the Malays of all classes, on this coast, take the same pride in heads as the Dyaks themselves, with the exception that they do not place them in their houses, or attach any superstitious ideas to them.

"I asked Matari what was the solemn form of agreement among his tribes; and he assured me the most solemn was drinking each other's blood, in which case it was considered they were brothers; but pledging the blood of fowls was another and less solemn form.

"On the 26th of January the *Royalist's* boat, with Captain Hart and Mr. Penfold, second mate, of the *Viscount Melbourne*, arrived here. The reason, it appears, of the *Royalist* coming was, to seek the missing crew of the *Viscount Melbourne*, a large ship wrecked on the Luconia shoal. The captain in the launch, with some *coolies*; the first and third mates, with Colonel Campbell of the 37th, M.N.I., in a cutter; the second mate, Mr. Penfold, and the surgeon, in the second cutter; a fourth boat with twenty-five lascars, and the jolly-boat, making in all five boats, left the vessel well provisioned, and steered in company for the coast, which they made somewhere between Borneo and Tanjong Barram. The fourth boat was missed the night they made the land; and being all at anchor, and the weather fine, it was strongly suspected that the twenty-five lascars deserted with her.

"The other four boats proceeded a day or two, when the first cutter, with Colonel Campbell on board, went in the evening in search of water; and though the rest showed lights all night, returned no more. They were, on the following day, attacked by a *prahu*, which fired into them and severely wounded one man, and succeeded in capturing the jolly-boat; but finding nothing in her, set her on fire—lascars and all. The crew, however, was rescued, and she was abandoned; and the two remaining boats, in course of time, arrived at Singapore. The *Royalist* was taken up by government to seek the missing boats, and just touched here for an hour or two, the boat coming up while the vessel kept the sea.

"*Feb. 9th.*—Mr. Williamson returned from Sanpro, where I sent him to watch a party of natives who had gone among the Dyaks; the Panglima Sadome, of the tribe of Sanpro, came with him, and brought the lamentable account of the death of eight more Dyaks, cut off by the Sakarrans. It frets me dreadfully; however, on the whole I see a vast improvement, and a degree of confidence in me arising among the Dyaks, greater than I expected.

"*14th.*—I have now entered on the most difficult task, and the one most likely to cause an ultimate failure in my undertaking, but which is indispensably necessary. I mean, the administration of justice. As long as my laws are applied to the people of the country, there is no trouble; but directly *equal* justice is administered, it causes heartburn and evasion; the *rajahs* and *pangerans* are surrounded by a gang of followers who heretofore have robbed, plundered, and even murdered, without inquiry being made. It was enough that a follower of the *rajah* was concerned, to hush up all wrongs; and any of the oppressed, who were bold enough to lodge a complaint, were sure to rue it.

"All the rascals and ruffians who follow the great men find this species of protection the best and the only reward; and as the slaves are looked upon as personal property, any punishment inflicted upon them is likewise inflicted upon their masters. I have all along foreseen these obstacles, and the necessity of at once combating them—whether successfully or not signifies little; but they must be encountered, and the result left to the Almighty.

"Equal justice is the groundwork of society; and unless it can be administered, there can be no hope of ultimate improvement. The country may have bad laws; but such laws as it has must be enforced, gently and mildly as may be toward the superiors, but strictly toward the guilty; and all crimes coming under my cognizance must meet with their punishment. These remarks are preliminary to two cases, in which the *rajah's* followers have been concerned.

"The first of these was a man stealing sago, which is stored without the houses at the water's edge; he was convicted. The other occurred sometime since, but has only just been traced. A party at night gutted a house, getting a booty of upward of 200 *reals*; the goods have been discovered; but the three followers of the *rajah* have absconded since the affair has been blown; whether to return or not is uncertain. There can be no doubt, however, that they have been sent away to keep clear of the consequences, by one of the *rajah's* brothers named Abdul Khadir, who, when they were off, accused two accomplices, people of the country!

"Another most shameful mode of exaction and tyranny is practiced by these Borneo people, particularly their *nakodas*. It consists in lending small sums of money to the natives (that is, Sarawak people), and demanding interest at the rate of fifty *per cent* per month; by this means a small sum is quickly converted into one which is quite out of the power of the poor man to pay; and he, his wife, and children, are taken to the house of the creditor to work for him, while the debt still accumulates, and the labour is endless. I intend to strike at this slavery in disguise, but not just yet; the suppression of robbery, the criminal department of justice, being more immediately important.

"*15th.*—I may, in continuation of yesterday, mention another instance in illustration of this oppressive system. Si Pata (a Siniawan), son of the *tumangong*, lost in gambling to Nakoda Ursat eighteen *reals*, which in eighteen months has now arisen to a debt of 170 *reals*; but all prospect of payment of such an accumulated sum being impossible from a poor man, Nakoda Ursat consigns the debt to Pangeran Abdul Khadir, who can demand it by fair means or by foul; and if Si Pata cannot pay, make his father pay. Thus a gambling transaction is run up to ten times its original amount, and a whole family involved in distress by these iniquitous proceedings.

"Such things must not be; and odious as they seem to a European, and indignant as they make him, yet he must not proceed with the strong hand. Reflection, too, teaches us that vice is comparative; and in forming a judgment, we must not forget a man's education, the society in which he lives, the absence of restraint, and the force of example from childhood; so that what would be heinous in a Christian long under a settled government, is light by comparison in a Malay, who is a nominal professor of Islam, and brought up with the idea that might makes right, and has no one external cause to deter him from crime.

"*March 12th.*—On the whole getting on very well, but with many reasons for vexation, and more for anxiety. The chief of these is, whether Mr. Bonham will come here, as I have suggested, or rather pressed. Another feature of inquietude is from the Chinese of Sipang, who certainly aim at greater power than I shall allow them, and perhaps, some day or other, it will come to a struggle.

"Petty troubles I do not reckon, though there are enow on all sides, and for the last few days I have felt as if sinking under them; but that is not my usual temperament. I now look impatiently for intelligence. Blow, fair breezes, and waft *Royalist* here!

"*25th.*—A period of wearing uncertainty since my last, having news neither of the *Royalist* nor of Mr. Bonham, and kept on the *qui vive* by a schooner or two at the entrance of the river. The plot thickens in and around; and for the sake of keeping up a register of events in something like order, I will here mention the leading features. Seriff Sahib, of Sadong, pretends to be friendly, but is treacherous in his heart, as is his brother, Seriff Muller of Sakarran. We have been quite clear of Dyaks, and our own tribes enjoying rest and peace; and one tribe from without, namely Serang, has come in and claimed my protection.

"The only tribe at all troublesome is the Singè, the chief of which (the Orang Kaya Parembam) is decidedly opposed to me, and swears by Macota. I am given to believe, however, that the majority of his people do not agree with him; and I shall dispossess him of his dignity, and substitute a friendly chief. The Singè Dyaks are the most powerful and numerous in my territory, and the only ones who have not been attacked and plundered by the Sakarrans.

"At Lundu are the Sibnowan Dyaks, under the Orang Kaya Tumangong; and the Lundu Dyaks, once a flourishing tribe, now, by ill-treatment of all sorts, reduced to twenty persons. I may mention among my other difficulties, that many, nay most, of the Dyak tribes are held as *private property*: any rascally Borneon making a present to the sultan, gets a grant of a Dyak tribe, originally to rule, now to plunder or sell; and in this way the portion of the Sibnowans settled at Lundu are under Bandar Sumsu; but, being a resolute people, he cannot do them much wrong. This Bandar Sumsu has lately been disturbing the Lundu Dyaks in the following manner: a Sibnowan Dyak lived with the Lundu Dyaks, which gave him an opening to demand of the Lundus the sum of fifty *reals* (100 *rupees*), which was paid; but unluckily the Sibnowan died in the course of a few months, still with the Lundus, and a farther sum of eighty *reals*, or 160 *rupees*, was demanded, which not being raised, the daughter of one of the head people was seized, and sold for that sum to a Chinaman!

"*Pangeran* Macota has likewise been injuring these poor people, though I shall find it difficult to bring it home to him. His agent, Bandar Dowud (a man involved in debt), took fifteen Dyak cloths and sold them, or rather forced them to take them, at an exorbitant rate; in a month or two after, he returns and demands 200 *reals* over and above the large price already paid for articles worth seven or eight *reals*; the poor Dyaks not being able to pay, he seizes the chief's daughter (a married woman), and demands four other women in lieu of the sum. Happily for the poor Dyaks, this news came to my ears, and I sent to Lundu in haste. They had all fled, having *stolen* their two women, one from each *bandar*, and carried them away.

"On the *patingi* and *tumangong* reaching Lundu, they found two of the tribe, one the *pangeran*, the other the father of the girl sold to the Chinaman, after a long search in the jungle. These two men I have now with me, and wait for the Orang Kaya Tumangong before going into the case. The *pangeran* is the same Dyak whose conversation I have detailed at large on my first visit to the place. He is a man of intelligence; and this tribe (if it may yet be so called) has always borne the character of being the most hospitable and generous among the Dyaks. I may at some future time revert to them.

"There is a rumour of war between the Sarebus and Sakarran Dyaks, in consequence of the former tribe seizing a Balow woman on the territory of the latter, and refusing to restore her. Let these two predatory tribes employ and weaken one another, and it will be well for us and all the other people of this country, and they will afterward be the more easily brought into subjection.

"From Borneo we have news, but as uncertain as everything else regarding the capital. A hundred vessels, it is reported, are coming to attack them; and they, in consequence, are building *a fort*. The *Royalist* had been there and departed.

"Pangeran Usop, it is said, was about to come here, when the arrival of the *Royalist* induced him to postpone his design.

"There is every reason to believe that the Chinese of Sambas, particularly those of Montrado, are extremely dissatisfied; and a report yesterday states that a man sent by the *sultan* to demand gold had been killed by them, and that the *sultan's* letter to the Kunsi, after being defiled, was publicly burned. Our own Chinese of Sipang are certainly intriguing with Sambas; and, as the *rajah* well expresses it, 'their clothes-box is here, but their treasure-chest is at Sambas.'

"It is impossible to say what quantity of gold the Kunsi may get; but their pretence that they *get none* must be false, when every common Malay obtains from half to one *bunkal* per month.

"To counteract the chance of evil, I have intimated that the Simbock Kunsi are to come here; and on the whole, they (of Sipang) have taken it more quietly than I expected. They are not in a state for war; but they have vague notions and intentions provided they can keep out opposition, to make this place subservient to them, as it would indeed be, provided they were allowed to strengthen themselves while the other parties remained stationary. But *divide and rule* is a good motto in my case; and the Chinese have overlooked the difference between this country and Sambas. There they have numerous rivers in the vicinity of their settlements—here but one; and, the Dyak population being against them, starvation would soon reduce them to terms. The *Royalist* arrived about the end of March, and sailed again on the 9th April.

"I have before mentioned the difficulty of administering justice; and experience teaches me that the risk to myself, on this score, is more to be apprehended than on any other. The forms I have not much alluded to; and the following is as nearly as possible the Malay custom:—The *rajah's* brothers and myself sit at one end of the long room in my house; at the sides are the Patingis and Tumangong, and other respectable people; in the centre the parties concerned; and, behind them, anybody who wishes to be present. We hear both parties; question, if necessary; and decide—and from this decision there is no appeal.

"One only condition I insist upon; and that is, that in any intricate case, or whenever I dread confederacy, I do not allow the witnesses to hear each other. The laws of evidence, in a *free country*, prohibit any leading questions being put to witnesses: here, for the purposes of justice, it is indispensable; for the people, being ruled by fear, and apprehensive of consequences, often falter before the face of the accused, and their testimony has to be wrung from them. To decide also according to the technicalities of construction would be here ridiculous, and defeat the ends of justice. The people are rude and uncivilized; their oppressors crafty and bold, who have no hesitation about lying, and bringing others to lie for them. Oaths are a farce to them.

"The aggrieved are timid, vacillating, and simple, and cannot readily procure even necessary evidence; for their witnesses are afraid to speak. Under these circumstances, I look at the leading features of the case, the probability, the characters, the position of parties, and determine according to my judgment. It is not, indeed, a very difficult task; for the disputes are generally glaring, and, when bolstered up, usually fail in their most important links; and at a touch of cross-questioning, the witnesses, resolved to tell the same story, fall into opposite ones. In one case, about a slave, three witnesses had resolved on the sex; but, questioned separately as to size and age, all disagreed. They were not prepared. One represented her a woman grown and marriageable; another, as high as my walking-stick; the third, a little child.

"I have now on hand a serious matter, of robbery to a large extent, and three of the *rajah's* followers are implicated. Would it were over and well!—but done it must be. How little can those at a distance know my difficulties—alone, unaided, the unceasing attention by day, the anxiety and sleeplessness by night, the mountain of doubt upon mountain piled, and the uncertainty of necessary support or assistance!

"The *pangeran* of the Lundu Dyaks lived with me three weeks, and I was able to do him substantial justice; and hope for the future that his life, and that of the remnant of his tribe, may be rendered more endurable.

"His residence with me was doubly advantageous, as it enabled me to ascertain his character, and him to see something of our habits and manners. The impression on my part was highly favourable; for I found him a quiet, intelligent man, and a keen observer; and I believe the impression he received was equally favourable. The *poetry* of the Dyak expressions is remarkable; and, like most wild people, they seem to delight in oratory, and to be a good deal swayed by it. For hours I have talked with the *pangeran*, listened to his history, heard his complaints, sympathized in the misfortunes of his tribe, and shuddered at the wrongs and sufferings they have endured.

"'We are few,' he exclaimed, 'and therefore our oppressions are aggravated; the same demands are made upon us as though we were many, and we have not the means of resisting or complying. We fly to the jungle; we are like deer—we have no home, no perch. Our wives and children are taken from us; our sufferings are very great.'

"On another occasion he said, 'I have felt my sufferings to be so great, that I wished to die, if Jovata would permit it. I wished to die; for I remembered how happy we were once, and how miserable now.' I could dwell largely on these and suchlike language and descriptions, which appear to me highly pathetic and touching—at least I found them so in reality; and I cannot forbear adding one or two more such, highly characteristic.

"'Our home,' said the *pangeran*, 'was a happy one; none who came to us wanted. The fruit on the trees was saved; the fish in the river near us was never destroyed. Rice was plenty; if it was scarce, we kept it, and fed ourselves upon vegetables, that we might give it to those who visited our habitation. The fish, the fruit, and the rice were preserved,[1] that the men of the seas (Malays) might eat of them; yet they had no pity on us. We were free men, yet they treated us worse than slaves. We are now but few; and unless you protect us, we shall soon cease to be.'

"Again: 'The *tumangong* was severe to us; and when Macota came, he said the *tumangong* was a bad man, and he would shield us; but he was much worse than the *tumangong*. Now, you say you will cherish us; we believe you; but you are at a distance, and perhaps may not be able.'

---

1. This I found on inquiry, to be strictly true—a most amiable trait!—B.

"Further: 'Pangeran Macota kept me nine months in his house, and wanted to make me a slave; but I escaped, and travelled through the woods, and swam the rivers, till I came to my own country. He thought the Dyak had no eyes except in the jungle; he thought he had no ears except to listen to the bird of omen; he thought he had no wit except to grow rice; but the Dyak saw, and heard, and understood, that while his words were sweet, his heart was crooked, and that, whether they were men of the sea or Dyaks, he deceived them with fair sayings; he said one thing to one man, and another to a second; he deceived with a honied mouth. I saw and understood it all while I lived in his house. How could I trust him afterward?'

"These expressions were concluded by significantly twisting his two fore-fingers round each other, to show the intrigues that were carried on. I grew very fond of this poor naked savage; for if honesty and a kind heart entitle a man to our esteem, he is worthy of it.

"I had a long conference with Si Nimook, the Sow Dyak, and hope to recover his wife. Amid all the wealth and all the charity of England, how well bestowed would a small portion be for the purpose of restoring one hundred and fifty women and children to their husbands and parents, and releasing them from slavery! A small rill from the plenteous river would cheer this distant misery, and bestow the blessing of fertility on the now barren soil of these poor Dyaks. Oh, that I had the brass to beg—to draw out a piteous tale so as to touch the heart!"

# CHAPTER 13

# Resolves to Proceed to Borneo Proper

The next portion of Mr. Brooke's *Journal* details another excursion up the country, and then proceeds to describe the early incidents of his infant government. As he advanced on his way, affairs began to assume more important aspects; and yet they could hardly be painted with greater force or interest than in his simple notes.

"*April 25th.*—Ascended the left-hand river, in order to introduce the Kunsi Simbock to their new territory; passed the night on a pebbly bank; moon at full, bright and unclouded, tingeing the luxuriant foliage, and glancing on the clear rapid stream. Four distinct and distant races met on this lonely and lovely spot—English, Chinese, Malays, and Dyaks! What a scope for poetry and reflection—the time, the clime, the spot, and the company!

"*26th.*—After our morning meal and bath, entered the small river Stabad, which, according to report, runs from a source two or three days' journey further into the interior. At present it is so obstructed by fallen trees, that we were forced to return, after ascending about four miles. We left our boats near its entrance, and walked to the small but steep mountain, Tubbang. Its length may be about 400 feet. After mounting, by a winding path, about half-way up toward the top, we arrived at the entrance of a cave, into which we descended through a hole. It is fifty or sixty feet long, and the far end is supported on a colonnade of stalactites, and opens on a sheer precipice of 100 or 150 feet.

"Hence the spectator can overlook the distant scene; the forest lies at his feet, and only a few trees growing from the rock reach nearly to the level of the grotto. The effect is striking and panoramic; the grotto cheerful; floored with fine sand; the roof groined like Gothic, whence the few clear drops which filter through form here and there the fantastic stalactites common to such localities. The natives report the cave to be the residence of a fairy queen; and they show her bed, pillow, and other of her household furniture. Within the cave we found a few remnants of human bones; probably some poor Dyak who had crawled there to die.

"Having finished our survey of the place, and wandered sufficiently about the mount, we re-embarked, and dropped a short way down the river, and started again into the jungle to look for antimony ore, but without success, our guide having forgotten the road. After a couple of hours' wandering, the latter part in a heavy storm of rain, we reached the boats; and I thence ascended to Suntah, where we were all glad to house ourselves, as the deluge continued.

"*27th.*—I will say nothing of my works at Suntah, except that they run away with my money, are badly conducted by my Chinese *hadji*, and, above all, that I have great reason to suspect the integrity and steadiness of this said *hadji*. I must therefore make up my mind either to change him when the business is finished, or to watch him very narrowly; for the honesty of a diamond-worker, like the virtue of Cæsar's wife, must be above suspicion, or he must be watched closely; but how?

"*28th.*—Descended the river, and, arriving at Sarawak, found both work and cause for inquietude. The *rajah* had heard of Dyak pirates, and dispatched four boats, two large and two small: the Snake, weakly manned by the *tumangong's* people, and the rest led by *pangeran*s (who neither work nor fight) and a wretched crew, chiefly Borneons. Mr. Crimble, taking my servant Peter and four Javanese, went most imprudently in the second of the large boats. The whole, being dispatched in haste (foolish haste), insufficiently provided in every respect, may fall into trouble, and involve me in very unpleasant circumstances.

"The other cause for uneasiness is the attack of a Chinese boat at the mouth of the river. The boat that attacked her is a small one, with eight or ten men, which came out of Sadong, and had been lying here for a week or more. She is commanded by a *pangeran* named Badrudeen, has some Illanuns on board, and is bound on a piratical cruise. As she descended the river, she met with the small China boat, likewise from Sambas, with eight men, which she treacherously assailed, desperately wounding one man and severely another; but the China boat's consort heaving in sight, the pirate pulled away. I must redress this, if it be in my power; and have ordered the Datus to gather men to follow the rascals, as it is probable they will be lurking not far from hence. In the mean time it gave me great pain dressing the hurts of these poor Chinese, one of whom I think must die, being cut along the back and side—across the body from the side nearly to the back-bone, a ghastly gaping wound, beside having his arm slashed through. The other man is very severely, and perhaps, without medical attend-ance, mortally, hurt, having his arm half cut through at the muscular development between the shoulder and elbow—poor fellow! I must say for the Chinese, they seem very grateful for any attention shown them.

"*29th*.—My birthday. Men collected, and tomorrow we start for Telang Telang. This morning, much to my relief, our fleet returned, after an encounter with thirteen Dyak boats. About one o'clock on the 28th, pulling into a bay between Morotaba and Tanjong Poe, they came unexpectedly on them. One Borneon boat had lagged behind; the *pangeran* who commanded deserted the second, and sought ref-uge with the Tumangong, trying to induce him to fly; and the crew of the third, a large boat with my two Europeans on board, was, by their account, in a state of fear, which totally incapacitated them from acting. All rose, none would pull; all shouted, none would serve the guns; all commanded, none obeyed; most were screaming out to run; all bellowing out, in hopes of frightening the enemy; none to direct the helm.

"The *tumangong*, with only seventeen men in all, insisted on ad-vance; and the Borneons, encouraged by threats from the Europe-ans, and the good example of the Javanese, did not fly. The two boats opened their fire; the Dyaks retreated in confusion and alarm: but from the tumult, the noise, and the rocking of the boat, Mr. Crimble could only fire three times with the bow six-pounder carronade, and from other guns loaded with grape and canister, while the rascally Borneons never fired at all. The Dyaks suffered loss, and left behind them clothes, rice, fish, cooking-pots, swords, &c.; and, considering the state of the Borneons, it was lucky the dread of our prowess put them to flight so easily. Crimble assured me that, with a Siniawan crew, he could have destroyed half their force. The Dyaks behaved very well, pulling off with great steadiness and without noise.

"*June 20th.*—The events of the month may be compressed into a narrative comprising the internal and external.

"The internal state of the country is decidedly improving and flourishing, and bears the aspect of gradually increasing prosperity. Justice has been strictly administered. Robberies, which a few months ago were of nightly occurrence, are now rarely heard of; and that vile intriguing to make poor people slaves, from debt or false claims, is entirely stopped.

"The people who had scattered at the close of the war have been collected, and are building their houses a short way up the river at the Campong Jekiso, which, when finished, will be a neat-looking village.

"The Pangeran Macota is intriguing; but as he is sure to do that, it need not be insisted upon.

"Muda Hassim is true and agreeable, and entirely reconciled to the *patingi* and *tumangongs*; so far, indeed, nothing can be better than our internal state: there is peace, there is plenty; the poor are not harassed, and justice is done to all.

"The Dyaks of the interior are improving and content, and gaining courage daily to complain of any wrong that may be offered them. To the *sena*, or forced trade, I have almost put a stop, by confiscating the goods wherever met with; and this plan once acted on, the Dyaks have not been slow to bring me bundles of *bidongs* (Dyak cloths), iron, and the like.

"The tribes that continue unsettled are the Suntah and Singè: the affairs of the latter I will mention hereafter.

"Suntah has been for a long time under the government of Seriff Sahib of Sadong, and through his *paternal* charge has dwindled away from four hundred to fifty or sixty families. Shortly after my assuming the reins of government, he dispatched (according to custom) a mixed party of Malays and Dyaks, and falling on my helpless tribe of San-pro, killed some, and carried away twenty women and children into captivity. I was not strong enough to resent the injury; but wrote him a strong letter, demanding the women, and telling him he was not to send, under any pretext, into my country.

"The women I did not get; but I heard that the communication frightened him: for, of course, they deem I am backed by all the power of my country. While the *Royalist* still lay here, I heard that his people were raising the revenue from the Suntah Dyaks; but it must be remarked, that the Suntah are on the edge of my territory, having left the former location. As this was done in the face of my caution not to intermeddle without my consent, I resolved at once to put the matter to the issue; and having armed four boats, went up and seized all the rice and *padi* collected for my neighbours' use.

"The Suntah Dyaks were and are alarmed to a pitiable degree; for they fear Seriff Sahib with good reason; and yet my being on the spot gave them no option of evading my demand. Thus the matter was brought to a crisis; and having taken the revenue (as it was called) for the poor Dyaks themselves, I shall be able to keep them from starvation, to the verge of which, so early in the season, they are already reduced. The Dyaks remain unsettled; but I am now in hopes of bringing them to the interior of the Quop, which is further within our own territory. Muda Hassim wrote to Seriff Sahib to tell him the Dyaks were no longer his, but mine; and Seriff Sahib, sore-hearted, conspired against us, and held for some time a higher tone than his wont.

"I shall now narrate my proceedings at the mountain of Singè, from which I have just returned. The mountain, with its groves of fruit-trees, has been already described; and as a preface to my present description, I must particularize the circumstances of the Dyak tribe of Singè. The tribe consists of at least 800 males, the most ignorant, and therefore the most wild, of the Dyaks of my country; and, from their position, they have never been overcome or ruined, and are therefore a rich community, and proportionately independent. Their old chief is by name Parembam, and the *panglima*, or head-warrior, his younger brother, by name Si Tummo.

"These men have for a very long time ruled this tribe; and the elder has certainly acquired from the Malays a portion of cunning and intrigue, and lost the general simplicity of the native Dyak character. He is unquestionably a man of ability. His sway, however, on the mountain has for a long time been unpopular; and a large proportion of the people, dissatisfied with his extortions, have been attached to a younger chief, by name Bibit. Some time past, finding it impossible to manage this old chief, Parembam, and being convinced that the change might readily be made, I called Bibit, and made him chief, or Orang Kaya of the tribe. Parembam neither was nor is inclined to give up his authority without a struggle; and though the mass adhere to the new chief, by title 'Steer Rajah,' yet Parembam's long-established customs, his great wealth, and his talents, render him a dangerous old man to the younger leader.

"One quality, however, Parembam is deficient in, as well as his brother the Panglima, and that is *bravery*; and on this much depends in a Dyak tribe. Steer Rajah, on the contrary, has always been renowned in war, and is the envied possessor of many heads. The Dyaks have among them a fashion which they call *bunkit*, or vaunting; for instance, in the present case Steer Rajah and Parembam dared each other to go on excursions to procure heads, *i. e.* against their enemies—this is *bunkit*. One of Steer Rajah's followers went accordingly, and quickly procured the head of a hostile warrior far out of my territory; and on the return of the party, Parembam in turn sent forty men to Simpoke, which is a tribe attached to Samarahan, and on our immediate border.

"Close to the Dyaks of Simpoke live a party of the Sigo Dyaks, who belong to me; and this party of Parembam's, confounding friends and enemies, killed some of the Sigo Dyaks—how many is not certain. The Sigos, taking the alarm, cut off their retreat, and killed two of the Singè Dyaks; and many beside were wounded by *sudas* and *ranjows*, and, all broken, fled back to their own country. Thus, though they obtained five heads, they lost two, and those belonging to their principal warriors. This news reaching me, I hurried up to the hill, and arrived just after part of the war-party had brought the heads.

"I may here remark, that I have positively forbidden the Dyak tribes within my territory to war one upon the other; and this, therefore, was a serious offence against me on the part of Parembam. At once to aim at more than this restriction would be fruitless, and even risk my ability to effect this first step on the road to improvement. I likewise came up here to go through the ceremony of installing the Orang Kaya Steer Rajah in his office; and thus I have had an excellent opportunity of seeing their customs and manners. What follows will be a personal narration, or nearly so, of what I have seen; and it applies, with slight difference, to almost all the interior tribes.

"On our ascending the mountain, we found the five heads carefully watched, about half a mile from the town, in consequence of the non-arrival of some of the war-party. They had erected a temporary shed close to the place where these miserable remnants of noisome mortality were deposited; and they were guarded by about thirty young men in their finest dresses, composed principally of scarlet jackets ornamented with shells, turbans of the native bark-cloth dyed bright yellow, and spread on the head, and decked with an occasional feather, flower, or twig of leaves. Nothing can exceed their partiality for these trophies; and in retiring from the 'war-path,' the man who has been so fortunate as to obtain a head hangs it about his neck, and instantly commences his return to his tribe.

"If he sleep on the way, the precious burden, though decaying and offensive, is not loosened, but rests on his lap, while his head (and nose!) reclines on his knees. The retreat is always silently made until close to home, when they set up a wild yell, which announces their victory and the possession of its proofs. It must, therefore, be considered, that these bloody trophies are the evidences of victory—the banner of the European, the flesh-pot of the Turk, the scalp of the North American Indian—and that they are torn from enemies, for taking heads is the effect and not the cause of war.

"On our reaching the *balei*, or public hall, of the Orang Kaya Steer Rajah, I immediately called a number of their chiefs together, and opened a conference with them on the subject of Parembam having attacked and killed the Dyaks of Sigo. They *all* disapproved of it most highly, asserting that the Sigos were their younger brothers; that no sufficient cause had ever existed; that Parembam had acted badly, and must pay to purchase *peace*. Were they, I asked, willing to force Parembam into payment? They were. Would they insist on the heads being restored to the Sigos, and receive those of their own people? They would!

"It may be observed, that their causes for war, as well as its progress and termination, are exactly the same as those of other people. They dispute about the limits of their respective lands; about theft committed by one tribe upon another; about occasional murders; the crossing each other on the war-path; and about a thousand other subjects.

"When a tribe is on a warlike excursion, it often happens that their track (or 'trail') is crossed by another tribe. Those who strike the trail guard it at some convenient spot, apprehending the party to be enemies; they plant *ranjows* in the path, and wait till the returning party are involved among them to make an attack. If enemies, and they succeed, all is well; but if friends, though no attack be made, it is a serious offence, and mostly gives occasion to war if not paid for. The progress of the contest consists in attacking each other by these surprises, particularly about the time of sowing, weeding, and cutting the rice-crops.

"When one party is weaker, or less active, or less warlike than the other, they solicit a peace through some tribe friendly to both, and pay for the lives they have taken: the price is about two gongs, value 33½ *reals*, for each life: thus peace is concluded. This is the custom with these Dyaks universally; but it is otherwise with the Sarebus and Sakarran. But Sarebus and Sakarran are not fair examples of Dyak life, as they are pirates as well as head-hunters, and do not hesitate to destroy all persons they meet with.

"Parembam, having been called before me, declared that these heads belonged to the Simpoke Dyaks, and that they had not attacked the Sigos. As I was not quite certain of the fact, I thought it unjust to proceed against him till I had stronger proof.

"On the following morning the heads were brought up to the village, attended by a number of young men all dressed in their best, and were carried to Parembam's house amid the beating of gongs and the firing of one or two guns. They were then disposed of in a conspicuous place in the public hall of Parembam. The music sounded and the men danced the greater part of the day; and toward evening carried them away in procession through all the *campongs* except three or four just about me. The women, in these processions, crowd round the heads as they proceed from house to house, and put *sirih* and betel-nut in the mouths of the ghastly dead, and welcome them!

"After this they are carried back in the same triumph, deposited in an airy place, and left to dry. During this process, for seven, eight, or ten days, they are watched by the boys of the age of six to ten years; and during this time they never stir from the public hall—they are not permitted to put their foot out of it while engaged in this sacred trust. Thus are the youths initiated.

"For a long time after the heads are hung up, the men nightly meet and beat their gongs, and chant addresses to them, which were rendered thus to me: 'Your head is in our dwelling, but your spirit wanders to your own country.' 'Your head and your spirit are now ours: persuade, therefore, your countrymen to be slain by us.' 'Speak to the spirits of your tribe: let them wander in the fields, that when we come again to their country we may get more heads, and that we may bring the heads of your brethren, and hang them by your head,' &c. The tone of this chant is loud and monotonous, and I am not able to say how long it is sung; but certainly for a month after the arrival of the heads, as one party here had had a head for that time, and were still exhorting it.

"These are their customs and modes of warfare; and I may conclude by saying that, though their trophies are more disgusting, yet their wars are neither so bloody, nor their cruelties so great, as those of the North American Indian. They slay all they meet with of their enemies—men, women, and children; but this is common to all wild tribes. They have an implacable spirit of revenge as long as the war lasts, retort evil for evil, and retaliate life for life; and, as I have before said, the heads are the trophies, as the scalps are to the red men. But, on the contrary, they never torture their enemies, nor do they devour them; and peace can always be restored among them by a very moderate payment. In short, there is nothing new in their feelings, or in their mode of showing them; no trait remarkable for cruelty; no head-hunting for the sake of head-hunting.

"They act precisely on the same impulses as other wild men: war arises from passion or interest; peace from defeat or fear. As friends, they are faithful, just, and honest; as enemies, blood-thirsty and cunning, patient on the war-path, and enduring fatigue, hunger, and want of sleep, with cheerfulness and resolution. As woodmen they are remarkably acute; and on all their excursions carry with them a number of *ranjows*, which, when they retreat, they stick in behind them, at intervals, at a distance of twenty, fifty, or a hundred yards, so that a hotly-pursuing enemy gets checked, and many severely wounded. Their arms consist of a sword, an iron-headed spear, a few wooden spears, a knife worn at the right side, with a *sirih*-pouch, or small basket. Their provision is a particular kind of sticky rice, boiled in bamboos. When once they have struck their enemies, or failed, they return, without pausing, to their homes.

"To proceed with my journal. My principal object in coming up the hill was, to appoint the Orang Kaya Steer Rajah as the chief, beside Pagise as *panglima*, or head warrior, and Pa Bobot as *pangeran*, or revenue officer. It was deemed by these worthy personages quite unfit that this ceremony should take place in the public hall or circular house, as that was the place wherein the heads are deposited, and where they hold councils of war.

"With the Dyaks, all council is divided into hot and cold; peace, friendship, good intentions, are all included under the latter head—war, &c., are under the former. Hot is represented by red, and cold by white. So in everything they make this distinction; and as the public hall is the place for war-councils and war-trophies, it is hot in the extreme, unfit for friendly conference. A shed was therefore erected close to the Orang Kaya's house, wherein the ceremony was to take place. About nine in the evening we repaired to the scene; loud music, barbarous but not unpleasing, resounded, and we took our seats on mats in the midst of our Dyak friends.

"A feast was in preparation; and each guest (if I may call them such) brought his share of rice in bamboos, and laid it on the general stock. As one party came up after another, carrying their burning logs, the effect was very good; and they kept arriving until the place and its vicinity was literally crammed with human beings. A large antique *sirih*-box was placed in the midst; and I contributed that greatest of luxuries, tobacco.

"The feast, in the mean time, was in preparation, some of the principal people being employed in counting the number who were to eat, and dividing the bamboos into exactly equal portions for each person. About six inches were allotted to every man; and it took a very long time to divide it, for they are remarkably particular as to the proper size and quantity to each share. The bamboos of rice being, however, at length satisfactorily disposed, the Orang Kaya produced as his share a large basin full of sauce, composed of salt and chilis, and a small stock of sweetmeats; and then the ceremony of his installation commenced as follows:

"A jacket, a turban, a cloth for the loins, and a *kris* (all of white) were presented to the chief as a token of *sejiek dingin*, or cold, *i.e.* good. The chief then rose, and, taking a white fowl and waving it over the eatables, repeated nearly the following words:—(The commencement, however, is curious enough to dwell upon: the opening is a sort of invocation, beginning with the phrase, '*Samungut, Simungi.*' *Samungut* is a Malay word, *Simungi* signifying the same in Dyak; the exact meaning it is difficult to comprehend; but it is here understood as some principle, spirit, or fortune, which is in men and things. Thus the Dyaks, in stowing their rice at harvest, do it with great care, from a superstitious feeling that the *Simungi* of the *padi* will escape. They now call this principle to be present—that of men, of pigs (their favourite animal), of *padi*, and of fruits.

"They particularly named my *Simungi*, that of my ancestors, of the *pangeran* from Borneo, of the *datus* and of their ancestors, and of the ancestors of their own tribe. They call them—that is, their *Simungi*— to be present. They then call upon Jovata to grant their prayer, that the great man from Europe, and the Datus, might hold the government for a length of time)—'May the government be cold' (good); 'May there be rice in our houses;' 'May many pigs be killed;' 'May male children be born to us;' 'May fruit ripen;' 'May we be happy, and our goods abundant;' 'We declare ourselves to be true to the great man and the *datus*; what they wish we will do, what they command is our

185

law.'

"Having said this and much more, the fowl was taken by a leading Malay, who repeated the latter words, while others bound strips of white cloth round the heads of the multitude. The fowl was then killed, the blood shed in a bamboo, and each man dipping his finger in the blood, touched his forehead and breast, in attestation of his fidelity. The fowl was now carried away to be cooked: and when brought back, placed with the rest of the feast, and the dancing commenced. The chief, coming forward, uttered a loud yell ending in 'ish,' which was oftentimes repeated during the dance. He raised his hands to his forehead, and taking a dish, commenced dancing to lively music. Three other old chief men followed his example; each uttering the yell and making the salute, but without taking the dish.

"They danced with arms extended, turning the body frequently, taking very small steps, and little more than lifting their feet from the ground. Thus they turned backward and forward, passed in and out of the inner rooms, and frequently repeating the yell, and making the salutation to me. The dish, in the mean time, was changed from one to the other: there was little variety, no gesticulation, no violence; and, though not deficient in native grace, yet the movements were by no means interesting. The dance over, the feast commenced; and everything was carried on with great gravity and propriety. I left them shortly after they began to eat, and retired, very fagged, to my bed, or rather, to my board; for sitting cross-legged for several hours is surely a great infliction.

"I may add to this account that, while writing it, the Dyak land-tribes of Siquong, Sibaduh, and Goon, sent their deputies to me. These people are not under any Malay government, and it is now for the first time they have trusted themselves as far as Sarawak. They have an objection to drinking the river-water, and expressed great surprise at the flood-tide. Their confidence is cheering to me, and will, I trust, be advantageous to themselves. Their trade in rice is very considerable: and toward Sambas they exchange eight or ten *pasus* of rice for one of salt.

"Our conference was pleasing. They desired protection, they desired trade. 'They had all heard, *the whole world had heard*, that *a son of Europe* was a friend to the Dyaks.' My visitors drank Batavia arrack with great gusto, declaring all the time it was not half so good as their own; however, at a pinch anything will do. Some other Dyaks met these strangers; they were not adversaries, and so they chewed *sirih*, and drank grog in company; but among enemies this may not be: they can neither eat nor drink in company without desiring a reconciliation. I may add, that the Siquong tribe consists of at least four hundred families, with forty public halls, or *baleis*, for heads. A Dyak family cannot be estimated at fewer than twelve people, which will give four thousand eight hundred or five thousand people. Sibaduh and Goon may be about seventy-five families: beside these, Si Panjong and Sam Penex want to come in to me, which will give one hundred and one more families. What might be done with these people, if I had a little more power and a little assistance!

"I was going to close my account of the Dyaks; but I had scarcely penned the last sentence when a large party of Singè Dyaks and five Dyaks of Sigo arrived—thus all these enemies meeting. In the conference which followed, the Singè allowed they were wrong in attacking Sigo, and laid all the blame on the old chief, Parembam. They likewise allowed it to be just that Parembam should be forced to pay, and conclude a peace. With the Goon and Sibaduh Dyaks they had long been at enmity; but they agreed to make peace if Sibaduh would pay two gongs, formerly demanded, as the price of peace. The Sibaduh, however, did not allow the justice of the demand; but the parties were reconciled so far as that each promised to maintain a truce and to eat together: and the Singès declared they would not attack the Sibaduhs on account of the two gongs, but obtain them in a friendly conference.

"I have (being hurried) briefly mentioned these circumstances, which took a long time to settle, as the Dyaks are very fond of speechifying, which they do sitting, without action or vivacity, but with great fluency, and using often highly metaphysical and elegant language. It was a great nuisance having fifty naked savages in the house all night, extended in the hall and the anterooms. They finished a bottle of gin, and then slept; and I could not avoid remarking that their sleep was light, such as temperance, health, and exercise bestow. During many hours I heard but one man snore, while half the number of Europeans would have favoured me with a concert sufficient to banish rest.

"I shall now briefly mention our *foreign policy* for the last few months.

"For a time we were annoyed with incessant reports of their coming to attack us in force; but, though scarcely believing they would be bold enough, I took precautions, pushed on the completion of our boats, built a fort, and made a fence round the village. These precautions taken, and fifteen boats in the water ready for action, I cared very little, though the news reached me that Byong, the Sarebus chief, had hung a basket on a high tree which was to contain my head.

"*Sadong.*—Our relations with Seriff Sahib were very unsettled; and by the bullying tone of the people of Singè I thought it probable he might be induced to measure his strength, backed by the Sakarran Dyaks, against us. I have already mentioned his attack upon my Dyaks of Sanpro, and the second dispute about the Suntah Dyaks; in the first of these he came off with impunity; in the second I met him with success, and out-manoeuvred him, and wrested the Dyaks from him. Shortly after the transactions at Suntah, a boat of Sakarran Dyaks came to Sarawak nominally *to trade*, but in reality to tamper with the fidelity of the *datus* and others. They proposed to the *tumangong* to join Seriff Sahib, stating that they were sent by him to try all the people here. 'They had been ruined here; Seriff Sahib would restore them their property; and if they left Muda Hassim, James Brooke, and the Chinese, they could afterward easily make a prey of the Dyaks and Chinese, with Seriff Sahib's assistance, and get plenty of slaves.'

"The plan proposed for the removal was as follows:—Seriff Sahib, with forty Malay boats, and the Sakarrans with one hundred boats, were to request permission from Muda Hassim to attack the Dyak tribe of Siquong, and under this pretence were to come up the river, when the *datus* were to join, with their wives and children, and all were to take flight together. The *tumangong* told me this as soon as he heard it himself; and, to make sure, I sent Patingi Gapoor to fish their story out of them, which he did most successfully. Being assured of the fact, I called the Dyaks, and, before some dozens of our people and one or two persons from Singè, taxed them with their guilt.

"They were obliged to confess, and insisted upon it that Seriff Sahib had sent them, &c. Many urged me to put these Dyaks to death; but the reluctance we all have to shedding blood withheld me, and I had no desire to strike at a wren when a foul vulture was at hand. I dismissed the emissaries scot-free, and then both Muda Hassim and myself indited letters to Seriff Sahib, that of Muda Hassim being severe but dignified. Before they were dispatched, an ambassador arrived from Singè with letters both to the *rajah* and myself, disclaiming warmly all knowledge of the treachery, swearing *the most solemn* oaths in proof of his truth, and declaring that, so far from having committed so shameful an action, he had never even dreamed of such a thing in his worst dreams, as he hoped that God would save him.

"Our letters were sent before his ambassador was received, and a second disclaimer, like the first, quickly reached us. Of course it was my policy, whatever my opinion might be, to receive his offers of friendship and to believe all he said; and, therefore, the matter ended, and ended so far well, that Seriff Sahib lowered his former tone; and, certainly, whatever he may desire in his heart, or *dream* of, he wants to be well with us here, and, I can see, fears us. I am content, because I really wish for peace, and not war; Muda Hassim is content, because he has humbled Seriff Sahib, and acted decisively; and the *seriff* is content as the fiend in the infernal regions. I leave it to all gentle readers to form their own opinion of his truth or treachery; but I must hint to them my private opinion that he did send agents to tempt, and would have gained the *datus* if he could; and as for his oaths, my belief is, he would swear a basketful of the most sacred before breakfast to support a lie, and yet not lose his appetite! The *datus* were too old, and knew him too well, to be caught in his trap.

"Seriff Sahib has now sent a fleet of boats up the Sarebus River; but the result I do not yet know.

"To conclude our foreign policy, I must mention Borneo Proper.

"My great object is to reconcile Muda Hassim and the sultan, and to restore the former to Borneo, before the coming of Mr. Bonham on his diplomatic mission. To effect this, I have resolved to proceed myself; and Muda Hassim, equally anxious, has letters and two of his brothers ready to accompany me. If we can gain this object, I shall be firmly established, and relieved from the intriguing, mean, base Borneons. And it will be an advantage to the government measure, in as far as they will be enabled to form their arrangements with all instead of a single faction of the Borneo *pangerans*. From all I hear, Muda Hassim is more powerful than either the sultan or Pangeran Usop; and if he appeals to arms, I am assured he will carry his point, and become the sovereign of Borneo virtually, if not nominally.

"The *Royalist* now waits for us at the mouth of the river, which I hope to reach on the 14th, this being the 12th July. Heigh for the sea once more! But yet, though I go, I take my cares with me, and but for the necessity, the absolute necessity, of bringing the Borneo question to a crisis, good or bad, I would fain stop where I am. For even during one short month's absence I fear my poor people will suffer from the intrigues of the rascally Borneo *pangerans*. In this I do not include Muda Hassim, who, with a most amiable private character, and with integrity and good faith, desires to do right, as far as his education and prejudices will permit. It is sad to reflect that this very prince, who really wishes to do good, and to conduce to the comfort of his people, should, from want of energy, have been so fearful an oppressor, through the agency of others; and it is not here alone that vile agents for vile purposes are plentiful."

# CHAPTER 14

# Sail for Singapore

After Mr. Brooke's return from his expedition against the Singè Dyak chief Parembam, he was visited by his friend Captain Elliott, of the Madras engineers, whose acquaintance I had the pleasure of subsequently making at Singapore. He is, as Mr. Brooke describes him, "a man of science and education, and the best of good fellows." During his stay at Sarawak, he established his observatory, and all its apparatus; and a shed (now converted into a goat-house) will always retain the appellation of "the Observatory." Mr. Brooke and Captain Elliott appear to have made some very amusing and agreeable excursions up the different rivers, an account of which is given in the journal; but I shall pass it over, as I am anxious to follow my friend through with his government up to the time of my meeting him at Singapore.

"*Thursday, July 14th.*—We were to have started on this most lucky day at ten o'clock, but what with innumerable preparations and delays, it was near six before the *rajah* was ready to dismiss the procession; and my alarm became considerable that, Friday (an unlucky day) having commenced by the native reckoning, we should again be postponed till Sunday. However, by making six o'clock five, and keeping back the watches to suit our purpose, our departure was achieved. The state spears and swords were brought forth. The letters for the sultan, in their brass tray covered with embroidered cloth, were duly mounted, with the greatest reverence, on the head of Bandar Sumsu; and nothing remained but to take leave.

"The *rajah* addressed a few words to his brothers, requesting them to tell the sultan that his heart was always with him; that he could never separate from him, whether far or near; and that he was, and always had been, true to his son. Budrudeen then rose, and approaching the *rajah*, seated himself close to him, bending his head to the ground over his hand, which he had grasped. The *rajah* hastily withdrew his hand, and clasping him round, embraced, kissing his neck.

"Both were greatly agitated and both wept, and I could have wept for company, for it was no display of state ceremony, but genuine feeling. It is seldom, very seldom, they show their feelings; and the effect was the more touching from being unexpected; beside, it is a part of our nature (one's better nature) to feel when we see others feel. Pangeran Marsale followed; both brothers likewise parted with Muda Mahammed in the same way, and they certainly rose in my opinion from this token of affection toward each other.

"My *adieus* followed; we all rose; the *rajah* accompanied us to the wharf; and as we embarked, I could see the tears slowly steal from his eyes. I could not help taking his hand, and bidding him be of good cheer; he smiled in a friendly manner, pressed my hand, and I stepped into my boat. Our gongs struck up; the barge, decorated with flags and streamers, was towed slowly along against the flood-tide; the guns fired from the wharf, from the Chinese houses, and from our fort, and we passed along in all the pomp and pride of *Sarawak state*. It was dusk when we got down to the first reach, and there we brought up to wait for the ebb."

I shall omit that part of my friend's journal containing his remarks and observations along the coast between Sarawak and the entrance of the Borneo River. On the 21st July his narration continues thus:

"I must now leave geography, and turn to politics. On casting anchor we acted on a plan previously formed, and sent off the gig, with Seriff Hussein and Nakoda Ahmed, to the city, to intimate my arrival, and that of the *rajah's* brothers, with letters from Muda Hassim. I trusted to their dread of and curiosity about the English expedition to insure my reception; but I gave particular directions, in case the sultan asked about me, that my ambassadors were to say I was here; that I had been corresponding about the English coming; that I was not a man in authority, or belonging to the East India Company; and that they were sure I should not land unless he invited me to come and see him. To show eagerness would have raised suspicion; backwardness excites the contrary feeling, and a desire to entertain some intercourse.

"*July 22nd.*—At the unconscionable hour of 2 a.m., a mob of *pangerans* came on board, in number not fewer than fifty, and with a multitude of followers. They awoke us out of our first sleep, and crowded the vessel above and below, so that we could scarce find room to make our toilet in public, while the heat was suffocating us. However, we did manage it, and sat talking till daylight. Our visitors were chiefly relations or adherents of Muda Hassim, and some of the first men in the country. Pangeran Budrudeen and Pangeran Marsale were in their glory, and happy; and it was evident at once that our affairs were likely to succeed to our heart's content.

"All were anxious and eager in inquiries about Muda Hassim, and wishing his return. The *sultan*, Pangeran Usop, Pangeran Mumin, and others declared, 'Borneo could never be well till he came back.' In short, it was clear that the country was in distress and difficulty from within: trade ruined, piracy abounding, the mouth of the river unsafe, their forts insulted by the pirates, the communication with their dependencies cut off, food dear, and the tobacco, which comes from the northward, not to be had. Everything conspires to forward Muda Hassim's views and mine; and during this conversation, it was evident they were looking to me as a friend.

"At daylight a boat from the *sultan* arrived to carry up the letters; but Budrudeen and his brother resolved to proceed first, in order to make sure of an honourable reception for the chop. At 7 o'clock there was a stir. I saw them over the side with delight, and gave them a salute with pleasure. Breakfast done, I was too happy to lie down, and slept till past midday, having then only to wait for Budrudeen's return.

"*23rd.*—Budrudeen came at 3 p.m., bringing with him good news of the most favourable reception from all parties, all wishing for reconciliation and the return of Muda Hassim. Tomorrow, boats are to come for the letters, which are to be conveyed in state. The day following I am to go up, and am likewise to be received in all honourable form.

"*24th.*—At 7 a.m. the state-boat, a shabby concern, decorated with yellow flags, arrived, and at eight the letters were borne away under a salute. Thus we had a second time the satisfaction of getting rid of the mob at an early hour.

"*25th.*—At 9½ a.m. I started with Williamson in the gig, with the long-boat in company, carrying the presents. On approaching the town, before the ebb had run long, it appeared to be a very Venice of hovels, a river Cybele rising from the water. For those who like it, the locality is not ill chosen. The hills recede from the river, and form an amphitheatre; and several other rivers or streams flowing in, cause a muddy deposit, on which the houses are built. At high water they are surrounded; at low water stand on a sheet of mud. On nearing it, we were encompassed by boats which preceded and followed us, and we passed the floating market, where women, wearing immense hats of palm-leaves, sell all sorts of edibles, balanced in their little canoes, now giving a paddle, now making a bargain, and dropping down with the tide, and again regaining their place when the bargain is finished.

"The first impression of the town is miserable. The houses are crowded and numerous, and even the palace does not present a more captivating aspect, for, though large, it is as incommodious as the worst. Our presentation was exactly similar to that of our first meeting with Muda Hassim at Sarawak, only the crowd was much greater. We had been seated but a few minutes when Pangeran Usop arrived, and directly afterward the *sultan*. He gave us tea, leaf-cigars, and *sirih*, and, in short, showed us every attention; and what was best of all did not keep us very long. Our apartment was partitioned off from the public hall, a dark-looking place, but furnished with a table brought by us, and three rickety chairs, beside mattresses and plenty of mats. We were kept up nearly all night, which, after the fatigues of the day, was hard upon us.

"Further observation confirmed us in the opinion that the town itself is miserable, and its locality on the mud fitted only for frogs or natives; but there is a level dry plain above the entrance of the Kiangi River, admirably suited for a European settlement; and across the Kiangi is swelling ground, where the residents might find delightful spots for their country-houses. The greatest annoyance to a stranger is the noisome smell of the mud when uncovered; and all plated or silver articles, even in the course of one night, get black and discoloured. The inhabitants I shall estimate moderately at 10,000, and the Kadien population are numerous amid the hills.

"*27th.*—Our objects in coming to Borneo were threefold. Firstly, to effect a reconciliation between the *sultan* and Muda Hassim; secondly, to gain the *sultan's* approval and signature to my holding Sarawak; and thirdly, to release the Kleeses [Hindoostanees] of the shipwrecked vessels, the *Sultana* and *Lord Melbourne*. The first object was gained at once, as the sultan seemed really overjoyed at being good friends with his uncle; and Pangeran Usop, from whom we anticipated difficulty, stepped forward directly to aid us while Pangeran Mumin was not averse.

"I will not now stop to sketch the characters of these worthies, as

I shall hereafter have a better knowledge of them; but I may remark, *en passant*, that it was evident, even to my inexperience, that no two of them were on good terms, and all probably united in a feeling that Muda Hassim's return would be a personal as well as public advantage. The other principal *pangerans*, namely, Tizudeen (the *sultan's* natural brother), Kurmaindar (the father of the country), Bahar (the *rajah's* brother-in-law), Tizudeen second (the *rajah's* natural brother), were all for Muda Hassim; and the population, as far as I could learn, decidedly desirous of his being restored to them.

"Each day I had several interviews with the *sultan*, in his *surow* or private room; and he assured me of his fondness for Muda Hassim, his wish to have him near him again, and the great benefit it would be. Moreover, he was pleased to express great personal regard for me; and every five minutes I had to swear 'eternal friendship,' while he, clasping my hand, kept repeating, 'amigo suya,' 'amigo suya,' meaning, *my* friend, *my* friend. At the same time he professed great readiness to give me Sarawak—inquired the amount of revenue—seemed satisfied, and said, 'I wish you to be there; I do not wish anybody else; you are my *amigo*, and it is nobody's business but mine; the country is mine, and if I please to give you all, I can.' His Majesty is very proud of displaying his very small smattering of Spanish or Portuguese; and almost all the higher people having acquired a few words, shows there must have been a communication at no very distant date. I was also warned not to care for any of the other *pangerans*,—not, indeed, to have anything to say to them.

"With this advice I took the liberty to dispense; and sent to Pangerans Mumin and Usop to intimate my wish to visit them. The former pleaded that his house was unfit to receive me; but the latter immediately sent a most polite message, that any time, either by day or night, he should be happy to see me; and accordingly I went. The house *and style* are the best in Borneo. I was politely and kindly greeted; and I soon found that I was with a man of sense and quickness. There was a little diplomacy at first on his part; but as I proceeded direct to my object, he at once laid it aside. In fact, candour is the basis of our right influence with the natives; and as I desired to make Pangeran Usop my friend, I went candidly to work, and immediately told him all that I had already told the *sultan*.

"The amount of my conversation was as follows: The first topic being the anticipated visit of the English, 'Were the English coming?' 'Was Mr. Bonham coming?' were the first questions; and 'With what intent?' I replied, that the English were certainly coming, but with no evil intentions; that it was true they were offended by the ill usage the captain and people of the *Sultana* had met with; yet that I had endeavoured to put it in the best light, and had urged that a friendly communication for the future was better than a retrospect which might give rise to unpleasant feelings: I was sure that the English desired a friendly intercourse; and I hoped, though I could not say, that they would look to the future, and not to the past. I had, I added, no authority; but my friendship for the *sultan* induced me to inform him what I had heard abroad. When Mr. Bonham came, he would be able to tell them all; but I could say now that I thought he would demand a treaty between Singapore and Borneo for the mutual protection of trade, and the care of individuals of each nation who were shipwrecked or otherwise sought protection at either place.

"On the whole, it is certain that the feelings of Borneo are decidedly friendly, and equally certain that the persons of influence will receive us in their warmest manner, and grant us everything, if we resort only to measures of conciliation. It never can be too often repeated, that conciliation is the only policy with Malays, and particularly the Borneons, who have very vague and confused ideas of our power. A harsh truth, a peremptory demand, they have never heard in their lives, and they will not hear it for the first time and remain friendly; for all who have the least acquaintance with the native character know their acute sense of false shame. To demand, therefore, of the chief here to acknowledge our superiority would, I am sure, be met with a haughty refusal. In a few years, if we proceed mildly to establish a beneficial influence, they will fall into our views without reserve; for, as I have often before stated, their government is in the last stage of destruction and decay.

"The reconciliation of Muda Hassim was soon complete; and as to the Kleeses of the Lord Melbourne, twenty in number, they were at once surrendered to me, with a request that I would forward them to Singapore as quickly as I could. The boat of the *Lord Melbourne* was likewise given to me. I had some scruples about three Kleeses of the *Sultana*, who had been sold at Malludu Bay, bought there by an Arab *seriff*, and brought here. By all their laws and customs they were his slaves, purchased at a distance, and, as I had no right to claim them (supposing even that to be just), and was resolved not to leave them in captivity, I paid a fair price for them at the rate of twenty-five dollars per man. I regret to add, there is one other man not in the place; and one is gone to Tutorga—about a day's journey hence.

"*28th.*—I may here draw a brief sketch of the principal personages of this most primitive court, beginning with its worthy head, the sultan.

"The *sultan* is a man past fifty years of age, short and puffy in person, with a countenance which expresses very obviously the imbecility of his mind. His right hand is garnished with an extra diminutive thumb, the natural member being crooked and distorted. His mind, indexed by his face, seems to be a chaos of confusion; without acuteness, without dignity, and without good sense. He can neither read nor write; is guided by the last speaker; and his advisers, as might be expected, are of the lower order, and mischievous from their ignorance and their greediness. He is always talking, and generally joking; and the most serious subjects never meet with five minutes' consecutive attention. The favourable side of his character is, that he is good-tempered and good-natured; by no means cruel; and, in a certain way, generous, though rapacious to a high degree. His rapacity, indeed, is carried to such an excess as to astonish a European, and is evinced in a thousand mean ways.

"The presents I made him were unquestionably handsome; but he was not content without begging from me the share I had reserved for the other *pangerans*; and afterward, through Mr. Williamson, solicited more trifles, such as sugar, penknives, and the like. To crown all, he was incessantly asking what was left in the vessel; and when told the truth,—that I was stripped as bare as a tree in winter,—he frequently returned to the charge. In the middle of the night, when our boat came up with some gifts for him, he slipped out his royal person, that he might see what packages there were. I must say, however, that this was not intended for me to know; and, personally, he did not behave very ill toward me, only dunning me occasionally. In regard to the Sarawak revenue, he was eager in his inquiries; and was very ready, on the strength of his thousand dollars, and my generosity, to give me a list of things which amounted to 10,000 dollars in value.

"I may note one other feature which marks the man. He requested, as the greatest favour,—he urged, with the earnestness of a child,—that I would send back the schooner before the month *Ramban* (*Ramadan* of the Turks); remarking, 'What shall I do during the fast without soft sugar and dates?' What effect the exaggerated promises of Mr. de Souza must have had on such a temper, may readily be imagined; and what the evil influence of such a prince on the country, needs not be stated; for, like other fools, he is difficult to guide where the object is right, and facile whenever it promises any immediate advantage. I will only add, that during my intercourse of six days, he has given me the impression that he is not in his right mind; and, at any rate, that flattery and bad counsel have deprived him of the little wit he might probably originally have possessed.

"Of Pangeran Mumin, the De Gadong and the *sultan's* son-in-law, I know little; and he is, in secret, a most determined opposer of mine; but I believe he, as well as most, is desirous of being good friends with the English, and will readily listen to any overtures which promise increase of trade. He seemed to me a shrewd, cunning man, fit for a *Nakoda*.

"Pangeran Usop is a man of middle age, short, active, and intelligent, and, I may add, ambitious. Pangeran Muda Hassim will throw himself into the arms of the English, from his partiality, and from the hope of a better order of things, and the eventual succession to the throne, to which he stands next,—the present sultan having no legitimate children.

"Two of my objects were thus achieved at once; and the Kleeses (twenty-three) were, much to their satisfaction, dispatched to the vessel in the Melbourne's gig. My own affair of Sarawak meets with some opposition from Mumin, who is decidedly friendly to Macota. The sultan, however, is steady to me, gabbles daily and hourly of his intentions; and Pangeran Usop likewise pushes on my suit with his influence, at the same time giving me this one piece of good advice, *viz.* that Muda Hassim must be induced to return to Borneo, for that two persons (Muda Hassim and myself) cannot govern together; and he added, 'If Muda Hassim returns, you will have a fine trade at Sarawak; but while he is there, no native *prahus* will visit the place.' This is true: I have no fear of ultimate success in my suit; but delay is formidable, and I have already intimated that I propose making my *congé* on the 2nd of August.

"*30th.*—I have little more to add about Borneo, save my plaint against our dungeon, though the said dungeon be honourably situated behind the throne, and within the royal apartments. Just below the town are several rills of the finest water; and the natives report that they issue from a small but deep lake at a very short distance. Beneath one of these spouts we each evening took a most delicious bath in water as cold as it is limpid. I am no great bustler at any time; but since being here, I have purposely abstained from all manifestation of curiosity, and never desired or requested to see much; it rouses suspicion, and suspicion rouses distrust, and distrust draws the *kris*. On the contrary, by being backward at first, you become subsequently a sort of domesticated animal, and privileged to use your eyes and limbs. Most Europeans do themselves great injury by searching the mountains and the waters, breaking the rocks, shooting the birds, and gathering the plants. The natives can never believe they would take so much trouble without being well paid by the value of the treasures found, or employed by the East India Company to espy their land, in order that the said company might seize it at their convenience.

"*31st.*—A conclave of *pangerans*, when it was finally resolved to grant the country of Sarawak to me as *rajah* or governor.

"*August 1st,* 1842.—An important day in my history, and I hope one which will be marked with a white stone in the annals of Sarawak. The letters to Muda Hassim being finished and signed, the contract giving me the government of Sarawak came under discussion, and was likewise completed by ten at night, signed, sealed, and witnessed. Thus I have gained every object for which I came to Borneo; and tomorrow, God willing, I take my leave.

"The miserable state of Borneo I have already mentioned; and it is now a saying of the Balagnini pirates, that '*it is difficult to catch fish, but easy to catch Borneons.*' Externally and internally they are equally wretched, and torn by factions; yet, on the whole, I am not inclined to judge harshly of the poorer order of them. They are a good-tempered, very hospitable, and unwarlike people, the victims of their *rajahs*; the oppressed, but not the oppressors. In this character, however, I do not reckon the *pangerans* and their followers. It is from these latter that Europeans take their estimate of the people generally, and consequently truly account them, from that standard, to be a wretched sample of humanity—mean, thievish, arrogant, insolent, and ready for any wickedness. The *pangerans* themselves are only a step better: but even here I must make a little allowance; for I believe their crimes arise more from their poverty and impunity than from any inherent viciousness.

"*3rd.*—The Pangerans Budrudeen and Marsale, and a host more, came on board this night, and kept us up as usual.

"*4th.*—Another mob arrived the middle of last night. I retreated from them, being far from well, and got some sleep. At 2 p.m. the letters came on board; were received with honours; and as soon as we could rid ourselves of our troublesome visitors, we dropped outside

Tanjong Sapo, and sailed the following day.

"The Kleeses sold at Malludu were brought from Ambun, and reported to the authorities that a European woman was detained there. I made particular inquires of the Borneon *pangerans*, and they said they had always understood that such was the case. Unhappy lady, if she be a lady! Is it a compassionate part to release her after many years of captivity?

"*14th.*—Anchored off the Morotaba, having had nothing but calms, light winds, and squalls.

"*15th.*—Got part of the way up the river, and at 8 p.m. dropped our anchor; and in about an hour later two boats started for Sarawak. The night was moonlight, with a cold breeze; and, after a pleasant pull, we arrived, and created as much sensation as we could desire. But it was better, and I was gratified with the intelligence that everything had gone on well during our absence. At break of day I went, fagged, to bed. So ended our mission to Borneo.

"On the evening of the 18th the *sultan's* letters were produced in all the state which could possibly be attained. On their arrival they were received and brought up amid large wax torches, and the person who was to read them was stationed on a raised platform; standing below him was the *rajah*, with a sabre in his hand; in front of the *rajah* was his brother, Pangeran Jaffer, with a tremendous *kempilan* drawn; and around were the other brothers and myself, all standing—the rest of the company being seated. The letters were then read, the last one appointing me to hold the government of Sarawak. After this the *rajah* descended, and said aloud, 'If any one present disowns or contests the *sultan's* appointment, let him now declare.' All were silent. He next turned to the Patingis, and asked them; they were obedient to the will of the *sultan*.

"Then came the other *pangerans*—'Is there any *pangeran* or any young *rajah* that contests the question? Pangeran Der Macota, what do you say?' Macota expressed his willingness to obey. One or two other obnoxious *pangerans* who had always opposed themselves to me were each in turn challenged, and forced to promise obedience. The *rajah* then waved his sword, and with a loud voice exclaimed, 'Whoever he is that disobeys the *sultan's* mandate now received, I will separate his skull;' at the moment some ten of his brothers jumped from the verandah, and, drawing their long *krisses*, began to flourish and dance about, thrusting close to Macota, striking the pillar above his head, pointing their weapons at his breast.

"This *amusement*, the violence of motion, the freedom from restraint, this explosion of a long pent-up animosity, roused all their passions; and had Macota, through an excess of fear or an excess of bravery, started up, he would have been slain, and other blood would have been spilt. But he was quiet, with his face pale and subdued, and, as shortly as decency would permit after the riot had subsided, took his leave. This scene is a custom with them; the only exception to which was, that it was pointed so directly at Macota. I was glad, at any rate, that all had gone off without bloodshed.

"*22nd.*—I found that though matters had been quiet during my absence, repeated efforts had been made to disturb the country. First, it was positively stated and industriously circulated that I was certain to be killed in Borneo; and next a report was propagated that 6000 Chinese were on their march from Sambas, with evil intentions. These rumours did not serve any object, and my return has set them at rest; but I regretted to hear that the Singè Dyaks had, contrary to my positive prohibition, killed a Dyak of Sanpro.

"Other affairs are prosperous. Macota is to be sent out of the country, and the *rajah* himself talks of returning to Borneo; and both these events will please me greatly.

"*January 1st,* 1843.—Another year passed and gone; a year, with all its anxieties, its troubles, its dangers, upon which I can look back with satisfaction—a year in which I have been usefully employed in doing good to others.

"Since I last wrote, the Dyaks have been quiet, settled, and improving; the Chinese advancing toward prosperity; and the Sarawak people, wonderfully contented and industrious, relieved from oppression, and fields of labour allowed them.

"Justice I have executed with an unflinching hand; and the amount of crime is certainly small—the petty swindling very great.

"The month of January was a dreary month. A sick man in the house, and very little medicine; and what was worse, the *Royalist* did not make her appearance. Yet both these troubles disappeared nearly together; for M'Kenzie got well, and the schooner, bringing with her Dr. Treacher, arrived. She had been detained undergoing some necessary repairs. The accession of a medical man is particularly valuable.

"I have nothing to say about the country, except that I have given Pangeran Macota orders to leave, which he is obeying in as far as preparing his boat; and I hope that in six weeks we shall be rid of his cunning and diabolically intriguing presence.

"The Rajah Muda Hassim, his brothers, and the tag-rag following, I also hope soon to be rid of; for although they behave far better than they did at first, it is an evil to have wheel within wheel; and these young *rajahs* of course expect, and are accustomed to, a license which I will not allow.

"Budrudeen is an exception—a striking and wonderful instance of the force of good sense over evil education.

"The rest of the people go on well; the time revolves quietly; and the Dyaks, as well as the Malays and Chinese, enjoy the inestimable blessing of peace and security. At intervals a cloud threatens the serenity of our political atmosphere; but it speedily blows over. However, all is well and safe; and so safe that I have resolved to proceed in person to Singapore.

"My motives for going are various; but I hope to do good, to excite interest, and make friends; and I can find no season like the present for my absence. It is now two years since I left Singapore, 'the boundary of civilization.' I have been out of the civilized world, living in a *demi*-civilized state, peaceably, innocently, and usefully.

"*Feb. 8th.*—After ten days' delay at the mouth of the river, got out."

## CHAPTER 15

# Return Royal Visit to the Dido

I have now followed Mr. Brooke's *journal* up to the time of our first meeting at Singapore, and his accompanying me to Sarawak, and have no remarks of my own to offer that could add in the slightest degree to its interest; happily, none such are needed. I had not yet seen my friend's journal when I arrived at Sarawak, nor was it until sometime after that I by degrees learned the progress of his infant government from its commencement. It was with unfeigned pleasure I then found that, while performing my duty in the suppression of piracy, I was, at the same time, rendering the greatest assistance and support to an individual in his praiseworthy, novel, and important position.

I had long felt a desire to explore the Island of Borneo, which the few travellers who have called there describe as not only one of the largest and most fertile in the world, but one of the most productive in gold and diamonds, and other rich minerals and ores; one from which the finest camphor known is brought into merchandise, and which is undoubtedly capable of supplying every kind of valuable spice, and articles of universal traffic and consumption. Yet, with all these capabilities and inducements to tempt the energetic spirit of trade, the internal condition of the country, and the dangers which beset its coasts, have hitherto prevented the interior from being explored by Europeans; and to prove how little we are acquainted even with its shores, I actually sailed by the best Admiralty chart eighty miles inland, and over the tops of mountains!

*May 4th*, 1843.—Passed through the Tambelans, a beautiful group of between 100 and 150 small islands. They are very extensive, and but thinly inhabited. There is good anchorage near some of them; but we had nothing less than twenty fathoms. They are placed so close together that, after passing the first, we were to all appearance completely land-locked in a magnificent and capacious harbour. The following morning we anchored off the mouth of the Sambas River, and sent the boats away to examine the creeks, islands, and rivers along the coast for traces of pirates—which were discovered by the remains of their fires on different parts, although no clew could be obtained as to the direction in which they had gone.

On the morning of the 8th I again sent the *pinnace* and two cutters, Mr. Partridge, Messrs. D'Aeth and Jenkins, with a week's provisions, the whole under the command of Lieutenant Wilmot Horton, Mr. Brooke kindly offering his assistance, which, from his knowledge of the Malay language, as well as of the kind of vessels used by the pirates, was thankfully accepted. I directed them to proceed to the Island of Marundum, and, after visiting the South Natunas, to rejoin the *Dido* at Sarawak. In the mean time I proceeded leisurely along the coast, anchoring where convenient, and finding regular soundings all the way in from four to ten fathoms: weather remarkably fine, and water smooth.

On the morning of the 9th, on rounding Tanjong Datu, we opened suddenly on a suspicious-looking boat, which, on making us out, ran for a small, deep bay formed by Cape Datu and the next point to the eastward. Standing a little further on, we discovered a second large boat in the offing, which likewise stood in shore, and afterward a third at the bottom of the bay. From the description I had received, I easily made these out to be Illanuns, an enterprising tribe of pirates, of whose daring adventures I had heard much. They inhabit a small cluster of islands off the N.E. coast of Borneo, and go out in large fleets every year to look for *prahus* bound to Singapore or the Straits; and, after capturing the vessels, reduce their crews to slavery. It is of a cruel nature; for Mr. Brooke observes:

> Nor is the slavery of that mild description which is often attributed to the Asiatics; for these victims are bound for months, and crowded in the bottom of the pirate vessels, where they suffer all the miseries which could be inflicted on board an African slaver.

Having fairly pinned these worthies into a corner, and knowing that the only two small boats I had left on board would stand no chance with them in pulling, to make sure of my prizes I loaded the two foremost guns on each side, and, having no proper chart of the coast, proceeded under easy sail, feeling my way into the bay with the lead. When just within musket-range, I let go the anchor, which was no sooner done than the three boats commenced making a move. I thought at first they were coming alongside to sue for pardon and peace; and my astonishment was great when I discovered that nothing was further from their intention.

One pulled away, close in shore, to the eastward, and the other two to the westward. They were rowed by about forty oars each, and appeared, from their swiftness, to be flying, and that, too, from under my very nose; and what rendered it still more ridiculous and disagreeable, owing to a strong ebb tide, the ship remained exactly in a position that no gun could be brought to bear on either side. The dingy and jolly-boat gave chase; but the pirates had the start, and it was useless; for although a few men were seen to drop from their oars in consequence of our fire of musketry from the forecastle, still their pace never slackened; and when they did come within the bearing of our guns, which they were obliged to do for a minute or two while rounding the points that formed the bay, though our thirty-two pound shot fell thickly about their heads, frequently dashing the spray all over them, not a man flinched from his oar.

We could not help admiring their plan of escape, and the gallant manner in which it was effected. I saw that it would be quite unavailing to attempt to catch the boats that had pulled to windward; but we lost no time in slipping our cable and making all sail in chase of the one that had gone to leeward. But the "artful dodger" was still too fast for us: we lost sight of him at dusk, close off the mouth of a river, up which, however, I do not think he went; for our two boats were there very shortly after him; and although they searched all night and next morning, they could discover no traces of the fugitive. Besides, these pirates have no friends among the inhabitants of the province of Sarawak who would have screened them from us; on the contrary, they would have put them to death if once in their power. I certainly never made so sure of anything in my life as of capturing the three *prahus* after I had seen them safe at the bottom of the little bay at Tanjong Datu: but *there is many a slip between the cup and the lip.*

We returned the following day to pick up the anchor and cable, and observed that it was a place well adapted as a rendezvous for pirates. The bay is studded with rocks; and, to my horror, I found that I had run Her Majesty's ship *Dido* inside two that were a-wash at low water! A mountain stream of most delicious water runs into the bay between two rocks, and the coast abounds with oysters.

On the 13th the *Dido* anchored off Tanjong Poe, outside the bar at the entrance of the river leading to Mr. Brooke's residence and seat of government, at the town of Sarawak, situated about twenty-four miles up. At half-tide on the following morning we crossed the bar, carrying no less than three and a half fathoms, and entered the beautiful river of Morotaba, which we ran up for the first fifteen miles under all sail, with a fresh, leading breeze. The *Dido* was the first square-rigged vessel that had ever entered those waters. We came to at the junction river which unites the two principal entrances to the Sarawak.

In the evening our boats returned on board from their expedition, having reached Sarawak the day previous by the western entrance. On leaving the *Dido*, on the morning of the 8th, they proceeded to the Island of Marundum, a favourite rendezvous for pirates, where they came on a fleet of the Illanum tribe, who, however, did not give them an opportunity of closing; but, cutting their *sampans* adrift, made a precipitate flight, opening fire as they ran out on the opposite side of a small bay, in which they had been watering and refitting. This, of course, led to a very exciting chase, with a running fire kept up on both sides; but the distance was too great for the range of the guns on either side; and the pirates, who, in addition to sailing well, were propelled by from forty to sixty oars each, made their escape.

It was not until nearly hull-down that they (probably out of bravado) ceased to fire their stern guns. As they went in the direction of the Natunas, our boats steered for those islands, and anchored under the south end of one of them. At daylight next morning, although in three fathoms water, the *pinnace*, owing to the great rise and fall of tide, grounded on a coral reef, and Lieutenant Horton and Mr. Brooke proceeded in one of the cutters to reconnoitre. As they neared the s.w. point, they were met by six *prahus*, beating their *tomtoms* as they advanced, and making every demonstration of fighting. Lieutenant Horton judiciously turned to rejoin the other boats; and the *pinnace* having, fortunately, just then floated, he formed his little squadron into line abreast, cleared for action, and prepared to meet his formidable-looking antagonists.

Mr. Brooke, however, whose eye had been accustomed to the cut and rig of all the boats in these seas, discovered that those advancing were not Illanuns, and fancied there must be some mistake. The Natunas people had been trading with Sarawak, and he was intimately acquainted with a rich and powerful chief who resided on the island;

he therefore raised a white flag of truce on his spy-glass, and from the bow of the *pinnace* hailed, waved, and made all the signs he could to warn them of the danger into which they were running; but a discharge of small arms was the only reply he got. They then detached their three smallest vessels inshore, so as to command a cross-fire, and cut off the retreat of our boats; and the rest advanced, yelling, beating their *tom-toms*, and blazing away with all the confidence of victory, their shot cutting through the rigging, and splashing in the water all around.

It was an anxious moment for the *Dido's* little party. Not a word was spoken. The only gun of the *pinnace* was loaded with grape and canister, and kept pointed on the largest *prahu*. The men waited, with their muskets in hand, for permission to fire; but it was not until within pistol-range that Lieutenant Horton poured into the enemy his well-prepared dose. It instantly brought them to a halt; yet they had the temerity to exchange shots for a few minutes longer, when the largest cried for quarter, and the other five made for the shore, chased by the two cutters, and keeping up a fire to the last.

The prize taken possession of by the *pinnace* proved to be a *prahu* mounting three brass guns, with a crew of thirty-six men, belonging to the Rajah of Rhio, and which had been dispatched by that chief to collect tribute at and about the Natunas islands. They had on board ten men killed, and eleven (four of them mortally) wounded. They affected the greatest astonishment on discovering that our boats belonged to a British man-of-war, and protested that it was all a mistake; that the island had lately been plundered by the Illanun pirates, for whom they had taken us; that the rising sun was in their eyes, and that they could not make out the colours, &c.

Lieutenant Horton, thinking that their story might possibly have some foundation in truth, and taking into consideration the severe lesson they had received, directed Dr. Simpson, the assistant-surgeon, to dress their wounds; and after admonishing them to be more circumspect in future, restored them their boat, as well as the others which belonged to the island, two of them being a trifle smaller, but of the same armament as the one from Rhio, and the remaining three still smaller, carrying twelve men each, armed with spears and muskets. These had been taken possession of by the cutters after they had reached the shore and landed their killed and wounded, who were borne away from the beach so smartly by the natives that our people had not time to ascertain the number hurt.

ATTACK ON THE H.M.S. DIDO'S PARTY BY THE SIRHASSAN

The surgeon went ashore, and dressed the wounds of several of them, an act of kindness and civilization far beyond their comprehension. The natives, however, appeared to bear us no malice for the injury we had inflicted on their countrymen, but loaded our boats with fruit, goats, and everything we required. It afforded some amusement to find that among the slightly wounded was Mr. Brooke's old, wealthy, and respectable friend already alluded to, who was not a little ashamed at being recognized; but piracy is so inherent in a Malay, that few can resist the temptation when a good opportunity for plunder presents itself. The fact, which I afterward ascertained, was, that they took our boats for some coming from a wreck with whatever valuables they could collect; and their not having seen anything of the ship rather strengthened this conjecture; the excuse they made for continuing the fight after they had discovered their mistake being that they expected no quarter.[1]

*May 16th.*—We proceeded up the river twelve miles further into the interior of this interesting country, and with my friend Mr. Brooke on board, approached Sarawak, his seat of government; in the reach before you near which, and off the right bank of the river, is a long and dangerous shelf of rocks. The deep channel which lies between the bank and the rocks is not more than sixty or seventy feet wide, and required some little care in passing; but, with the exception of the flying jibboom, which got nipped off in the branch of a magnificent overhanging tree, we anchored without accident in six fathoms water, and greatly astonished the natives with a royal salute in honour of Muda Hassim, the Rajah of Borneo. During the whole morning large boats, some carrying as many as two hundred people, had been coming down the river to hail Mr. Brooke's return; and one of the greatest gratifications I had was in witnessing the undisguised delight, mingled with gratitude and respect, with which each head man welcomed their newly-elected ruler back to his adopted country.

Although many of the Malay chiefs had every reason to expect that in the *Dido* they saw the means by which their misdeeds were to be punished, they showed their confidence in Mr. Brooke by bringing their children with them—a sign peculiar to the Malay. The scene was both novel and exciting; presenting to us, just anchored in a large

---

1. I am happy to say that the Lords of the Admiralty have since been pleased to promote Lieutenant Wilmot Horton and Mr. W. L. Partridge, mate, who commanded the *pinnace*, for their gallantry on this occasion.—H. K.

fresh-water river, and surrounded by a densely-wooded jungle, the whole surface of the water covered with canoes and boats dressed out with their various-coloured silken flags, filled with natives beating their tom-toms, and playing on their wild and not unpleasant-sounding wind-instruments, with the occasional discharge of firearms. To them it must have been equally striking and extraordinary (as few of them had ever seen any larger vessel than their own war-boats, or a European, until Mr. Brooke's arrival) to witness the *Dido* anchored almost in the centre of their town, her mast-heads towering above the highest trees of their jungle; the loud report of her heavy two-and-thirty pounder guns, and the running aloft, to furl sails, of 150 seamen, in their clean white dresses, and with the band playing, all which helped to make an impression that will not easily be forgotten at Sarawak.

I was anxious that Mr. Brooke should land with all the honours due to so important a personage, which he accordingly did, under a salute. The next business was my visit of ceremony to the *rajah*, which was great fun, though conducted in the most imposing manner. The band, and the marines, as a guard, having landed, we (the officers) all assembled at Mr. Brooke's house, where, having made ourselves as formidable as we could with swords and cocked hats, we marched in procession to the royal residence, His Majesty having sent one of his brothers, who led me by the hand into his presence. The palace was a long, low shed, built on piles, to which we ascended by a ladder. The audience-chamber was hung with red and yellow silk curtains, and round the back and one side of the platform occupied by the *rajah* were ranged his ministers, warriors, and men-at-arms, bearing spears, swords, shields, and other warlike weapons.

Opposite to them were drawn up our royal marines, the contrast between the two body-guards being very amusing. Muda Hassim is a wretched-looking, little man; still there was a courteous and gentle manner about him that prepossessed us in his favour, and made us feel that we were before an individual who had been accustomed to command. We took our seats in a semicircle, on chairs provided for the occasion, and smoked cigars and drank tea. His majesty chewed his *sirih*-leaf and betel-nut, seated with one leg crossed under him, and playing with his toes. Very little is ever said during these audiences, so we sat staring at one another for half an hour with mutual astonishment; and, after the usual compliments of wishing our friendship might last as long as the moon, and my having offered him the *Dido*

The rajah's palace

and everything else that did not belong to me in exchange for his house, we took our leave.

*May 19th.*—This was the day fixed for the *rajah's* visit to the *Dido*, about which he appeared very anxious, although he had seldom been known to go beyond his own threshold. For this ceremony all the boats, guns, tom-toms, flags, and population were put in requisition; and the procession to the ship was a very gorgeous and amusing spectacle. We received him on board with a royal salute. He brought in his train a whole tribe of natural brothers. His guards and followers were strange enough, and far too numerous to be admitted on the *Dido's* deck, so that as soon as a sufficient number had scrambled on board, the sentry had orders to prevent any more from crowding in; but whether, in so doing, the most important personages of the realm were kept out, we did not ascertain.

One fellow succeeded in obtaining a footing with a large yellow silk canopy, a corner of which having run into the eye of one of the midshipmen, the bearer missed his footing, and down came the whole concern—as I was informed, by *accident!* The party assembled in my cabin, and the remarks were few, nor did they manifest great astonishment at anything. In fact, a Malay never allows himself to be taken by surprise. I believe, however, the *rajah* did not think much of my veracity, when I informed him that this was not the largest ship belonging to Her Britannic Majesty, and that she had several mounting upward of 100 guns, though he admitted that he had seen a grander sight than any of his ancestors.

There was much distress depicted in the royal countenance during his visit which I afterward ascertained was owing to his having been informed that he must not spit in my cabin. On leaving the ship, whether the cherry brandy he had taken made him forget the directions he had received, I do not know, but he squirted a mouthful of red betel-nut juice over the white deck, and then had the temerity to hold out his hand to the first lieutenant, who hastily applied to him the style (not royal) of "a dirty beast," which not understanding, he smiled graciously, taking it as some compliment peculiar to the English.

This farce over, I had now some time to look about me, and to refit my ship in one of the prettiest spots on earth, and as unlike a dockyard as anything could be.

Mr. Brooke's then residence, although equally rude in structure with the abodes of the natives, was not without its English comforts of sofas, chairs, and bedsteads. It was larger than any of the others, but being, like them, built on piles, we had to mount a ladder to get into it. It was situated on the same side of the river (the right bank), next to, but rather in the rear of, the *rajah's* palace, with a clear space of about 150 yards between the back and the edge of the jungle. It was surrounded by palisades and a ditch, forming a protection to sheep, goats, pigeons, cats, poultry, geese, monkeys, dogs, ducks, and, occasionally, bullocks.

The house consisted of but one floor. A large room in the centre, neatly ornamented with every description of firearms, in admirable order and ready for use, served as an audience and mess-room; and the various apartments round it as bed-rooms, most of them comfortably furnished with matted floors, easy chairs, pictures, and books, with much more taste and attention to comfort than bachelors usually display. In one corner of the square formed by the palisades were the kitchen and offices. The Europeans with Mr. Brooke consisted of Mr. Douglas, formerly in the navy, a clever young surgeon, and a gentleman of the name of Williamson, who, being master of the native language, as well as active and intelligent, made an excellent prime minister.

Besides these were two others, who came out in the yacht, one an old man-of-war's man, who kept the arms in first-rate condition, and another worthy character, who answered to the name of Charley, and took care of the accounts and charge of everything. These were attended by servants of different nations. The cooking establishment was perfect, and the utmost harmony prevailed. The great feeding-time was at sunset, when Mr. Brooke took his seat at the head of the table, and all the establishment, as in days of yore, seated themselves according to their respective grades. This hospitable board was open to all the officers of the *Dido*; and many a jovial evening we spent there.

All Mr. Brooke's party were characters—all had travelled; and never did a minute flag for want of some entertaining anecdote, good story, or song, to pass away the time; and it was while smoking our cigars in the evening that the natives, as well as the Chinese who had become settlers, used to drop in, and, after creeping up according to their custom, and touching the hand of their European *rajah*, retire to the further end of the room, and squat down upon their haunches, remain a couple of hours without uttering a word, and then creep out again. I have seen sixty or seventy of an evening come in and make this sort of *salaam*. All the Malays were armed; and it is reckoned an insult for one of them to appear before a *rajah* without his *kris*. I could not help remarking the manly, independent bearing of the half-savage and nearly naked mountain Dyak compared with the sneaking deportment of the Malay.

The following little adventure was told me during my stay at Sarawak, by Dr. Treacher, who had lately joined Mr. Brooke, his former medical attendant having returned to England. It appears that Dr. Treacher received a message by a confidential slave that one of the ladies of Macota's *harem* desired an interview, appointing a secluded spot in the jungle as the rendezvous. The doctor, being aware of his own good looks, fancied he had made a conquest, and, having got himself up as showily as he could, was there at the appointed time. He described the poor girl as both young and pretty, but with a dignified and determined look, which at once convinced him that she was moved to take so dangerous a step by some deeper feeling than that of a mere fancy for his person.

She complained of the ill treatment she had received from Macota, and the miserable life she led, and avowed that her firm resolve was to destroy (not herself, gentle creature! but) him; for which purpose she wanted a small portion of arsenic. It was a disappointment that he could not comply with her request; so they parted—he full of pity and love for her, and she, in all probability, full of contempt for a man who felt for her wrongs, but would not aid in the very simple means she had proposed for redressing them.

While at Singapore, Mr. Whitehead had kindly offered to allow his yacht, the *Emily*, a schooner of about fifty tons, with a native crew, to bring our letters to Borneo, on the arrival at Singapore of the mail from England. About the time she was expected, I thought it advisable to send a boat to cruise in the vicinity of Cape Datu, in case of her falling in with any of these piratical gentry. The *Dido's* largest boat, the *pinnace*, being under repair, Mr. Brooke lent a large boat which he had had built by the natives at Sarawak, and called the *Jolly Bachelor*. Having fitted her with a brass six-pounder long gun, with a volunteer crew of a mate, two midshipmen, six marines, and twelve seamen, and a fortnight's provisions, I dispatched her under the command of the second lieutenant, Mr. Hunt; Mr. Douglas, speaking the Malayan language, likewise volunteered his services.

One evening, after they had been about six days absent, while we were at dinner, young Douglas made his appearance, bearing in his arms the captured colours of an Illanun pirate. It appears that the day after they had got outside they observed three boats a long way in the offing, to which they gave chase, but soon lost sight of them, owing to their superior sailing. They, however, appeared a second and a third time, after dark, but without the *Jolly Bachelor* being able to get near them; and it now being late, and the crew both fatigued and hungry, they pulled inshore, lighted a fire, cooked their provisions, and then hauled the boat out to her grapnel, near some rocks, for the night; lying down to rest with their arms by their sides, and muskets round the mast, ready loaded.

Having also placed sentries and lookout men, and appointed an officer of the watch, they one and all (sentries included, I suppose), owing to the fatigues of the day, fell asleep! At about three o'clock the following morning, the moon being just about to rise, Lieutenant Hunt happening to be awake, observed a savage brandishing a *kris*, and performing his war-dance on the bit of deck, in an ecstasy of delight, thinking, in all probability, of the ease with which he had got possession of a fine trading-boat, and calculating the cargo of slaves he had to sell, but little dreaming of the hornets' nest into which he had fallen. Lieutenant Hunt's round face meeting the light of the rising moon, without a turban surmounting it, was the first notice the pirate had of his mistake.

He immediately plunged overboard; and before Lieutenant Hunt had sufficiently recovered his astonishment to know whether he was dreaming or not, or to rouse his crew up, a discharge from three or four cannon within a few yards, and the cutting through the rigging by the various missiles with which the guns were loaded, soon convinced him there was no mistake. It was as well the men were still lying down when this discharge took place, as not one of them was hurt; but on jumping to their legs, they found themselves closely pressed by two large war-*prahus*, one on each bow. To return the fire, cut the cable, man the oars, and back astern to gain room, was the work of a minute; but now came the tug of war; it was a case of life and death.

Our men fought as British sailors ought to do; quarter was not expected on either side; and the quick and deadly aim of the marines prevented the pirates from reloading their guns. The Illanun *prahus* are built with strong bulwarks or barricades, grape-shot proof, across the fore part of the boat, through which ports are formed for working the guns; these bulwarks had to be cut away by round shot from the *Jolly Bachelor* before the musketry could bear effectually. This done, the grape and canister told with fearful execution.

In the meantime, the *prahus* had been pressing forward to board, while the *Jolly Bachelor* backed astern; but, as soon as this service was achieved, our men dropped their oars, and, seizing their muskets, dashed on: the work was sharp, but short, and the slaughter great. While one pirate boat was sinking, and an effort made to secure her, the other effected her escape by rounding the point of rocks, where a third and larger *prahu*, hitherto unseen, came to her assistance, and putting fresh hands on board, and taking her in tow, succeeded in getting off, although chased by the *Jolly Bachelor*, after setting fire to the crippled prize, which blew up and sunk before the conquerors got back to the scene of action.

While there, a man swam off to them from the shore, who proved to be one of the captured slaves, and had made his escape by leaping overboard during the fight. The three *prahus* were the same Illanun pirates we had so suddenly come upon off Cape Datu in the *Dido*, and they belonged to the same fleet that Lieutenant Horton had chased off the Island of Marundum. The slave prisoner had been seized, with a companion, in a small fishing canoe, off Borneo Proper; his companion suffered in the general slaughter. The sight that presented itself on our people boarding the captured boat must indeed have been a frightful one.

None of the pirates waited on board for even the chance of receiving either quarter or mercy, but all those capable of moving had thrown themselves into the water. In addition to the killed, some lying across the thwarts, with their oars in their hands, at the bottom of the *prahu*, in which there was about three feet of blood and water, were seen protruding the mangled remains of eighteen or twenty bodies.

During my last expedition I fell in with a slave belonging to a Malay chief, one of our allies, who informed us that he likewise had been a prisoner, and pulled an oar in one of the two *prahus* that attacked the *Jolly Bachelor*; that none of the crew of the captured *prahu* reached the shore alive, with the exception of the lad that swam off to our people; and that there were so few who survived in the second *prahu*, that, having separated from their consort during the night, the slaves, fifteen in number, rose and put to death the remaining pirates, and then ran the vessel into the first river they reached, which proved to be the *Kaleka*, where they were seized, and became the property of the governing *datu*; and my informant was again sold to my companion, while on a visit to his friend the *datu*. Each of the attacking *prahus* had between fifty and sixty men, including slaves, and the larger one between ninety and a hundred. The result might have been very different to our gallant but dozy *Jolly Bachelors.*

I have already mentioned the slaughter committed by the fire of the *pinnace*, under Lieutenant Horton, into the largest Malay *prahu*; and the account given of the scene which presented itself on the deck of the defeated pirate, when taken possession of, affords a striking proof of the character of these fierce rovers; resembling greatly what we read of the Norsemen and Scandinavians of early ages. Among the mortally wounded lay the young commander of the *prahu*, one of the most noble forms of the human race; his countenance handsome as the hero of Oriental romance, and his whole bearing wonderfully impressive and touching. He was shot in front and through the lungs, and his last moments were rapidly approaching. He endeavoured to speak, but the blood gushed from his mouth with the voice he vainly essayed to utter in words.

Again and again he tried, but again and again the vital fluid drowned the dying effort. He looked as if he had something of importance which he desired to communicate, and a shade of disappointment and regret passed over his brow when he felt that every essay was unavailing, and that his manly strength and daring spirit were dissolving into the dark night of death. The pitying conquerors raised him gently up, and he was seated in comparative ease, for the welling out of the blood was less distressing; but the end speedily came: he folded his arms heroically across his wounded breast, fixed his eyes upon the British seamen around, and, casting one last glance at the ocean—the theatre of his daring exploits, on which he had so often fought and triumphed—expired without a sigh.

The spectators, though not unused to tragical and sanguinary sights, were unanimous in speaking of the death of the pirate chief as the most affecting spectacle they had ever witnessed. A sculptor might have carved him as an Antinous in the mortal agonies of a Dying Gladiator.

The leaders of the piratical *prahus* are sometimes poetically addressed by their followers as *matari, i. e.,* the sun; or *bulan*, the moon; and from his superiority in every respect, physical and intellectual, the chief whose course was here so fatally closed seemed to be worthy of either celestial name.

# CHAPTER 16

# Ascent of the River

*May 21st.*—I received intimation that the *rajah* had written a letter, and wished me to appoint a time and place, that it might be presented in due form. Accordingly I attended in Mr. Brooke's hall of audience on the following day, where I found collected all the chiefs, and a crowd of natives, many of them having already been informed that the said letter was a requisition for me to assist in putting down the hordes of pirates who had so long infested the coast. I believe many of those present, especially the Borneons, to have been casually concerned, if not deeply implicated, in some of their transactions. After I had taken my seat with Mr. Brooke at the head of the table, the *rajah's* sword-bearers entered, clearing the way for the huge yellow canopy, under the shade of which, on a large brass tray, and carefully sewn up in a yellow silk bag, was the letter, from which it was removed, and placed in my hands by the Pangeran Budrudeen. I opened the bag with my knife, and giving it to an interpreter, he read it aloud in the Malayan tongue. It was variously received by the audience, many of whose countenances were far from prepossessing.

The following is a copy of the letter, to which was affixed the *rajah's* seal:

This friendly epistle, having its source in a pure mind, comes from Rajah Muda Hassim, next in succession to the royal throne of the kingdom of Borneo, and who now holds his court at the trading city of Sarawak, to our friend Henry Keppel, head captain of the war-frigate belonging to Her Britannic Majesty, renowned throughout all countries—who is valiant and discreet, and endowed with a mild and gentle nature:

This is to inform our friend that there are certain great pirates, of the people of Sarebus and Sakarran, in our neighbourhood, seizing goods and murdering people on the high seas. They have more than three hundred war-*prahus*, and extend their ravages even to Banjarmassim; they are not subject to the government of Bruni (Borneo); they take much plunder from vessels trading between Singapore and the good people of our country.

It would be a great service if our friend would adopt measures to put an end to these piratical outrages.

We can present nothing better to our friend than a *kris*, such as it is.

*20th day of Rahial Akhir, 1257.*

To which I sent the following reply:—

Captain Keppel begs to acknowledge the receipt of the Rajah Muda Hassim's letter, representing that the Dyaks of Sarebus and Sakarran are the pirates who infest the coast of Borneo, and do material damage to the trade of Singapore.

Captain Keppel will take speedy measures to suppress these and all other pirates, and feels confident that Her Britannic Majesty will be glad to learn that the Rajah Muda Hassim is ready to co-operate in so laudable an undertaking.

Not being prepared for the oriental fashion of exchanging presents, I had nothing to offer to his *rajah*ship; but I found out afterward that Mr. Brooke had (unknown to me) sent him a clock in my name. The royal *kris* was handsome, the handle of carved ivory, with a good deal of gold about it.

This information about the pirates gave me good ground to make a beginning; and having arranged with Mr. Brooke to obtain all necessary intelligence relative to their position, strength, and numbers,[1] I determined on attacking them in their strongholds, commencing with the Sarebus, who, from all accounts, were by far the most strongly fortified. Mr. Brooke accepted my invitation to accompany us, as well as to supply a native force of about three hundred men, who, should

1. Piratical habits are so interwoven with the character of these Sarebus people, that the capture at sea of a few *prahus* would have but small effect in curing the evil; while a harassing duty is encountered, the result is only to drive the pirates from one cruising-ground to another; but, on the contrary, a system which joins conciliation with severity, aiming at the correction of the native character as well as the suppression of piracy, and carrying punishment to the doors of the offenders, is the only one which can effectually eradicate an evil almost as disgraceful to those who permit it as to the native states engaged in it.

we succeed in the destruction of the pirate forts, would be useful in the jungle. Mr. Brooke's going to join personally in a war against (in the opinion of the *datus*) such formidable opponents as the Sakarran and Sarebus pirates—who had never yet been conquered, although repeatedly attacked by the united forces of the surrounding *rajahs*—was strongly opposed by the chiefs.

On his informing them that he should go, but leaving it optional whether they would accompany him or not, their simple reply was, "What is the use of our remaining? If you die, we die; and if you live, we live; we will go with you." Preparations for the expedition were accordingly commenced.

No place could have suited us better for a refit. Within a few yards of the ship was a Chinese workshop. Our boats were hauled up to repair under sheds, and we drew our fresh water alongside; and while the *Dido* was at Sarawak, Mr. Jago, the carpenter, built a very beautiful thirty-foot gig, having cut the plank up in the Chinaman's sawpit.

While these works were in progress, I accompanied Mr. Brooke up the river. The *Royalist* having been dispatched to Singapore with our letters, we started on our pleasure-excursion. With the officers from the *Dido* and the chiefs, who always accompany the "*Tuan Besar*," we mustered about sixty persons; and with our guns, walking-sticks, cigars, and a well supplied commissariat, determined to enjoy ourselves.

We were not long in making the acquaintances of the chiefs. Men who had formerly rebelled, who were conquered by Mr. Brooke, and had their (forfeited) lives saved, their families restored to them, and themselves finally reinstated in the offices they had previously held—these men were very naturally and faithfully attached. Our young gentlemen found their Malayan names difficult to remember, so that the gallant old Patingi Ali was seldom called any other name than that of "Three-Fingered Jack," from his having lost part of his right hand; the *tumangong* was spoken of as the "Father of Hopeful," from one of his children, a fine little fellow, whom he was foolishly attached to, and seldom seen without.

Der Macota, who had sometime before received the appellation of "the Serpent," had, ever since he got his orders to quit, some six months before, been preparing his boats, but which were ready in an incredibly short time after the *Dido's* arrival; and thus Mr. Brooke got rid of that most intriguing and troublesome rascal; a person who had, from the commencement, been trying to supplant and ruin him. He it was that gave the Sakarran pirates permission to ascend the river for the purpose of attacking the comparatively defenceless mountain Dyaks; and he it was that persecuted the unfortunate young Illanun chief, Si Tundo, even to his assassination. He was at last got rid of from Sarawak, but only to join and plan mischief with that noted piratical chief, Seriff Sahib; he, however, met his deserts.

We ascended the river in eight or ten boats. The scene to us was most novel, and particularly fresh and beautiful. We stopped at an empty house on a cleared spot on the left bank during the ebb-tide, to cook our dinner; in the cool of the afternoon we proceeded with the flood; and late in the evening brought up for the night in a snug little creek close to the Chinese settlement. We slept in native boats, which were nicely and comfortably fitted for the purpose. At an early hour Mr. Brooke was waited on by the chief of the Kunsi; and on visiting their settlement he was received with a salute of three guns. We found it kept in their usual neat and clean order, particularly their extensive vegetable gardens; but being rather pressed for time, we did not visit the mines, but proceeded to the villages of different tribes of Dyaks living on the Sarambo mountain, numbers of whom had been down to welcome us, very gorgeously dressed in feathers and scarlet.

The foot of the mountain was about four miles from the landing-place; and a number of these kind savages voluntarily shouldered our provisions, beds, bags, and baggage, and we proceeded on our march. We did not expect to find quite a turnpike-road; but, at the same time, I, for one, was not prepared for the dance led us by our wild cat-like guides through thick jungle, and alternately over rocky hills, or up to our middles in the soft marshes we had to cross. Our only means of doing so was by feeling on the surface of the mud (it being covered in most places about a foot deep with grass or discoloured water) for light spars thrown along lengthwise and quite unconnected, while our only support was an occasional stake at irregular distances, at which we used to rest, as the spars invariably sunk into the mud if we attempted to stop; and there being a long string of us, many a fall and flounder in the mud (gun and all) was the consequence.

The ascent of the hill, although as steep as the side of a house, was strikingly beautiful. Our resting-places, unluckily, were but few; but when we did reach one, the cool, fresh breeze, and the increasing extent and variety of scene—our view embracing, as it did, all the varieties of river, mountain, wood, and sea—amply repaid us for the exertion of the lower walk; and, on either hand, we were sure to have a pure cool rivulet tumbling over the rocks. While going up, however, our whole care and attention were requisite to secure our own safety; for it is not only one continued climb up ladders, but such ladders! They are made of the single trunk of a tree in its rough and rounded state, with notches, not cut at the reasonable distance apart of the ratlins of our rigging, but requiring the knee to be brought up to the level of the chin before the feet are sufficiently parted to reach from one step to another; and that, when the muscles of the thigh begin to ache, and the wind is pumped out of the body, is distressing work.

We mounted, in this manner, some 500 feet; and it was up this steep that Mr. Brooke had ascended only a few months before, with two hundred followers, to attack the Singè Dyaks. He has already described the circular halls of these Dyaks, in one of which we were received, hung round, as the interior of it is, with hundreds of human heads, most of them dried with the skin and hair on; and to give them, if possible, a more ghastly appearance, small shells (the cowry) are inserted where the eyes once were, and tufts of dried grass protrude from the ears. But my eyes soon grew accustomed to the sight; and by the time dinner was ready (I think I may say *we*) thought no more about them than if they had been as many cocoa-nuts.

Of course the natives crowded round us; and I noticed that with these simple people it was much the same as with the more civilized, and that curiosity was strongest in the gentler sex; and again, that the young men came in more gorgeously dressed, wearing feathers, neck-laces, armlets, ear-rings, bracelets, beside jackets of various-coloured silks, and other vanities—than the older and wiser chiefs, who en-cumbered themselves with no more dress than what decency actually required, and were, moreover, treated with the greatest respect.

We strolled about from house to house without causing the slight-est alarm: in all we were welcomed, and invited to squat ourselves on their mats with the family. The women, who were some of them very good-looking, did not run from us as the plain-headed Malays would have done; but laughed and chatted to us by signs in all the conscious-ness of innocence and virtue.

We were fortunate in visiting these Dyaks during one of their grand festivals (called Maugut); and in the evening, dancing, singing, and drinking were going on in various parts of the village. In one house there was a grand *fête*, in which the women danced with the men. The dress of the women was simple and curious—a light jacket open in front, and a short petticoat not coming below the knees, fitting close, was hung round with jingling bits of brass, which kept "making music" wherever they went. The movement was like all other native dances—graceful, but monotonous. There were four men, two of them bearing human skulls, and two the fresh heads of pigs; the women bore wax-lights, or yellow rice on brass dishes. They danced in line, moving backward and forward, and carrying the heads and dishes in both hands; the graceful part was the manner in which they half turned the body to the right and left, looking over their shoulders and holding the heads in the opposite direction, as if they were in momentary expectation of someone coming up behind to snatch the nasty relic from them. At times the women knelt down in a group, with the men leaning over them. After all, the music was not the only thing wanting to make one imagine oneself at the opera. The necklaces of the women were chiefly of teeth—bears' the most common—human the most prized.

In an interior house at one end were collected the relics of the tribe. These consisted of several round-looking stones, two deer's heads, and other inferior trumpery. The stones turn black if the tribe is to be beaten in war, and red if to be victorious; any one touching them would be sure to die; if lost, the tribe would be ruined.

The account of the deer's heads is still more curious: A young Dyak having dreamed the previous night that he should become a great warrior, observed two deer swimming across the river, and killed them; a storm came on with thunder and lightning, and darkness came over the face of the earth; he died immediately, but came to life again, and became a *rumah guna* (literally a *useful house*) and chief of his tribe; the two deer still live, and remain to watch over the affairs of the tribe. These heads have descended from their ancestors from the time when they first became a tribe and inhabited the mountain. Food is always kept placed before them, and renewed from time to time.

While in the circular building, which our party named "the scullery," a young chief (Meta) seemed to take great pride in answering our interrogatories respecting different skulls which we took down from their hooks: two belonged to chiefs of a tribe who had made a desperate defence; and judging from the incisions on the heads, each of which must have been mortal, it must have been a desperate affair. Among other trophies was half a head, the skull separated from across between the eyes, in the same manner that you would divide that of a hare or rabbit to get at the brain—this was their division of the head of an old woman, which was taken when another (a friendly) tribe was present, who likewise claimed their half. I afterward saw these tribes share a head.

But the skulls, the account of which our informant appeared to dwell on with the greatest delight, were those which were taken while the owners were asleep—cunning with them being the perfection of warfare. We slept in their "scullery;" and my servant Ashford, who happened to be a sleep-walker, that night jumped out of the window, and unluckily on the steep side; and had not the ground been well turned up by the numerous pigs, and softened by rain, he must have been hurt.

*May 25th.*—Having returned to our boats, we moved up another branch of the river, for the purpose of deer-shooting, and landed under some large shady trees. The sportsmen divided into two small parties, and, under the guidance of the natives, went in search of game, leaving the remainder of the party to prepare dinner against our return.

The distance we had to walk to get to our ground was what our guides considered nothing—some five miles through jungle; and one of the most distressing parts in jungle-walking is the having to climb over the fallen trunks of immense trees.

A short time before sunset we came to a part of the jungle that opened on to a large swamp, with long rank grass about six feet high, across which was a sort of Dyak bridge. The guide having made signs for me to advance, I cautiously crept to the edge of the jungle; and after some little trouble, and watching the direction of his finger, I observed the heads of two deer, male and female, protruding just above the grass at about sixty yards' distance. From the manner the doe was moving about her long ears, it had, to my view, all the appearance of a rabbit. Shooting for the pot, I selected her.

As soon as I fired, some of my boat's crew made a dash into the grass; and in an instant three of them were nearly up to their chins in mud and water, and we had some difficulty in dragging them out: Our Malay guide more knowingly crossed the bridge; and being acquainted with the locality, reached the deer from the opposite side, taking care to utter a prayer and cut the throat with the head in the direction of the Prophet's tomb at Mecca, without which ceremony no true follower of Islam could partake of the meat. The doe was struck just below the ear; and my native companion appeared much astonished at the distance and deadly effect with which my smooth-bored *Westley Richards* had conveyed the ball.

The buck had got off before the smoke had cleared sufficiently for me to see him. From what I had heard, I was disappointed at not seeing more game. The other party had not killed anything, although they caught a little fawn, having frightened away the mother.

My time was so occupied during my stay in Borneo, that I am unable to give any account of the sport to be found in the island. Neither had Mr. Brooke seen much of it; unless an excursion or two he had made in search of new specimens of the ourang-outang, or *mias*, may be brought under that head. This excursion he performed not only with the permission and under the protection, but as the guest, of the piratical chief Seriff Sahib; little thinking that, in four years afterward, he would himself, as a powerful *rajah*, be the cause of destroying his town, and driving him from the country.

So much for sporting. The pleasure, I believe, increases in proportion to the risk. But, while on the subject, I may mention that of pig-shooting, which I found an amusement not to be despised, especially if you approach your game before life is extinct. The jaws are long, tusks also, and sharp as a razor; and when once wounded, the animals evince a strong inclination to return the compliment: they are active, cunning, and very fast. I shot several at different times. The natives also describe a very formidable beast, the size of a large bullock, found farther to the northward, which they appear to hold in great dread. This I conceive to be a sort of bison; and if so, the sporting in Borneo altogether is not so bad.

The following day we went to other ground for deer; but the Dyaks had now enjoyed peace so long that the whole country was in a state of cultivation; and after scrambling over tracts of wild-looking country, in which Mr. Brooke, two years before, had seen the deer in hundreds, we returned to our boats, and down the river to Sarawak.

We now began to prepare in earnest for work of another sort. The news of our intended attack on the Sarebus pirates had soon reached them, and spread all over the country; and we had daily accounts of the formidable resistance they intended to make. By the 4th July our preparations were complete, and the ship had dropped down to the mouth of the river. I forgot to mention that all the adjoining *seriffs* had, in the greatest consternation, sent me assurances of their future good intentions. Seriff Jaffer, who lived with an industrious but warlike race of Dyaks up the Linga River, a branch of the Batang Lupar, had never been known to commit piracy, and had been frequently at war with both the Sarebus and Sakarrans, offered to join our expedition.

From Seriff Sahib, who lived up a river at Sadong, adjoining the Sarebus territory, and to whom the "Serpent" Macota had gone, Mr.

Brooke and myself had invitations to partake of a feast on our way to the Sarebus River. This was accompanied with a present of a couple of handsome spears and a porcupine, and also an offer to give up the women and children he had, with the assistance of the Sakarran pirates, captured from the poor Sow Dyaks up the Sarawak.

Farther to the eastward, and up the Batang Lupar, into which the Sakarran runs, lived another powerful *seriff* by the name of Muller, elder brother and coadjutor of Seriff Sahib. These all, however, through fear at the moment, sent in submissive messages; but their turn had not yet come, and we proceeded toward the Sarebus.

The island of Burong, off which the *Dido* was to remain at anchor, we made the first place of rendezvous. The force from the *Dido* consisted of her *pinnace*, two cutters, and a gig; beside which Mr. Brooke lent us his native-built boat, the *Jolly Bachelor*, carrying a long six-pounder brass gun and thirty of our men; also a large tope of thirty-five tons, which carried a well-supplied commissariat, as well as ammunition.

The native force was extensive; but I need only mention the names of those from Sarawak. The three chiefs (the Tumangong and two Patingis, Gapoor and Ali) had two large boats, each carrying about 180 men. Then there was the *rajah's* large, heavy boat, with the rascally Borneons and about 40 men, and sundry other Sarawak boats; and, beside, a Dyak force of about 400 men from the different tribes of Lundu, Sow, Singè, &c. Of course, it caused some trouble to collect this wild, undisciplined armament, and two or three successive points of rendezvous were necessary; and it was the morning of the 8th before we entered the river.

Lieutenant Wilmot Horton was to command the expedition; with him, in the *pinnace*, were Mr. W. L. Partridge, mate; Dr. Simpson, assistant-surgeon; Mr. Hallowes, midshipman; fourteen seamen, and five marines. In the first cutter was Mr. D'Aeth, Mr. Douglas, from Sarawak, and Mr. Collins, the boatswain; in the second cutter, Mr. Elliott, the master, and Mr. Jenkins, midshipman. The *Jolly Bachelor* was commanded by Lieutenant Tottenham, and Mr. Comber, midshipman, with Mr. Brooke's medical friend, Dr. Treacher, and an amateur gentleman, Mr. Ruppel, from Sarawak.

The force from the *Dido* was about 80, officers and men. The command of the boats, when sent away from a man-of-war, is the perquisite of the first lieutenant. My curiosity, however, would not allow me to resist the temptation of attending the party in my gig; and I had my friend Mr. Brooke as a companion, who was likewise attended by a sampan and crew he had taken with him to Sarawak from Singapore. His coxswain, Seboo, we shall all long remember: he was civil only to his master, and, I believe, brave while in his company. He was a stupid-looking and powerfully-built sort of savage, always praying, eating, smiling, or sleeping. When going into action, he always went down on his knees to pray, holding his loaded musket before him. He was, however, a curious character, and afforded us great amusement—took good care of himself and his master, but cared for no one else.

In the second gig was Lieutenant E. Gunnell, whose troublesome duty it was to preserve order throughout this extensive *musketoe* fleet, and to keep the natives from pressing too closely on the rear of our boats—an office which became less troublesome as we approached the scene of danger. The whole formed a novel, picturesque, and exciting scene; and it was curious to contemplate the different feelings that actuated the separate and distinct parties—the odd mixture of Europeans, Malays, and Dyaks, the different religions, and the eager and anxious manner in which all pressed forward. The novelty of the thing was quite sufficient to excite our Jacks, after having been cooped up so long on board ship, to say nothing of the chance of a broken head.

Of the Malays and Dyaks who accompanied us, some came from curiosity, some from attachment to Mr. Brooke, and many for plunder, but I think the majority to gratify revenge, as there were but few of the inhabitants on the north coast of Borneo who had not suffered more or less from the atrocities of the Sarebus and Sakarran pirates—either their houses burned, their relations murdered, or their wives and children captured and sold into slavery.

We did not get far up the river the first day, as the tope was very slow, and carried that most essential part of all expeditions, the commissariat. Patingi Ali, who had been sent the day before to await the force in the mouth of the Sarebus, fell in with five or six native boats, probably on the look-out for us, to which he gave chase, and captured one, the rest retreating up the river.

On the 9th June, 1843, we had got some thirty miles in the same direction; everything was in order; and, as we advanced, I pulled from one end of my little fleet to the other, and felt much the same sort of pride as Sir William Parker must have experienced when leading seventy-five sail of British ships up the Yeang-tse Keang River into the very heart of the Celestial Empire. It rained hard; but we were well supplied with *kajans*, a mat admirably adapted to keep out the wet; and securely covered in, my gig had all the appearance of a native boat, especially as I had substituted paddles for oars.

In this manner I frequently went a little in advance of the force; and on the 9th I came on a couple of boats, hauled close in under the jungle, apparently perfectly unconscious of my approach. I concluded them to be part of the small fleet of boats that had been chased, the previous day, in the mouth of the river; and when abreast of them, and within range, I fired from my rifle. The crews of each boat immediately precipitated themselves into the water, and escaped into the jungle. They were so closely covered in, that I did not see any one at first; but I found that my ball had passed through both sides of an iron kettle, in which they were boiling some rice. How astonished the cook must have been! On coming up, our Dyak followers dashed into the jungle in pursuit of the fugitives, but without success.

We moved on leisurely with the flood-tide, anchoring always on the ebb, by which means we managed to collect our stragglers and keep the force together. Toward the evening, by the incessant sound of distant gongs, we were aware that our approach was known, and that preparations were making to repel us. These noises were kept up all night; and we occasionally heard the distant report of ordnance, which was fired, of course, to intimidate us. During the day, several deserted boats were taken from the banks of the river and destroyed, some of them containing spears, shields, and ammunition, with a few firearms.

The place we brought up at for the night was called Boling; but here the river presented a troublesome and dangerous obstacle in what is called the bore, caused by the tide coming in with a tremendous rush, as if an immense wave of the sea had suddenly rolled up the stream, and, finding itself confined on either side, extended across, like a high bank of water, curling and breaking as it went, and, from the frightful velocity with which it passes up, carrying all before it. There are, however, certain bends of the river where the bore does not break across: it was now our business to look out for and gain these spots between the times of its activity. The natives hold them in great dread.

From Boling the river becomes less deep, and not safe for large boats; so that here we were obliged to leave our *tope* with the commissariat, and a sufficient force for her protection, as we had received information that thirteen piratical boats had been some time cruising outside, and were daily expected up the river on their return, when our unguarded tope would have made them an acceptable prize. In addition to this, we were now fairly in the enemy's country: and for all we knew, hundreds of canoes might have been hid in the jungle, ready to launch. Just below Boling, the river branches off to the right and left; that to the left leading to another nest of pirates at Pakoo, who are (by land) in communication with those of Paddi, the place it was our intention to attack first.

Having provisioned our boats for six days, and provided a strong guard to remain with the tope, the native force not feeling themselves safe separated from the main body,—we started, a smaller and more select party than before, but, in my opinion, equally formidable, leaving about 150 men. This arrangement gave but little satisfaction to those left behind, our men not liking to exchange an expedition where a fight was certain, for a service in which it was doubtful, although their position was one of danger, being open to attack from three different parts of the river. Our party now consisted of the *Dido's* boats, the three *datus* from Sarawak, and some Sow Dyaks, eager for heads and plunder. We arrived at our first resting-place early in the afternoon, and took up a position in as good order as the small space would admit.

I secured my gig close to the bank, under the shade of a large tree, at some little distance from the fleet of boats; and, by myself, contemplated my novel position—in command of a mixed force of 500 men, some seventy miles up a river in the interior of Borneo; on the morrow about to carry all the horrors of war among a race of savage pirates, whose country no force had ever yet dared to invade, and who had been inflicting with impunity every sort of cruelty on all whom they encountered, for more than a century.

As the sun went down, the scene was beautiful, animated by the variety and picturesque appearance of the native *prahus*, and the praying of the Mussulman, with his face in the direction of the Prophet's tomb, bowing his head to the deck of his boat, and absorbed in devotions from which nothing could withdraw his attention. For a time— it being that for preparing the evening meal—no noise was made: it was a perfect calm; and the rich foliage was reflected in the water as in a mirror, while a small cloud of smoke ascended from each boat, to say nothing of that from my cigar, which added much to the charm I then experienced.

Late in the evening, when the song and joke passed from boat to boat, and the lights from the different fires were reflected in the water, the scenery was equally pleasing; but later still, when the lights were out, there being no moon, and the banks overhung with trees, it was so dark that no one could see beyond his own boat.

A little after midnight, a small boat was heard passing up the river, and was regularly hailed by us in succession; to which they replied, "We belong to your party." And it was not until the yell of triumph, given by six or eight voices, after they had (with a strong flood-tide in their favour) shot past the last of our boats, that we found how we had been imposed on.

# CHAPTER 17

# Triumphant Return to Sarawak

*June 11th.*—We moved on immediately after the passing up of the bore, the dangers of which appeared to have been greatly exaggerated. The beating of gongs and discharge of cannon had been going on the whole of the previous night.

The scenery improved in beauty every yard that we advanced; but our attention was drawn from it by the increase of yelling as we approached the scene of action. Although as yet we had only heard our enemies, our rapid advance with a strong tide must have been seen by them from the jungle on the various hills which now rose to our view.

Being in my gig, somewhat ahead of the boats, I had the advantage of observing all that occurred. The scene was the most exciting I ever experienced. We had no time for delay or consideration: the tide was sweeping us rapidly up; and had we been inclined to retreat then, we should have found it difficult. A sudden turn in the river brought us (Mr. Brooke was by my side) in front of a steep hill which rose from the bank. It had been cleared of jungle, and long grass grew in its place. As we hove in sight, several hundred savages rose up, and gave one of their war-yells: it was the first I had heard. No report from musketry or ordnance could ever make a man's heart feel so *small* as mine did at that horrid yell: but I had no leisure to think. I had only time for a shot at them with my double barrel, as they rushed down the steep, while I was carried past. I soon after heard the report of our large boat's heavy gun, which must have convinced them that we likewise were prepared.

On the roof of a long building, on the summit of the hill, were several warriors performing a war-dance, which it would be difficult to imitate on such a stage. As these were not the forts we were in search of, we did not delay longer than to exchange a few shots in sweeping along.

Our next obstacle was more troublesome, being a strong barrier right across the river, formed of two rows of trees placed firmly in the mud, with their tops crossed and secured together by rattans; and along the fork, formed by the crossing of the tops of these stakes, were other trees firmly secured. Rapidly approaching this barrier, I observed a small opening that might probably admit a canoe; and gathering good way, and putting my gig's head straight at it, I squeezed through. On passing it the scene again changed, and I had before me three formidable-looking forts, which lost not a moment in opening a discharge of cannon on my unfortunate gig. Luckily their guns were properly elevated for the range of the barrier; and, with the exception of a few straggling grape-shot that splashed the water round us, the whole went over our heads.

For a moment I found myself cut off from my companions, and drifting fast upon the enemy. The banks of the river were covered with warriors, yelling and rushing down to possess themselves of my boat and its crew. I had some difficulty in getting my long gig round, and paddling up against the stream; but, while my friend Brooke steered the boat, my cockswain and myself kept up a fire with tolerable aim on the embrasures, to prevent, if possible, their reloading before the *pinnace*, our leading boat, could bring her twelve-pound carronade to bear. I was too late to prevent the *pinnace* falling athwart the barrier, in which position she had three men wounded.

With the assistance of some of our native followers, the rattan-lashings which secured the heads of the stakes were soon cut through; and I was not sorry when I found the *Dido's* first cutter on the same side with myself. The other boats soon followed; and while the *pinnace* kept up a destructive fire on the fort, Mr. D'Aeth, who was the first to land, jumped on shore, with his crew, at the foot of the hill on the top of which the nearest fort stood, and at once rushed for the summit. This mode of warfare—this dashing at once in the very face of their fort—was so novel and incomprehensible to our enemies, that they fled, panic-struck, into the jungle; and it was with the greatest difficulty that our leading men could get even a snap-shot at the rascals as they went.

That evening the country was illuminated for miles by the burning of the capital, Paddi, and adjacent villages; at which work, and plundering, our native followers were most expert.

At Paddi the river branches off to the right and left; and it was on the tongue of land formed by them that the forts were very cleverly placed. We took all their guns, and burned the stockades level with the ground.

The banks of the river were here so confined, that a man might with ease throw a spear across; and, as the jungle was close, it was necessary to keep pretty well on the alert. For the greater part of the night, the burning of the houses made it as bright as day. In the evening, Drs. Simpson and Treacher amputated a poor fellow's arm close to the shoulder, which, in the cramped space of the boat, was no easy operation. He was one of our best men, and captain of the forecastle on board the *Dido*.

Early on the following morning (12th) our boats, with the exception of the *Jolly Bachelor*, now become the hospital, proceeded up the two branches of the river; almost all the native force remaining to complete the work of destruction.

An accident had nearly occurred at this period. A report had reached us that several large boats—supposed to be a fleet of Sarebus pirates returning from a cruise—were in the river; and knowing that they could not well attack and pass our force at Boling without our hearing of it, I took no further notice of the rumour, intending to go down in my gig afterward and have a look at them. While we were at breakfast in the *Jolly Bachelor*, a loud chattering of many voices was heard, attended by a great beating of *tom-toms*; and suddenly a large *prahu*, crowded with savages, came sweeping round the bend of the river, rapidly nearing us with a strong flood-tide. As she advanced, others hove in sight.

In a moment pots and spoons were thrown down, arms seized, and the brass six-pounder, loaded with grape and canister, was on the point of being fired, when Williamson, the only person who understood their character, made us aware that they were a friendly tribe of Dyaks, from the River Linga, coming to our assistance, or, more likely, coming to seek for plunder and the heads of their enemies, with whom they had for many years been at war. Those in the leading boat had, however, a narrow escape. I had already given the order to fire; but luckily the priming had been blown off from the six-pounder. Had it not been so, fifty at least out of the first hundred would have been sent to their long homes. They were between eight and nine hundred strong.

The scene to me was indeed curious and exciting: for the wild

The attck on Paddi by the boats of H.M.S. Dido

appearance of these fellows exceeded anything I had yet witnessed. Their war-dresses—each decorating himself according to his own peculiar fancy, in a costume the most likely at once to adorn the wearer and strike terror into the enemy—made a remarkable show. Each had a shield and a handful of spears; about one in ten was furnished with some sort of firearm, which was of more danger to himself or his neighbour than to anyone else. They wore short padded jackets, capable of resisting the point of a wooden spear.

The first thing necessary was to supply each with a strip of white calico, to be worn in the head-dress as a distinguishing mark, to prevent our people knocking them over if met by accident while prowling about the jungle. We also established a watchword, "*Datu*," which many of them, who had great dread of the white men, never ceased to call out. Sheriff Jaffer, in command of their force, had promised to join us from the beginning; but as they did not make their appearance off the mouth of the river, we thought no more of them. It was necessary to dispatch messengers up the rivers to inform our boats of this re-enforcement, as in all probability an attack would have been made immediately on the appearing in sight of so formidable a force.

At 10 a.m. our boats returned, having gone up the right-hand branch as far as it was practicable. That to the left having been obstructed by trees felled across the stream, was considered, from the trouble taken to prevent our progress, to be the branch up which the enemy had retreated, and not being provisioned for more than the day, they came back, and started again in the afternoon with the first of the flood-tide. Of this party Lieutenant Horton took charge, accompanied by Mr. Brooke. It was a small, but an effective, and determined, and well-appointed little body, not likely to be deterred by difficulties. A small native force of about forty men accompanied them, making, with our own, between eighty and ninety people. The forts having been destroyed, no further obstacles were expected to our advance beyond the felling of trees and the vast odds as to numbers in case of attack, the pirates being reckoned to be about six thousand Dyaks and five hundred Malays.

The evening set in with rain and hazy weather. Our native skirmishing parties were returning to their boats and evening meals; our advancing party had been absent about an hour and a half, and I had just commenced a supper in the *Jolly Bachelor* on ham and poached eggs, when the sound of the *pinnace's* twelve-pounder carronade broke through the stillness of the night. This was responded to by one of those simultaneous war-yells apparently from every part of the country. My immediate idea was that our friends had been surrounded. It was impossible to move so large a boat as the *Jolly Bachelor* up to their assistance; nor would it be right to leave our wounded without a sufficient force for their protection. I immediately jumped into my gig, taking with me a bugler, whom I placed in the bow, and seeing our arms in as perfect readiness as the rain would allow us to keep them in, I proceeded to join the combatants.

Daylight had disappeared, as it does in tropical climates, immediately after the setting of the sun. The tide had just turned against me; and as I advanced up the river, the trees hung over many parts, nearly meeting across; at the same time the occasional firing that was kept up assured me that the enemy were on the alert, and with all the advantages of local knowledge and darkness on their side. From the winding of the stream, too, the yells appeared to come from every direction, sometimes ahead and sometimes astern.

I had pulled, feeling my way, for nearly two hours, when a sudden and quick discharge of musketry, well on my left hand, intimated to me that I was approaching the scene of action; and, at the same time, passing several large canoes hauled up on the bank, I felt convinced that my anticipation was right, that our party were surrounded, and that we should have to fight our way to each other. My plan was to make it appear as if I was bringing up a strong re-enforcement; and the moment the firing ceased, I made the bugler strike up "Rory O'More," which was immediately responded to by three British cheers, and then followed a death-like stillness—if anything, more unpleasant than the war-yell—and I could not help feeling certain that the enemy lay between us.

The stream now ran rapidly over loose stones. Against the sky, where the jungle had been cleared, I could distinctly see the outlines of human beings. I laid my double-barrel across my knees, and we pulled on. When within shot-range, I hailed, to make certain, and receiving no answer, after a second time, I fired, keeping the muskets of the gig's crew ready to repel the first attack in case the enemy did not decamp. My fire was answered by Lieutenant Horton, "We are here, sir." At first I was much distressed from the fear that I might have hurt anyone. They had not heard me hail, owing, I suppose, to the noise of the water rushing over the stones; and they had not hailed me, thinking that I must of course know that it was them, and the enemy being in the jungle all round, they did not like to attract attention to where they were.

I found they had taken up a very clever position. The running stream had washed the ground away on the right bank, leaving a sort of little, deep bay, just big enough to hold the boats, from which the bank rose quite perpendicularly. On the top of this bank the jungle had been cleared for about thirty yards, and on this Lieutenant Gunnel, with seven royal marines, was posted as a rear-guard. This was an important position, and one of danger, as the jungle itself was alive with the enemy; and although the spears were hurled from it continually during the night, no shot was thrown away unless the figure of the pirate could be distinctly seen.

It continued to rain: the men wore their great-costs for the purpose of keeping their pieces dry; and several times, during that long night, I observed the muskets of these steady and good men brought to the shoulder and again lowered without firing, as that part of the jungle whence a spear had been hurled to within a few feet of where they stood did not show a distinct form of anything living. The hours were little less interesting for those who, in the boats below, stood facing the opposite bank of the river with their arms in their hands. It appears that the enemy had come down in great force to attack the boats from that side; and as the river was there very shallow, and the bottom hard, they could, by wading not more than knee-deep, have approached to within five or six yards of them; but in the first attack they had lost a great many men, and it is supposed that their repeated advances throughout the night were, more to recover their dead and wounded than to make any fresh attack on our compact little force, whose deadly aim and rapid firing must have astonished them, and who certainly were, one and all, prepared to sell their lives as dearly as possible.

To the left of our position, and about 200 yards up the river, large trees were being felled during the night; and by the torch-lights showing the spot, the officer of the boat, Mr. Partridge, kept up a very fair ball-practice with the *pinnace's* gun. Toward morning a shot fell apparently just where they were at work; and that being accompanied by what we afterward ascertained caused more horror and consternation among the enemy than any thing else, a common signal sky-rocket, made them resign the ground entirely to us. The last shot, too, that was fired from the *pinnace* had killed three men.

As daylight broke I found that most of our party had squatted down with their guns between their knees, and, being completely exhausted, had fallen asleep in spite of the rain. Few will ever forget that night. There were two natives and one marine only of our party badly wounded; the latter was struck by a rifle shot, which entered his chest and lodged in his shoulder; and this poor fellow, a gallant young officer named Jenkins, already distinguished in the Chinese war, volunteered to convey in the second gig, with four boys only, down to the Jolly Bachelor. He performed this duty, and was again up with the party before daylight.

At daylight we found the pirates collecting in some force above us; and several shots were fired, as if to try the range of their rifles; but they took good care not to come within reach of our muskets. Shortly after, the tide beginning to rise, we made preparations for ascending further up the river. This was more than they bargained for, as we were close to where they had removed their families, with such little valuables as they could collect, when we so unexpectedly carried their forts and took possession of their town; and we were not sorry on observing, at that moment, a flag of truce advance from their party down the stream, and halt half way to our position. We immediately sent an unarmed Malay to meet them; and after a little talk, they came to our boats. The message was, that they were ready to abide by any terms we might dictate. I promised that hostilities should cease for two hours; but told them we could treat only with the chiefs, whose persons should be protected, and I invited them to a conference at 1 p.m.

In the meanwhile, having first sent notice by the messengers, I took advantage of the time, and ascended in my gig, without any great difficulty, above the obstruction they had been so busy throwing across the river during the night. The news that hostilities were to cease was not long in being communicated; and, by the time I had got up, the greatest confidence appeared to be established. Having pulled up into shoal water, and where the river widened, the banks were soon covered with natives; and some seventy or eighty immediately laid aside their spears and walked off to my boat, the whole of which, together with its crew, they examined with the greatest curiosity.

In the heat of the day we indulged in a most refreshing bath under the shade of overhanging trees, the bottom of the river being fine sand and pebbles worn smooth by the running stream.

At the appointed hour the chiefs made their appearance, dressed in their best, but looking haggard and dejected. Mr. Brooke, the "*Tuan Besar*," or great man, officiated as spokesman.

He fully explained that our invasion of their country, and destruction of their forts and town, was not for the purposes of pillage or gain to ourselves, but as a punishment for their repeated and aggravated acts of piracy; that they had been fully warned, for two years before, that the British nation would no longer allow the native trade between the adjacent islands and Singapore to be cut off and plundered, and the crews of the vessels cruelly put to death, as they had been.

They were very humble and submissive; admitted that their lives were forfeited, and if we said they were to die, they were prepared; although, they explained, they were equally willing to live. They promised to refrain forever from piracy, and offered hostages for their good behaviour.

Mr. Brooke then explained how much more advantageous trade would be than piracy, and invited them to a further conference at Sarawak, where they might witness all the blessings resulting from the line of conduct he had advised them to follow. If, on the other hand, we heard of a single act of piracy being committed by them, their country should be again invaded and occupied; and their enemies, the whole tribe of Linga Dyaks, let loose upon them, until they were rooted out and utterly destroyed.

To other questions they replied, that although the chief held communication, and was in the habit of cruising with the people of the other settlements of Pakoo and Rembas, still they could not hold themselves responsible for their good conduct; and as both held strongly fortified positions (of course supposed by themselves to be impregnable), they did not think that they would abstain altogether from piracy unless we visited and inflicted a similar chastisement to that they themselves had suffered. They also stated that, although they never would again submit to the orders of the great and powerful chiefs, Seriffs Sahib and Muller, still they could not join in any expedition against them or their old allies, their blood-thirsty and formidable neighbours in the Sakarran River.

On our return to the still smoking ruins of the once picturesque town of Paddi, we found that Seriff Jaffer, with his 800 warriors, had not been idle. The country round had been laid waste. All had been desolated, together with their extensive winter-stores of rice. It was a melancholy sight; and, for a moment, I forgot the horrid acts of piracy and cruel murders of these people, and my heart relented at what I had done—it was but for a few minutes.

Collecting our forces, we dropped leisurely down the river, but not without a parting yell of triumph from our Dyak force—a yell that must have made the hearts of those quail whose wives and children lay concealed in the jungle near to where we had held our conference.

We arrived at Boling soon after midnight, where we found the tope, with our provision, quite safe. Several shots had been fired at her the night before; and large parties had repeatedly come down to the banks, and endeavoured to throw spears on board.

At daylight (Wednesday, 14th) we lost no time in completing to four days' provisions, and starting, with the flood-tide, for Pakoo. It took us until late in the evening before we appeared in sight of two newly-built stockades, from which the pirates fled, panic-struck, without firing a shot, on our first discharge. We had evidently come on them before they were prepared, as we found some of the guns in the forts with the slings still on by which they had been carried.

The positions of the forts here, as at Paddi, were selected with great judgment; and had their guns been properly served, it would have been sharp work for boats. The same work of destruction was carried on; but the town was larger than at Paddi, and night setting in, the conflagration had a grand effect.

Although the greater part of their valuables had been removed, the place was alive with goats and poultry, the catching of which afforded great sport for our men. Some of the Singè Dyaks succeeded in taking the heads of a few pirates, who probably were killed or wounded in the forts on our first discharge. I saw one body afterward without its head, in which each passing Dyak had thought proper to stick a spear, so that it had all the appearance of a huge porcupine.

The operation of extracting the brains from the lower part of the skull, with a bit of bamboo shaped like a spoon, preparatory to preserving, is not a pleasing one. The head is then dried, with the flesh and hair on it, suspended over a slow fire, during which process the chiefs and elders of the tribe perform a sort of war-dance.

Soon after daylight the following morning (Thursday, 15th) the chiefs of the tribe came down with a flag of truce, when much the same sort of conference took place as at Paddi. They were equally submissive, offering their own lives, but begging those of their wives and children might be spared. After promising to accede to all we desired, they agreed to attend the conference about to assemble at Sarawak, where the only terms on which they could expect lasting peace and mutual good understanding would be fully explained and discussed.

Like their friends at Paddi, they were of opinion that their neighbours at Rembas would not abstain from piracy until they had received convincing proof that the power existed which was capable and determined to put down piracy. All these misguided people appeared not only to listen to reason, but to be open to conviction; and I am far from imputing to them that treachery so commonly attributed to all classes of Malays. The higher grades, I admit, are cunning and deceitful; but subsequent events during the last two years have proved the truth and honesty of the intentions of these people. They have strictly adhered to their promises; and have since, although surrounded by piratical tribes, been carrying on a friendly trade with Sarawak.

Our next point of attack was Rembas. Although there was a nearer overland communication between those places, the distance by water was upward of sixty miles; but the strong tides were of great assistance, as we could always rest when they were against us. High water was the only time, however, that suited us for landing, as the fall of tide left a considerable space of soft mud to wade through before reaching *terra firma*: this was sufficiently unpleasant to our men, without the additional trouble of having to load and fire when in that position; besides, when stuck fast in the mud, you become a much easier object to be fired at.

At Rembas the tide was not up until just before daylight; and, having no moon to light us, a night attack was not considered advisable; so that we brought up about a quarter tide below the town, on the evening of the 16th. As Rembas contained a larger proportion of Malays (who are always well supplied with firearms) than the other settlements, though we had not experienced any opposition at Pakoo, we fully expected they would here make a better stand.

We advanced early in the morning, and soon came up with a succession of formidable barriers, more troublesome to cut through than any we had before encountered. About a mile below the town we landed 700 of the Linga Dyaks on the left bank of the river, who were to separate into two divisions—commanded by Seriff Jaffer and his son, a remarkably fine and spirited youth—and creep stealthily through the jungle, for which the country was well adapted, so as to get to the rear of the town and forts, and make a simultaneous attack on the first shot being fired from our boats.

The last barrier (and there were four of them) was placed just within point-blank range; the gig being a light boat, I managed to haul her over, close to the bank, and advanced so as to be both out of sight and out of range; and just as our first boat came up with the barrier, I pushed out from under the bank, and opened a fire of musketry on the stockade, which was full of men. This, with the war-yell that followed from their rear (both unexpected), together with their fears having been already worked upon by the destruction of Paddi and defeat of Pakoo, threw them into the greatest confusion. They fled in all directions, without provoking us by firing a shot, although we found the guns loaded.

Seriff Jaffer and his Dyaks were gratified by having all the fighting to themselves, and by some very pretty hand-to-hand encounters. We were much amused, afterward, by their own account of the heroic deeds they had performed. Lives were lost on both sides, and heads taken. This Rembas was by far the largest and strongest place we had assaulted. We found some very large war-boats, both fitted and building; one measured ninety-two feet in length, with fourteen beam; and in addition to the usual good supply of fruit, goats, and poultry, our men were gratified by finding several bullocks. The plunder was great; and although, with the exception of the guns, of no value to us, it was very much so to our native followers.

After we had destroyed everything, we received a flag of truce, when similar explanations and promises were made as at Paddi and Pakoo; and here ended for the present, the warlike part of our expedition. The punishment we had inflicted was severe, but not more than the crime of their horrid piracies deserved. A few heads were brought away by our Dyak followers, as trophies; but there was no unnecessary sacrifice of life, and I do not believe there was a woman or child hurt. The destruction of these places astonished the whole country beyond description. In addition to the distance and difficulty of access to their strongly-fortified positions, they looked for protection from the bore that usually ran up the Sarebus, and which they imagined none but their own boats could manage.

As the different Malay chiefs heard that, in ten days, a handful of white men had totally destroyed their strongholds, they shook their heads, and exclaimed, "God is great!" and the Dyaks declared that the *Tuan Besar* (Mr. Brooke) had charmed the river to quiet the bore,[1] and that the whites were invulnerable. Although this expedition would have a great moral effect on all the more respectable and thinking natives, inasmuch as the inhabitants of the places destroyed were looked upon, from the large proportion of Malays, as more civilized than their formidable and savage neighbours, the Dyaks inhabiting the Sakarran

---

1. It had never been known so quiet as during the days we were up their river.

River; still, it was not to be supposed, when the settlements of Paddi, Pakoo, and Rembas could not be responsible for the good behaviour of one another, that it was probable the severe lesson taught them would have any great effect on the Sakarrans.

On regaining the *tope* at Boling, we found our assistant surgeon, Dr. Simpson, who had been left in charge of the sick, laid up with fever and ague. For convenience's sake, the wounded men had been removed to a large native boat; and while the doctor was passing along the edge of the boat, his foot slipped, he fell overboard, and not being much of a swimmer, and a strong tide running, he was a good while in the water, though a native went after him. He had, for some time past, been in bad health; but the cold he then caught brought on inflammation in the lungs, under the effects of which he sank soon after our return to Singapore. Poor Simpson! he was not only clever in his profession, but endeared to us all by his kind and gentle manner, so grateful to the sick. There were few of us, while in China, who had not come under his hands, and experienced his tender, soothing, and unremitting attention.

We now gave our native followers permission to depart to their respective homes, which they did loaded with *plunder*, usually, in India, called *loot*; ourselves getting under weigh to rejoin the *Dido* off the island of Burong, and from thence we proceeded to the mouth of the Morotaba, where, leaving the ship, Mr. Brooke and I went in my boat, with two others in attendance, to take leave of the *rajah*, prior to my return to Singapore and China. Although the greater part of the native boats attached to the expedition had already arrived at Sarawak, the *rajah* had sent them back, some miles down the river, with as many others as he could collect, gorgeously dressed out with flags, to meet Mr. Brooke and myself, the heroes of the grandest expedition that had ever been known in the annals of Malayan history.

Our approach to the grand city was, to them, most triumphant, although to us a nuisance. From the moment we entered the last reach, the saluting from every gun in the capital that could be fired without bursting was incessant; and as we neared the royal residence, the yells, meant for cheers, and the beating of gongs, intended to be a sort of "See, the conquering hero comes!" were quite deafening. The most minute particulars of our deeds, of course greatly exaggerated, had been detailed, long before our arrival, by the native chiefs, who were eye-witnesses; and when we were seated in the *rajah's* presence, the royal countenance relaxed into a smile of real pleasure as he turned his wondering eyes from Mr. Brooke to myself and back again. I suppose he thought a great deal of us, as he said little or nothing; and, as we were rather hungry after our pull, we were very glad to get away once more to Mr. Brooke's hospitable board, to which we did ample justice.

My stay at Sarawak was but of short duration, as, before I had time to carry out the arrangements I had made to put down this horrid traffic, the *Dido* was, owing to some changes in the distribution of the fleet, recalled to China.

As the tide would not suit for my return to the *Dido* until two o'clock the following morning, we sat up until that hour, when, with mutual regret, we parted. I had just seen enough of Borneo and my enterprising friend, Mr. Brooke, to feel the deepest interest in both. No description of mine can in any way give my readers a proper idea of the character of the man I had just then left; and however interesting his journal may appear in the reading, it is only by being in his company, and by hearing him advocate the cause of the persecuted inland natives, and listening to his vivid and fair description of the beautiful country he has adopted, that one can be made to enter fully into and feel what I would fain describe, but cannot.

We parted; and I did not then expect to be able so soon to return and finish what I had intended, *viz.*, the complete destruction of the strongholds belonging to the worst among the pirate hordes, so long the terror of the coast, either by capturing or driving from the country the piratical Seriffs Sahib and Muller, by whose evil influence they had been chiefly kept up. From all that I had seen, the whole country appeared to be a large garden, with a rich and varied soil, capable of producing anything. The natives, especially the mountain Dyaks, are industrious, willing, inoffensive, although a persecuted race; and the only things wanted to make the country the most productive and happiest in the world were, the suppression of piracy, good government, and opening a trade with the interior, which could not fail of success. All these I saw partially begun; and I felt assured that with the assistance of a vessel of war, and the countenance only of the government, Mr. Brooke would, although slowly, yet surely, bring about their happy consummation.

# CHAPTER 18

# Ludicrous Midnight Alarm

*June 24th.*—I reached the *Dido* at 8 o'clock, and immediately got under weigh. After remaining twenty-four hours to water at Singapore, I sailed for Hong Kong. My time, during the year that I was absent from Borneo, if not quite so usefully, was not unpleasantly passed. We lay a few months in the Canton River. In addition to having good opportunities of seeing the natives of China in their domestic state, I witnessed one of those most curious and extraordinary sights that occasionally occur during the winter months in the city of Canton, namely, a fire. The one I saw was about the most extensive that had ever been experienced; and the *Dido's* crew had the gratification of being of some assistance in the protection of British property. From China the *Dido* accompanied the commander-in-chief, in the Cornwallis, to the Spanish colony at Manilla, which is a place that few forget; and a short description of our visit there has been given in an interesting little work, written by Captain Cunynghame.

On my return to Hong Kong, I had the gratification of receiving on board the *Dido*, Major-General Lord Saltoun and his staff, consisting of two old and esteemed friends of mine, Captain, now Major Arthur Cunynghame, his lordship's *aide-de-camp*, and Major Grant, of the 9th Lancers, who had been adjutant-general to the forces. A more agreeable cruise at sea I never experienced. We called at the island of Pinang, in the Malacca Straits, on our way, where we again fell in with the admiral; and I was most agreeably surprised at meeting my friend Mr. Brooke, who had come on to Singapore to meet Sir William Parker, and had followed him up in the *Wanderer*, commanded by my friend Captain Henry Seymour,—that vessel, in company with the *Harlequin*, Captain the Hon. George Hastings, and the H. C. steamer *Diana*, having just returned from an expedition to Acheen, whither they had been dispatched by the commander-in-chief, to inquire into and demand redress for an act of piracy, committed on an English merchant-vessel.

An account of the expedition has already been published. The pirates had made a desperate resistance, and several lives were lost, and many severely wounded on our side; among the latter was my friend Mr. Brooke (in the head and arm), for which I took the liberty of giving him a lecture on his rashness, he having quite sufficient ground for fighting over in his newly-adopted country. He was much pleased at the admiral's having promised that the *Dido* should return again to the Straits station as soon as she had completed her voyage to Calcutta.

On the 11th March, 1844, we anchored off the grand City of Palaces, and well does it merit the name. We could not have, timed our visit better. The governor-general, the Earl of Ellenborough, was being *fêted* on his return from the frontiers, which *fêtes* were continued on the arrival, a few days after ourselves, of the *Cornwallis* at Kedgeree, when the flag of Sir William Parker was shifted to the *Dido*. The admiral experienced the same style of hospitable entertainment that had previously been given to General Sir Hugh Gough on his return from the Chinese expedition.

At Calcutta I was kindly invited by the "Tent Club," and introduced to that noble and most exciting of all field-sports, "Hog-hunting in India;" but with which the pleasures of the day did not cease. The subsequent convivial meeting was a thing not easily to be forgotten. Although under a tent pitched by the edge of the jungle, thirty miles from the city, none of the comforts of the house were wanting; there were the *punkah* and the *hookah*, those luxuries of the East, to say nothing of heaps of ice from the far West, which aided considerably the consumption of champagne and claret; and to better all these good things, every man brought with him the will and the power to please and to be pleased.

A few days before my departure from Calcutta, the governor-general finding it necessary to send treasure to China, the admiral desired me to receive it on board. Although a welcome cargo, it delayed for a couple of months my return to Borneo. I found Mr. Brooke awaiting my arrival at Singapore; but as I could not then receive him on board, Captain Hastings took him over to Sarawak in the Harlequin.

On arriving at Hong Kong, Rear-Admiral Sir T. Cochrane appointed Mr. Frederick Wade as first lieutenant, Lieutenant Wilmot Horton having been promoted to the rank of commander for his gallant defence when the *Dido's* boats were attacked by the very superior force of pirates off the island of Sirhassan.

Having landed the treasure at Hong Kong, and completed stores and provisions, I sailed from Macao on the 21st June, and working down against the monsoon, arrived at Singapore on the 18th July. I here found letters from Mr. Brooke, stating that the Sakarrans had been out in great force; and although he was not aware of any danger to himself or his settlement, still, by coming over quickly, I might have a fair chance of catching and crushing them in the very act of piracy. I lost no time in preparing for another expedition. The government at Calcutta had become fully sensible of the necessity of protecting the native trade to Singapore, and had sent down the *Phlegethon* steamer, of light draught of water, and better adapted to service in the straits or rivers than any of Her Majesty's larger vessels. She was, moreover, fitted in every way for the peculiar service on which she was to be employed, with a zealous, experienced, and active commander, F. Scott,[1] as well as a fine enterprising set of young officers. I lost no time in making application for her to the resident counsellor, Mr. Church (in the absence of Colonel Butterworth, the Governor of the Straits), who immediately placed her at my disposal; and with such means, I was anxious to commence operations as speedily as possible, leaving the *Vixen* and *Wolverine* to perform the other duties of the station.

*Thursday, 25th July.*—Sailed from Singapore, having dispatched the *Phlegethon* the previous night, with orders to rendezvous at the entrance to the Morotaba, which we entered in the evening of the 29th; and anchoring the ship inside the river, I went on in the steamer to within four miles of Sarawak, when I pulled up in my gig, accompanied by the *Dido's pinnace*, that I might, by firing her carronade as a signal, be enabled to give notice of our approach, not feeling myself quite secure from a shot from the forts, which were very judiciously placed so as to command the last reach approaching the town, as I knew that before Mr. Brooke's return they had been put in a state of defence, and a regular watch kept, by self-appointed officers, sleeping on their arms. I, however, got up without accident, in time to receive a hearty welcome, about daylight.

Not expecting to revisit Borneo during the period that the ship had to run before completing her usual time of commission, it was gratifying for me to read in my friend's journal, alluding to my former

---

1. I have lately heard, with much regret, of the death of this valuable officer.

visit;

I came myself in the *Dido*; and I may say that her appearance was the consummation of my enterprise." "The natives saw directly that there was a force to protect and to punish; and most of the chiefs, conscious of their evil ways, trembled; Muda Hassim was gratified, and felt that this power would exalt his authority both in Borneo and along the coast, and he was not slow in magnifying the force of the *Dido*. The state in which Captain Keppel and his officers visited the *rajah* all heightened the effect; and the marines and the band excited the admiration and the fears of the natives. I felt the *rajah's* hand tremble at the first interview; and not all the well-known command of countenance, of which the natives are masters, could conceal his emotion.

Gentle reader, excuse my vanity if I continue a little further with my friend's journal, although it gets rather personal:

I believe the first emotion was anything but pleasurable; but Captain Keppel's conciliatory and kind manner soon removed any feeling of fear; and was all along of the greatest use to me in our subsequent doings. The first qualification, in dealing with a Malay, is a kind and gentle manner; for their habitual politeness is such that they are hurt by the ordinary *brusquerie* of the European.

I shall not go over the chase of the three boats of the Balagnini pirates, or the attack made on the *Dido's* boats by the Sirhassan, people, except to remark, that in the latter case, I am sure Lieutenant Horton acted rightly in sparing their lives and property; for, with these occasional pirates, a severe lesson, followed by that degree of conciliation and pardon which shall best insure a correction of their vices, is far wiser and preferable to a course of undistinguishing severity.

I found Sarawak much altered for the better, and the population considerably increased. Mr. Brooke had established himself in a new house built on a beautiful and elevated mound, from which the intriguing Macota had just been ejected on my first visit. Neat and pretty-looking little Swiss cottages had sprung up on all the most picturesque spots, which gave it quite a European look. He had also made an agreeable addition to his English society; and a magazine of English merchandise had been opened to trade with the natives, together with many other improvements.

On the other hand, Seriff Sahib, not deterred, as I had anticipated he would be, by the example I made of his neighbours in the Sarebus, had taken measures for withdrawing from the adjoining river of Sadong, where he had been living in a comparatively unguarded state, and had, during the last nine months, been making busy preparations for fortifying himself at a place called Patusen, up the Batang Lupar. He had lately got things in a forward state, had called out a large fleet of Sakarrans as an escort; and being puffed up with his own power and importance, had thought proper to prolong the performance of his voyage, of about 100 miles, from his residence in Sadong to his fortified position at Patusen, for three weeks or a month, during which time he had dispatched small parties of his fleet, which consisted of upward of 150 war-*prahus*, on piratical excursions.

These robbers had, in addition to their piracies on the high seas, scoured the coast in all directions, and committed the greatest atrocities, attended with some of the most cruel murders. One sample will be sufficient to show their brutal character:—A detachment of three of their boats, having obtained information that a poor Dyak family, belonging to a tribe in Mr. Brooke's territory, had come down from their mountain to cultivate a small portion of land nearer the coast, and, for their better security, had made their dwelling in the upper branches of a large tree on the outskirts of the forest, determined to destroy them. Their little children were playing in the jungle when the pirates were seen approaching the tree with their diabolical war-yells. As the poor man did not descend immediately on being summoned, he was shot; when other ruffians, to save their ammunition, mounted the tree, murdered the woman, and returned in triumph to their boats with the heads of both victims. The children, who had witnessed this from their hiding-places, succeeded in getting to Sarawak.

Taking advantage of Mr. Brooke's unusually long absence, Sarawak itself was threatened, and open defiance hurled at any European force that should dare approach Patusen. Reports, too, had been industriously spread that Mr. Brooke never intended to return; and when he did get back to his home, he found the town guarded and watched like a besieged city. With his usual nerve and decision he withdrew his men from the forts, and sent to Seriff Sahib to inform him that he should suffer for his temerity.

A letter I received from him is so characteristic, and gives so lively a description of these events, that I am tempted to print it.

My Dear Keppel,

It is useless applying a spur to a willing horse; so I will only tell you that there is plenty to do here, and the sooner you can come the better for all of us, especially your poor friends the Dyaks. Bring with you as much force as you can to attack Sakarran.

The case stands thus:—Seriff Sahib, quite frightened at Sadong since last year, enraged likewise at his loss of power and his incapability of doing mischief, collected all the Sakarran Dyaks, and was joined by many of the Dyaks of Sarebus and some Balows. He likewise had a good many Malays, and bullied everyone in his vicinity. This force met at the entrance of the Sadong Delta, and committed depredations. They were not less than 200 Dyak boats, and some 15 or 20 armed Malay *prahus*, beside others. Just as they were collected, the Harlequin appeared off the coast, and had the *Dido* been with us, we might have *had them all*; but the opportunity will never again occur. Seriff Sahib, with this force, has started today for Sakarran, and I was not strong enough with my eight native boats to attack him.

It is really greatly to be lamented, because we should most completely have crushed the head of the snake. We must, however, make the best of it. It is his intention, on his arrival at Sakarran, to fortify and wait for our attack, and in the mean time to send out his Dyaks along the coast and inland to such places as they dare venture to attack.

Come then, my dear Keppel, for there is plenty to do for all hands. I have ordered a gun-boat from Mr. Goldie, to make our force stronger; and had I possessed such a one the day before yesterday, I would have pulled away for the Sadong today.

"My regards to all. I still propose Pepper-Pot Hall for your residence. I only wish I felt *quite sure* that Fortune had it in store that you would be here on your return from China. That dame, however, seems to delight in playing me slippery tricks just at present; and never was the time and tide so missed before, which would have led to fortune, as the other day. All the queen's ships and all the queen's men could not bring such a chance together again.

Ever, my dear Keppel, your sincere friend,

Captain the Hon. Henry Keppel.                    J. Brooke.

No one could have been more disappointed or have regretted more than my gallant friend Captain Hastings, that his orders did not admit of any delay, or of his attacking that redoubtable pirate Seriff Sahib, especially as he had a small score to settle with that kind of gentry, having had his first lieutenant, H. Chads, severely wounded in two places, and several men killed, in the affair at Acheen Head. It was, however, all for the best, as the few boats that the Harlequin could have sent would have stood but a poor chance against upward of 200 war-*prahus*, all fitted and prepared for fight.

On the 1st of August, with the *Dido* and *Phlegethon* at anchor off Sarawak, the warlike preparations were going on rapidly. I had saluted and paid my visit to Muda Hassim; he was delighted to see me again, and we went through the form of holding several conferences of war in his *divan*. He appears to be a good well-meaning man, well inclined toward the English, moderately honest, and, if roused, I daresay not without animal courage; and altogether, with the assistance of his clever younger brother, Budrudeen, a very fit person to govern that part of Borneo of which he is *rajah*.

During my absence, Sarawak had been visited by H.M.S. *Samarang*, Captain Sir Edward Belcher, who had received directions to call on and communicate with Mr. Brooke. In dropping down the river the *Samarang* grounded on a long shelf of rocks, at the top of high water, and with the ebb-tide rolled over, filling with the succeeding flood. She was nearly a fortnight in this position, but was ultimately saved by the skill and almost unparalleled perseverance (aided by such assistance of men and spars as Mr. Brooke could afford) of her captain, officers, and crew—a feat that must have given the natives a good idea of what British seamen are capable of. This accident delayed for a short time a visit that was afterward made by Sir Edward Belcher, accompanied by Mr. Brooke, to Borneo Proper. A hurried inspection of the capabilities of that part of the coast took place; and the fact of there being coal on the island was ascertained.

I received a second letter from Muda Hassim, of which the following is a translation:

This comes from Pangeran Muda Hassim, Rajah of Borneo, to our friend Captain Keppel, in command of Her Britannic Majesty's ship.

(*After the usual compliments*):

We beg to let our friend Captain Keppel know, that the pirates of Sakarran, whom we mentioned last year, still continue their piracies by sea and land; and that many Malays, under Seriff Sahib, who have been accustomed to send or to accompany the pirates and to share in their spoils, have gone to the Sakarran River, with a resolve of defending themselves rather than accede to our wishes that they should abandon piracy.

Last year Captain Belcher told the sultan and myself, that it would be pleasing to the Queen of England that we should repress piracy; and we signed an agreement, at his request, in which we promised to do so; and we tell our friend of the piracies and evil actions of the Sakarran people, who have, for many years past, done much mischief to trade, and make it dangerous for boats to sail along the coast; and this year many *prahus*, which wanted to sail to Singapore, have been afraid. We inform our friend Captain Keppel of this, as we desire to end all the piracy, and to perform our agreement with the Queen of England.

*Monday, 5th August, 1844,* being the morning fixed for the departure of our expedition against the Sakarran pirates, the *Phlegethon* steamer weighed at 8 o'clock, and proceeded down the river to await at the mouth the collection of our force. Among those who accompanied us from Sarawak was the Pangeran Budrudeen, the intelligent brother of the *rajah* already noticed. This was a great and unusual event in the royal family; and the departure from the *rajah's* wharf, which I viewed from Mr. Brooke's house, on the opposite bank of the river, was intended to be very imposing. The barge of state was decked out with banners and canopies; all the chiefs attended, with the Arab priest Mudlana at their head, and the barge pushed off amid the firing of cannon, and a general screech, invoking the blessing of Mahomet.

Having seen the last boat off, Mr. Brooke and myself took our departure in the gig, when another and last farewell salute was fired from the *rajah's* wharf.

Three hours brought us to the steamer, anchored off the fishing huts at the mouth of the river. Here we heard that a small boat from the enemy's country had, under the pretence of trading, just been in to spy into our force, but decamped again on the appearance of the steamer. We now all got fairly away together, the smaller boats keeping near the shoals in shore, while the steamer was obliged to make an offing some miles from the coast. From the masthead we distinctly made out the small boat that had left the mouth of the river before, both pulling and sailing in the direction of the Batang Lupar, up which the

Sakarran country lies; and as it was desirable that the pirates should not get information of our approach, at dusk, being well in advance, and our auxiliary force following, I dispatched Mr. Brooke's Singapore sampan and one of the *Dido's* cutters in chase. At half-past nine we anchored in the stream within the entrance.

We were fortunate at Sarawak in picking up two excellent and intelligent pilots, who had long known the whole river, and had themselves been several times forced to serve in the boats while on their piratical excursions.

*Tuesday 6th.*—With the flood-tide arrived all the well appointed and imposing little fleet, and with them the cutter and *sampan* with two out of the three men belonging to the boat of which they had been in chase; the third having been speared by Seboo, on showing a strong inclination to run a-muck in his own boat, *i. e.* to sell his life as dearly as he could. From these men we obtained information that Seriff Sahib was fully prepared for defence—that his harem had been removed—and that he would fight to the last. We also learned that Macota, better known among us by the name of the "Serpent," and often mentioned in Mr. Brooke's journal, was the principal adviser, in whose house the councils of war were generally held.

We anchored, in the afternoon, off the mouth of the River Linga; and while there we dispatched a messenger to Seriff Jaffer to caution him against giving any countenance or support to either of the Seriffs Sahib and Muller, on whose punishment and destruction we were determined.

The Batang Lupar, as far as this, is a magnificent river, from three to four miles wide, and, in most parts, from five to seven fathoms water.

*Wednesday, 7th.*—We weighed at daylight, but were obliged to anchor again before appearing in sight of Patusen, until the tide should rise sufficiently to enable us to pass a long flat shoal, over which, during the spring-tides, a bore rushes with frightful velocity.

We now collected our boats, and made our arrangements as well as we could, for attacking a place we had not yet seen. We had now a little more difficulty in keeping our native force back, as many of those who had accompanied the expedition last year had gained so much confidence that the desire of plunder exceeded the feeling of fear.

After weighing at 11, with a strong tide sweeping us up, we were not many minutes in coming in sight of the fortifications of Patusen; and indeed they were not to be despised. There were five of them, two not quite finished. Getting suddenly into six feet water, we anchored the steamer; not so formidable a berth, although well within musket-range, as we might have taken up had I been aware of the increasing depth of water nearer the town; but we approached so rapidly there was no time to wait the interpretation of the pilot's information.

The *Dido* and *Phlegethon's* boats were not long in forming along-side. They were directed to pull in shore, and then attack the forts in succession; but my gallant first-lieutenant, Wade, who had the command, was the first to break the line, and pull directly in the face of the largest fort. His example was followed by the others; and dividing, each boat pulled for that which appeared to the officer in command to be the one most likely to make a good fight. The forts were the first to open fire on both steamer and boats, which was quickly and smartly returned. It is impossible to imagine a prettier sight than it was from the top of the *Phlegethon's* paddle-box. It was my intention to have fired on the enemy from the steamer, so as to draw their attention off the boats; but owing to the defective state of the detonating priming-tubes, the guns from the vessel did not go off, and the boats had all the glory to themselves.

They never once checked in their advance; but the moment they touched the shore the crews rushed up, entering the forts at the embrasures, while the pirates fled by the rear.

In this sharp and short affair we had but one man killed, poor John Ellis, a fine young man, and captain of the main-top in the *Dido*. He was cut in two by a cannon-shot while in the act of ramming home a cartridge in the bow-gun of the *Jolly Bachelor*. Standing close to poor Ellis at the fatal moment was a fine promising young middy, Charles Johnson, a nephew of Mr. Brooke's, who fortunately escaped unhurt. This, and two others badly wounded, were the only accidents on our side.

Our native allies were not long in following our men on shore. The killed and wounded on the part of the pirates must have been considerable. Our followers got several heads. There were no fewer than sixty-four brass guns of different sizes, beside many iron, found in and about the forts: the latter we spiked and threw into the river. The town was very extensive; and after being well looted, made a glorious blaze.

Our Sarawak followers, both Malays and Dyaks, behaved with the greatest gallantry, and dashed in under the fire of the forts. In fact, like their country, anything might be made of them under a good government; and such is their confidence in Mr. Brooke's judgment, and their attachment to his person, that he might safely defy in his own stronghold the attacks of any foreign power.

After our men had dined, and had a short rest during the heat of the day, we landed our whole force in two divisions—and a strange but formidable-looking force they made—to attack a town situated about two miles up, on the left bank of a small river called the Grahan, the entrance to which had been guarded by the forts; and immediately after their capture the tide had fallen too low for our boats to get up. Facing the stream, too, was a long stockade; so that we determined on attacking the place in the rear, which, had the pirates only waited to receive us, would have caused a very interesting skirmish. They, however, decamped, leaving everything behind them.

In this town we found Seriff Sahib's residence, and, among other things, all his curious and extensive wardrobe. It was ridiculous to see our Dyaks dressed out in all the finery and plunder of this noted pirate, whose very name, a few days previous, would have made them tremble. Goats and poultry there were in abundance. We likewise found a magazine in the rear of the *seriff's* house, containing about two tons of gunpowder; also a number of small barrels of fine powder, branded "Dartford," in exactly the same state as it had left the manufactory in England. It being too troublesome and heavy to convey on board the steamer, and each of our native followers staggering up to his knees in mud, under a heavy load of plunder, I had it thrown into the river.

It was evident how determined the chief had been to defend himself, as, beside the defences already completed, eight others, in different states of forwardness, were in the course of erection; and had the attack been delayed a few weeks, Patusen would not have been carried by boats without considerable loss of life. It was the key to this extensive river; the resort of the worst of pirates; and each chief had contributed his share of guns and ammunition toward its fortification and defence.

We returned to our boats and evening meal rather fatigued, but much pleased with our day's work, after ascending nearly seventy miles from the mouth of the river. The habitations of 5000 pirates had been burnt to the ground; four strong forts destroyed, together with several hundred boats; upward of sixty brass cannons captured, and about a fourth that number of iron spiked and thrown into the river, beside vast quantities of other arms and ammunition; and the powerful Seriff Sahib, the great pirate-patron for the last twenty years, ruined past recovery, and driven to hide his diminished head in the jungle.

The 8th and 9th were passed in burning and destroying the rest of the straggling town, and a variety of smaller boats, which were very numerous. I had also an account to settle with that cunning rascal Macota, for his aiding and abetting Seriff Sahib in his piracies. He had located himself very pleasantly near a bend in the river, about a mile above Seriff Sahib's settlement, and was in the act of building extensive fortifications, when I had the satisfaction of anticipating the visit and some of the compliments he would have conferred on my friend Mr. Brooke at Sarawak. Budrudeen, the *rajah's* brother, had likewise been duped by this fellow, and was exceedingly anxious to insert the blade of a very sharp and beautiful *kris* into the body of his late friend. Mr. Brooke, however, was anxious to save his life, which he afterward had the satisfaction of doing.

I shall never forget the tiger-like look of the young *Pangeran* when we landed together in the hopes of surprising the "Serpent" in his den; but he was too quick for us, having decamped with his followers, and in so great a hurry as to leave all his valuables behind—among them a Turkish pipe, some chairs once belonging to the Royalist, and other presents from Mr. Brooke. Everything belonging to him was burnt or destroyed save some handsome brass guns. There was one of about 12 cwt. that had been lent by the sultan when Macota was in favour, and which I returned to Budrudeen for his brother.

We were here joined by a large number of the Linga Dyaks, the same force that had joined us the year previous, while up the Sarebus, but unaccompanied by Seriff Jaffer, of whom it was not quite clear that he had not been secretly aiding the pirates. I sent them back with assurances to their chiefs that they should not be molested unless they gave shelter or protection to either Seriff Sahib or Muller. Seriff Sahib, with a considerable body of followers, escaped inland in the direction of the mountains, from the other side of which he would be able to communicate with the River Linga. Macota was obliged to fly up the river toward the Undop, on which the village and residence of Seriff Sahib's brother, Seriff Muller, was situated.

Having destroyed every boat and sampan, as well as house or hut, on the 10th, as soon as the tide had risen sufficiently to take us over the shoals, we weighed, in the steamer, for the country of the Sakarran Dyaks, having sent the boats on before with the first of the flood.

About fifteen miles above Patusen is the branch of the river called the Undop: up this river I dispatched Lieutenant Turnour, with Mr.

Comber, in the *Jolly Bachelor*, and a division of our native boats, while we proceeded to where the river again branches off to the right and left, as on the tongue of land so formed we understood we should find a strong fort; beside, it was the highest point to which we could attempt to take the steamer. The branch to the left is called the Sakarran; that to the right retains the name of Lupar, inhabited chiefly by Sakarrans. We found the place deserted and the houses empty. Knowing that these people depended almost entirely for protection on the strongly fortified position at Patusen, I did not expect any similar opposition from either Seriff Muller or the desperate bloodthirsty Sakarrans, and consequently divided my force into three division—the one, already mentioned, under Lieutenant Turnour, up the Undop; another, under Mr. D'Aeth, up the Lupar; while Lieutenant Wade, accompanied by Mr. Brooke, ascended the Sakarran.

I had not calculated on the disturbed and excited state in which I found the country; and two wounded men having been sent back from the Undop branch with accounts of the pirates, chiefly Malays, who were collected in great numbers, both before and in the rear of our small force; and an attempt having been made to cut off the bearer of this information, Nakoda Bahar, who had had a very narrow escape, and had no idea of taking back an answer unless attended by a European force,—I determined on sending assistance. But I had some difficulty in mustering another crew from the steamer, and was obliged to leave my friend Capt. Scott, with only the idlers, rather critically situated.

I deemed it advisable to recollect my whole force; and before proceeding to the punishment of the Sakarrans, to destroy the power and influence of Seriff Muller, whose town was situated about twenty miles up, and was said to contain a population of 1500 Malays, independently of the surrounding Dyak tribes. Having dispatched boats with directions to Lieutenant Wade and Mr. D'Aeth to join us in the Undop, I proceeded in my gig to the scene of action, leaving the steamer to maintain as strict a blockade of the Sakarran and Lupar branches as, with their reduced force, they were capable of. On my joining Lieutenant Turnour, I found him just returned from a very spirited attack which he had made, assisted by Mr. Comber, on a stockade situated on the summit of a steep hill; Mr. Allen, the master, being still absent on a similar service, on the opposite side of the river.

The gallant old chief Patingi Ali was likewise absent, in pursuit of the enemy that had been driven from the stockades, with whom he had had a hand-to-hand fight, the whole of which—being on the rising ground—was witnessed by our boats' crews, who could not resist hailing his return from his gallant achievement with three hearty British cheers. This had the effect of giving such an impulse to his courage, that, in a subsequent affair, it unhappily caused a serious loss among this active and useful branch of our force.

We had now to unite in cutting our way through a barrier across the river similar to that described in the attack on the Sarebus, which having passed, we brought up for the night close to a still more serious obstacle, being a number of huge trees felled, the branches of which meeting midway in the river, formed apparently an insurmountable obstacle to our progress. But *patience and perseverance overcome all difficulties*; and by night only three of the trees remained to be cleared away. We were now within a short distance of their town, so that we could distinctly hear the noise and confusion which our advance had occasioned.

On the right bank, and about fifty yards in advance of the barrier, stood a farm-house, which we considered it prudent to occupy for the night, for which advanced post we collected about fifty volunteers. These consisted of Messrs. Steward, Williamson, and Comber; a corporal and four marines; my gig's crew; and a medley of picked men from our Dyak and Malay followers; not forgetting my usual and trusty attendant John Eager with his bugle, the sounding of which was to be the signal for the whole force to come to the rescue, in the event of surprise—not at all improbable from the nature of our warfare and our proximity to the enemy's town.

And here a most ludicrous scene occurred during the night. Having placed our sentries and lookout men, and given "*Tiga*" as the watchword, we were, shortly after midnight, suddenly aroused from sound sleep by a Dyak war-yell, which was immediately responded to by the whole force. It was pitch dark: the interior of our farmhouse, the partitions of which had been removed for the convenience of stowage, was crowded to excess. In a moment every man was on his legs: swords, spears, and *krisses* dimly glittered over our heads. It is impossible to describe the excitement and confusion of the succeeding ten minutes: one and all believed that we had been surrounded by the enemy, and cut off from our main party.

I had already thrust the muzzle of my pistol close to the heads of several natives, whom, in the confusion, I had mistaken for Sakarrans; and as each in his turn called out "*Tiga*," I withdrew my weapon to apply it to somebody else; until, at last, we found that we were all "*Tigas.*" I had prevented Eager, more than once, from sounding the alarm, which, from the first, he had not ceased to press me for permission to do. The Dyak yell had, however, succeeded in throwing the whole force afloat into a similar confusion, and not hearing the signal, they concluded that they, and not we, were the party attacked. The real cause we afterward ascertained to have arisen from the alarm of a Dyak, who dreamt, or imagined, that he felt a spear thrust upward through the bamboo-flooring of our building, and immediately gave his diabolical yell. The confusion was ten times as much as it would have been had the enemy really been there. So ended the adventures of the night in the wild jungle of Borneo.

# CHAPTER 19

# The Dido Sails for England

At daylight we were joined by Lieutenant Wade and Mr. Brooke—their division making a very acceptable increase to our force—and by 8 o'clock the last barrier was cut through between us and Seriff Muller's devoted town. With the exception of his own house, from which some eight or nine Malays were endeavouring to move his effects, the whole place was deserted. They made no fight; and an hour afterward the town had been plundered and burnt. The only lives lost were a few unfortunates, who happened to come within range of our musketry in their exertions to save some of their master's property. A handsome large boat, belonging to that chief, was the only thing saved; and this I presented to Budrudeen.

After a short delay in catching our usual supply of goats and poultry, with which the place abounded, we proceeded up the river in chase of the chief and his people; and here again we had to encounter the same obstacle presented by the felled trees thrown across the river—if possible of increased difficulty, owing to their greater size and the narrow breadth of the stream; but although delayed we were not to be beaten. We ascertained that the pirates had retreated to a Dyak village, situated on the summit of a hill, some twenty-five miles higher up the Undop, five or six miles only of which we had succeeded in ascending, as a most dreary and rainy night closed in, during which we were joined by Mr. D'Aeth and his division from the Lupar River.

The following morning, the 13th of August, at daybreak, we again commenced our toilsome work. With the gig and the lighter boats we succeeded better; and I should have despaired of the heavier boats ever getting up, had they not been assisted by an opportune and sudden rise of the tide, to the extent of twelve or fourteen feet, though with this we had to contend against a considerably increased strength of current. It was on this day that my ever active and zealous first lieutenant, Charles Wade, jealous of the advanced position of our light boats, obtained a place in my gig. That evening the *Phlegethon's* first and second cutters, the *Dido's* two cutters, and their gigs, were fortunate enough to pass a barrier composed of trees evidently but recently felled; from which we concluded ourselves to be so near the enemy, that, by pushing forward as long as we could possibly see, we might prevent further impediments from being thrown in our way. This we did; but at 9 p.m. arriving at a broad expanse of the river, and being utterly unable to trace our course, we anchored our advanced force for the night.

On Wednesday, 14th, we again pushed on at daylight. We had gained information of two landing-places leading to the Dyak village on the hill, round three-fourths of the foot of which the Undop flowed. The first landing-place we had no trouble in discovering, from the number of deserted boats collected near it. Leaving these to be looted by our followers, we proceeded in search of the second, which we understood was situated more immediately under the village, and which, having advanced without our guides, we had much difficulty in finding. The circuit of the base of the hill was above five miles. In traversing this distance, we had repeated skirmishing with straggling boats of the enemy, upon whom we came unexpectedly.

During this warfare, Patingi Ali, who, with his usual zeal, had here come up, bringing a considerable native force of both Malays and Dyaks, was particularly on the alert; and while we in the gig attacked the large war-*prahu* of Seriff Muller himself—the resistance of whose followers was only the discharge of their muskets, after which they threw themselves into the river, part only effecting their escape—the Patingi nearly succeeded in capturing that chief in person. He had escaped from his *prahu* into a remarkably beautiful and fast-pulling sampan, in which he was chased by old Ali, and afterward only saved his life by throwing himself into the water, and swimming to the jungle; and it was with no small pride that the gallant old chief appropriated the boat to his own use.

In the *prahu* were captured two large brass guns, two smaller ones, a variety of small arms, ammunition, provisions, colours and personal property, among which were also two pair of handsome jars of English manufacture. After this, having proceeded some considerable distance without finding the second landing-place, we put in close to a clear green spot, with the intention of getting our breakfasts, and of waiting the arrival of the other boat with the guides.

While our crew were busily employed cooking, Lieutenant Wade and myself fancied we heard the suppressed voices of many people not far distant, and taking up our guns we crept into the jungle. We had not penetrated many yards before I came in sight of a mass of boats concealed in a snug little inlet, the entrance to which had escaped our notice. These were filled with the piratical Dyaks and Malays, and on shore at various points were placed armed sentinels. My first impulse was to conceal ourselves until the arrival of our force; but my rash, though gallant friend deemed otherwise; and without noticing the caution of my upheld hand, dashed in advance, discharging his gun, and calling upon our men to follow.

It is impossible to conceive the consternation and confusion this our sudden sally occasioned among the pirates. The confused noise and scrambling from their boats I can only liken to that of a suddenly-roused flock of wild ducks. Our attack from the point whence it came was evidently unexpected; and it is my opinion that they calculated on our attacking the hill, if we did so at all, from the nearest landing-place, without pulling round the other five miles, as the whole attention of their scouts appeared to be directed toward that quarter.

A short distance above them was a small encampment, probably erected for the convenience of their chiefs, as in it we found writing materials, two or three desks of English manufacture, on the brass plate of one of which, I afterward noticed, was engraved the name of "*Mr. Wilson.*" To return to the pirates: with our force, such as it was—nine in number—and headed by Lieutenant Wade, we pursued our terrified enemy, who had not the sense or courage to rally in their judiciously selected and naturally protected encampment, but continued their retreat (firing on us from the jungle) toward the Dyak village on the summit of the hill.

We here collected our force, reloaded our firearms; and Lieutenant Wade, seeing from this spot the arrival at the landing-place of the other boats, again rushed on in pursuit. Before arriving at the foot of the steep ascent on the summit of which the before-mentioned Dyak village stood, we had to cross a small open space of about sixty yards, exposed to the fire from the village as well as the surrounding jungle. It was before crossing this plain that I again cautioned my gallant friend to await the arrival of his men, of whom he was far in advance; and almost immediately afterward he fell mortally wounded at my feet, having been struck by two rifle-shots, and died instantaneously.

I remained with the body until our men came up, and giving it in charge, we carried the place on the height without a check or further accident. The Dyak village we now occupied I would have spared, as on no occasion had we noticed any of the tribe fighting against us; but it was by shot fired from it that poor Wade was killed, and the work of destruction commenced simultaneously with the arrival of our men. It was most gratifying to me throughout the expedition to observe the friendly rivalry and emulation between the crews of the *Phlegethon* and the *Dido's* boats. On this occasion the former had the glory of first gaining the height; and one of the officers of the former, Mr. Simpson, wounded, with a pistol-shot, a man armed with a rifle, supposed to have been the person who had slain our first-lieutenant.

I may here narrate a circumstance, from which one may judge of the natural kind-heartedness of my lamented friend. During the heat of the pursuit, although too anxious to advance to await the arrival of his men, he nevertheless found time to conceal in a place of security a poor terrified Malay girl whom he overtook, and who, by an imploring look, touched his heart. The village and the piratical boats destroyed, and the excitement over, we had time to reflect on the loss we had sustained of one so generally beloved as the leader of the expedition had been among us all. Having laid the body in a canoe, with the British union-jack for a pall, we commenced our descent of the river with very different spirits from those with which we had ascended only a few hours before. In the evening, with our whole force assembled, we performed the last sad ceremony of committing the body to the deep, with all the honours that time and circumstance would allow. I read that beautiful, impressive service from a prayer-book, the only one, by the by, in the expedition, which he himself had brought, as he said, "in case of accident."

Before we again got under weigh, several Malay families, no longer in dread of their piratical chief, Seriff Muller, who had fled nobody knew whither, gave themselves up to us as prisoners, trusting to the mercy of a white man; the first instance of any of them having done so. We heard, also, that Macota had retreated with the *seriff;* and on examination we found the papers captured in the encampment belonged to them, exposing several deep intrigues and false statements addressed to the sultan, the purport of which was to impress his mind with the belief of a hostile intention on the part of the British government toward his country. We brought-up for the night off the still-burning ruins of Seriff Muller's town.

THE FUNERAL OF LIEUTENANT WADE

On Thursday the 15th we again reached the steamer. We found her prepared for action, having been much annoyed during the night by the continued Dyak war-yells—sounds, to uninitiated ears, as unpleasant as those of musketry. Having driven away the two principal instigators and abettors of all the piracies committed along the coast of Borneo and elsewhere, and destroyed their strongholds, it now remained for us to punish the pirates themselves as far as lay in our power. The Sakarran Dyaks being the only ones now remaining who had not received convincing proofs that their brutal and inhuman trade would be no longer allowed, the 15th and 16th were passed on board the steamer, to rest the men after the severe fatigue encountered up the Undop, and in making preparations for an advance up the Sakarran.

During the night of the 16th, several of our native followers were wounded. Their boats not being furnished with anchors, and the river being deep, they were obliged to make fast to the bank, which in the dark afforded great facility for the enemy to creep down through the jungle unperceived, so close as to fire a shot and even thrust their spears through the thin mat covering of the boats. One poor fellow received a shot in his lungs, from which he died the following day; a Dyak likewise died from a spear-wound; and in the morning we witnessed the pile forming for burning the Dyak, and the coffin making for conveying the body of the Malay to Sarawak, his native place; both parties having an equal horror of their dead falling into the hands of the enemy, although differing in their mode of disposing of them.

On Saturday, the 17th, the expedition, consisting of the *Dido's pinnace*, her two cutters and gig, the *Jolly Bachelor*, and the *Phlegethon's* first and second cutters and gig, started up the Sakarran. A small division of light native boats, under the command of the brave old Patingi Ali, were selected to keep as a reconnoitering party with our leading boats, while the remaining native force, of above thirty boats, followed as a reserve. We advanced the first day some twenty miles without so much as seeing a native, although our progress was considerably delayed by stopping to burn farm-houses, and a number of war-*prahus* found concealed in the jungle or long grass on either side of the river. We brought up early in the afternoon, for the purpose of strongly fortifying ourselves, both ashore and afloat, against surprise before the night set in, by which time it would have taken a well-disciplined and powerful force to have dislodged us.

This evening we had unusually fine weather; and we squatted

265

down to our meal of curry and rice with better appetites and higher spirits than we had done for some days. We advanced the following day: and although we reached several villages, the grain had been removed from them all; which, in all probability, was done immediately upon their hearing of the fall of their supposed impregnable Patusen. In the evening we took the same precautions as on the preceding night, considering that our enemies were not to be despised.

Owing to heavy rains which fell during the night, and caused a strong current, our progress was considerably retarded. The scenery was beautiful—more so than in any of the rivers we had yet visited. We likewise now repeatedly fell in with small detachments of the enemy, and spears were thrown from the banks, which added considerably to our excitement and amusement. On every point we found the remains of the preceding night's watch-fires, so that news of our approach would have been conveyed rapidly along. While leading in the gig with a select few of our followers, we came suddenly on a boat full of warriors, all gorgeously dressed, and apparently perfectly unconscious of our approach. The discharge of our muskets and the capsizing of their war-boat was the work of an instant; but most of their crew saved their lives by escaping into the jungle.

This evening, Sunday, the 18th, we experienced some difficulty in finding a suitable place for our bivouac. While examining the most eligible-looking spot on the bank of the river, the crew of one of the *Phlegethon's* boats, having crept up the opposite bank, came suddenly on a party of Dyaks, who saluted them with a war-yell and a shower of spears; and it was absurd to see the way in which they precipitated themselves into the water again to escape from this unexpected danger. The Dyaks, too, appear to have been equally surprised. The place we selected for the night was a large house about forty yards from the edge of the river; and for a musket-range around which we had not much difficulty in clearing the ground. Here we all united our different messes, and passed a jovial evening.

The night, however, set in with a most fearful thunder-storm, accompanied by the most vivid flashes of lightning I ever witnessed. The rain continued to fall in torrents; it cleared up at daylight, when we proceeded. As yet the banks of the river had been a continued garden, with sugarcane plantations and banana-trees in abundance. As we advanced, the scenery assumed a wilder and still more beautiful appearance, presenting high steep points, with large overhanging trees, and occasionally forming into pretty picturesque bays, with sloping banks. At other times we approached narrow gorges, looking so dark that, until past, you almost doubted there being a passage through. We were in hopes that this morning we should have reached their capital, a place called Karangan, supposed to be about ten miles farther on.

At 9 o'clock Mr. Brooke, who was with me in the gig, stopped to breakfast with young Jenkins in the second cutter. Not expecting to meet with any opposition for some miles, I gave permission to Patingi Ali to advance cautiously with his light division, and with positive instructions to fall back upon the first appearance of any natives. As the stream was running down very strong, we held on to the bank, waiting for the arrival of the second cutter. Our *pinnace* and second gig having both passed up, we had remained about a quarter of an hour, when the report of a few musket-shots told us that the pirates had been fallen in with. We immediately pushed on; and as we advanced, the increased firing from our boats, and the war-yells of some thousand Dyaks, let us know that an engagement had really commenced.

It would be difficult to describe the scene as I found it. About twenty boats were jammed together, forming one confused mass; some bottom up; the bows or sterns of others only visible; mixed up, pell-mell, with huge rafts; and among which were nearly all our advanced little division. Headless trunks, as well as heads without bodies, were lying about in all directions; parties were engaged hand to hand, spearing and *krissing* each other; others were striving to swim for their lives; entangled in the common *mêlée* were our advanced boats; while on both banks thousands of Dyaks were rushing down to join in the slaughter, hurling their spears and stones on the boats below.

For a moment I was at a loss what steps to take for rescuing our people from the embarrassed position in which they were, as the whole mass (through which there was no passage) were floating down the stream, and the addition of fresh boats arriving only increased the confusion. Fortunately, at this critical moment one of the rafts, catching the stump of a tree, broke this floating bridge, making a passage, through which (my gig being propelled by paddles instead of oars) I was enabled to pass.

It occurred to Mr. Brooke and myself simultaneously, that, by advancing in the gig, we should draw the attention of the pirates toward us, so as to give time for the other boats to clear themselves. This had the desired effect. The whole force on shore turned, as if to secure what they rashly conceived to be their prize.

We now advanced mid-channel: spears and stones assailed us from both banks. My friend Brooke's gun would not go off; so giving him the yoke-lines, he steered the boat while I kept up a rapid fire. Mr. Allen, in the second gig, quickly coming up, opened upon them, from a Congreve-rocket tube, such a destructive fire as caused them to retire panic-struck behind the temporary barriers where they had concealed themselves previous to the attack upon Patingi Ali, and from whence they continued, for some twenty minutes, to hurl their spears and other missiles.

Among the latter may be mentioned short lengths of bamboo, one end heavily loaded with stone, and thrown with great force and precision; the few firearms of which they were possessed were of but little use to them after the first discharge, the operation of reloading, in their inexperienced hands, requiring a longer time than the hurling of some twenty spears. The *sumpitan* was likewise freely employed by these pirates; but although several of our men belonging to the *pinnace* were struck, no fatal results ensued, from the dextrous and expeditious manner in which the wounded parts were excised by Mr. Beith, the assistant-surgeon; any poison that might remain being afterward sucked out by one of the comrades of the wounded men.

As our force increased, the pirates retreated from their position, and could not again muster courage to rally. Their loss must have been considerable; ours might have been light, had poor old Patingi Ali attended to orders.

It appears that the Patingi (over-confident, and probably urged on by Mr. Steward, who, unknown to me, was concealed in Ali's beat when application was made by that chief for permission to proceed in advance for the purpose of reconnoitring), instead of falling back, as particularly directed, on the first appearance of any of the enemy, made a dash, followed by his little division of boats, through the narrow pass above described. As soon as he had done so, huge rafts of bamboo were launched across the river, so as to cut off his retreat. Six large war-*prahus*, probably carrying 100 men each, then bore down—three on either side—on his devoted followers; and one only of a crew of seventeen that manned his boat escaped to tell the tale. When last seen by our advanced boats, Mr. Steward and Patingi Ali were in the act (their own boats sinking) of boarding the enemy. They were doubtless overpowered and killed, with twenty-nine others, who lost their lives on this occasion. Our wounded in all amounted to fifty-six.

A few miles higher up was the town and capital of Karangan, which place it was their business to defend, and ours to destroy, and this we succeeded in effecting without further opposition. We ascended a short distance above this, but found the river impracticable for the further progress of the boats; but our object having been achieved, the expedition may be said to have closed, as no more resistance was offered; so we dropped leisurely down the river, and that evening reached our resting-place of the previous night: but having burnt the house in the morning, we were obliged to sleep in our boats, with a strong guard on shore.

Attempts were made to molest the native boats by hurling spears into them from the jungle under cover of the night; but after a few discharges of musketry the enemy retired, leaving us to enjoy another stormy and rainy night as we best could.

On the 20th we reached the steamer, where we remained quiet all the next day, attending to the wounded, and ascertaining the exact extent of our loss. On the 22nd we again reached Patusen. We found everything in the same wretched state as when we left; and a pile of firewood, previously cut for the use of the steamer, had not been removed. After dark a storm of thunder, lightning, and heavy rain, came on as usual, and with it a few mishaps. A boat belonging to the old *tumangong* was capsized by the bore, by which his plunder, including a large brass gun, was lost, and the crew with difficulty saved their lives.

At eight we heard the report of a gun, which was again repeated much nearer at nine; and before a signal-rocket could be fired, or a light shown, we were astonished by being hailed by the boats of a British man-of-war; and the next moment Captain Sir E. Belcher, having been assisted by a rapid tide, came alongside the steamer with the welcome news of having brought our May letters from England. On the arrival of the *Samarang* off the Morotaba, Sir Edward heard of the loss we had sustained; and, with his usual zeal and activity, came at once to our assistance, having brought his boats no less than 120 miles in about thirty hours.

At the moment of his joining us, our second mishap occurred. The night, as previously mentioned, was pitch dark, and a rapid current running, when the cry of "a man overboard" caused a sensation difficult to describe. All available boats were immediately dispatched in search; and soon afterward we were cheered by the sound of "all right." It appears that the news of the arrival of the mail was not long in spreading throughout our little fleet, when Mr. D'Aeth, leaving the first cutter in a small sampan, capsized in coming alongside the steamer; the man in the bow (who composed the crew) saved himself by catching hold of the nearest boat; Mr. D'Aeth would have been drowned had he not been an excellent swimmer. This was not the last of our mishaps; for we had no sooner arranged ourselves and newly-arrived visitors from the *Samarang* comfortably on board the steamer from the pelting rain, than the accustomed and quick ear of Mr. Brooke heard the cry of natives in distress. Jumping into his Singapore sampan, he pushed off to their assistance, and returned shortly afterward, having picked up three, half drowned, of our Dyak followers, whom he had found clinging to the floating trunk of a tree. They too had been capsized by the bore; when, out of eleven composing the crew, only these three were saved—although the Dyaks are invariably expert swimmers.

On the 23rd, after waiting to obtain meridian observations, we moved down as far as the mouth of the River Linga, and then dispatched one of our Malay chiefs to the town of Bunting to summon Seriff Jaffer to a conference. This, however, he declined on a plea of ill health, sending assurance, at the same time, of his goodwill and inclination to assist us in our endeavours to suppress piracy.

On the night of the 24th, we once again reached Sarawak, where the rejoicings of the previous year, when we returned from a successful expedition, were repeated. On the third evening after our return, we were just settling down to enjoy a little rest, having got our sick and wounded into comfortable quarters, and were beginning heartily to indulge in the comforts of a bed after our fatigue and harassing duties in open boats during the previous three weeks, when information arrived that Seriff Sahib had taken refuge in the Linga River, where, assisted by Seriff Jaffer, he was again collecting his followers. No time was to be lost; and on the 28th, with the addition of the *Samarang's* boats, we once more started, to crush, if possible, this persevering and desperate pirate; and, in the middle of the night, came to an anchor inside the Linga River.

When our expedition had been watched safely outside the Batang Lupar, on its return to Sarawak, all those unfortunate families that had concealed themselves in the jungle, after the destruction of the different towns of Patusen and Undop, had emerged from their hiding-places, and, embarking on rafts, half-ruined boats, or, in short, anything that would float, were in the act of tiding and working their passage toward the extensive and flourishing town of Bunting. Their dismay can well be imagined, when, at daylight on the morning of the 29th, they found themselves carried by the tide close alongside

the long, black, terror-spreading steamer, and in the midst of our augmented fleet. Escape to them was next to hopeless; nor did the softer
sex seem much to mind the change—probably thinking that to be
swallowed up by the white man was not much worse than dying in
the jungle of starvation. I need not say that, instead of being molested,
they were supplied with such provisions and assistance as our means
would permit us to afford, and then allowed to pass quietly on; in addition to which we dispatched several of our native followers into the
Batang Lupar, to inform the poor fugitives that our business was with
the chiefs and instigators of piracy, and not to molest the misguided
natives.

With the ebb tide a large number of boats came down from the
town—the news of our arrival having reached them during the
night—containing the principal chiefs, with assurances of their pacific
intentions, and welcoming us with presents of poultry, goats, fruit,
&c., which we received, paying the fair market-price for them, either
by way of barter or in hard dollars. They assured us that Seriff Sahib
should not be received among them; but that they had heard of his
having arrived at Pontranini, on a small tributary stream some fifty
miles above their town. We immediately decided on proceeding in
pursuit before he could have time to establish himself in any force.

It was also evident that the Balow Dyaks, who inhabit this part of
the country, were decidedly in favour of our operations against Seriff
Sahib, although afraid—on account of Seriff Jaffer and his Malays—to
express their opinions openly. We also ascertained that Macota, with
a remnant of his followers, was hourly expected in the mouth of the
river, from the jungle, into which he had been driven during the fight
on the Undop heights. Knowing that it would fare badly with this
treacherous and cunning, although now harmless chief, should he fall
into the hands of any of our native followers, I dispatched two boats
to look out for and bring him to us alive. This they succeeded in doing, securing him in a deep muddy jungle, into which he had thrown
himself upon perceiving the approach of our men. Leaving him a prisoner on board the *Phlegethon*, we, with the floodtide pushed forward
in pursuit of Seriff Sahib.

For two days we persevered in dragging our boats, for the distance
of twenty miles, up a small jungly creek, which, to all appearance, was
impassable for anything but canoes. But it had the desired effect, proving to the natives what determination could achieve in accomplishing our object, even beyond the hopes of our sanguine Balow Dyak

guides. The consequence was, that Seriff Sahib made a final and pre-cipitate retreat, across the mountains, in the direction of the Pontiana River. So close were we on his rear—harassed as he was by the Balow Dyaks, who had refused him common means of subsistence—that he threw away his sword, and left behind him a child whom he had hitherto carried in the jungle; and this once dreaded chief was now driven, single and unattended, out of the reach of doing any further mischief.

The boats returned, and took up a formidable position off the town of Bunting, where we summoned Seriff Jaffer to a conference. To this he was obliged to attend, as the natives had learnt that we were not to be trifled with, and would have forced him on board rather than have permitted their village to be destroyed. With Pangeran Budrudeen, acting as the representative of the sultan, Seriff Jaffer was obliged to resign all pretensions to the government of the province over which he had hitherto held sway, since it was considered, from his being a Malay and from his relationship to Seriff Sahib, that he was an unsafe person to be intrusted With so important a post.

A second conference on shore took place, at which the chiefs of all the surrounding country attended, when the above sentence was confirmed. On this occasion I had the satisfaction of witnessing what must have been—from the effect I observed it to have produced on the hearers—a fine piece of oratory, delivered by Mr. Brooke in the native tongue, with a degree of fluency I had never witnessed before, even in a Malay. The purport of it, as I understood, was, to point out emphatically the horrors of piracy on the one hand, which it was the determination of the British government to suppress, and on the other hand, the blessings arising from peace and trade, which it was equally our wish to cultivate; and it concluded by fully explaining, that the measures lately adopted by us against piracy were for the protec-tion of all the peaceful communities along the coast. So great was the attention bestowed during the delivery of this speech that the drop-ping of a pin might have been heard.

From these people many assurances were received of their anxi-ety and willingness to cooperate with us in our laudable undertaking; and one and all were alike urgent that the government of their river should be transferred to the English.

On the 4th September the force again reached Sarawak, and thus terminated a most successful expedition against the worst pirates on the coast of Borneo.

We found the Samarang off the Morotaba entrance, when Mr. Brooke and myself became the guests of Sir Edward Belcher for several days, during which time we made excursions to all the small islands in that neighbourhood, discovered large quantities of excellent oysters, and had some very good hog-shooting. Afterward, accompanied by the boats of the Samarang, we paid a visit to the Lundu Dyaks, which gave them great delight. They entertained us at a large feast, when the whole of the late expedition was fought over again, and a war-dance with the newly-acquired heads of the Sakarran pirates was performed for our edification. Later in the evening, two of the elder chiefs got up, and, walking up and down the long gallery, commenced a dialogue, for the information, as they said, of the women, children, and poorer people who were obliged to remain at home.

It consisted in putting such questions to one another as should elicit all the particulars of the late expedition, such as, what had become of different celebrated Sakarran chiefs (whom they named)? how had they been destroyed? how did they die? by whom had they been slain? &c. All these inquiries received [289]the most satisfactory replies, in which the heroic conduct of themselves and the white men was largely dwelt upon. While this was performing, the two old warriors, with the heads of their enemies suspended from their shoulders like a soldier's *cartouch*-box, stumped up and down, striking the floor with their clubs, and getting very excited. How long it lasted none of our party could tell, as one and all dropped off to sleep during the recital. Mr. Brooke has given so good a description of these kind and simple people that I need not here farther notice them.

Shortly after our return to the *Samarang*, she, getting short of provisions, sailed for Singapore, and Mr. Brooke and myself went up to Sarawak, where the *Dido* was still lying. Great rejoicings and firing of cannon, as on a former occasion, announced our return; and, after paying our respects to the *rajah*, we visited the *tumangong* and *patingis*.

A curious ceremony is generally performed on the return of the chiefs from a fortunate war expedition, which is not only done by way of a welcome back, but is supposed to insure equal success on the next excursion. This ceremony was better performed at the old *tumangong's* than at the other houses. After entering the principal room we seated ourselves in a semicircle on the mat floor, when the old chief's three wives advanced to welcome us, with their female relatives, all richly and prettily dressed in *sarongs* suspended from the waist, and silken scarfs worn gracefully over one shoulder, just hiding or exposing as

War dance of the Lundu Dyaks

much of their well-shaped persons as they thought most becoming.

Each of these ladies in succession taking a handful of yellow rice, threw it over us, repeating some mystical words, and dilating on our heroic deeds, and then they sprinkled our heads with gold-dust. This is generally done by grating a lump of gold against a dried piece of shark's skin. Two of these ladies bore the pretty names of Inda and Amina. Inda was young, pretty, and graceful; and although she had borne her husband no children, she was supposed to have much greater influence over him than the other two. Report said that she had a temper, and that the *tumangong* was much afraid of her; but this may have been only Sarawak scandal. She brought her portion of gold-dust already grated, and wrapped up in a piece of paper, from which she took a pinch; and in reaching to sprinkle some over my head, she, by accident, put the prettiest little foot on to my hand, which, as she wore neither shoes nor stockings, she did not hurt sufficiently to cause me to withdraw it. After this ceremony we (the warriors) feasted and smoked together, attended on by the ladies.

Another conference with Muda Hassim took place, and I subsequently quitted Sarawak for Singapore, intending to re-provision the *Dido* at that port, and then return to Sarawak, in order to convey the *rajah* and his suite to Borneo Proper. At Singapore, however, I found orders for England, and sailed accordingly; but the service alluded to was readily performed by Sir Edward Belcher, in H.M.S. *Samarang*, accompanied by the H.C.'s steamer *Phlegethon*.

On my return to England I had the gratification to learn that Mr. Brooke had been appointed agent for the British government in Borneo, and that Captain Bethune, R.N., C.B., had been dispatched on special service to that island: events I cannot but consider of great importance to the best interests of humanity, and to the extension of British commerce throughout the Malayan Archipelago.

CHAPTER 20

# Returns Home

The return to England of Captain Bethune, C.B., bringing with him a further portion of Mr. Brooke's *Journal* to my charge, enables me to afford my readers some interesting details relative to the important events that have occurred in Borneo subsequent to my departure from Sarawak.

"*January*, 1845.—The departure of the *Dido* left me sad and lonely, for Captain Keppel had been really my companion and friend; and he so thoroughly entered into my views for the suppression of piracy, and made them his own, that I may not expect any successor to act with the same vigour and the same decision. Gallant *Didos*! I would ask no further aid or protection than I received from you. Sir Edward Belcher, with the *Phlegethon* in company, arrived not long after the *Dido's* departure, and conveyed the Rajah Muda Hassim and his train to Borneo Proper. H.M.S. *Samarang* and *Phlegethon* visited and examined Labuan, and proceeded thence to Ambun. Ambun is a miserable village; and it at once gave the lie to the report of a European female being there in captivity, for no *poor Orang Kaya* could retain such a prize. The inhabitants of Ambun are Badjows, and the country people or Dyaks of the interior are called Dusuns, or villagers.

"I saw many of them, and they appeared a gentle mild race, and far less warlike by account than our Dyaks. They are not tattooed, and the *sumpitan* is unknown amongst them. Leaving Ambun, which is situated in a pretty bay, we proceeded to Tampasuk, a considerable town, inhabited by Illanuns and Badjows. This is a piractical town; and I was informed by an Arab in captivity there that scarcely a week passes without strife and contention amongst themselves. There likewise I received information respecting the Balagnini, the great pirates

276

of these seas. They are represented as in habiting numerous small islands in the vicinity of Sooloo: their origin is Badjow. I apprehend there would be little difficulty in breaking their power, and curing the propensity to piracy.

"This cruise being over, I established myself quietly at Sarawak. The country is peaceable; trade flourishes; the Dyaks are content; the Malays greatly increased in number—in short, all goes well. I received a visit from Lingire, a Dyak chief of Sarebus. At first he was shy and somewhat suspicions; but a little attention soon put him at his ease. He is an intelligent man; and I hail with pleasure his advent to Sarawak, as the dawn of a friendship with the two pirate tribes. It is not alone for the benefit of these tribes that I desire to cultivate their friendship, but for the greater object of penetrating the interior through their means. There are no Malays there to impede our progress by their lies and their intrigues; and, God willing, these rivers shall be the great arteries by which civilization shall be circulated to the heart of Borneo.

"*14th.*—The Dyaks of Tumma, a runaway tribe from Sadong, came down last night, as Bandar Cassim of Sadong wishes still to extract property from them. Bandar Cassim I believe to be a weak man, swayed by stronger-headed and worse rascals; but, now that Seriff Sahib and Muda Hassim are no longer in the country, he retains no excuse for oppressing the poor Dyaks. Si Nankan and Tumma have already flown, and most of the other tribes are ready to follow their example, and take refuge in Sarawak. I have fully explained to the *bandar* that he will lose all his Dyaks if he continues his system of oppression, and more especially if he continues to resort to that most hateful system of seizing the women and children.

"I had a large assembly of natives, Malay and Dyaks, and held forth many good maxims to them. At present, in Sarawak, we have Balows and Sarebus, mortal enemies; Lenaar, our extreme tribe, and our new Sadong tribe of Tumma. Lately we had Kantoss, from near Sarambow, in the interior of Pontiana; Undops, from that river; and Badjows, from near Lantang—tribes which had never thought of Sarawak before, and perhaps never heard the name. Oh, for power to pursue the course pointed out!

"*16th.*—The Julia arrived, much to my relief; and Mr. Low, a botanist and naturalist, arrived in her. He will be a great acquisition to our society, if devoted to these pursuits. The same day that the Julia entered, the Ariel left the river. I dismissed the Tumma Dyaks; rewarned

Bandar Cassim of the consequences of his oppression; and had a parting interview with Lingire. I had another long talk with Lingire, and did him honour by presenting him with a spear and flag, for I believe he is true, and will be useful; and this Orang Kaya Pa-muncha, the most powerful of these Dyaks, must be mine. Lingire described to me a great fight he once had with the Kayans, on which occasion he got ninety-one heads, and forced a large body of them to retire with inferior numbers. I asked him whether the Kayans used the *sumpitan?* he answered, 'Yes.' 'Did many of your men die from the wounds?' 'No; we can cure them.' This is one more proof in favour of Mr. Crawfurd's opinion that this poison is not sufficiently virulent to destroy life when the arrow is (as it mostly is) plucked instantly from the wound.

"*26th.*—Linn, a Sakarran chief, arrived, deputed (as he asserted, and I believe truly) by the other chiefs of Sakarran to assure me of their submission and desire for peace. He likewise stated, that false rumours spread by the Malays agitated the Dyaks; and the principal rumour was, that they would be shortly attacked again by the white men. These rumours are spread by the Sariki people, to induce the Sakarrans to quit their river and take refuge in the interior of the *Rejong*; and once there, the Sakarrans would be in a very great measure at the mercy of the Sariki people. This is a perfect instance of Malay dealing with the Dyaks; but in this case it has failed, as the Sakarrans are too much attached to their country to quit it. I am inclined to believe their professions; and at any rate it is convenient to do so and to give them a fair trial.

"*28th.*—How is it to be accounted for, that the Malays have so bad a character with the public, and yet that the few who have had opportunities of knowing them well speak of them as a simple and not unamiable people? With the vulgar, the idea of a Malay—and by the Malay they mean the entire Polynesian race, with the exception of the Javanese—is that of a treacherous, blood-thirsty villain; and I believe the reason to be, that from our first intercourse to the present time, it is the *pangerans* or *rajahs* of the country, with their followers, who are made the standard of Malay character. These *rajahs*, born in the purple; bred amid slaves and fighting-cocks, inheriting an undisputed power over their subjects, and under all circumstances, whether of riches or poverty, receiving the abject submission of those around their persons, are naturally the slaves of their passions—haughty, rapacious, vindictive, weak, and tenacious unto death of the paltry punctilio of their court The followers of such *rajahs* it is needless to describe; they are the tools of the *rajah's* will, and more readily disposed for evil than for good; unscrupulous, cunning, intriguing, they are prepared for any act of violence.

"We must next contrast these with a burly, independent trader, eager after gain; probably not over-scrupulous about the means of obtaining it, ignorant of native character, and heedless of native customs and native etiquette. The result of such a combination of ingredients causes an explosion on the slightest occasion. The European is loud, contemptuous, and abusive; the Malay cool and vindictive. The regal dignity has been insulted; the *rajah* has received 'shame' before his court; evil counsellors are at hand to whisper the facility of revenge, and the advantages to be derived from it. The consequence too frequently follows—the captain and crew are *krissed*, and their vessel seized and appropriated. The repeated tragedy shocks the European mind; and the Malay has received, and continues to this day to receive, a character for treachery and bloodthirstiness.

"Even in these common cases an allowance must be made for the insults received, which doubtless on numerous occasions were very gross, and such flagrant violations of native customs as to merit death in native eyes; and we must bear in mind, that we never hear but one side of the tale, or only judge upon a bloody fact. It is from such samples of Malays that the general character is given by those who have only the limited means of trade for forming a judgment; but those who have known the people of the interior and lived among them, far removed from the influence of their *rajahs*, have given them a very different character. Simple in their habits, they are neither treacherous nor bloodthirsty; cheerful, polite, hospitable, gentle in their manners, they live in communities with fewer crimes and fewer punishments than most other people of the globe.

"They are passionately fond of their children, and indulgent even to a fault; and the ties of family relationship and good feeling continue in force for several generations. The feeling of the Malay, fostered by education, is acute, and his passions are roused if shame be put upon him; indeed, this dread of shame amounts to a disease; and the evil is, that it has taken a wrong direction, being more the dread of exposure or abuse, than shame or contrition for any offence.

"I have always found them good-tempered and obliging, wonderfully amenable to authority, and quite as sensible of benefits conferred, and as grateful, as other people of more favoured countries. Of course there is a reverse to this picture. The worst feature of the Malay character is the want of all candour or openness, and the restless spirit of cunning intrigue which animates them, from the highest to the lowest. Like other Asiatics, truth is a rare quality among them. They are superstitious, somewhat inclined to deceit in the ordinary concerns of life, and they have neither principle nor conscience when they have the means of oppressing an infidel, and a Dyak who is their inferior in civilization and intellect.

"If this character of the Malay be summed up, it will be anything but a bad one on the whole; it will present a striking contrast to the conduct and character of the *rajahs* and their followers, and I think will convince any impartial inquirer, that it is easily susceptible of improvement. One of the most fertile sources of confusion is, classing at one time all the various nations of the Archipelago under the general name of Malay, and at another restricting the same term to one people, not more ancient, not the fountain-head of the others, who issued from the centre of Sumatra, and spread themselves in a few parts of the Archipelago.

"The French, the German, the English, Scotch, and Irish are not more different in national character than the Malay, the Javanese, the Bugis, the Illanun, and the Dyak; and yet all these are indiscriminately called Malay, and a common character bestowed upon them. It would be as wise and as sensible to speak of a European character.

"*31st.*—Started on a short excursion up the country, and slept at Siniawan. Here I found a young *pangeran* (who came from Sambas with Mr. Hupé, a German missionary) enchained in the delights of opium. He left Sarawak for Sambas two months since, proceeded five hours' journey, and has since been smoking the drug and sleeping alternately. His life passes thus: between four and five he wakes, yawns, and smokes a pipe or two, which fits him for the labours of taking his guitar and playing for an hour. Then follows a slightly tasted meal, a pipe or two succeeds, and content and merriment for another hour or two. About eight o'clock the gentleman reclines, and pipe succeeds pipe till, toward daylight, he sinks intoxicated and stupid on his pillow, to wake up again in due course to play again the same part. Poor wretch! two months of this life of dissipation have reduced him to a shadow—two more months will consign him to his grave.

"*Feb. 1st.*—Started after breakfast, and paddled against a strong current past Tundong, and, some distance above, left the main stream and entered the branch to the right, which is narrower, and rendered difficult of navigation by the number of fallen trees which block up the bed, and which sometimes obliged us to quit our boat, and remove all the *kajang* covers, so as to enable us to haul the boat under the huge trunks. The main stream was rapid and turbid, swollen by a fresh, and its increase of volume blocked up the waters of the tributary, so as to render the current inconsiderable.

"The Dyaks have thrown several bridges across the rivers, which they effect with great ingenuity; but I was surprised on one of these bridges to observe the traces of the severe flood which we had about a fortnight since. The water on that occasion must have risen twenty feet perpendicularly, and many of the trees evidently but recently fallen, are the effects of its might. The walk to Rat, or Ra-at, is about two miles along a decent path. Nothing can be more picturesque than the hill and the village. The former is a huge lump (I think of granite), almost inaccessible, with bold bare sides, rising out of a rich vegetation at the base, and crowned with trees. The height is about 500 feet; and about a hundred feet lower is a shoulder of the hill on which stands the eagle-nest-like village of Ra-at, the ascent to which is like climbing by a ladder up the side of a house.

"This is one of the dwelling-places of the Sow Dyaks, a numerous but dispersed tribe. Their chief, or *orang kaya*, is an imbecile old man, and the virtual headship is in the hands of Nimok, of whom more hereafter. Our friends seemed pleased to see us, and Nimok apologized for so few of his people being present, as the harvest was approaching; but being anxious to give a feast on the occasion of my first visit to their tribe, it was arranged that tomorrow I should shoot deer, and the day following return to the mountain. The views on either side from the village are beautiful—one view enchanting from its variety and depth, more especially when lighted up by the gleam of a showery sunshine, as I first saw it. Soon, however, after our arrival, the prospect was shut out by clouds, and a soaking rain descended, which lasted for the greater part of the night.

"*2nd.*—Started after breakfast, and after a quiet walk of about three hours through a pleasant country of alternate hill and valley, we saw the valley of Nawang below us. Nawang is the property of the Singè Dyaks, and is cultivated by poor families, at the head of which is Niarak. The house contained three families, and our party was distributed among them, ourselves, *i. e.* Low, Crookshank, and myself, occupying one small apartment with a man, his wife, and daughter. The valley presented one of the most charming scenes to be imagined—a clearing amid hills of moderate elevation, with the distant mountains in the background; a small stream ran through it, which, being damned in several places, enables the cultivator to flood his *padi*-fields. The *padi* looked beautifully green. A few palms and plantains fringed the farm at intervals, while the surrounding hills were clothed in their native jungle. Here and there a few workmen in the fields heightened the effect; and the scene, as evening closed, was one of calm repose, and, I may say, of peace.

"The cocoa-nut, the betel, the sago, and the *gno* or *gomati*, are the four favourite palms of the Dyaks. In their simple mode of life, these four trees supply them many necessaries and luxuries. The sago furnishes food; and after the pith has been extracted, the outer part forms a rough covering for the rougher floor, on which the farmer sleeps. The leaf of the sago is preferable for the roofing of houses to the *nibong*. The *gomati*, or *gno*, gives the black fibre which enables the owner to manufacture rope or cord for his own use; and over and above, the toddy of this palm is a luxury daily enjoyed.

"When we entered, this toddy was produced in large bamboos, both for our use and that of our attendant Dyaks; I thought it, however, very bad. In the evening we were out looking for deer, and passed many a pleasant spot which once was a farm, and which will become a farm again. These the Dyaks called *rapack*, and they are the favourite feeding-grounds of the deer. To our disappointment we did not get a deer, which we had reckoned on as an improvement to our ordinary dinner-fare. A sound sleep soon descended on our party, and the night passed in quiet; but it is remarkable how vigilant their mode of life renders the Dyaks. Their sleep is short and interrupted; they constantly rise, blow up the fire, and look out on the night: it is rarely that some or other of them are not on the move.

"Yearly the Dyaks take new ground for their farm; yearly they fence it in, and undergo the labour of reclaiming new land; for seven years the land lies fallow, and then may be used again. What a waste of labour! more especially in these rich and watered valleys, which, in the hands of the Chinese, might produce two crops yearly.

"*3rd.*—Took leave of this pleasant valley, and by another and shorter road than we came reached Ra-at. We arrived in good time on the hill, and found everything prepared for a feast. There was nothing new in this feast. A fowl was killed with the usual ceremony; afterward a hog. The hog is paid for by the company at a price commensurate with its size: a split bamboo is passed round the largest part of the body, and knots tied on it at given distances; and according to the number of these knots are the number of *pasus* or *padi* for the price.

"Our host of Nawang, Niarak, arrived to this feast with a plentiful supply of toddy; and before the dance commenced, we were requested to take our seats. The circumstances of the tribe, and the ability of Nimok, rendered this ceremony interesting to me. The Sow tribe has long been split into four parties, residing at different places. Gunong Sow, the original locality, was attacked by the Sakarran Dyaks, and thence Nimok and his party retired to Ra-at. A second smaller party subsequently located at or near Bow, as being preferable; while the older divisions of Jaguen and Ahuss lived at the places so named. Nimok's great desire was to gather together his scattered tribe, and to become *de facto* its head.

"My presence and the *datus'* was a good opportunity for gathering the tribe; and Nimok hoped to give them the impression that we countenanced his proposition. The dances over, Nimok pronounced an oration: he dwelt on the advantages of union; how desirous he was to benefit his tribe; how constantly it was his custom to visit Sarawak in order to watch over the interests of the tribe—the trouble was his, the advantage theirs; but how, without union, could they hope to gain any advantage—whether the return of their remaining captive women, or any other? He proposed this union; and that, after the *padi* was ripe, they should all live at Ra-at, where, as a body, they were always ready to obey the commands of the *Tuan Besar* or the *datu*.

"This was the substance of Nimok's speech. But the effect of his oratory was not great; for the Bow, and other portions of the tribe, heard coldly his proposition, though they only opposed it in a few words. It was evident they had no orator at all a match for Nimok: a few words from Niana drew forth a second oration. He glanced at their former state; he spoke with animation of their enemies, and dwelt on their great misfortune at Sow; he attacked the Singè as the cause of these misfortunes: and spoke long and eloquently of things past, of things present, and things to come.

"He was seated the whole time; his voice varied with his subject, and was sweet and expressive; his action was always moderate, principally laying down the law with his finger on the mats. Niarak, our Singè friend, attempted a defence of his tribe; but he had drunk too freely of his own *arrack*; and his speech was received with much laughter, in which he joined. At this juncture I retired, after saying a few words; but the talk was kept up for several hours after, amid feasting and drinking.

"*4th.*—After breakfast, walked to our boats, and at six p.m. reached home, just in time; weather very rainy.

"*10th.*—Nothing to remark in these days, except the ordinary course of business and of life.

"*13th.*—The *tumangong* returned from Sadong, and brought me a far better account of that place than I had hoped for. It appears that they really are desirous to govern well, and to protect the Dyaks; and fully impressed with the caution I gave them, that unless they protect and foster their tribes, they will soon lose them from their removal to Sarawak.

"One large tribe, the Maluku, a branch of the Sibnowans, are, it appears, very desirous of being under my protection. It is a tempting offer, and I should like to have them; but I must not deprive the rulers of Sadong of the means of living comfortably, and the power of paying revenue. Protect them I both can and will. There are great numbers of Sarawak people at Sadong, all looking out for birds-nests; new caves have been explored; mountains ascended for the first time in the search. It shows the progress of good government and security, and, at the same time, is characteristic of the Malay character. They will endure fatigue, and run risks, on the chance of finding this valuable commodity; but they will not labour steadily, or engage in pursuits which would lead to fortune by a slow progress.

"*15th.*—Panglima Laksa, the chief of the Undop tribe, arrived, to request, as the Badjows and Sakarrans had recently killed his people, that I would permit him to retort. At the same time came Abong Kapi, the Sakarran Malay, with eight Sakarran chiefs, named Si Miow, one of the heads, and the rest Tadong, Lengang, Barunda, Badendang, Si Bunie, Si Ludum, and Kuno, the representatives of other heads. Nothing could be more satisfactory than the interview, just over. They denied any knowledge or connection with the Badjows, who had killed some Dyaks at Undop, and said all that I could desire. They promised to obey me, and look upon me as their chief: they desired to trade, and would guaranty any Sarawak people who came to their river; but they could not answer for all the Dyaks in the Batang Lupar.

"It is well known, however, that the Batang Lupar Dyaks are more peaceable than those of Sakarran, and will be easily managed; and as for the breaking out of these old feuds, it is comparatively of slight importance, compared to the grand settlement; for as our influence increases we can easily put down the separate sticks of the bundle. There is a noble chance, if properly used! It may be remarked that many of their names are from some peculiarity of person, or from some quality. *Tadong* is a poisonous snake; but, on inquiry, I found the young chief so named had got the name from being black. They are certainly a fine-looking race.

"*17th.*—Plenty of conferences with the Sakarran chiefs; and, as far as I can judge, they are sincere in the main, though some reserves there may be. Treachery I do not apprehend from them; but, of course, it will be impossible, over a very numerous, powerful, and warlike tribe, to gain such an ascendency of a sudden as at once to correct their evil habits."

Here again Mr. Brooke appears to have been placed on the horns of a dilemma by his ignorance of the views of the British Government. Had his position in Borneo been certain—had he either been supported or deserted—his path of policy would have been clear; whereas he evidently did not know what the morrow would bring forth; whether it would find him with an English force at his back, or abandoned to his own resources.

CHAPTER 21

# Mr. Brooke's Memorandum on the Piracy of the Malayan Archipelago

I cannot afford my readers a more accurate idea of the present state of piracy in the Malayan Archipelago, of the best mode of suppressing it, and of the vast field which the island of Borneo offers for the extension of British commerce, than by quoting a few of Mr. Brooke's observations on these important subjects, written before the operations of the squadron under command of Rear-Admiral Sir Thomas Cochrane took place, of which an account will be given in Chapter 22. With reference to the first topic, piracy, Mr. Brooke remarks:—

"The piracy of the Eastern Archipelago is entirely distinct from piracy in the Western world; for, from the condition of the various governments, the facilities offered by natural situation, and the total absence of all restraint from European nations, the pirate communities have attained an importance on the coasts and islands most removed from foreign settlements. Thence they issue forth and commit depredations on the native trade, enslave the inhabitants at the entrance of rivers, and attack ill-armed or stranded European vessels; and roving from place to place, they find markets for their slaves and plunder.

"The old-established Malay governments (such as Borneo and Sooloo), weak and distracted, are, probably without exception, participators in or victims to piracy; and in many cases both—purchasing from one set of pirates, and enslaved and plundered by another; and while their dependencies are abandoned, the unprotected trade languishes from the natural dread of the better-disposed natives to undertake a coasting voyage.

"It is needless to dwell upon the evil effects of piracy; but before venturing an opinion on the most effectual means of suppression, I propose briefly to give an account of such pirate communities as I am acquainted with.

"The pirates on the coast of Borneo may be classed into those who make long voyages in large heavy-armed *prahus*, such as the Illanuns, Balignini, &c., and the lighter Dyak fleets, which make short but destructive excursions in swift *prahus*, and seek to surprise rather than openly to attack their prey. A third, and probably the worst class, are usually half-bred Arab *seriffs*, who, possessing themselves of the territory of some Malay state, form a nucleus for piracy, a rendezvous and market for all the roving fleets; and although occasionally sending out their own followers, they more frequently seek profit by making advances, in food, arms, and gunpowder, to all who will agree to repay them at an exorbitant rate in slaves.

"The Dyaks of Sarebus and Sakarran were under the influence of two Arab *seriffs*, who employed them on piratical excursions, and shared in equal parts the plunder obtained. I had once the opportunity of counting ninety-eight boats about to start on a cruise; and reckoning the crew of each boat at the moderate average of twenty-five men, it gives a body of 2450 men on a piratical excursion. The piracies of these Arab *seriffs* and their Dyaks were so notorious, that it is needless to detail them here; but one curious feature, which throws a light on the state of society, I cannot forbear mentioning. On all occasions of a Dyak fleet being about to make a piratical excursion, a gong was beat round the town ordering a particular number of Malays to embark; and in case anyone failed to obey, he was fined the sum of thirty rupees by the *seriff* of the place.

"The blow struck by Captain Keppel of Her Majesty's ship *Dido* on these two communities was so decisive as to have put an entire end to their piracies; the leaders Seriff Sahib and Seriff Muller have fled, the Malay population has been dispersed, and the Dyaks so far humbled, as to sue for protection; and in future, by substituting local Malay rulers of good character in lieu of the piratical *seriffs*, a check will be placed on the Dyaks, and they may be broken of their piratical habits, in as far as interferes with the trade of the coast.

"The next pirate horde we meet with is a mixed community of Illanuns and Badjows (or sea-gipsys) located at Tampasuk, a few miles up a small river; they are not formidable in number, and their depredations are chiefly committed on the Spanish territory; their market, until recently, being Bruni, or Borneo Proper. They might readily be dispersed and driven back to their own country; and the Dusuns, or

287

villagers (as the name signifies), might be protected and encouraged. Seriff Houseman, a half-bred Arab, is located in Malludu Bay, and has, by account, from fifteen hundred to two thousand men with him. He is beyond doubt a pirate direct and indirect, and occasionally commands excursions in person, or employs the Illanuns of Tampasuk, and others to the eastward, who for their own convenience make common cause with him. He has no pretension to the territory he occupies; and the authority he exerts (by means of his piratical force) over the interior tribes in his vicinity, and on the island of Palawan, is of the worst and most oppressive description. This *seriff* has probably never come in contact with any Europeans, and consequently openly professes to hold their power in scorn.

"To my own knowledge Seriff Houseman seized and sold into slavery a boat's crew (about twenty men) of the *Sultana*, a merchant ship, which was burned in the Palawan passage. Within the last few months he has plundered and burned a European vessel stranded near the Mangsi Isles; and to show his entire independence of control, his contempt for European power, and his determination to continue in his present course, he has threatened to attack the city of Bruni, in consequence of the Bruni government having entered into a treaty with Her Majesty's government for the discouragement and suppression of piracy.

"This fact speaks volumes; an old-established and recognized Malay government is to be attacked by a lawless adventurer, who has seized on a portion of its territory, and lives by piracy, for venturing to treat with a foreign power for the best purposes. If any further proof of piracy were requisite, it would readily be established by numerous witnesses (themselves the victims), and by the most solemn declaration of the Bruni authorities, that peaceful traders on the high seas have been stopped by the *prahus* of this *seriff* and his allies, their vessel seized, their property plundered, and their persons enslaved; numerous witnesses could attest their having been reduced to slavery and detained in the very household of Seriff Houseman! When, however, the facts of his having sold into slavery the crew of a British vessel (which has been established before the Singapore authorities) come to be known, I conceive every other proof of the character of this person is completely superfluous.

"The indirect piracy of Seriff Houseman is even more mischievous than what is directly committed; for he supplies the Balagnini (a restless piratical tribe, hereafter to be mentioned) with food, powder, arms, salt, &c. under the agreement that they pay him on their return from the cruise, at the rate of five slaves for every 100 *rupees'* worth of goods. The Balagnini are in consequence enabled, through his assistance, to pirate effectively, which otherwise they would not be able to do; as, from their locality, they would find it difficult to obtain firearms and gunpowder.

"The most detestable part of this traffic, however, is Seriff Houseman selling, in cold blood, such of these slaves as are Borneons, to Pangeran Usop, of Bruni, for 100 *rupees* for each slave, and *Pangeran* Usop reselling each for 200 *rupees* to their relations in Bruni. Thus, this vile *seriff* (without taking into account the enormous prices charged for his goods in the first instance) gains 500 *per cent* for every slave, and Pangeran Usop clears 100 *per cent* on the flesh of his own countrymen, thereby *de facto* becoming a party to piracy, though doubtless veiled under the guise of compassion.

"More might be added on the subject of the piracies committed by this *seriff*; and it could easily be shown that the evils accruing from them affect, not only the peaceful trader, but extend to the peaceful agriculturist; but, for the sake of brevity, I deem it sufficient to add, that he exercises the same malign influence on the north coast as Seriff Sahib exercised on the northwest; and that, having surrounded himself by a body of pirates, he arrogates the rights of sovereignty, defies European power, contemns every right principle, and threatens the recognized and legitimate governments of the Archipelago.

"The Balagnini inhabit a cluster of small islands somewhere in the vicinity of Sooloo; they are of the Badjow or sea-gipsy tribe, a wandering race, whose original country has never been ascertained. At present, as far as I can learn, they are not dependent on Sooloo, though it is probable they may be encouraged by some of the *rajahs* of that place, and that they find a slave market there.

"The Balagnini cruise in large *prahus*, and to each *prahu* a fleet *sampan* is attached, which, on occasion, can carry from ten to fifteen men. They seldom carry large guns, like the Illanuns, but in addition to their other arms, big *lelas* (brass pieces, carrying from a one to a three pound ball), spears, swords, &c. They use long poles with barbed iron points, with which, during an engagement or flight, they hook their prey. By means of the fleet *sampans* already mentioned, they are able to capture all small boats; and it is a favourite device with them to disguise one or two men, while the rest lie concealed in the bottom of the boat, and thus to surprise *prahus* at sea, and fishermen or others at the mouths of rivers.

"By being disguised as Chinese they have carried off numbers of that nation from the Sambas and Pontiana Rivers. The cruising-grounds of these pirates are very extensive; they frequently make the circuit of Borneo, proceed as far as the south of Celebes, and in the other direction have been met off Tringanu, Calantan, and Patani. Gillolo and the Moluccas lie within easy range, and it is probable that Papua is occasionally visited by them. It will readily be conceived how harassing to trade must be the continued depredations of the Balagnini pirates, and more especially to the trade of Bruni, which seems, from the unwarlike habits of the natives, the chosen field of their operations.

"The number of Borneons yearly taken into slavery is very considerable, as a fleet of six or eight boats usually hangs about the island of Labuan, to cut off the trade, and to catch the inhabitants of the city. The Borneons, from being so harassed by these pirates, call the easterly wind 'the pirate wind.' The Balagnini commence cruising on the northwest coast about the middle of March, and return, or remove to the eastern side of the island, about the end of November.

"Of Magindano, or Mindanao, we are at the present time very ignorant; but we know that the inhabitants are warlike and numerous, and that that part of the island called Illanun Bay sends forth the most daring pirates of the Archipelago. The first step requisite is to gain more information concerning them, to form an acquaintance with some of their better-disposed chiefs, and subsequently we might act against them with a suitable force; but it would be rash and premature, in the present state of our knowledge, to come in contact with them in their own country. On one occasion I met eighteen Illanun boats on neutral ground, and learned from their two chiefs that they had been two years absent from home; and from the Papuan negro-slaves on board it was evident that their cruise had extended from the most eastern islands of the Archipelago to the north-western coast of Borneo.

"Having now enumerated the pirates I have become acquainted with since my residence in Sarawak, I shall proceed to offer an opinion of the best mode for the suppression of piracy in these seas.

"In the first place, a blow should be struck at the piratical communities with which we are already acquainted, and struck with a force which should convince all other pirates of the hopelessness of resistance; subsequently the recognized Malay governments may be detached from all communication with pirates; and, joining conciliation with punishment, laying down the broad distinction of piracy and no piracy, we may foster those who abandon their evil habits, and punish those who adhere to them.

"A system of supervision will, however, be necessary to carry out these measures: our knowledge of the native states must be improved; and as we become able to discriminate between the good and the bad, our sphere of action may be enlarged, and we may act with decision against all descriptions of pirates; against the indirect as well as the direct pirate; against the receiver of stolen goods as well as the thief; and against the promoter as well as the actual perpetrator of piracy.

"I would especially urge that, to eradicate the evil, the pirate-haunts must be burned and destroyed, and the communities dispersed; for merely to cruise against pirate-*prahus*, and to forbear attacking them until we see them commit a piracy, is a hopeless and an endless task, harassing to our men, and can be attended with but very partial and occasional success; whereas, on the contrary principle, what pirate would venture to pursue his vocation if his home be endangered—if he be made to feel in his own person the very ills he inflicts upon others?

"A question may arise as to what constitutes piracy; and whether, in our efforts to suppress it, we may not be interfering with the right of native states to war one upon another. On the first point, it appears clear to me, that the plunder or seizure of a peaceful and lawful trader on the high seas constitutes an act of piracy, without any reference to the nation or colour of the injured party; for if we limit our construction of piracy, we shall, in most cases, be in want of sufficient evidence to convict, and the whole native trade of the Archipelago will be left at the mercy of pirates, much to the injury of our own commerce and of our settlement of Singapore.

"On the second point, we can only concede the right of war to recognized states; and even then we must carefully avoid introducing the refinements of European international law among a rude and semi-civilized people, who will make our delicacy a cloak for crime, and declare war merely for the sake of committing piracy with impunity. On the contrary, all chiefs who have seized on territory and arrogate independence (making this independence a plea for piracy) can never be allowed the right of declaring war, or entering on hostilities with their neighbours; for, as I have before remarked, all native trade must in that case be at an end, as the piratical chiefs, no longer in dread of punishment from European powers, would doubtless declare war against every unwarlike native state which they did not need as a market for the sale of their slaves and plunder.

"Practically acting, however, on the broad principle, that the seizure of any lawful trader constitutes piracy, I consider no injustice could be done to the native states, and no interference occur with their acknowledged rights; for in practice it would be easy to discriminate a war between native nations from the piracies of lawless hordes of men; and without some such general principle, no executive officer could act with the requisite decision and promptitude to insure the eradication of this great evil.

"With a post such as is proposed to be established, our measures for the suppression of piracy (after the punishment of Seriff Houseman and the Balagnini) would advance step by step, as our knowledge increased, and with alternate conciliation and severity, as the case might require. By detaching the recognised governments from the practice, and gradually forming among the chief men a friendly and English party opposed to piracy, we should, I doubt not, speedily obtain our principal object of clearing the sea of marauders, and ultimately correct the natural propensity of the natives for piracy.

"In order to extend our commerce in these seas generally, and more particularly on the N.W. coast of Borneo, it is requisite, 1st, that piracy be suppressed; 2ndly, that the native governments be settled, so as to afford protection to the poorer and producing classes; and, 3rdly, that our knowledge of the interior should be extended, and our intercourse with the various tribes more frequent.

"That our commerce may be largely extended is so clear that I shall not stop to detail the productions of the island of Borneo, as it will suffice here to state generally that all authorities agree in representing it as one of the richest portions of the globe, and in climate, soil, and mineral and vegetable productions, inferior to no portion of the same extent.

"If these opinions be true—and from my experience I believe them to be so—it follows that the materials for an extensive and extended trade exist, and only require development, while a numerous and industrious, though wild population, which inhabits the interior, is debarred from all intercourse with Europeans from the badness of Malay government.

"On the first requisite for the development of commerce I need add nothing further, as it is a duty incumbent on all governments to eradicate piracy at any cost; and in the present case it would not be found a difficult or tedious task.

"A post like Labuan or Balambangan would, beyond doubt, give an impetus to trade, merely from the freedom from all restrictions, and the absence of all exactions, which the natives would enjoy; and (piracy being checked) countries which now lie fallow would, from their proximity, be induced to bring their produce into market.

"This limited extension is, however, of little moment when compared with the results which must attend our exerting a beneficial influence over the native governments for the purposes of affording protection to the poorer classes, insuring safety to the trader, and opening a field for the planter or the miner.

"The slightest acquaintance with the northwest coast of Borneo would convince any observer of the ease with which these objects might be effected; for the native government, being in a state of decadence, requires protection, and would willingly act justly toward traders and capitalists, and encourage their enterprises, in order to continue on friendly terms with any European power located in their vicinity. The numerous rivers on the coast, with their local rulers, are harassed by the demands of every petty *pangeran*; and while the sovereign is defrauded of his revenue, which the people would cheerfully pay, and his territory ruined, this host of useless retainers (acting always in his name) gain but very slight personal profits to counterbalance all the mischief they do.

"The principal feature is the weakness of the governments, both of the capital and its dependencies; and in consequence of this weakness there is a strong desire for European protection, for European enterprise, and for any change effected by Europeans. Supposing Labuan to be taken as a naval post, I consider that European capital might with safety be employed in Bruni.

"In the rivers contiguous to Sarawak the presence of Europeans would be hailed with joy, not only by the Dyaks, but by the Malays; and subsequently it would depend on their own conduct to what degree they retained the goodwill of the natives; but with ordinary conciliation, and a decent moral restraint on their actions, I feel assured that their persons and property would be safe, and no obstruction offered to fair trade or to mining operations.

"Supposing, as I have before said, the occupation of Labuan by the English, our influence over the government of Bruni would be complete; and one of our principal objects would be to maintain this ascendency, as a means of extending our trade.

"Our position at Labuan would, it must be borne in mind, differ from the position we occupied in relation to the native princes in Singapore. In the latter case, the native princes were without means, without followers, and with a paltry and useless territory, and became our pensioners. In the case of Labuan, we shall have an acknowledged independent state in our vicinity; and for the prosperity of our settlement we must retain our ascendency by the support of the government of Muda Hassim. Let our influence be of the mildest kind; let us, by supporting the legitimate government, ameliorate the condition of the people by this influence; let us pay every honour to the native princes; let us convince them of our entire freedom from all selfish views of territorial aggrandizement on the mainland of Borneo, and we shall enjoy so entire a confidence that virtually the coast will become our own without the trouble or expense of possession.

"I have impressed it on the Rajah Muda Hassim and Pangeran Budrudeen, that the readiest and most direct way of obtaining revenues from their various possessions will be by commuting all their demands for a stated yearly sum of money from each; and by this direct taxation, to which Muda Hassim and his brother seem ready to accede, the system of fraud and exaction would be abolished, the native mind tranquillized, and the legitimate government would become the protector rather than the oppressor of its dependencies. By this measure, likewise, a tone might be imparted to the native chiefs and rulers of rivers, and the people at large taught to feel that, after the payment of a specified sum, a right existed to resist all extra demands.

"Beside this, these *rajahs* are convinced that a certain yearly revenue is what they require, and is the only means by which they can retain their independence; and I have impressed it on their minds that, to gain a revenue, they must foster trade and protect Europeans in their dealings.

"If Labuan were English, and if the sea were clear of pirates, I see no obstacle to bringing these and other measures into immediate operation; and I am assured we should have the sincere and hearty cooperation of the Borneon government.

"Since the advent of Europeans in the Archipelago, the tendency of the Polynesian governments generally has been to decay; here the experiment may be fairly tried on the smallest scale of expense, whether a beneficial European influence may not reanimate a falling state, and at the same time extend our own commerce. We are here devoid of the stimulus which has urged us on to conquest in India. We incur no risk of the collision of the two races: we occupy a small station in the vicinity of a friendly and unwarlike people; and we aim at the development of native countries through native agency.

"If this tendency to decay and extinction be inevitable; if this adaptation of European policy to a native state be found unable to arrest the fall of the Borneon government, yet we shall retain a people already habituated to European manners, industrious interior races, and at a future period, if deemed necessary, settlements gradually developed in a rich and fertile country. We shall have a post in time of war highly advantageous as commanding a favourable position relative to China, we shall extend our commerce, suppress piracy, and prevent the present and prospective advantages from falling into other hands; and we shall do this at small expense.

"I own the native development through their own exertions is but a favourite theory; but whatever may be the fate of the government of Borneo, the people will still remain; and if they be protected and enabled to live in quiet security, I cannot entertain a doubt of the country's becoming a highly productive one, eminently calculated as a field for British enterprise and capital.

"If the development of the resources of the country can be effected by its native rulers it will be a noble task performed; but if it fail, the people of the coast will still advance and form governments for themselves under British influence.

"In concluding this hasty and general view of the subject, I may remark that commerce might be extended and capital laid out on the northwest coast of Borneo, to an amount to which it is difficult to fix limits, as the country is capable of producing most articles of commerce in demand from this quarter of the world, and the natives (who, as far as we know them, are an unwarlike, mild, and industrious race) would receive our manufactures, from which they are now in a great measure debarred. I have not alluded to any other countries of the Archipelago: for we must first become acquainted with them; we must become intimate, cultivate an English party, and accustom them to our manners; and probably the same conciliatory policy, the same freedom from design, which has succeeded in Borneo, will succeed elsewhere, if pushed with temper and patience.

"The general principle ought to be—to encourage established governments, such as those of Borneo and Sooloo, provided they will with all sincerity abandon piracy, and assist in its suppression; but at the same time, by supervision to convince ourselves of the fact, and keep them in the right path; for all treaties with these native states (and we have had several) are but so much waste paper, unless we see them carried into execution.

"I have now only to mention the third means for the extension of commerce. Our intercourse with the natives of the interior should be frequent and intimate: these people (beyond where I am acquainted with them) are represented as very numerous, hospitable, and industrious; and a friendly intercourse would develop the resources of their country, draw its produce to our markets, and give the natives a taste for British manufactures. This intercourse, however, must be prudently introduced and carefully advanced; for to bring these wild people into contact with ignorant and arrogant Europeans would produce bloodshed and confusion in a month.

"In Borneo, it is an advantage that the two races cannot come in collision; for from its climate it precludes all idea of colonization; and that which is next to an impossibility, the maintaining a good understanding between ignorant civilized men and ignorant savages. It is a field for commerce and capital, but no violent change of native customs should be attempted; and in this way alone, by gradual means, can we really benefit the natives and ourselves. When we consider the amount of produce obtained from the countries of the Archipelago, and their consumption of British manufactures, under the worst forms of government, living in a state of distraction and insecurity, and exposed to the depredations of pirates at sea, we may form some idea how vast may be the increase, should peace and security be introduced among them; and judging of the future by the past—by the limited experiment made at Sarawak—we may hope that the task is neither so difficult nor so uncertain as was formerly supposed."

# CHAPTER 22

# Returns to Sarawak

"*February 25th.*—Borneo River, H.M.S. *Driver*. Scarcely, on the 17th, had I finished writing, when a boat from Her Majesty's steamer *Driver*, bringing Captain Bethune and my friend Wise, arrived. How strange, the same day, and almost the same hour, I was penning my doubts and difficulties, when a letter arrives from Lord Aberdeen appointing me confidential agent in Borneo to her majesty, and directing me to proceed to the capital, with a letter addressed to the sultan and the Rajah Muda Hassim, in reply to the documents requesting the assistance of the British government to effect the suppression of piracy.

"My friend Wise I was glad to see, and a few hours' conversation convinced me how greatly I have been indebted to his exertions for success and my present position. His knowledge of trade, his cheerfulness regarding our pecuniary future, all impart confidence. Thus I may say, without much self-flattery, that the first wedge has been driven which may rive Borneo open to commerce and civilization, which may bestow happiness on its inhabitants. Captain Bethune is commissioned to report on the best locality for a settlement or station on the N.W. coast. I will only say here that no other person's appointment would have pleased me so well: he is intelligent, educated, and liberal, and in concert with him I am too happy to work.

"On the 18th of February the *Driver* arrived; on the 21st left Sarawak, and at noon of the 24th arrived at the anchorage in Borneo River, having towed the gun-boat against the N.E. monsoon. Mr. Williamson was dispatched to Borneo, and found all right. They were delighted with our coming and our mission, and the sultan himself has laid aside his fears. A few presents have been sent, which will delight the natives, and all will prosper.

"*26th.*—Budrudeen arrived, and from him I learned the politics of Borneo since my last visit, when Muda Hassim was reinstated in authority.

"As my mission refers more especially to piracy, I may here notice Muda Hassim's measures relative to that subject. Shortly after his arrival he addressed a letter to the Illanuns of Tampasuk, informing them of the engagement with the English to discourage and suppress piracy, advising them to desist, and ordering them not to visit Borneo until he (Muda Hassim) was convinced they were pirates no longer. This is good and candid. Muda Hassim at the same time requested Seriff Schaik to address a communication to Seriff Houseman of Malludu, acquainting him with his engagements, and the resolve of the Europeans to suppress piracy, adding that he was friends with the English, and no man could be friends with the English who encouraged piracy.

"The answer to this letter of Seriff Schaik, as far as I have yet learned, is a positive defiance. Three months since, I am informed, a brig or schooner was wrecked at a place called Mangsi, and she has been completely plundered and burned by Seriff Houseman: her cargo consisted of red woollens, fine white cloths, Turkey red cotton handkerchiefs, tin, pepper, Malacca canes, rattans, &c., &c. This evidently is a vessel bound to China, whether English or not is doubtful: the crew have not been heard of or seen here; and it is to be hoped may have reached Manilla.

"*28th.*—Borneo, or Bruni city. Left the Driver at 9 a.m. in the gunboat, with the *pinnace* and cutter in company: a fine breeze carried us to Pulo Chermin, and nearly the whole way to Pulo Combong, where we met with the state-boat bearing the letter. We entered the town straggling, and *the letter* having been received with firing of guns, banners displayed, and all the respect due to a royal communication, we were dragged in haste to the audience; the *sultan* on his throne, Muda Hassim and every principal *pangeran* waiting for us—Pangeran Usop to boot. The letter was read; twenty-one guns fired. I told them in all civility that I was deputed by Her Majesty the Queen to express her feelings of good will, and to offer every assistance in repressing piracy in these seas. The *sultan* stared. Muda Hassim said, 'We are greatly indebted; it is good, very good.' Then, heated, and sunburned, and tired, we took leave, and retired to the house prepared for us.

"*March, 1st.*—A long conference with Budrudeen, when, I believe, we exhausted all the important topics of Borneo politics: subsequently we visited Muda Hassim and the *sultan*. The latter was profuse in his kind expressions, and inquired of the interpreter when the English would come to Labuan, adding, 'I want to have the Europeans near me.' On this head, however, he gained no information. The presents were given to the *sultan* and *rajah*.

"*5th*.—In the evening visited Muda Hassim, and heard news from Malludu, which, divested of exaggerations, amounted to this: that Seriff Houseman was ready to receive us; was fortified, and had collected a fleet of boats; and that if the English did not come and attack him, he would come and attack Borneo, because they were in treaty with Europeans. After leaving Muda Hassim, paid the *sultan* a visit.

"*10th*.—I have nothing to say of our departure. Budrudeen accompanied us to the Mooarra, and thence, on Friday evening, we crossed to the anchorage of Labuan.

"*12th*.—Labuan. An island of about fifty feet high; twenty-five miles in circumference; woody; timber good; water from wells and a few small streams, which, after a drought, are dry; natives say water never fails. Anchorage good for the climate; well protected from the N.E.; not extensive; situation of contemplated town low; climate healthy, *i.e.*, the same as Borneo; soil, as far as seen, sandy or light sandy loam. Coal found near the extreme N.E. point: by native reports it is likewise to be found in many other places; traces of coal are frequent in the sandstone strata. Anchorage not difficult of defence against a European enemy; entrance sufficiently broad and deep between two islands, with a shoal: vide chart.

"The island of Labuan, for the purposes of refuge for shipwrecked vessels, of a windward post relative to China, for the suppression of piracy, and the extension of our trade, is well suited; it is no paradise, and any other island, with good climate, wood, and water, would suit as well. Its powerful recommendation is its being in the neighbourhood of an unwarlike and friendly people. There is no other island on the N.W. coast, and the abandoned Balambangan, to the northward of Borneo, is the only other place which could by possibility answer. The comparison between Balambangan and Labuan may be stated as follows: Balambangan, as a windward post relative to China, is superior, and it commands in time of war the inner passage to Manilla, and the eastern passages to China by the Straits of Makassar.

"Of its capabilities of defence we know nothing. It was surprised by the Sooloos. Its climate was not well spoken of. The island is larger than that of Labuan, and, as far as we know, has no coal. The great, and to me conclusive consideration against Balambangan is, that it is in the very nest of pirates, and surrounded by warlike and hostile people; and that to render it secure and effective, at least double the force would be necessary there that would suffice at Labuan. If Labuan succeeds and pays its own expenses, we might then take Balambangan; for the next best thing to a location on the main is to influence the people thereon by a succession of insular establishments.

"Yesterday we made an agreeable excursion to the n.e. point of Labuan; near the point it is picturesque, the cliffs are bold and cave-worn; the trees hang over the cliffs, or encroach on the intermediate sands, till they kiss the wave. Near a small cavern we discovered a seam of coal, which afforded us employment while Captain Bethune and Mr. Wise walked to obtain a view of the southern coast of the island.

"*Bruni, 21st May, 1845.*—After a longer time passed in Singapore than I wished, we at length started, in the *Phlegethon* steamer, for this city. At Singapore I had several interviews with Sir Thomas Cochrane.

"*22nd.*—On the authority of Sulerman, an intelligent Meri man, I am told that the tree below the town is the real *upas*, called by the Meri men *tajim*—the Borneons call it *upas*. *Bina* (the name we formerly got from a Borneon for *upas*) is, by Sulerman's statement, a thin creeper, the root or stem of which, being steeped in water, is added to the *upas*, to increase the poisonous quality; it is not, however, poisonous in itself. There is another creeper, likewise called *bina*, the leaves of which are steeped and mixed with the *upas*, instead of the stem of the first sort. This information may be relied on (in the absence of personal knowledge), as the man is of a tribe which uses the *sumpitan*, and is constantly in the habit of preparing the poison.

"*August 8th.*—Off Ujong Sapo, at the entrance of Borneo River. The time since I last added to my most desultory journal is easily accounted for. I have been at Singapore and Malacca, and am now anchored off Borneo Proper, with seven vessels, and an eighth is hourly expected. It is difficult, with such a force, to be moderate; and, with Sir Thomas Cochrane's other duties and engagements, it is probably impossible to devote any length of time on this coast; yet moderation and time are the key-stones of our policy. I have settled all the ceremonial for a meeting between the sultan and the admiral.

"The Pangeran Budrudeen came on board H.M.S. *Agincourt*, with every circumstance of state and ceremony, and met the admiral, I acting as interpreter. It was pleasing to witness his demeanour and bearing, which proved that, in minds of a certain quality, the power of command, though over savages, gives ease and freedom. The ship, the band, the marines, the guns, all excited Budrudeen's attention. On the 9th, it is arranged that the admiral shall meet the *sultan* and the *rajah*.

"*9th.*—In the course of the day, after the audience had terminated, the admiral made his demand of reparation on the sultan and Muda Hassim for the detention and confinement of two British subjects subsequent to their agreement with the British government. Of course, the *sultan* and the *rajah* replied that they were not in fault; that the act was Pangeran Usop's, and that he was too powerful for them to control by force. If Sir Thomas Cochrane would punish him, they should be much obliged, as they desired to keep the treaty inviolate.

"*10th.*—Pangeran Usop had to be summoned; come he would not, and yet I was in hopes that, when he saw the overwhelming force opposed to him, his pride would yield to necessity. About 2 p.m. the steamers took up their positions; the marines were landed, everything was prepared, yet no symptom of obedience. At length a single shot was fired from the *Vixen*, by the Admiral's order, through the roof of Usop's house, which was instantly returned, thus proving the folly and the temper of the man. In a few minutes his house was tenantless, having been overwhelmed with shot.

Usop was a fugitive; the amount of mischief done inconsiderable, and no damage except to the guilty party. Twenty captured guns the admiral presented to the *sultan* and the *rajah*; two he kept, from which to remunerate the two detained men. So far nothing could be more satisfactory. Usop has been punished severely, the treaty strictly enforced, and our supremacy maintained. No evil has been done except to the guilty; his house and his property alone have suffered, and the immediate flight has prevented the shedding of blood.

"*11th.*—At midday the Admiral, with the *Vixen* and *Nemesis*, went down the river, leaving the Pluto to me, to follow in next day.

"*12th.*—This morning I visited the *sultan* in company with Muda Hassim. By twelve at night the *Pluto* was anchored in the creek at Labuan, and on the 13th I once more took up my quarters aboard the flag-ship.

"*14th.*—Wooding.

"*16th.*—Last evening anchored within the point called in the chart Sampormangio, or, properly, Sampang Mengayu, which, being translated, signifies piratical or cruising waiting-place. The weather was thick and squally, and it was late before the *Dædalus* and *Vestal* arrived with their tows, the *Nemesis* and *Pluto*, the former frigate having carried away her mizzen top-mast.

"*17th.*—Squadron under weigh pretty early, getting into Malludu Bay. After breakfast, had a very heavy squall. *Agincourt* heeled to it, and sails of various sorts and sizes were blowing about in ribbons aboard some of the ships: afterward brought up nearly off the Melow River.

"*18th.*—*Vixen, Nemesis, Pluto*, and boats, proceeded up the bay, and anchored as near as possible to the entrance of the Marudu, or Malludu River. The character of Malludu Bay generally may be described as clear of danger, with high, wooded banks on either side, till in the bight, when the land gets flat and mangrovy, and the water shallow, and where the mouths of several small rivers are seen, one of which is Malludu.

"*19th.*—On the 19th of August was fought the celebrated battle of Malludu; the boats, 24 in number, and containing 550 marines and blue-jackets, having left the previous afternoon. As I was not present, I can say only what I heard from others, and from what I know from subsequently viewing the position. A narrow river with two forts mounting eleven or twelve heavy guns (and defended by from 500 to 1000 fighting men), protected by a strong and well-contrived boom, was the position of the enemy. Our boats took the bull by the horns, and indeed had little other choice; cut away part of the boom under a heavy fire; advanced, and carried the place in a fight protracted for fifty minutes.

"The enemy fought well and stood manfully to their guns; and a loss of six killed, two mortally and fifteen severely wounded, on our side, was repaid by a very heavy loss of killed and wounded on theirs. Gallant Gibbard,[1] of the *Wolverine*, fell mortally wounded while working at the boom, axe in hand. In short, the engagement was severe and trying to our men from the fire they were exposed to. At two minutes to nine, aboard the *Vixen*, we heard the report of the first heavy gun, and it was a time of anxiety and uneasiness till the first column of

---

1. Leonard Gibbard made his first trip to sea under my charge in 1834, when I commanded the *Childers* in the Mediterranean, and at that early age gave promise of what he afterward proved himself to be—a gallant officer and thorough seaman. Poor fellow! he was always a general favourite wherever he went—H. K.

black smoke proclaimed that the village was fired.

"I may here mention that before the fight commenced a flag of truce came from the enemy, and asked for me. Captain Talbot (in command) offered to meet Seriff Houseman either within or without the boom, provided his whole force was with him. Seriff Houseman declined; but offered (kind man!) to admit two gigs to be hauled over the boom. No sooner was this offer declined, and the flag returned the second time with a young *seriff*, son of Seriff Layak of Bruni, than the enemy opened fire, which was promptly returned. Had Captain Talbot entered as proposed, I deem it certain he would never have quitted the place alive; for the *seriff* and his followers had made themselves up to fight, and nothing but fight. Many chiefs were killed; two or three *seriffs* in their large turbans and flowing robes; many Illanuns in their gay dresses and golden charms; many Badjows; many slaves—among them a captive Chinaman; many were wounded; many carried away; and many left on the ground dead or dying.

"*20th.*—On the evening of the 19th a detachment of ten boats, with fresh men and officers, quitted the Vixen, and arrived at the forts shortly after daylight. I accompanied this party; and the work of destruction, well begun yesterday, was this day completed. Numerous proofs of the piracies of this *seriff* came to light. The boom was ingeniously fastened with the chain cable of a vessel of 300 or 400 tons; other chains were found in the town; a ship's long-boat; two ship's bells, one ornamented with grapes and vine leaves, and marked '*Wilhelm Ludwig, Bremen;*' and every other description of ship's furniture. Some half-piratical boats, Illanun and Balagnini, were burned; twenty-four or twenty-five brass guns captured; the iron guns, likewise stated to have been got out of a ship, were spiked and otherwise destroyed. Thus has Malluda ceased to exist; and Seriff Houseman's power received a fall from which it will never recover.

"Amid this scene of war and devastation was one episode which moved even harder hearts than mine. Twenty-four hours after the action, a poor woman, with her child of two years of age, was discovered in a small canoe; her arm was shattered at the elbow by a grape shot; and the poor creature lay dying for want of water in an agony of pain, with her child playing round her and endeavouring to derive the sustenance which the mother could no longer give. This poor woman was taken on board the *Vixen*, and in the evening her arm was amputated. To have left her would have been certain death; so I was strongly for the measure of taking her to Sarawak, where she can be protected.

"To all my inquiries she answered, 'If you please to take me, I shall go. I am a woman, and not a man; I am a slave, and not a free woman: do as you like.' She stated too, positively, that she herself had seen Seriff Houseman wounded in the neck, and carried off; and her testimony is corroborated by two Manilla men, who, among others, ran away on the occasion, and sought protection from us, who likewise say that they saw the *seriff* stretched out in the jungle, but they cannot say whether dead or wounded. The proof how great a number must have been killed and wounded on their part is, that on the following day ten dead men were counted lying where they fell; among them was Seriff Mahomed, the bearer of the flag of truce, who, though offered our protection, fought to the last, and in the agonies of death threw a spear at his advancing foes.

"The remnant of the enemy retired to Bungun; and it will be some time before we learn their real loss and position. It is needless here to say anything on the political effects to be expected from the establishment of a government in Bruni, and the destruction of this worst of piratical communities. When I return to Bruni, and see how measures advance, I may mention the subject again; but I will venture here to reurge, that mere military force, however necessary, cannot do what it is desirable should be done. Supervision and conciliation must go hand in hand with punishment; and we must watch that the snake does not again rear his head through our neglect. The keystone is wanting as yet, and must be supplied if possible; we must, to back the gallant deeds of the admiral and fleet, continue to pursue a steady course of measures. In the evening returned to the *Vixen*.

"*21st.*—The morning quiet. After breakfast, under weigh; proceeded off the River Bankoka, where we found the *Cruiser* at anchor. As there was nothing to detain us, crossed over to the squadron—remained an hour aboard *Agincourt*; then rejoined Sir Thomas Cochrane aboard *Vixen*, and before dinner-time were at anchor in the northeast side of Balambangan. Our woman prisoner doing well, and pleased with the attention paid her.

"*23rd.*—Southwestern harbour of Balambangan. Yesterday examined the N.E. harbour; a dreary-looking place, sandy and mangrovy, and the harbour itself filled with coral patches; here the remains of our former settlement were found: it is a melancholy and ineligible spot. The S.W. harbour is very narrow and cramped, with no fitting site for a town, on account of the rugged and unequal nature of the ground; and if the town were crammed in between two eminences, it would be deprived of all free circulation of air. Water is, I hear, in sufficient quantity, and good. On the whole, I am wretchedly disappointed with this island; it has one, and only one recommendation, *viz.*, that it is well situated in the Straits for trading and political purposes; in every other requisite it is inferior to Labuan. Balambangan is commercially and politically well placed. Labuan, though inferior, is not greatly inferior in these points; the harbour, the aspect, the soil, are superior: it may probably be added, that the climate is superior likewise; and we must remember that those who had an opportunity of trying both places give the preference to Labuan.

"Then, on other points, Labuan has a clear advantage. It commands the coal; it is in the vicinity of a friendly people, and settlement may be formed with certainty and at a moderate expense, and with small establishments. Can this be done at Balambangan? I own I doubt it; the people in the vicinity we know nothing of, but we shall find them, in all probability, hostile. The Sooloos we are already too well acquainted with. The Illanuns are in the vicinity. In the case of Labuan, the details of the first establishment (no small step) can be clearly seen and arranged; but I do not see my way regarding Balambangan. The matter is of secondary importance, but a languishing settlement at first is to be dreaded; food will be scarce, and houses difficult to build; while at Labuan the population of Bruni are at our disposal, and the government our own. I leave others to judge whether a superior (but somewhat similar) position, commercially and politically, will outweigh the other disadvantages mentioned, and repay us for the extra expenses of the establishment; but, for myself, I can give a clear verdict in favour of Labuan.

"*24th.*—Buried poor Mr. East, of the *Agincourt*, on Balambangan. Gibbard, poor, gallant fellow, was consigned to the deep a day or two before.

"*25th.*—A day of disaster and parting: the morning blowy, with an unpleasant sea. *Vestal* ran ashore on a coral-patch, but soon swung off. I was very sorry to part with the *Agincourt*. Farewell, gallant *Agincourts!* farewell, kind admiral! farewell, the pride, pomp, and panoply of a flag-ship liner! My occupation's over for the present, and I retire with content to solitude and the jungle of Sarawak. I step down the huge side, wave a parting *adieu*, jump on the *Cruiser's* deck—the anchor is weighed, and away we fly.

"*30th.*—Coming down in Her Majesty's ship *Cruiser*, and now off Ujong Sapo. On our passage we had some good views of Kina Balow, and from various points; judging the distance by the chart, the angle of elevation gives the mountain not less than 12,000 feet and up to 14,000; the latter result agreeing with the computation of the master of the *Dædalus*.

"*31st.*—Started for Bruni, and half way met a boat with Pangeran Illudeen, bringing the news of the place. Two days after the admiral and his steamers left, Pangeran Usop seized the hill behind his late house with 300 Kadiens, and commenced an attack on the town. Pangeran Budrudeen on this mustered about the like number and mounted the hill, and by a fire of musketry dislodged the enemy, who retired, stood again, were again defeated, and finally dispersed. This victory raised the courage of the Brunions, and a counter-attack was planned, when the arrival of Her Majesty's ship *Espiegle* delayed them. As the officers of the *Espiegle* and the *rajah* could not speak a word of each other's language, the boat only stayed a few hours, and went away in ignorance of the condition of the town.

"After her departure, Budrudeen gathered about a thousand men of all arms, with some hundred muskets; and leaving Bruni at three o'clock in the morning, reached the landing-place at 6 a.m., and at eight marched for Barukas, where they arrived at one o'clock. On the way the Kadiens humbled themselves, and begged their houses might be spared, which were spared accordingly. On reaching Baruukas, they found Pangeran Usop had been deserted by the Kadiens, and was in no way expecting their coming. The few persons who remained fled ignominiously, Pangeran Usop showing them the example; and his women, children, gold, and other property, fell into the hands of his victors.

"The same evening Budrudeen returned to the city in triumph; and there can be no doubt these vigorous measures have not only settled them in power, but have likewise raised the spirits of their adherents, and awed the few who remain adverse. 'Never,' the Brunions exclaim, 'was such a war in Bruni. Pangeran Budrudeen fights like a European; the very spirit of the Englishman is in him; he has learned this at Sarawak.' Fortune favoured Usop's escape. He fled to the seashore near Pulo Badukan, and there met a boat of his entering from Kimanis: he took possession and put out to sea, and returned with her to that place.

"Budrudeen we found in active preparation for pursuit. A dozen war-*prahus* were nearly ready for sea, and this force starts directly we depart.

"Budrudeen's vigour has given a stimulus to this unwarlike people, and he has gained so great a character—victory sits so lightly on his plume—that his authority will now be obeyed; while Usop, in consequence of his cowardly flight (for so they deem it), from the want of energy he has displayed, has lost character as well as wealth, and would scarce find ten men in Bruni to follow him. Unluckily for himself, he was a great boaster in the days of his prosperity; and now the contrast of his past boasting with his present cowardice is drawn with a sneer. 'His mouth was brave,' they exclaim, 'but his heart timid.' 'He should have died as other great men have died, and not have received such shame; he should have *amoked*,[2] or else given himself up for execution.' This seems to be the general impression in the city.

"My mind is now at rest about the fate of my friends; but I still consider a man-of-war brig coming here every month or two as of great importance; for it will be necessary for the next six months to consolidate the power of Muda Hassim and Budrudeen; and if, with the new order of things, they constantly see white faces, and find that they are quiet and inoffensive, the ignorant terror which now prevails will abate. Besides this, we might find the opportunity a favourable one for becoming acquainted with the Kadiens and the Marats, and giving them just impressions of ourselves; for I have no doubt that on the late occasion the Kadiens were worked upon by all kinds of false reports of the pale faces taking their lands, burning their houses, &c., &c., &c.

"We only see the effects; we do not see (until we become very well acquainted with them) the strings which move the passions of these people. The Kadiens are, however, an unwarlike and gentle race, and have now given in their submission to Muda Hassim. I do not mention the sultan, because, as I before said, he is so imbecile that, as regards public affairs, he is a cipher: he will some day cease to be sultan, and give place to a better man.

"Our interview with the *rajah*, with Budrudeen, and all the other host of our acquaintance, was quite a triumph—they hot with their success, and we bringing the account of Malludu's sanguinary fight. Happy faces and wreathed smiles supplied the place of the anxious and

---

2. *Anglicè*, run-a-muck.

doubtful expression which I had left them wearing. All vied in their attentions; fruit enough to fill a room: the luscious durian, the delicate *mangosteen* and *lousch*, the grateful *rombusteen*, the *baluna, pitabu, mowha, plantain*, &c., &c., were showered upon us from all quarters. The *rajah* daily sent a dinner; all was rejoicing, and few or no clouds lowered in the distance. I was proud and happy; for I felt and feel that much of this has been owing to my exertions. I will not stop to say how or why; but I first taught them to respect and to confide in Englishmen, and no one else has yet untaught them this lesson.

"*September 3rd.*—After parting interviews we quitted the city at two, and arrived aboard Her Majesty's ship *Cruiser* at eight p.m. Tomorrow morning we sail for Sarawak, where, at any rate, I hope for rest for a month or two.

"*19th.*—Sarawak. Thus concludes a large volume. Captain Bethune and myself, with Commander Fanshawe and a party of *Cruisers*, returned from a five days' excursion among the Dyaks, having visited the Suntah, Stang, Sigo, and Sanpro tribes. It was a progress; at each tribe there was dancing, and a number of ceremonies. White fowls were waved as I have before described, slaughtered, and the blood mixed with *kunyit*, a yellow root, &c., &c., which delightful mixture was freely scattered over them and their goods by me, holding in my hand a dozen or two women's necklaces. Captain Bethune has seen and can appreciate the Dyaks: tomorrow he leaves me, and most sorry shall I be to lose him. A better man or a better public servant is not to be found.

"Among my Dyak inquiries, I found out that the name of their god is Tuppa, and not Jovata, which they before gave me, and which they use, but do not acknowledge. Tuppa is the great god; eight other gods were in heaven; one fell or descended into Java—seven remained above; one of these is named Sakarra, who, with his companions and followers, is (or is in) the constellation of a cluster of stars, doubtless the Pleiades; and by the position of this constellation the Dyaks can judge good and bad fortune. If this cluster of stars be high in the heavens, success will attend the Dyak; when it sinks below the horizon, ill luck follows; fruit and crops will not ripen; war and famine are dreaded. Probably originally this was but a simple and natural division of the seasons, which has now become a gross superstition.

"The progress is ended; tomorrow I shall be left in the solitude and the quiet of the jungle: but, after witnessing the happiness, the plenty, the growing prosperity of the Dyak tribes, I can scarcely believe that I could devote my life to better purpose, and I dread that a removal might destroy what I have already done.

"We must now wait the decision of government with patience. Captain Bethune, in making his report, will have the advantage of real substantial personal knowledge. I esteem him highly, and regard him as a man of the most upright principles, who is not, and will not be swayed in his duty by any considerations whatever. I am glad we are to stand the ordeal of such a man's inquiry."

CHAPTER 23

# British Settlements in 1775

I will now endeavour to make the reader better acquainted with
the nature of a country and people so imperfectly known, by offering
that general view of its past events and present condition which will
make the information respecting them more intelligible, as well as applicable to new circumstances and future measures.

By looking at the map, it will be seen that the island of Borneo extends over 11 degrees of latitude and as many of longitude, from 4° N.
to 7° S., and 108° to 119° E. The N.W. coast is but thinly populated;
and the natives who inhabit the banks of some of the beautiful rivers differ, as has been already stated, from each other in manners and
customs, and have but little communication among themselves. The
S., E., and N.E. coasts of Borneo are also but thinly inhabited, and very
little known. There are various divisions of Malays, as well as different
tribes of Dyaks, who live in an unsettled state, and occasionally make
war on one another: their principal occupation, however, is piracy.

The north part of the island was once in the possession of the East
India Company, who had a settlement and factory on the island of
Balambangan, which was attacked in 1775, when in a weak and unguarded state, by a powerful piratical tribe of Sooloos, who surprised
the fort, put the sentries to death, and turned the guns on the troops,
who were chiefly Buguese (or Bugis) Malays. Those who escaped got
on board the vessels in the harbour, and reached the island of Labuan,
near the mouth of the Borneo river; while the booty obtained by
the pirates was estimated at 375,000*l.* From that time to this these
atrocious pirates have never been punished, and still continue their
depredations.

The remainder of the coast on the N.W. is now called Borneo
Proper, to distinguish it from the name that custom has given to the

whole island, the original name of which was Kalamantan, and Bruni that of the town now called Borneo. The latter was probably the first part of the coast ever visited by Europeans, who consequently extended the appellation to the island itself. The town of Borneo, situated on the river of that name, was, until the last few years, a port of some wealth, and carrying on an extensive trade, which has been ruined entirely by the rapacity of the Malay chiefs, who have now but little control over that part of Borneo Proper which lies to the northward of the river.

The province of Sarawak is situated at the S.W. end of Borneo Proper, and was formally ceded in perpetuity by the sultan in 1843 to Mr. Brooke, who, indeed, had possessed the almost entire management of the district for the two previous years.

"It extends from Tanjong Datu (I quote from Mr. Brooke's description of his territory) to the entrance of the Samarahan River, a distance along the coast of about sixty miles in an E.S.E. direction, with an average breadth of fifty miles. It is bounded to the westward by the Sambas territory, to the southward by a range of mountains which separate it from the Pontiana River, and to the eastward by the Borneon territory of Sadong. Within this space then are several rivers and islands, which it is needless here to describe at length, as the account of the river of Sarawak will answer alike for the rest.

"There are two navigable entrances to this river, and numerous smaller branches for boats, both to the westward and eastward; the two principal entrances combine at about twelve miles from the sea, and the river flows for twenty miles into the interior in a southerly and westerly direction, when it again forms two branches—one running to the right, the other to the left hand, as far as the mountain range. Beside these facilities for water-communication, there exist three other branches from the easternmost entrance, called Morotaba, one of which joins the Samarahan River, and the two others flow from different points of the mountain range already mentioned. The country is diversified by detached mountains, and the mountain range has an elevation of about three thousand feet.

"The aspect of the country may be generally described as low and woody at the entrance of the rivers, except a few high mountains; but in the interior undulating in parts, and part presenting fine level plains. The climate may be pronounced healthy and cool, though for the six months from September to March a great quantity of rain falls. During my three visits to this place, which have been prolonged to eight months, and since residing here, we have been clear of sickness, and during the entire period not one of three deaths could be attributed to the effects of climate. The more serious maladies of tropical climates are very infrequent; from fever and dysentery we have been quite free, and the only complaints have been rheumatism, colds, and ague; the latter, however, attacked us in the interior, and no one has yet had it at Sarawak, which is situated about twenty-five miles from the mouth of the river.

"The soil and productions of this country are of the richest description, and it is not too much to say, that, within the same given space, there are not to be found the same mineral and vegetable riches in any land in the world. I propose to give a brief detail of them, beginning with the soil of the plains, which is moist and rich, and calculated for the growth of rice, for which purpose it was formerly cleared and used, until the distractions of the country commenced. From the known industry of the Dyaks, and their partiality to rice-cultivation, there can be little doubt that it would become an article of extensive export, provided security were given to the cultivator and a proper remuneration for his produce.

"The lower grounds, beside rice, are well adapted for the growth of sago, and produce canes, rattans, and forest-timber of the finest description for ship-building and other useful purposes. The Chinese export considerable quantities of timber from Sambas and Pontiana, particularly of the kind called Balean by the natives, or the lion-wood of the Europeans; and at this place it is to be had in far greater quantity and nearer the place of sale. The undulating ground differs in soil, some portions of it being a yellowish clay, while the rest is a rich mould; these grounds, generally speaking, as well as the slopes of the higher mountains, are admirably calculated for the growth of nutmegs, coffee, pepper, or any of the more valuable vegetable productions of the tropics. Beside the above mentioned articles, there are birds-nests, bees-wax, and several kinds of scented wood, in demand at Singapore, which are all collected by the Dyaks, and would be gathered in far greater quantity provided the Dyak was allowed to sell them.

"Turning from the vegetable to the mineral riches of the country, we have diamonds, gold, tin, iron, and antimony ore certain; I have lately sent what I believe to be a specimen of lead ore to Calcutta; and copper is reported. It must be remembered, in reading this list, that the country is as yet unexplored by a scientific person, and that the inquiries of a geologist and a mineralogist would throw further light on the minerals of the mountains, and the spots where they are to be found in the greatest plenty.

"The diamonds are stated to be found in considerable numbers, and of a good water; and I judge the statement to be correct from the fact that the diamond-workers from Sandak come here and work secretly, and the people from Banjamassim, who are likewise clever at this trade, are most desirous to be allowed to work for the precious stone. Gold of a good quality certainly is to be found in large quantities. The eagerness and perseverance of the Chinese to establish themselves is a convincing proof of the fact; and ten years since a body of about 3000 of them had great success in procuring gold by their ordinary mode of trenching the ground.

"The quantity of gold yearly procured at Sambas is moderately stated at 130,000 *bunkals*, which, reckoned at the low rate of 20 Spanish dollars a *bunkal*, gives 2,600,000 Spanish dollars, or upward of half a million sterling. The most intelligent Chinese are of opinion, that the quantity here exceeds that at Sambas; and there is no good reason to suppose it would fall short of it were once a sufficient Chinese population settled in the country.

"Antimony ore is a staple commodity, which is to be procured in any quantity. Tin is said to be plentiful, and the Chinese propose working it; but I have had no opportunity of visiting the spot where it is found. Copper, though reported, has not been brought; and the iron ore I have examined is of inferior quality. The specimen of what I supposed to be lead ore has been forwarded to Calcutta, and it remains to be seen what its value may be. And beside the above-mentioned minerals, there can be little doubt of many others being discovered, if the mountain range was properly explored by any man of science. Many other articles of minor importance might be mentioned; but it is needless to add to a list which contains articles of such value, and which would prove the country equal in vegetable and mineral productions to any in the world.

"From the productions (continues Mr. Brooke) I turn to the inhabitants, and I feel sure that in describing their sufferings and miseries I shall command the interest and sympathy of every person of humanity, and that the claims of the virtuous and most unhappy Dyaks will meet with the same attention as those of the African. And these claims have the advantage, that much good may be done without the vast expenditure of lives and money which the exertions on the African coast yearly demand, and that the people would readily appreciate the good that was conferred upon them, and rapidly rise in the scale of civilization."

The inhabitants may be divided into three different classes, *viz.* the Malays, the Chinese, and the Dyaks; of the two former little need be said, as they are so well known.

The Dyaks (or more properly Dyak) of Borneo offer to our view a primitive state of society; and their near resemblance to the Tarajahs of Celebes,[1] to the inland people of Sumatra, and probably to the Arafuras of Papua,[2] in customs, manners, and language, affords reason for the conclusion that these are the aboriginal race of the Eastern Archipelago, nearly stationary in their original condition. While successive waves of civilization have swept onward the rest of the inhabitants, while tribes as wild have arisen to power, flourished, and decayed, the Dyak in his native jungles still retains the feelings of earlier times, and shows the features of society as it existed before the influx of foreign races either improved or corrupted the native character.

The name "Dyak" has been indiscriminately applied to all the wild people on the island of Borneo; but as the term is never so used by themselves, and as they differ greatly, not only in name, but in their customs and manners, we will briefly, in the first instance, mention the various distinct nations, the general locality of each, and some of their distinguishing peculiarities.

1st. The Dusun, or villagers of the northern extremity of the island, are a race of which Mr. Brooke knows nothing personally; but the name implies that they are an agricultural people: they are represented as not being tattooed, as using the *sumpitan*, and as having a peculiar dialect.[3]

2nd. The Murut. They inhabit the interior of Borneo Proper. They are not tattooed, always use the *sumpitan*, and have a peculiar dialect. In the same locality, and resembling the Murut, are some tribes called the Basaya.

---

1. See *Prichard's Researches*, 1826, which, meagre as they must have been from the want of data, tell us in two or three pages nearly all we know on the subject. That able investigator states that the Dyaks of Borneo resemble the Taraj of Celebes.
2. With regard to the Arafuras, or Haraforas, it is stated that they are termed in some districts Idaan, in others Murut, and in others Dayaks. See Raffles' *Java*. And Leyden assures us that all these varieties were originally called Idaan.
3. A singular contrast to preceding accounts, which represent the north and northeastern population not only as pirates, called Tiran or Zedong, but even as cannibals. Near them there appear to be the piratical nests of Magindano, Sooloo, &c.

3rd. The Kadians (or Idaans of voyagers) use the *sumpitan*, and have likewise a peculiar dialect; but in other respects they nowise differ from the Borneons, either in religion, dress, or mode of life. They are, however, an industrious, peaceful people, who cultivate the ground in the vicinity of Borneo Proper, and nearly as far as Tanjong Barram. The wretched capital is greatly dependent upon them, and, from their numbers and industry, they form a valuable population. In the interior, and on the Balyet River, which discharges itself near Tanjong Barram, is a race likewise called Kadian, not converted to Islam, and which still retains the practice of "taking heads."

4th. The Kayan. The Kayans are the most numerous, the most powerful, and the most warlike people in Borneo. They are an inland race, and their locality extends from about sixty miles up the country from Tanjong Barram to the same extent farther into the interior, in latitude 3° 30' N., and thence across the island to probably a similar distance from the eastern shore. Their customs, manners, and dress are peculiar, and present most of the characteristic features of a wild and independent people. The Malays of the N.W. coast fear the Kayans, and rarely enter their country; but the Millanows are familiar with them, and there have thence been obtained many particulars respecting them. They are represented as extremely hospitable, generous, and kind to strangers, strictly faithful to their word, and honest in their dealings; but on the other hand, they are fierce and bloodthirsty, and when on an expedition, slaughter without sparing. The Kayans are partially tattooed, use the *sumpitan*, have many dialects, and are remarkable for the strange and apparently mutilating custom adopted by the males, and mentioned by Sir Stamford Raffles.

5th. To the southward and westward of Barram are the Millanows,[4] who inhabit the rivers not far from the sea. They are, generally speaking, an intelligent, industrious, and active race, the principal cultivators of sago, and gatherers of the famous camphor *barus*. Their locality extends from Tanjong Barram to Tanjong Sirak. In person they are stout and well-made, of middling height, round good-tempered countenances, and fairer than the Malays. They have several dialects among them, use the *sumpitan*, and are not tattooed. They retain the practice of taking heads, but they seldom seek them, and have little of

4. There are several rivers, Meri, Bentulu, &c., the inhabitants of which, says Mr. Brooke, I class under the general term Millanow, as their dialects show a very close connection, and their habits are the same. Evidently from language they are civilized tribes of Kayans.

the ferocity of the Kayan.

6th. In the vicinity of the Kayans and Millanows are some wild tribes, called the Tatows, Balanian, Kanowit, &c. They are probably only a branch of Kayans, though differing from them in being elaborately tattooed over the entire body. They have peculiar dialects, use the *sumpitan*, and are a wild and fierce people.

7th. The Dyak. They are divided into Dyak Darrat and Dyak Laut, or land and sea Dyaks. The Dyak Lauts, as their name implies, frequent the sea; and it is needless to say much of them, as their difference from the Dyak Darrat is a difference of circumstances only. The tribes of Sarebus and Sakarran, whose rivers are situated in the deep bay between Tanjong Sipang and Tanjong Sirak, are powerful communities, and dreadful pirates, who ravage the coast in large fleets, and murder and rob indiscriminately; but this is by no means to be esteemed a standard of Dyak character. In these expeditions the Malays often join them, and they are likewise made the instruments for oppressing the Laut tribes. The Sarebus and Sakarran are fine men, fairer than the Malays, with sharp keen eyes, thin lips, and handsome countenances, though frequently marked by an expression of cunning.

The Balows and Sibnowans are amiable tribes, decidedly warlike, but not predatory; and the latter combines the virtues of the Dyak character with much of the civilization of the Malays. The Dyak Laut do not tattoo, nor do they use the *sumpitan*; their language assimilates closely to the Malay, and was doubtless originally identical with that of the inland tribes. The name of God among them is Battara (the Avatara of the Hindoos). They bury their dead, and in the graves deposit a large portion of the property of the deceased, often to a considerable value in gold ornaments, brass guns, jars, and arms. Their marriage ceremony consists in two fowls being killed, and the forehead and breast of the young couple being touched with the blood; after which the chief, or an old man, knocks their heads together several times, and the ceremony is completed with mirth and feasting. In these two instances they differ from the Dyak Darrat.

It must be observed that the Dyak also differs from the Kayan in not being tattooed; and from the Kayan Millanows, &c., in not using the *national* weapon—the *sumpitan*. The Kayan and the Dyak, as general distinctions, though they differ in dialect, in dress, in weapons, and probably in religion, agree in their belief of similar omens, and, above all, in their practice of taking the heads of their enemies; but with the

Kayan this practice assumes the aspect of an indiscriminate desire of slaughter, while with the Dyak it is but the trophy acquired in legitimate warfare. The Kadians form the only exception to this rule, in consequence of their conversion to Islam; and it is but reasonable to suppose, that with a slight exertion in favour of Christianity, others might be induced to lay aside this barbarous custom.

With respect to the dialects, though the difference is considerable, they are evidently derived from a common source; but it is remarkable that some words in the Millanow and Kayan are similar to the Bugis and Badjow language. This intermixture of dialects, which can be linked together, appears to be more conclusive of the common origin of the wild tribes and civilized nations of the Archipelago than most other arguments; and if Marsden's position be correct (which there can be little or no reason to doubt), that the Polynesian is an original race with an original language,[5] it must likewise be conceded that the wild tribes represent the primitive state of society in these islands.

We know little of the wild tribes of Celebes beyond their general resemblance to the Kayans of the east coast of Borneo; and it is probable that the Kayans are the people of Celebes, who crossing the Strait of Makassar, have in time by their superior prowess possessed themselves of the country of the Dyaks. Mr. Brooke (from whom I am copying this sketch) is led to entertain this opinion from a slight resemblance in their dialects with those used in Celebes, from the difference in so many of their customs from those of the Dyaks, and from the Kayans of the *northwest coast of Borneo* having one custom in common with the wild tribe of Minkoka in the Bay of Boni.

Both the Kayans and Minkokas on the death of a relative seek for a head; and on the death of their chief many human heads must be procured: which practice is unknown to the Dyak. It may further be remarked, that their probable immigration from Celebes is supported by the statement of the Millanows, that the Murut and Dyak give place to the Kayan whenever they come in contact, and that the latter people have depopulated large tracts in the interior, which were once occupied by the former.

Having thus briefly noticed the different wild people of the island, I proceed with the more particular task of describing the Dyak Darrats.

The locality of these Dyaks may be marked as follows:—The Pon-

5. Leyden concluded that the language was allied to the Batta and Tagala, and the whole derived from and varieties of the primitive tongue of the Philippine Islands.

tiana River, from its mouth, is traced into the interior toward the northward and westward, until it approaches at the farthest within 100 miles of the northwest coast; a line drawn in latitude 3° N. till it intersects the course of the Pontiana River will point out the limit of the country inhabited by the Dyak. Within this inconsiderable portion of the island, which includes Sambas, Landak, Pontiana, Sangow, Sarawak, &c., are numerous tribes, all of which agree in their leading customs, and make use of nearly the same dialect. Personally (writes our sole authority for any intelligence respecting them), I am acquainted only with the tribes of Sarawak and some tribes further in the interior beyond the government of the Malays, who inhabit the country between Sarawak and Landak; and the description of one tribe will serve as a description of all, so little do they vary.

Before, however, I say anything of the character of the Dyaks, or their temper, it will be necessary to describe briefly the government under which they live, and the influence it has upon them; and if afterward in the recital there appear some unamiable points in their character, an allowance will be made for their failings, which those who rule them would not deserve.

The Dyaks have from time immemorial been looked upon as the bondsmen of the Malays, and the *rajahs* consider them much in the same light as they would a drove of oxen—*i. e.* as personal and disposable property. They were governed in Sarawak by three local officers, called the Patingi, the Bandar, and the Tumangong. To the Patingi they paid a small yearly revenue of rice, but this deficiency of revenue was made up by sending them a quantity of goods—chiefly salt, Dyak cloths, and iron—and demanding a price for them six or eight times more than their value. The produce collected by the Dyaks was also monopolized, and the edible birds-nests, bees-wax, &c. &c. were taken at a price fixed by the Patingi, who moreover claimed mats, fowls, fruits, and every other necessary at his pleasure, and could likewise make the Dyaks work for him for merely a nominal remuneration.

This system, not badly devised, had it been limited within the bounds of moderation, would have left the Dyaks plenty for all their wants; or had the local officers known their own interest, they would have protected those upon whom they depended for revenue, and under the worst oppression of one man the Dyaks would have deemed themselves happy. Such unfortunately was not the case; for the love of immediate gain overcame every other consideration, and by degrees old-established customs were thrown aside, and new ones substituted in their place. When the Patingi had received all he thought proper to extort, his relatives first claimed the right of arbitrary trade, and gradually it was extended as the privilege of every respectable person in the country to *serra*[6] the Dyaks.

The poor Dyak, thus at the mercy of half the Malay population, was never allowed to refuse compliance with these demands; he could plead neither poverty, inability, nor even hunger, as an excuse, for the answer was ever ready: "Give me your wife or one of your children;" and in case he could not supply what was required, the wife or the child was taken, and became a slave. Many modes of extortion were resorted to; a favourite one was convicting the Dyak of a fault and imposing a fine upon him. Some ingenuity and much trickery were shown in this game, and new offences were invented as soon as the old pleas would serve no longer; for instance, if a Malay met a Dyak in a boat which pleased him, he notched it, as a token that it was his property; in one day, if the boat was a new one, perhaps three or more would place their marks on it; and as only one could get it, the Dyak to whom the boat really belonged had to pay the others *for his fault.*

This, however, was only "a fault;" whereas, for a Dyak to injure a Malay, directly or indirectly, purposely or otherwise, was a *high offence,* and punished by a proportionate fine. If a Dyak's house was in bad repair, and a Malay fell in consequence and was hurt, or pretended to be hurt, a fine was imposed; if a Malay in the jungle was wounded by the springs set for a wild boar, or by the wooden spikes which the Dyaks for protection put about their village, or scratched himself and said he was injured, the penalty was heavy; if the Malay was *really hurt,* ever so accidentally, it was the ruin of the Dyak. And these numerous and uninvited guests came and went at pleasure, lived in free quarters, made their requisitions, and then forced the Dyak to carry away for them the very property of which he had been robbed.

This is a fair picture of the governments under which the Dyaks live; and although they were often roused to resistance, it was always fruitless, and only involved them in deeper troubles; for the Malays could quickly gather a large force of sea Dyaks from Sakarran, who were readily attracted by hope of plunder, and who, supported by the fire-arms of their allies, were certain to overcome any single tribe that held out.

The misfortunes of the Dyaks of Sarawak did not stop here. An-

6. Probably a Dyak phrase for levying exactions on the oppressed people. It is not Malay.

timony ore was discovered; the cupidity of the Borneons was roused; then *pangerans* struggled for the prize; intrigues and dissensions ensued; and the inhabitants of Sarawak in turn felt the very evil they had inflicted on the Dyaks; while the Dyaks were compelled, amid their other wrongs, to labour at the ore without any recompense, and to the neglect of their rice-cultivation. Many died in consequence of this compulsory labour, so contrary to their habits and inclinations; and more would doubtless have fallen victims, had not civil war rescued them from this evil, to inflict upon them others a thousand times worse.

Extortion had before been carried on by individuals, but now it was systematized; and *pangerans* of rank, for the sake of plunder, sent bodies of Malays and Sakarran Dyaks to attack the different tribes. The men were slaughtered, the women and children carried off into slavery, the villages burned, the fruit-trees cut down,[7] and all their property destroyed or seized. The Dyaks could no longer live in tribes, but sought refuge in the mountains or the jungle, a few together; and as one of them pathetically described it—"We do not live," he said, "like men; we are like monkeys; we are hunted from place to place; we have no houses; and when we light a fire, we fear the smoke will draw our enemies upon us."

In the course of ten years, under the circumstances detailed—from enforced labour, from famine, from slavery, from sickness, from the sword—one half of the Dyak population[8] disappeared; and the work

7. The utter destruction of a village or town is nothing to the infliction of cutting down the fruit-trees. The former can be rebuilt, with its rude and ready materials, in a few weeks; but the latter, from which the principal subsistence of the natives is gathered, cannot be suddenly restored, and thus they are reduced to starvation.

8. The grounds for this opinion are an estimate personally made among the tribes, compared with the estimate kept by the local officers before the disturbance arose; and the result is, that only two out of twenty tribes have not suffered, while some tribes have been reduced, from 330 families to 50; about ten tribes have lost more than half their number; one tribe of 100 families has lost all its women and children made slaves; and one tribe, more wretched, has been reduced from 120 families to 2, that is, 16 persons; while two tribes have entirely disappeared. The list of the tribes and their numbers formerly and now are as follows:—Suntah, 330—50; Sanpro, 100—69; Sigo, 80—28; Sabungo, 60—33; Brang, 50—22; Sinnar, 80—34; Stang, 80—30; Samban, 60—34; Tubbia, 80—30; Goon, 40—25; Bang, 40—12; Kujjuss, 35—0; Lundu, 80—2; Sow, 200—100; Sarambo, 100—60; Bombak, 35—35; Paninjow, 80—40; Singè, 220—220; Pons, 20—0; Sibaduh, 25—25. Total, formerly, 1795—now, 849 families; and reckoning eight persons to each family, the amount of population will be, formerly, 14,360—now, 6792: giving a decrease of population in ten years of 846 families, or 7568 persons!

of extirpation would have gone on at an accelerated pace, had the remnant been left to the tender mercies of the *pangerans*; but chance (we may much more truly say Providence) led our countryman Mr. Brooke to this scene of misery, and enabled him, by circumstances far removed beyond the grounds of calculation, to put a stop to the sufferings of an amiable people.

There are twenty tribes in Sarawak, on about fifty square miles of land. The appearance of the Dyaks is prepossessing: they have good-natured faces, with a mild and subdued expression; eyes set far apart, and features sometimes well formed. In person they are active, of middling height, and not distinguishable from the Malays in complexion. The women are neither so good-looking nor well-formed as the men, but they have the same expression, and are cheerful and kind-tempered. The dress of the men consists of a piece of cloth about fifteen feet long, passed between the legs and fastened round the loins, with the ends hanging before and behind; the head-dress is composed of bark-cloth, dyed bright yellow, and stuck up in front so as to resemble a tuft of feathers. The arms and legs are often ornamented with rings of silver, brass, or shell; and necklaces are worn, made of human teeth, or those of bears or dogs, or of white beads, in such numerous strings as to conceal the throat.

A sword on one side, a knife and small betel-basket on the other, complete the ordinary equipment of the males; but when they travel they carry a basket slung from the forehead, on which is a palm-mat, to protect the owner and his property from the weather. The women wear a short and scanty petticoat, reaching from the loins to the knees, and a pair of black bamboo stays, which are never removed except the wearer be *enceinte*. They have rings of brass or red bamboo about the loins, and sometimes ornaments on the arms; the hair is worn long; the ears of both sexes are pierced, and earrings of brass inserted occasionally; the teeth of the young people are sometimes filed to a point and discoloured, as they say that "Dogs have white teeth." They frequently dye their feet and hands of a bright red or yellow colour; and the young people, like those of other countries, affect a degree of finery and foppishness, while the elders invariably lay aside all ornaments, as unfit for a wise person or one advanced in years.

In character the Dyak is mild and tractable, hospitable when he is well used, grateful for kindness, industrious, honest, and simple; neither treacherous nor cunning, and so truthful that the word of one of them might safely be taken before the oath of half-a-dozen Borneons. In their dealings they are very straightforward and correct, and so trustworthy that they rarely attempt, even after a lapse of years, to evade payment of a just debt. On the reverse of this picture there is little unfavourable to be said; and the wonder is, they have learned so little deceit or falsehood where the examples before them have been so rife. The temper of the Dyak inclines to be sullen; and they oppose a dogged and stupid obstinacy when set to a task which displeases them, and support with immovable apathy torrents of abuse or entreaty. They are likewise distrustful, fickle, apt to be led away, and evasive in concealing the amount of their property; but these are the vices rather of situation than of character, for they have been taught by bitter experience that their rulers set no limits to their exactions, and that hiding is their only chance of retaining a portion of the grain they have raised. They are, at the same time, fully aware of the customs by which their ancestors were governed, and are constantly appealing to them as a rule of right, and frequently arguing with the Malay on the subject.

Upon these occasions they are silenced, but not convinced; and the Malay, while he evades or bullies when it is needful, is sure to appeal to these very much-abused customs whenever it serves his purpose. The manners of the Dyaks with strangers are reserved to an extent rarely seen among rude or half-civilized people; but on a better acquaintance (which is not readily acquired), they are open and talkative, and, when heated with their favourite beverage, lively, and evincing more shrewdness and observation than they have gained credit for possessing. Their ideas, as may well be supposed, are very limited; they reckon with their fingers and toes, and few are clever enough to count beyond twenty; but when they repeat the operation, they record each twenty by making a knot on a string.

Like other wild people, the slightest restraint is irksome, and no temptation will induce them to stay long from their favourite jungle. It is there they seek the excitement of war, the pleasures of the chase, the labours of the field, and the abundance of fruit in the rich produce which assists in supporting their families. The pathless jungle is endeared to them by every association which influences the human mind, and they languish when prevented from roaming there as inclination dictates.

With reference to the gradual advance of the Dyaks, Mr. Brooke observes in an early part of his journal:—"The peaceful and gentle aborigines—how can I speak too favourably of their improved condition? These people, who, a few years since, suffered every extreme of misery from war, slavery, and starvation, are now comfortably lodged, and comparatively rich. A stranger might now pass from village to village, and he would receive their hospitality, and see their *padi* stored in their houses. He would hear them proclaim their happiness, and praise the white man as their friend and protector. Since the death of Parembam, no Dyak of Sarawak lost his life by violence, until a month since, when two were cut off by the Sakarran Dyaks.

None of the tribes have warred among themselves; and I believe their war excursions to a distance in the interior have been very few, and those undertaken by the Sarambos. What punishment is sufficient for the wretch who finds this state of things so baleful as to attempt to destroy it? Yet such a wretch is Seriff Sahib. In describing the condition of the Dyaks, I do not say that it is perfect, or that it may not be still further improved; but with people in their state of society innovations ought not rashly or hastily to be made; as the civilized being ought constantly to bear in mind, that what is clear to him is not clear to a savage; that intended benefits *may* be regarded as positive injuries; and that his motives are not, and scarcely can be, appreciated! The greatest evil, perhaps, from which the Dyaks suffer, is the influence of the *datus* or chiefs; but this influence is never carried to oppression, and is only used to obtain the expensive luxury of 'birds-nests' at a cheap rate. In short, the Dyaks are happy and content; and their gradual development must now be left to the work of time, aided by the gentlest persuasion, and advanced (if attainable) by the education of their children."

The latest accounts from Sarawak describe the increasing prosperity of that interesting settlement. Among other recent intelligence I have heard from Mr. Brooke that Seriff Sahib died of a broken heart, shortly after his arrival at the Pontiana River.

# CHAPTER 24

# Governor Crawfurd's Opinions Thereon

The establishment of a British settlement on the northwest coast of Borneo, and the occupation of the island of Labuan, are measures that have for some time past been under consideration by Her Majesty's government; and I am courteously enabled to lay before my readers the valuable opinions of Mr. Crawfurd (late Governor of Singapore) on this subject:

"I am of opinion (Mr. Crawfurd writes) that a settlement on the northwest coast of Borneo—that is, at a convenient point on the southern shore of the China Sea—would be highly advantageous to this country, as a coal *depôt* for steam navigation; as a means of suppressing Malayan piracy; as a harbour of refuge for ships disabled in the China Sea; and finally, as a commanding position during a naval war.

"The island of Labuan has been pointed out for this purpose; and as far as our present limited knowledge of it will allow me to judge, it appears to possess all the necessary qualities for such a settlement.

"The requisite properties are, salubrity of climate, a good *harbor*, a position in the track of steam-navigation, conveniency of position for ships disabled in typhoons, conveniency of position for our cruisers during war, and a locality strong and circumscribed by nature, so as to be readily capable of cheap defence.

"Labuan lies in about 6° of north latitude, and consequently the average heat will be about 83° of Fahrenheit; the utmost range of the thermometer will not exceed ten degrees. In short, the year is a perpetual hot summer. It is, at the same time, well ventilated by both monsoons; and being near twenty miles from the marshy shores of the Borneo River, there is little ground to apprehend that it will be found unhealthy, even if those shores themselves had been ascertained to be so, which, however, is not the case; for, in proof of their salubrity, it may be stated, that the town of Borneo is healthy, although it stands, and has stood for centuries, on the flooded banks of the river; the houses being built on posts, and chiefly accessible by boat.

"With respect to harbour, a most essential point, I do not perceive that the island is indented by any bay or inlet that would answer the purpose of one.[1] The channel, however, which lies between it and the mainland of Borneo is but seven miles broad, and will probably constitute a spacious and convenient harbour. The name of the island itself, which means anchorage, I have no doubt is derived from the place affording shelter to native shipping, and those probably, in most cases, fleets of pirate *prahus*. This channel is again further restricted by four islets, and these, with four more lying to the southwest, will afford shelter in the southwest or mild monsoon; protection is given in the northeast, the severest monsoon, by Labuan itself: and I may add, that the island is, by four degrees of latitude, beyond the extreme southern limit of the typhoons of the Chinese Sea.

"In the channel between Labuan and the main, or rather between Labuan and the islets already mentioned, the soundings on the Admiralty chart show that vessels drawing as much as eighteen feet water may anchor within a mile of the shore, and the largest vessels within a mile and a half; a convenience for shipping which greatly exceeds that of Singapore. One of the advantages of Labuan will be that it will prove a port of refuge for shipping disabled in the storms of the Chinese Seas. Many examples, indeed some of recent occurrence, might be adduced to show the need there is of such a port.

"Labuan lies nearly in the direct track both of steam and sailing navigation from India to China, during the northeast, the worst and severest of the two monsoons; and is as intermediate a position between Singapore and Hong Kong as can be found, being 700 miles from the former and 1000 from the latter.

"The insular character and narrow limits of Labuan will make it easily and cheaply defensible. The extreme length of the island appears to be about six miles, its greatest breadth about four and a half, and probably its whole area will not be found to exceed thirty square miles.

"From the rude tribes of the immediate vicinity no hostile attack

---

1. Sir Edward Belcher has since surveyed Labuan in Her Majesty's ship *Samarang*, and finding an excellent harbour, named it Victoria Bay.—H. K.

is to be apprehended that would make the present erection of forts or batteries necessary. No Asiatic enemy is at any time to be feared that would make such defences requisite. In five-and-twenty years it has not been found imperative to have recourse to them at Singapore. It is only in case of war with a naval power that fortifications would be required; but I am not informed what local advantages Labuan possesses for their erection. A principal object of such fortifications would be the defence of the shipping in the harbour from the inroads of an enemy's cruisers.

"At one point the soundings, as given in the Admiralty chart, are stated nine fathoms, within three quarters of a mile of the shore; and I presume that batteries within this distance would afford protection to the largest class of merchantmen. In Singapore Roads no class of shipping above mere native craft can lie nearer than two miles of the shore; so that in a war with a European naval power, the merchant shipping there can only be defended by Her Majesty's navy.

"One of the most striking national advantages to be expected from the possession of Labuan would consist in its use in defending our own commerce, and attacking that of opponents, in the event of a naval war. Between the eastern extremity of the Straits of Malacca and Hong Kong, a distance of 1700 miles, there is no British harbour, and no safe and accessible port of refuge; Hong Kong is, indeed, the only spot within the wide limits of the Chinese Sea for such a purpose, although our legitimate commercial intercourse within it extends over a length of 2000 miles. Everywhere else, Manilla and the newly opened ports of China excepted, our crippled vessels or our merchantmen pursued by the enemy's cruisers, are met by the exclusion or extortion of semi-barbarous nations, or in danger of falling into the power of robbers and savages.

"Labuan fortified, and supposing the Borneon coal to be as productive and valuable in quality as it is represented, would give Great Britain in a naval war the entire command of the China Sea. This would be the result of our possessing or commanding the only available supply of coal, that of Bengal and Australia excepted, to be found in the wide limits which extend east of the continents of Europe and America.

"The position of Labuan will render it the most convenient possible for the suppressing of piracy. The most desperate and active pirates of the whole Indian Archipelago are the tribes of the Sooloo group of islands lying close to the north shore of Borneo, and the people of the north and northeastern coast of Borneo itself; these have of late years proved extremely troublesome both to the English and Dutch traders; both nations are bound by the Convention of 1824 to use their best endeavours for the suppression of piracy, and many efforts have certainly been made for this purpose, although as yet without material effect in diminishing the evil.

"From Labuan, these pirates might certainly be intercepted by armed steamers far more conveniently and cheaply than from any other position that could be easily pointed out: indeed, the very existence of a British settlement would tend to the suppression of piracy.

"As a commercial *depôt*, Labuan would have considerable advantages by position; the native trade of the vicinity would of course resort to it, and so would that of the north coast of Borneo, of the Sooloo Islands, and of a considerable portion of the Spice Islands. Even for the trade of the Philippines and China, it would have the advantage over Singapore of a voyage by 700 miles shorter; a matter of most material consequence to native commerce.

"With all the countries of the neighbourhood lying west of Labuan I presume that a communication across both monsoons might be maintained throughout the year. This would include a portion of the east coast of the Malay peninsula, Siam, and part of Cochin China.

"Labuan belongs to that portion of the coast of Borneo which is the rudest. The Borneons themselves are of the Malay nation, originally emigrants from Sumatra, and settled here for about six centuries. They are the most distant from their original seat of all the colonies which have sprung from this nation. The people from the interior differ from them in language, manners, and religion, and are divided into tribes as numerous and as rude as the Americans when first seen by Europeans.

"From such a people we are not to expect any valuable products of art or manufacture, for a British mercantile *depôt*. Pepper is, however, produced in considerable quantity, and the products of the forests are very various, as bees-wax, gum-benjamin, fine camphor, camphor oil, esculent swallows' nests, canes and rattans, which used to form the staple articles of Borneon import into Singapore. The Borneon territory opposite to Labuan abounds also, I believe, in the palm which yields sago, and indeed the chief part of the manufactured article was thirty years ago brought from this country. The Chinese settlers would, no doubt, as in Singapore and Malacca, establish factories for its preparation according to the improved processes which they now practice at those places.

"There may be reason to expect, however, that the timber of the portion of Borneo referred to may be found of value for ship-building; for Mr. Dalrymple states that in his time, above seventy years ago, Chinese junks of 500 tons burden used to be built in the river of Borneo. As to timber well-suited for boats and house-building, it is hardly necessary to add that the northwest coast of Borneo, in common with almost every other part of the Archipelago, contains a supply amounting to superfluity.

"I may take this opportunity of stating, as evidence of the conveniency of this portion of Borneo for a commercial intercourse with China, that down to within the last half century a considerable number of Chinese *junks* were engaged in trading regularly with Borneo, and that trade ceased only when the native government became too bad and weak to afford it protection. Without the least doubt this trade would again spring up on the erection of the British flag at Labuan. Not a single Chinese junk had resorted to the Straits of Malacca before the establishment of Singapore, and their number is now, of one size or another, and exclusive of the junks of Siam and Cochin China, not less than 100.

"From the cultivation of the land I should not be disposed to expect anything beyond the production of fresh fruits and esculent vegetables, and when the land is cleared, of grass for pasture. The seas in this part of the world are prolific in fish of great variety and great excellence; and the Chinese settlers are found everywhere skilful and industrious in taking them.

"Some difficulty will, in the beginning, be experienced with respect to milk, butter, and fresh meat: this was the case at first in Singapore, but the difficulty has in a good measure been overcome. The countries of the Archipelago are generally not suited to pasture, and it is only in a few of them that the ox and buffalo are abundant. The sheep is so nowhere, and for the most part is wanting altogether; cattle, therefore, must be imported.

"As to corn, it will unquestionably be found far cheaper to import than to raise it. Rice will be the chief bread-corn, and will come in great abundance and cheapness from Siam and Cochin China. No country within 700 miles of Singapore is abundant in corn, and none is grown in the island: yet from the first establishment of the settlement to the present time, corn has been both cheap and abundant, there has been wonderfully little fluctuation, there are always stocks, and for many years a considerable exportation. A variety of pulses, vegetable oil, and culinary salt, will be derived from the same countries, as is now done in abundance by Singapore.

"The mines of antimony are 300 miles to the southwest of Labuan, and those of gold on the west and the south coasts; and I am not aware that any mineral wealth has been discovered in the portion of Borneo immediately connected with Labuan, except that of coal—far more important and valuable, indeed, than gold or antimony. The existence of a coal-field has been traced from Labuan to the islands of Kayn-arang—which words, in fact, mean coal island—to the island of Chermin, and from thence to the mainland over a distance of thirty miles. With respect to the coal of Labuan itself, I find no distinct statement beyond the simple fact of the existence of the mineral; but the coal of the two islands in the river, and of the main, is proved to be—from analysis and trial in steam-navigation—superior to nearly all the coal which India has hitherto yielded, and equal to some of our best English coals. This is the more remarkable, as it is known that most surface-minerals, and especially coals, are inferior to the portions of the same veins or beds more deep-seated.

"Nearly as early as the British flag is erected, and, at all events, as soon as it is permanently known to be so, there may be reckoned upon with certainty a large influx of settlers. The best and most numerous of these will be the Chinese. They were settled on the Borneo river when the Borneo government, never very good, or otherwise than comparatively violent and disorderly, was most endurable.

"Borneo is, of all the great islands of the western portion of the Archipelago, the nearest to China, and Labuan and its neighbourhood the nearest point of this island. The distance of Hong Kong is about 1000 miles, and that of the island of Hainan, a great place for emigration, not above 800; distances which to the Chinese *junks*—fast sailers before the strong and favourable winds of the monsoons—do not make voyages exceeding four or five days. The coasts of the provinces of Canton and Fokien have hitherto been the great hives from which Chinese emigration has proceeded; and even Fokien is not above 1400 miles from Labuan, a voyage of seven or eight days. Chinese trade and immigration will come together. The northwest coast of Borneo produces an unusual supply of those raw articles for which there is always a demand in the markets of China; and Labuan, it may be reckoned upon with certainty, will soon become the seat of a larger trade with China than the river of Borneo ever possessed.

"I by no means anticipate the same amount of rapid advance in population, commerce, or financial resources for Labuan, that has distinguished the history of Singapore, a far more centrical position for general commerce; still I think its prospect of success undoubted; while it will have some advantages which Singapore cannot, from its nature, possess. Its coal-mines, and the command of the coal-fields on the river of Borneo, are the most remarkable of these; and its superiority as a post-office[2] station necessarily follows. Then it is far more convenient as a port of refuge; and, as far as our present knowledge will enable us to judge, infinitely more valuable for military purposes, more especially for affording protection to the commerce which passes through the Chinese Sea, amounting at present to probably not less than 300,000 tons of shipping, carrying cargoes certainly not under the value of 15,000,000*l.* sterling.

"Labuan ought, like Singapore, to be a free port; and assuredly will not prosper if it is not. Its revenue should not be derived from customs, but, as in that settlement, from excise duties: upon the nature of these, as it is well known, it is unnecessary to enlarge. They covered during my time, near twenty years ago, and within five years of the establishment of the settlement, the whole charges of a small but sufficient garrison (100 *sepoys*), and a moderate but competent civil establishment.

"The military and civil establishments have been greatly increased of late years; but the revenue, still in its nature the same, has kept pace with them. During my administration of Singapore, the municipal charges fell on the general fund; but they are at present amply provided for from a distinct source, chiefly an assessment on house-property.

"If the military and civil charges of Labuan are kept within moderate bounds, I make no doubt but that a similar excise revenue will be adequate to cover the charges of both, and that in peace at least the state need not be called on to make any disbursement on its account; while during a naval war, if the state make any expenditure, it will be fully compensated by the additional security which the settlement will afford to British commerce, and the annoyance it will cause to the enemy.

"As to the disposal of the land, always a difficult question in a new

2. *Vide* Mr. Wise's Plan, following, for accelerating the communication between Great Britain and China, viz. the conveyance of the mails from Hong Kong to Suez (*via* Ceylon) direct. Submitted to Her Majesty's Government, 14th September, 1843; adopted 20th June, 1845.

and unoccupied colony, the result of my own inquiries and personal experience lead me to offer it as my decided conviction that the most expedient plan—that which is least troublesome to the government, most satisfactory to the settler, and ultimately most conducive to the public prosperity—is to dispose of it for a term of years, that is, on long leases of 1000 years, or virtually in perpetuity; the object in this case of adopting the leasehold tenure being, by making the land a chattel interest, to get rid of the difficulties in the matter of inheritance and transfer, which, under the administration of English law, and in reference more particularly to the Asiatic people who will be the principal landowners, are incident to real property. Town allotments might be sold subject to a considerable quit-rent, but allotments in the country for one entirely nominal. Those of the latter description should be small, proportionate with the extent of the island, and the time and difficulty required in such a climate to clear the land, now overgrown for the most part with a stupendous forest of evergreen trees, and the wood of which is too abundant to be of any value, certainly for the most part not worth the land-carriage of a couple of furlongs.

"A charter for the administration of justice should be as nearly as possible contemporaneous with the cession. Great inconvenience has resulted in all our Eastern settlements of the same nature with that speculated on at Labuan, from the want of all legal provision for the administration of justice; and remembering this, it ought to be guarded against in the case of Labuan.

"Whether in preparing for the establishment of a British settlement on the coast of Borneo, or in actually making one, Her Majesty's ministers, I am satisfied, will advert to the merits and peculiar qualifications of Mr. Brooke. That gentleman is unknown to me, except by his acts and writings; but, judging by these, I consider him as possessing all the qualities which have distinguished the successful founders of new colonies; intrepidity, firmness, and enthusiasm, with the art of governing and leading the masses. He possesses some, moreover, which have not always belonged to such men, however otherwise distinguished; a knowledge of the language, manners, customs, and institutions of the natives by whom the colony is to be surrounded; with benevolence and an independent fortune, things still more unusual with the projectors of colonies. Toward the formation of a new colony, indeed, the available services of such a man, presuming they are available, may be considered a piece of good fortune."

"Mem.—I have adopted an average rate of seven miles per hour

# Suggestions for Accelerating the Communication Between Great Britain and China.

| Proposed Route from Hong Kong to London, and vice versâ. | Course. | Distance, Miles. | Average Rate per Hour, Miles. | Interval under Weigh. Days. Hours. | | Interval at Anchor. Days. Hours. | | Total Interval. Days. Hours. | | Duties at Anchor. |
|---|---|---|---|---|---|---|---|---|---|---|
| Hong Kong to Pulo Labuan | S. 2° 18′ E. | 1009 | 7 | 6 | — | 1 | 12 | 7 | 12 | To receive Coal.[1] |
| Pulo Labuan to Singapore | S. 69 23 W. | 707 | — | 4 | 6 | — | 12 | 4 | 18 | To receive Coal, land and receive Mails. |
| Singapore to Malacca | S. 64 48 W. 19 N. 51 41 W. 103 | 122 | — | — | 18 | — | 6 | 1 | — | To land and receive Mails. |
| Malacca to Pinang | N. 30 37 W. | 222 | — | 1 | 8 | — | 16 | 2 | — | To receive Coal, land and receive Mails. |
| Pinang to Ceylon[2] | N. 82 24 W. 303 S. 80 45 W. 916 | 1219 | — | 7 | 6 | 2 | 12 | 8 | 18 | Ditto Ditto |
| Ceylon to Aden | As now performed by the Peninsular and Oriental Steam Navigation Co., detention of 2 days included | | | | | 11 | — | | | |
| Aden to Suez | Ditto Ditto | | | | | 8 | — | | | |
| Suez to Alexandria | Ditto all stoppages included | | | | | 3 | — | | | |
| Alexandria to Malta | Ditto Ditto | | | | | 4 | — | | | |
| Malta to Marseilles | As now performed by H.M. Post-Office Packets, ditto | | | | | — | 4 | | | |

Note 1. above. The Borneo coal-mines would also serve to keep the Hong Kong, Singapore, and Pinang stations supplied with fuel for Steam Vessels carrying the Mails between Hong Hong and Suez direct.

Note 2. above. Receiving at Ceylon the Outward Overland Mail from England, and returning therewith to China.

Marseilles Ditto by regular course of Post ditto     5    —
to London
Total Interval from Hong Kong to London, and vice versâ, by the   59    —
proposed Route. Days

as a fair estimate of the speed well-appointed Steam Vessels, of moderate size and power, will be enabled to accomplish and maintain, throughout the proposed Route, at all seasons of the year; for, during the whole distance from Pinang to Aden, and *vice versâ*, neither monsoon, from the course steered, becomes at any period a directly adverse wind, an advantage which the route hitherto observed does not possess. Assuming that the Hon. East India Company continue the management of the Bombay line, and that the Peninsular and Oriental Steam Navigation Company are encouraged to render their operations more comprehensive, by the establishment of branch steamers between Ceylon and Singapore, to which latter port Her Majesty's steam vessels on the China station could convey the mails from Hong Kong, this all-important object might, without difficulty, be attained.

"The advantages to the Straits settlements, consequent on the adoption of improved arrangements, require no comment; and the *practicability* of effecting a very considerable acceleration of the communication with China is evident from the simple fact that the average interval which has occurred in the transmission of letters from China, by the last twenty Overland Mails (irrespective of the unfortunate July mail from Bombay), exceeds the period occasionally occupied by fast-sailing ships, in accomplishing the voyage *viâ* the Cape of Good Hope.

"London, 14th Sept. 1843.[3]

"Henry Wise,

"13, Austin Friars.

"P.S.—*Oct. 9th.* The arrival at Suez on the 16th *ult.* of the H.C.S. Akbar, in *forty-six* days from Hong Kong, after accomplishing the passage down the China seas, against the S.W. monsoon—unassisted also by any previously arranged facilities for coaling, exchange of steamers at Aden, and other manifest advantages requisite for the proper execution of this important service, confirms the correctness of my estimate for performing the voyage from Hong Kong to Suez, or *vice versâ, viz. forty-three* days, including stoppages."

---

3. Date of submitting the above proposed route and estimate to Her Majesty's Government for consideration.

# Concluding Observations
## FIRST EDITION

The recent proceedings of Government in following up the impression made upon Malay piracy, as related in these pages; the appointment of Mr. Brooke as British Agent in Borneo, armed with the moral and physical power of his country; the cession of the island of Labuan to the British crown; and the great advance already made by the English ruler of Sarawak, in laying broad foundations for native prosperity, while extending general security and commerce; all combine to add an interest to the early individual steps which have led to measures of so much national consequence.

Deeply as I felt the influence of that individual on the condition of Borneo, and the Malayan Archipelago generally, while employed there, and much as I anticipated from his energetic character, extraordinary exertions, and enlarged views for the future, I confess that my expectations have been greatly increased by the progress of events since that period. It needed nothing to confirm my faith in the results that were sure to follow from his enlightened acts—from his prudence and humanity in the treatment of his Dyak subjects, and the neighbouring and interior independent tribes—from his firm resistance to the Malay tyranny exercised upon the aborigines, and his punishment of Malay aggression, wherever perpetrated.

But when I see these elements of good wisely seconded by the highest authorities of England, I cannot but look for the consummation of every benefit desired, much more rapidly and effectively than if left to the efforts of a private person, even though that person were a Brooke! If the appearance of H.M.S. *Dido* on the coast and at Sarawak produced a salutary effect upon all our relations with the inhabitants, it may well be presumed that the mission of Captain Bethune, and the expedition under Rear-Admiral Sir Thomas Cochrane, must have greatly improved and extended that wholesome state of affairs. Indeed, it is evident, by the complete success which attended Mr. Brooke's official visit to Borneo Proper in H.M.S. *Driver*, after receiving dispatches from Lord Aberdeen appointing him British agent in the island, carried out by Captain Bethune in November, 1844, that the presence of a British force in those seas was alone necessary to enable him to suppress piracy, and perfect his plans for the establishment of a native government which should not oppress the country, and which should cultivate the most friendly intercourse with us.

Thus we find the piratical Pangeran Usop put down, and Muda Hassim exercising the sovereign power in the name of his imbecile nephew, who still retains the title of sultan. The principal chiefs, and men distinguished by talent and some acquaintance with foreign affairs, are now on our side; and it only requires to support them in order that civilization may rapidly spread over the land, and Borneo become again, as it was one or two centuries ago, the abode of an industrious, rich, pacific, and mercantile people, interchanging products with all the trading nations of the world, and conferring and reaping those blessings which follow in the train of just and honourable trade wheresoever its enterprising spirit leads in the pursuit of honest gain. As the vain search for the philosopher's stone conducted to many a useful and valuable discovery, so may we be assured that the real seeking for gold through the profitable medium of commerce has been, is, and will be the grand source of filling the earth with comfort and happiness.

Among the numerous visions of this kind which open to our sense while reflecting on the new prospects of this vast island—so little known, yet known to possess almost unbounded means to invite and return commercial activity—is the contemplation of the field it presents to missionary labours. When we read Mr. Brooke's description of the aboriginal Dyak, and observe what he has himself done in one locality within the space of four or five short years, what may we not expect to be accomplished by the zeal of Christian missions judiciously directed to reclaim such a people from utter barbarism, and induce them to become true members of a faith which teaches forbearance and charity between man and man, and inculcates, with the love and hope of heaven, an abhorrence of despotism and blood, and a disposition to live in good-will and peace with all our fellow-creatures? There are here no prejudices of caste, as in India, to impede the missionaries' progress.

Mr. Brooke has pointed out what may be effected in this way, and we have only to say amen to his prayer, with an earnest aspiration that it may be speedily fulfilled.

Having enjoyed the pleasure of communicating to the public this satisfactory description of the *status quo* in Borneo to the latest period (September, 1845), I venture to congratulate them upon it. Thus far all is well and as it should be, and promising the happiest issue; but I hope I may not be charged with presumption in offering an opinion from my experience in this quarter, and respectfully suggesting that, in addition to a permanent British settlement at Labuan, it will be absolutely necessary to proceed with the suppression of Malay piracy, by steadily acting against every pirate-hold.

Without a continued and determined series of operations of this sort, it is my conviction that even the most sanguinary and fatal on-slaughts will achieve nothing beyond a present and temporary good. The impression on the native mind is not sufficiently lasting: their old impulses and habits return with fresh force; they forget their heavy retribution; and in two or three years the memory of them is almost entirely effaced. Till piracy be completely suppressed there must be no relaxation; and well worth the perseverance is the end in view, the welfare of one of the richest and most improvable portions of the globe, and the incalculable extension of the blessings of Britain's prosperous commerce and humanizing dominion.

In looking forward to the certain realization of these prospects, I may mention the important circumstance of the discovery of coal in abundance for the purposes of steam navigation. The surveys already made afford assurances of this fact, and the requisite arrangements are in progress for opening and working the mines. It is generally known that the Dutch assert very wide pretensions to colonies and monopolies in those seas. A treaty has been concluded between the Netherlands government and England; and although that important document contains no reference whatever to Borneo, it is most desirable for the general extension of commerce that no national jealousies, no ideas of conflicting interests, no encroaching and ambitious projects, may be allowed to interfere with or prevent the beneficial progress of this important region.

With such a man as Mr. Brooke to advise the course most be-coming, disinterested, and humane for the British empire to pursue, it is not too much to say that, if the well-being of these races of our fellow-creatures is defeated or postponed, the crime will not lie at our door. The sacrifices we have made to extinguish slavery throughout the world are a sure and unquestionable pledge that we will do our utmost to extirpate the horrid traffic in those parts, and to uproot the system of piracy that feeds it. It is the bounden duty of both Holland and Great Britain to unite cordially in this righteous cause. The cry of nature is addressed to them; and if rejected, as surely as there is justice and mercy in the Providence which overrules the fate of nations, no blessing will prosper them, but wealth, and dominion, and happiness will pass away from them forever. Mr. Brooke invokes their co-operation, and his noble appeal cannot be withstood.

The central position of Labuan is truly remarkable. That island is distant from

| Hong Kong | 1009 miles. |
| Singapore | 707 " |
| Siam | 984 " |
| Manilla | 650 " |

On the other hand, Mr. Brooke's territory of Sarawak is distant from

| Singapore | 427 miles |
| Labuan | 304 " |
| Hong Kong | 1199 " |

How direct and central are these valuable possessions for the universal trade of the East!

# Postscript
## SECOND EDITION

June 6th, 1846.

In the foregoing remarks with which I closed the first edition of this book, I ventured to congratulate the public on the cheerful aspect of affairs in Borneo at the latest period of which accounts had then reached me. I could then say, with a joyful heart, "Thus far all is well and as it should be, and promising the happiest issue." But now I must write in a different strain. The mischiefs I pointed out above as likely to ensue from a desultory and intermittent mode of dealing with Malay piracy have revealed themselves even sooner and in a more formidable manner than I had anticipated. The weak and covetous *sultan* of Borneo has, with more than the usual fickleness of Asiatics, already forgotten the lessons we gave him and the engagements he solemnly and voluntarily contracted with us.

Mr. Brooke's faithful friends, Muda Hassim and the Pangeran Budrudeen, with numbers of their families and retainers, have been basely murdered by their treacherous kinsman, because of their attachment to the English and their unswerving determination to put down piracy; and what is worst of all, Mr. Brooke's arch-enemy, the subtle and indefatigable villain Macota, the man whose accursed head was thrice saved by my too-generous friend, has now returned triumphantly to the scene of his former crimes, and is commissioned by the sultan to take Mr. Brooke's life by poison, or by any other of those treacherous arts in which there is no more consummate adept than Macota. I could trust securely to Mr. Brooke's gallantry and skill for the protection of his life against the attacks of open foes; and my only fears arise when I reflect on his utter insensibility to danger, and think how the admirable qualities of his own guileless, confiding nature may facilitate the designs of his enemies.

H.M.S. *Hazard*, from Hong Kong, having touched at Bruni about the end of March last, was boarded by a native, who gave the captain such information as induced him to sail with all speed for Sarawak; and there this man made the following deposition:—

Japper, a native of Bruni, deposes that he was sent aboard H.M.S. *Hazard* by the Pangeran Muda Mahomed, to warn the captain against treachery, and to communicate the following details to Mr. Brooke at Sarawak.

The Rajah Muda Hassim was raised by the sultan to the title of Sultan Muda (or young sultan), and, together with his brothers and followers, was living in security, when he was attacked by orders of the *sultan* at night, and together with thirteen of his family, killed in different places. Four brothers, *viz.* Pangeran Muda Mahomed, Pangeran Abdul Kader, Pangeran Abdulraman, and Pangeran Mesahat, together with several young children of the Rajah Muda Hassim, alone survive. The deponent Japper was in attendance on his lord, the Pangeran Budrudeen, at the time of the attack. The *pangeran*, though surprised by his enemies, fought for some time, and when desperately wounded, retired outside his house with his sister and another woman named Koor Salem. The deponent was there and was wounded, as were both the women.

The Pangeran Budrudeen ordered deponent to open a keg or cask of gunpowder, which he did; and the last thing his lord did was to take his ring from his finger and desire the deponent to carry it to Mr. Brooke; to bid Mr. Brooke not to forget him, and not to forget to lay his case before the Queen of England. The deponent then quitted his lord, who was with the two women, and immediately after his lord fired the powder, and the three were blown up. The deponent escaped with difficulty; and a few days afterward, the ring intrusted to his charge, was taken from him by the *sultan*. The *sultan*, and those with him, killed the Rajah Muda Hassim and his family, because he was the friend of the English and wanted to suppress piracy.

The *sultan* has now built forts and defied the English. He talked openly of cutting out any vessel that arrived; and two *Pangerans* went down, bearing the flag of the Rajah Muda Hassim, to look at the vessel, and to kill the captain if they could get him ashore. The deponent had great difficulty in getting to the ship; and should his flight be discovered, he considers the lives of the surviving portion of the Rajah Muda Hassim's family will be in danger. The deponent did what he was ordered, and what his late lord, the Pangeran Budrudeen, desired him to do. The sultan had a man ready to send, named Nakoda Kolala, to Kaluka, to request that Pangeran Macota would kill Mr. Brooke by treachery or poison.

(*Signed*)

J. Brooke.

Having put Mr. Brooke on his guard, the *Hazard* proceeded to Singapore, whence the H.E.I.C. war-steamer *Phlegethon* would be immediately dispatched to Sarawak.

ADDITIONAL CHAPTER

# Admiral Sir Thomas Cochrane Sails for Borneo

BY WALTER K. KELLY

On receipt of the intelligence referred to in Captain Keppel's post-
script to the second edition, Admiral Sir Thomas Cochrane at once
determined to bring Sultan Omar to a strict reckoning for the atrocities imputed to him. Touching with the fleet at Sarawak on the 24th
of June, 1846, he invited the Government Agent, Mr. Brooke, to accompany him to Bruni, and assist in the intended investigation. Meanwhile, that gentleman had taken such steps as his means enabled him to
adopt towards checking the further development of the calamity that
had occurred. He had visited several parts of the coast in the *Phlegethon*, to ascertain the feelings of the inhabitants, and to prevent them
from following the *sultan's* example, should they be so disposed.

But everywhere he found the people loud in their condemnation of the *sultan's* proceedings, and greatly disaffected towards his
government. It was only from the northward that news of a different complexion was received. The Illanun pirates in that quarter were
busily bestirring themselves, actuated, of course, by the belief that the
government of Bruni was again prepared to make common cause
with them. In fact, by the flagrant violation of his engagements, solemnly and voluntarily entered into with the British authorities, and
by the murder of his relatives solely on account of their fidelity to the
faith of treaties, to the law of nations, and to the true interests of their
country and of mankind, the *sultan* had unequivocally avowed himself
a pirate. Such appears to have been the view taken of the case by our
Admiral.

On the 4th of July, the Admiral, accompanied by Mr. Brooke, arrived off Mooarro island, at the entrance of the Bruni River, where they learned several particulars respecting the recent murders, and found that rumour, instead of exaggerating the reality, had fallen far short of it. The Rajah Muda Hassim, one of his sons, Pangeran Budrudeen, seven brothers, one sister, other relations, and about a similar number of other persons, had perished simultaneously. Two of the remaining princes were subsequently put to death upon its being discovered that Si Japper had fled to Mr, Brooke with information of what had occurred; and of the whole family there remained in existence only two brothers, and the son and heir of the *rajah*. These three owed their safety to the protection of the most powerful remaining *pangeran*, named Mumim, who, although son-in-law of the *sultan*, disapproved of the deed, but confined his interference to the protection of those parties. In one of his despatches to the Admiralty, Sir Thomas Cochrane says:

The cause of this sudden change of conduct on the part of the *sultan* (who, their Lordships are already aware, is a very weak as well as ill-conditioned character) was the fate that had attended Pangeran Usop, whom, their Lordships will remember, I, at the *sultan's* request, last year attacked and drove from the city, and who was subsequently taken and put to death by Budrudeen, in consequence of an attack he made upon it after my departure. It would appear that the *sultan's* reputed son, a man of worthless character, Pangeran Hassim, had married Usop's daughter; and, partaking of his father-in-law's hostility to the English, and disposition to piracy, as well as deeply resenting his fall, and exercising the very great influence he had over the mind of the *sultan*, he, in conjunction with a very clever and artful man, named Hadgi Samod, at last brought His Highness to consent to this deed of revenge.

Our informants further stated, that so soon as this crime had been perpetrated, the *sultan* began to place the river and city in a state of defence; and Commander Egerton, of the Hazard, corroborated the statement that a trap had been laid for him to get him to the city, and, as alleged by the informants, with the view of putting him to death.

Under all the foregoing circumstances, and those considerations alluded to in my letter, No. 95, before referred to, there did not appear to me the shadow of a doubt as to my right, with reference to those principles which govern European states under similar circumstances, to proceed with an armed force, and demand an explanation of these hostile deeds.

When off the island of Chermin, at the mouth of Bruni River, the Admiral received a sort of apologetic letter from the Sultan, offering a vague explanation of the treatment complained of by Commander Egerton, of the Hazard, and requesting in general terms that "his friend should not believe anything Si Japper might have stated." The letter contained no more explicit allusion to the recent transactions, nor did it prohibit an approach by an armed force, or threaten resistance.

On the 8th of July the fleet passed the bar and ascended the river, the *Phlegethon* leading the way, and sounding. On approaching Pulo Bangore, five forts opened to view, admirably placed for denying a passage beyond them. A gun was fired from one of the forts, and the largest of them hoisted a flag, which Mr. Brooke recognised as that of his murdered friend, Muda Hassim. For a while some doubt was felt on board the flag-ship as to whether this was not intended as an intimation that the English should be received as friends. But they were not long left in suspense upon the subject, as the moment the *Phlegethon* had passed the narrows, the battery commenced a spirited fire, which was promptly returned. The five forts were stormed, the guns destroyed, and the magazine blown up.

Higher up the river there was a heavy battery, *à fleur d'eau*, consisting of eight brass and two iron guns, from 68 to 9 pounders, supported by five other heavy works on hills not far in the rear. The main battery pointed directly down to a bend of the river, from which it was distant about 800 yards, and round which the fleet had to turn. As soon as the ships appeared in sight, all these batteries commenced a sharp and extremely well-directed fire upon them, seconded by a play of musketry from the woods on the right, to which the *Spiteful*, the flag-ship, was obliged to submit without retaliation. Her position was for a while very critical, with the beach but a few yards beyond her paddle-boxes, the *Royalist* in tow, and the boats filled with the whole of the landing force.

The utmost silence and attention were required to prevent the whole being thrown on shore. But the *Phlegethon* soon put an end to the crisis. The fire from her ship-guns, from the battery of field-pieces placed round her bows, and from the brigade of rockets planted upon her bridge, together with the now rapid progress of the whole force directly up the river, so astonished and dismayed the enemy that they fled before the steamers could reach their works, or the storming party carry out the service intended for it. The marines under Captain Hawkins immediately took possession of the heights that command the town. These operations were not accomplished without loss; two men having been killed, and seven wounded.

The city was found entirely deserted by the inhabitants, and the *sultan* had fled into the interior. A force of nearly 500 men, under Captain Mundy, was sent in pursuit of him on the 10th. Mr. Brooke accompanied the expedition, which was directed against Damuan, a village 30 miles from Bruni, where the *sultan* was supposed to have determined on making a stand. On their way they arrived at the village of Kabran, where they found a large house deserted by its owners, but full of valuable property secured in massive chests; also arms, ammunition, &c. both for great guns and small arms, and several tin cases of fine English powder, all of which belonged to Hadgi Hassim. The magazines, ammunition, and property were destroyed, and six Spanish brass guns of considerable size and great beauty, which we found on an adjacent eminence, were carried off.

After two ineffectual attempts to continue its march to Damuan, under heavy rain and through a deeply flooded country, the expedition returned to Bruni; whence it started again to take a new route on the morning of the 13th. This time it succeeded in reaching Damuan; but too late to capture the *sultan*, who had already fled further inland. The destruction of some household furniture belonging to the *sultan*, magazines of powder, ammunition for guns of different calibre, and a considerable quantity of cartridges, admirably made, for musketry, was all that could be effected.

At Bruni the Admiral managed, through Japper, to open a communication with those of the dispersed inhabitants who were friendly to the British; and on the day following the occupation of the city, he was visited by Pangerans Mumim, Buher, and Muda Mohammed. As the *sultan* had fled, and they were, in fact, without a government, the Admiral "invited them to come to some determination as to the course they would pursue for the well-being of their country;" but they appeared to be entirely paralysed.

"Pangeran Mumim," the Admiral observes "although condemning the *sultan's* proceedings, and himself very respectable in character, yet was most timid, and seemed to have an aversion to setting the *sultan* aside; and the others, although very violent against him, had neither talent nor weight to undertake the formation of a new government."

"Mr. Brooke landed on the following day, and at Mumim's house had a meeting on an enlarged scale, and stated to it my readiness to assist them in any measure that would have the effect of putting an end to the existing anarchy, or that might give permanent security to life and property. But on this and subsequent occasions he found the same timidity and irresolution to prevail as at their conference with me. In point of fact, the massacre had been of that sweeping character, as to cut off every man of weight or intelligence, and leave the survivors in an irrecoverable state of helplessness and dismay.

"In the meantime, the common people had recovered from their panic, and commenced returning to the town; and by the fourth or fifth day nearly every house was inhabited, and the same busy scene presented itself as on ordinary occasions, the boats flocking round the ships to sell or exchange their produce, with as much confidence as in any English port; and I am persuaded nothing would have been more gratifying to them than to have learned from me that I was authorised to establish an Englishman (such a one, for instance, as Mr. Brooke) as their governor and chief, under whom they would have felt confident of the undisturbed enjoyment of the produce of their industry, and of protection from uncertain and despotic exactions."

Having remained eleven days at the city with- out any prospect of securing a definite and satisfactory arrangement, the Admiral, with Mr. Brooke's concurrence, addressed a proclamation to the chief person actually in the place, to be given to the *sultan* on his return, detailing the whole of the proceedings between him and the British authorities during the past twelve months; pointing out the unprincipled conduct of the *sultan*; shewing how entirely he and his subjects were at the Admiral's mercy, and threatening him with the most vigorous retaliation should he ever again evince hostility towards Great Britain. The document was read to the assembled authorities, merchants, &c, who seemed perfectly pleased with its contents, and no less so with the intimation that a ship of war was to be left with them until Mr. Brooke's return. The meeting having broken up, the Admiral sailed northward, taking Mr. Brooke with him.

Previously to this, the researches of our countrymen had been rewarded by the discovery of a very fine seam of coal on the mainland, of the same quality as the Kiangi coal. It is very favourably circumstanced for working, being fourteen feet broad, and dipping at an angle of 25° into a low hill, separated by only a mile of level ground from the harbour of Mooarro. Report states that there are numerous other beds in the same neighbourhood.

The Admiral's next visit was to the Ulanun pirates, on whom he inflicted severe punishment, including the destruction of their strongholds on the rivers Tampassok and Fandassar. He then left Captain Mundy of the *Iris* to finish the work so well begun, by settling accounts with some of the pirates who had not yet been made to feel our force; and who, under the directions of Hadgi Samod, the *sultan's* general, were still carrying on hostilities against the native tribes that were friendly to the English. Nothing could exceed the glee with which our sailors engaged in this service. A very animated description of the operations is given by Captain Mundy in a letter dated August 28, 1846, from which the following is an extract:

On the 7th instant, I parted company with the commander-in-chief; and no sooner was the squadron out of sight than I sent Lieutenant Little away with my boats and five days' provisions, with orders to cruise that time along the coast and join me 100 miles to the southward. The Admiral's orders to me were to carry on the war against the Illanun rascals by sea and land, according to my discretion, and to look after the *sultan's* first chieftain, Hadgi Samod, who had been the principal adviser of the *sultan* in the hostile measures against us; and who, it was now reported, had sought refuge somewhere amongst the piratical tribes.

On the 12th I anchored at Ambong, and Lieutenant Little joined me. He had captured and destroyed one piratical *prahu*, and had burnt a large Illanun village, after sustaining an attack from a large body of pirates, who threw spears from the banks at the boats, but were eventually driven off with the loss of several killed and wounded. No one was injured on our side, though the spears stuck into the sides of our boats—these fellows rushing down within ten yards of the *pinnace*, hurling their darts, and holding up their large wooden shields to protect them from musketry.

On the 14th we anchored off Kimanis, where Mr. Brooke received information that Hadgi Samod had fortified himself in the Mambacoot River, distant only six miles; and that nine gun-boats, which had been sent from Borneo to attack him, had found his position too strong, and had therefore decided to remain off Kimanis till the arrival of the frigate. I gave directions therefore to Mr. Little to be ready with all the boats of the Iris at daylight the. following morning, assisted by the *Phlegethon* cutters, and to proceed to attack this noted chief wherever he might be found. Mr. Brooke and I commenced business by sending a messenger to the Dyak chief, desiring him to give up Hadgi Samod, and enter into friendly communication with us.

The return message was an insolent bit of bravado, desiring us to come and take him, and that they were not afraid of our shot, which they would catch in their hands and throw back at our boats.

Neither Mr. Brooke nor myself had intended to take any active part in the expedition; but the unlooked-for, and, I may add, extraordinary circumstance of the sudden arrival of thirty war *prahus*, carrying twenty guns and about four hundred men, under their chiefs, inhabiting districts for twenty miles round, for the purpose of paying their respects to the English *rajah*, and to assure him of their anxiety for legitimate commerce, and their wish to be friends of England, entirely altered the position of affairs. Mr. Brooke, with his accustomed decision, after a lengthened discussion with their chieftains, declared it to be his belief that they were honest men, and that it would be very impolitic on our part to refuse the offer of their aid, and that he should wish to accompany them. Of course I acquiesced immediately, and it was arranged that we should go together in the gig, thus putting implicit confidence in their faith, whilst Lieutenant Little could always keep his force compactly together, ready to act on the first semblance of treachery.

At five a.m. on the 18th, the boats were in movement. At eight I crossed the bar in a beautiful new gig the Admiral gave me, the principal *pangeran* of our new allies shewing the channel. Lieutenant Little's force came next, and about a quarter of a mile in the rear the large fleet of *prahus*. It was a picturesque scene; boat after boat dashing through the surf with their gaudy flags and long streamers, and then shooting into the unruffled stream beyond, and taking up their assigned positions, which were well under command of my guns and rockets. Our force now commenced pulling up against a strong ebb; and, after three good hours at the oars, the first attempt to oppose our progress appeared in large rafts floating down, and soon afterwards the report of guns in the distance was heard. On pulling swiftly round a point to clear one of the rafts, the gig being then about fifty yards ahead of the main division, we came suddenly upon a long line of thick bamboo stakes fixed across the stream, with an immense boom attached to them, but which, owing to the freshes, had swung athwart.

Facing these defences, only eighty yards distant, a fort had been erected, which, as soon as our boats came into view, opened fire. Before the enemy could reload, I fell back upon the gunboats, and ordered Mr. Little to give way and 'at them.' He was soon followed by the barge and cutter, and the action became general,—shot, rockets, and musketry; but, owing to the strength of the tide, it was ten minutes before my first lieutenant could get over the short distance; and when he finally captured the fort, he found it had been armed with small swivelguns only, which the defenders had managed to carry into the jungle. One of our native allies recognised Hadgi Samod and his Bornean sub-officers in the battery.

Having demolished the fort and destroyed the magazines, ammunition, &c, we pushed on without losing time; and observing, as we passed a narrow creek, a *prahu* endeavouring to escape, we dashed at her and captured her; the crew, who escaped, leaving behind their spears, *krises*, and *sumpitans, i. e.* quivers of poisoned arrows. The country was now extremely beautiful. The interior of the houses was extremely neat,—mats, threshing and knitting machines, ordinary implements, and other furniture, in capital order; and had it not been for the numerous human skulls suspended from the ceiling in regular festoons, with the thigh and arm bones occupying the intervening spaces, and other ornaments peculiar to the wildest class of Dyaks, I should have fancied myself in a civilised land.

At three p.m., on coming to a turn of the river, a magnificent mansion presented itself to our view, the verandah of which gave a frontage of 200 feet by 20 in breadth. It was close to the river, and partially concealed by cocoanut-trees. One of these had been cut down, and of it a kind of abatis was made, from behind which, as our boats advanced, a masked battery was opened.

These guns were quickly silenced, and I was not long in jumping on *terra firma*, rifle in hand. The enemy were driven into the interior, carrying off their killed and wounded. The house was soon in flames; and amongst the internal decorations consumed were fifty human skulls, and as many packages of human bones—many of them evidently the. latest gifts of the Dyak gentlemen to their lady-loves; for you must know that no aristocratic youth dare venture to pay his addresses to the fair one unless he throws at the blushing maidens feet a net full of skulls at the same time that he offers his hand and heart.

At four p.m. we bivouacked for the night; and early in the morning of the 17th a deserter from Hadgi Samod swam across the river to our camp, and informed us that his chief had retreated in despair to the houses at the head of the river. At early dawn, therefore, we were on his track, and in half an hour a cheer from the headmost boats signalised that the last refuge of the enemy was in sight. A few strokes more and our guns and rockets were in play; and after a vain endeavour of the resolute chief by musketry and sumpets to oppose our steady advance, he was compelled to abandon his fortress and retreat into the wilderness. Having burnt all the buildings of those inhabitants who had taken an active part against us, we returned down the river, and were on board the ship by sunset. Our loss was one seaman of the *Iris* killed, and four wounded; two of the *Phlegethon's*, and eight of our native allies wounded.

The native chiefs rendezvoused at the *Phlegethon*, where we entertained them till a late hour, each of them swearing to protect the persons and property of all shipwrecked or distressed Europeans who might be driven upon their iron-bound coast; and I really hope we have made a commencement in the good work of rendering these seas secure for the peaceful trader. The wonderful effect of our Congreve rockets gave them an idea of our power; whilst our uniform kindness to all the unpiratical tribes plainly bespoke our anxiety to be friendly with the good.

After the termination of the proceedings against the Illanuns, Mr. Brooke returned to Bruni to complete the task of re-establishing order there, which the Admiral had confided to his experienced judgment. Then, having made a short stay in the city, he returned to Sarawak, taking with him the remains of Muda Hassim's family, among the rest his young son, the heir presumptive to the throne of Borneo. Let us hope that the boy, thus early removed from contaminating associations, and trained up under so kind and judicious a guardian, will one day prove a compensation to his country for the disastrous loss it sustained in the premature death of his brave, upright, intelligent, and docile uncle, Budrudeen.

In his dealings towards the humbled and fugitive *sultan*, Mr. Brooke appears to have acted in all respects as became his own high character and his station as a servant of the British crown. Had he chosen, as Rajah of Sarawak, to pursue his righteous quarrel to the uttermost against his delinquent feudal chief, he might easily have found specious arguments to justify such a course, and precedents in abundance as well in European as in Asiatic history. But he was not the man to sacrifice a great opportunity of doing good to the satisfaction of a merely personal vengeance. It was his duty, as British agent, above all things to uphold the fair fame of his country for equity and moderation; and from that duty, he never swerved either in this or in any other instance.

The *sultan* was no longer dangerous; his teeth had been drawn; the mass of his people both feared and respected the English; and the presence of our ships on the coast would effectually prevent any outbreak of a hostile spirit. Meanwhile, Bruni was without a government, or the means of constructing one; so that it was evidently both safe and expedient to permit Omar to return to his capital, in order that the administrative routine might resume its ordinary course under the sanction and prestige of his name. With the consent, therefore, of our agent, the *sultan* re-entered Bruni within a month after his flight from it; and he wrote Mr. Brooke a very humble letter, entreating forgiveness of the past, and making strong promises of future good behaviour. He also addressed a penitent letter to Her Majesty, Queen Victoria, in which he renewed and ratified his two former engagements.

Captain Mundy visited the *sultan* in state on the 19th of September, and thus describes the interview:

Early on that morning I despatched all the boats, armed, under Lieutenant Heath, taking with him the detachment of marines, and gave him orders to moor the force in line of battle in front of the *sultan's* new palace, and land the marines on the platform commanding the entrance of the hall of audience, and there wait my arrival. I left the *Iris* at 7h. 30m. a.m., and pulling the seventeen miles in three hours and a half, found all ready for my reception. As I stepped on shore I was received under a salute of fifteen guns by Pangeran Mumim, and the *sultan* met me at the threshold of the hall. Here the marines were drawn up,

350

directly enfilading the divan; and as they presented arms, I observed the old monarch tremble in his slippers; for he evidently entertained some slight suspicion that, as he well merited punishment, I would act as his highness would certainly have done in my place—namely, kidnap him by treachery.

The *sultan* appeared about sixty years of age, his countenance denoting imbecility, not untinctured with hypocrisy. He has two thumbs on his right hand, is five feet five inches in height, thin, and meagre of limb. He was well dressed, and his manner and deportment thoroughbred; and he was treated with great respect by the numerous princes and magnates who thronged the *salle*. After presenting my officers, I told him that I had words for his private ear, and must speak with him alone. He led me immediately to an antechamber commanding a view of the river. He then ordered a large wax taper to be lit and placed before us, explaining that this light was witness of the purity of his heart, and of the oath which he was ready to make of his goodwill towards his sister the Queen of England.

I then gave him, through my interpreter, the following information: that England would insist upon his ministers being good men, favourable to Europeans and to lawful commerce, exact in the observance of treaties, and active in discountenancing piracy; that a grave outrage had been committed by firing on the British flag, and that I could not say what redress would be considered sufficient. The *sultan* assured me in reply, that he was ready to submit to any terms which the Admiral might dictate; that he would deliver up four of the princes who had been active in the late hostilities against us; and that for the future his government should be strictly just. I told him he was sure to receive justice from our government, and that all depended upon his own conduct; and I ended by remarking that it would be much more agreeable for me to protect his new palace and capital, than to receive orders to inflict upon it the same chastisement with which we had visited Tampassok, Pandassar, and Mambacoot.

The *sultan* again swore by the Prophet, in honour of whom he had just fasted thirty days, that his heart was in the right place; that he had never forgotten the kindness of the Admiral to him last year; and that he had given positive orders to Hadgi Samod, who commanded the forts, not to fire on us, but that that chieftain would not obey him.

After a few more words I took my leave, and re-embarked; and I will now only add, that it is my firm opinion that he will hereafter submit to any demands made by Mr. Brooke, who is, indeed, *de facto, sultan* of the whole territory from Point Api to Malludu, a coast of seven hundred miles. What an extraordinary position for an English gentleman to be placed in! And how has he managed to receive the homage of so vast a population? By unremitting kindness and attention to the natives of every description, during a six years' residence. What could be more extraordinary than the gathering of the *rajahs* off Kimanis, last month, just before we attacked Mambacoot? people who had never seen him, and who had only heard from others of his benevolence and good government at Sarawak.

Then how romantic his march against the *sultan* into the interior!—ending by the total submission of the most ancient Mahomedan sovereign of the East, who, I forgot to mention, told me that his family had supplied the last twenty-five reigning princes, of whom his highness was exceedingly proud, and which he hoped would be considered by our government as a reason for supporting him on the throne.

Thus far events have fully justified the wise forbearance manifested towards this weak and despicable offender by the British Admiral, and by Mr. Brooke, acting under his authority. According to the last accounts from Borneo Proper, the *sultan* remained deeply impressed by the stern lesson he had received; the people of the coast were quiet, and eager for trade; and the Illanun pirates were said to have removed from their untenable quarters on the Tampassok and the Pandassar to Tunka, a piratical place on the eastern coast, remote from the broad commercial highway guarded by our ships. And now at length we may confidently hope that this happy state of things will be permanent. The crowning act has been put to the history of the initiatory struggles for the establishment of British commerce and British influence in the vast and teeming regions of the Indian Archipelago. After such long disheartening delays, attended with such deplorable consequences, the flag of Great Britain now waves over Labuan, a pledge of safety to the peaceful trader, a terror to the pirate and the oppressor.

The ceremony of taking possession of the island and its dependencies was performed on the 24th of December last by Captain Mundy. The *Iris* and *Wolf*, which had been despatched on this service, dressed ship; royal salutes were fired; marines and small-armed men landed; and Pangeran Mumim, the prime minister of Borneo, with many chiefs, and a multitude of Malays and Dyaks, attended on shore. Their picturesque *prahus*, anchored close to the beach, with flags and banners, had a beautiful effect. Captain Mundy had on the 18th concluded a treaty with the *sultan*, by which the island was ceded for ever to Her Majesty the Queen of Great Britain, and stipulations were made for the suppression of piracy all along the coast.

These matters were explained to the assembled natives in a short speech, delivered by Captain Mundy, and put into Malay by Lieutenant Heath. The prospect of protection and peaceful trade delighted the Borneans; and the only drawback to the satisfaction universally expressed by them was, that they could not at once settle on the island. Numbers of persons had repaired thither with that intention, and were with difficulty restrained from so doing by the authority of the Admiral, until further instructions should have been received from this country. A colony will of course be founded in Labuan, nor can its existence be long held in abeyance; but it is right that the basis should be laid without precipitation.

In order, therefore, to avoid the mischiefs incident to crude and hasty measures of colonisation, Captain Mundy was directed by his instructions to raise no fortifications, form no establishments on shore, and allow no settlers. Labuan is for the present a naval station, and no more; but the time is at hand when it will become a second Singapore. Several merchants on the latter island have signified their intention to remove their establishments to Labuan, whenever the place shall be ready for their reception.

The gratification we feel in recording an event of such high promise in the history of commerce and civilisation is impaired by one unhappy circumstance. The officers and crews of the two vessels suffered severely from sickness at Labuan; and Messrs. Gordon and Airey, the commander of the *Wolf* and the master of the *Iris*, fell victims to the jungle-fever. The former dying on the island, was buried there; the latter expired a few days after his return to Singapore. The sickness that prevailed among the sailors has been ascribed to their imprudent indulgence in the wild fruits of the island, to over-exertion and needless exposure, &c. These things may have done some hurt; but the main cause of the sickness is too obvious to be mistaken.

The ceremony of hoisting the flag was performed on a large space, cleared of jungle, and levelled expressly for that purpose. It is very strange that the officers engaged in the of such a proceeding. In all tropical climates, deadly *miasmata* continue for a long while to hang over newly-made surfaces of earth, and malignant fevers surely await the white men who are rash enough to take up their abode on such spots before they have been sufficiently exposed to wind and sun.

There is nothing, therefore, in the unfortunate incidents that have marked our taking possession of Labuan which should warrant a belief in the insalubrity of the island. Probably there is no spot within the tropics where European life is exposed to fewer risks from natural causes. The soil of the island is light and porous; it contains few or no morasses; and its situation exposes it to the action of the prevailing winds, which sweep perpetually up and down those seas. For nine months of the year it is supplied abundantly with water; and if during the other three months this article of primary necessity be less plentiful, it is still in no worse a predicament than Singapore itself. On the north of the island there are several small runnels which would appear to be supplied by perennial sources; and it will everywhere be easy to construct tanks and reservoirs.

Notwithstanding the lively and hopeful interest now so generally felt in this country with regard to our prospects in the far East, it is not perhaps superfluous to insist on the great advantages which cannot but accrue to us from the step we have just taken. In attempting to estimate the national importance of our new possession, our conjectures are far more likely to fall short of the reality than to exceed it. For a great commercial people we have certainly exhibited no extraordinary sagacity or quickness of perception in this matter and others connected with it. Thirty years of stolid indifference to an immense fortune that lay at our feet cannot be thought of without humiliation. Happily, the present generation of merchants, shipowners, and statesmen, appear to be heartily ashamed of the blunders and the supineness of their predecessors, and eager to seize the opportunities still open to them.

The capabilities of Labuan have been shrewdly scanned by those who can best turn them to good account, and their value is recognised in every great centre of trade throughout the empire. In the memorial presented last year to the then First Lord of the Treasury by the Directors of the Manchester Chamber of Commerce and Manufactures, we find the following pregnant passage relating to Labuan:

> It is most conveniently situated for the prosecution and protection of our China trade; it would serve as a point of refuge

for our shipping in case of distress; it would form a bulwark in case of war, and a restraining terror to pirates. It would establish a centrical depot for trade, not only for the whole of the immense cluster of prolific islands in its own vicinity, but for the more distant marts of Siam and the Philippine Islands, and might open the unexplored regions of Japan. Possessing coals itself, it also, by its geographical position, commands a boundless supply of that commodity from the mainland of Borneo; whilst it is so happily situated as to be but a few miles out of the best track to China during the n.e. monsoon.

The memorialists pointedly complain of the obstacles that have hitherto prevented the extension and security of their trade in the Asiatic Archipelago, making it always a precarious source of gain, and often an occasion of heavy losses. Its uncertainty and irregularity, they say, have been "greatly aggravated by the total absence of British influence throughout the whole of the islands stretching from the Straits of Malacca almost to our Australian possessions. Although the British Government has not yet thought fit to create an influence in this important quarter, yet has the Dutch Government been constantly and wisely vigilant in spreading its power there; and it is a source of regret to your memorialists that a field for enterprise so useful and so improvable should be abandoned to the grasp of a power of whose interpretation of treaties (as in the case of Java), British merchants have so much cause to complain, and whose general policy in those distant regions is marked by exclusiveness and rapacity."

These very significant hints have not been disregarded by the present Administration. It seems bent on emulating the better part of the Dutch policy in the East, as the Dutch on their part have begun to relax the restrictive rigour of their commercial system in imitation of our example. They have seen in the prosperity of Singapore the advantages which a total absence of commercial restrictions can confer on a small island, destitute of internal resources adequate for the support of its inhabitants, and situated at the embouchure of straits difficult of navigation. Profiting by the lesson, they have declared Macassar a free port from the first day of this year. In all sincerity we congratulate them on this wise beginning of reformation. If they will fairly follow out the same principle to all its consequences, they will find in the long-run that the commercial rivalry which they seem to dread so intensely at our hands, is really the most fortunate thing that could befall them.

Already they partially discern the erroneous nature of the theories which have hitherto presided over their system in the East; and the more they divest themselves of their narrow jealousies, the better will it be for themselves, as well as for us and others. There is no grosser fallacy than the old trading maxim, that what one gains another loses; on the contrary, in proportion as traffic is freed from the factitious impediments with which ignorance and wilfulness have hitherto surrounded it, the comfortable truth will become apparent, that the gain of one is the gain of all. The Dutch may be assured that there is room enough for them and us in the vast regions which they have hitherto monopolised with such inadequate result. It is manifest that they need our co-operation; for alone they have been unable to clear the waters round their colonies of pirates, or to develop the great natural resources of the countless shores over which they affect to claim suzerainty.

We will help them to do the work which has proved too much for their unaided strength, and will seek no more than our fair share in the profits of the enterprise. We will respect their rights of possession wherever they can reasonably substantiate them, but elsewhere we will not suffer them any longer to play the dog in the manger. Let them pay us the moderate compliment to suppose that we too, like themselves, have grown wiser by experience; and while they laugh at our expense over the egregious folly of a colonial minister, who made them a present of Java, the most precious of all their possessions, let them reflect that a new generation has arisen, which may not be quite so gullible as their fathers, or so magnanimously indifferent to their own interests.

In anticipation of the extended trade which is about to spring up in the Indian Archipelago, Her Majesty's ministers have deemed it expedient to provide for its better regulation by the appointment of a general superintendent and protector. The measure once resolved on, it was impossible that they should waver for a moment in their choice of the individual to fill the office. The Queen's commission has gone out to Sarawak, appointing Mr. Brooke "Her Majesty's Commissioner and Consul-general to the *sultan* and Independent Chiefs of Borneo."

By the last overland mail (April 23rd), accounts have been received from Mr. Brooke, dated Penang, 5th March. He was there awaiting the arrival of Rear-admiral Inglefield in H.M.S. *Vernon*, and was to return with that officer to Labuan and Borneo Proper. Lieutenant Heath of H. M. S. *Wolf* had transmitted to Rear-admiral Sir Thomas Cochrane a most favourable report from Labuan, happily confirming the remarks we have made above on the general salubrity of the island. The subtle fever-fiend that had been so incautiously roused from his slumbers in the jungle, had spent his strength in the first onset, and had left the officers and men of the Wolf unmolested, and in the enjoyment of sound health. The news from the mainland of Borneo was no less satisfactory.

# Appendix

## No. 1

TREATY BETWEEN HIS BRITANNIC MAJESTY AND THE KING OF THE NETHERLANDS, RESPECTING TERRITORY AND COMMERCE IN THE EAST INDIES. SIGNED AT LONDON, MARCH 17, 1824.

In the name of the most holy and undivided Trinity.

His Majesty the King of the United Kingdom of Great Britain and Ireland, and His Majesty the King of the Netherlands, desiring to place upon a footing mutually beneficial their respective possessions and the commerce of their subjects in the East Indies, so that the welfare and prosperity of both nations may be promoted in all time to come, without those differences and jealousies which have, in former times, interrupted the harmony which ought always to subsist between them? and being anxious that all occasions of misunderstanding between their respective agents may be, as much as possible, prevented; and in order to determine certain questions which have occurred in the execution of the Convention made at London on the 13th of August, 1814, in so far as it respects the possessions of His Netherland Majesty in the East, have nominated their Plenipotentiaries, that is to say:

His Majesty the King of the United Kingdom of Great Britain and Ireland, the Right Honourable George Canning, a member of His said Majesty's most honourable Privy Council, a member of Parliament, and His said Majesty's principal Secretary of State for Foreign Affairs;—and the Right Honourable Charles Watkin Williams Wynn, a member of His said Majesty's most honourable Privy Council, a member of Parliament, Lieutenant-Colonel Commandant of the Montgomeryshire Regiment of Yeomanry Cavalry, and President of His said Majesty's Board of Commissioners for the affairs of India:

And His Majesty the King of the Netherlands, Baron Henry Fagel, member of the Equestrian Corps of the Province of Holland, Counsellor of State, Knight Grand Cross of the Royal Order of the Belgic Lion, and of the Royal Guelphic Order, and Ambassador Extraordinary and Plenipotentiary of His said Majesty to His Majesty the King of Great Britain; and Anton Reinhard Falck, Commander of the Royal Order of the Belgic Lion, and his said Majesty's Minister of the Department of Public Instruction, National Industry, and Colonies:

Who, after having mutually communicated their full powers, found in good and due form, have agreed on the following Articles.

*Article 1.* The high contracting parties engage to admit the subjects of each other to trade with their respective possessions in the Eastern Archipelago, and on the continent of India, and in Ceylon, upon the footing of the most favoured nation; their respective subjects conforming themselves to the local regulations of each settlement.

*Article 2.* The subjects and vessels of one nation shall not pay, upon importation or exportation, at the ports of the other in the Eastern Seas, any duty at a rate beyond the double of that at which the subjects and vessels of the nation to which the port belongs are charged.

The duties paid on exports or imports at a British port on the continent of India, or in Ceylon, on Dutch bottoms, shall be arranged so as in no case to be charged at more than double the amount of the duties paid by British subjects, and on British bottoms.

In regard to any article upon which no duty is imposed, when imported or exported by the subjects or on the vessels of the nation to which the port belongs, the duty charged upon the subjects or vessels of the other shall in no case exceed six per cent.

*Article 3.* The high contracting parties engage that no treaty hereafter made by either, with any native power in the Eastern Seas, shall contain any article tending, either expressly or by the imposition of unequal duties, to exclude the trade of the other party from the ports of such native power: and that if, in any treaty now existing on either part, any article to that effect has been admitted, such article shall be abrogated upon the conclusion of the present treaty.

It is understood that before the conclusion of the present treaty, communication has been made by each of the contracting parties to the other of all treaties or engagements subsisting between each of them respectively and any native power in the Eastern. Seas ;. and that the like communication shall be made of all such treaties concluded by them respectively hereafter.

*Article 4.* Their Britannic and Netherland Majesties engage to give strict orders as well to their civil and military authorities as to their ships of war, to respect the freedom of trade, established by Articles 1., 2., and 3.; and in no case to impede a free communication of the natives in the Eastern Archipelago with the ports of the two governments respectively, or of the subjects of the two governments with the ports belonging to native powers.

*Article 5.* Their Britannic and Netherland Majesties in like manner engage to concur effectually in repressing piracy in those seas: they will not grant either asylum or protection to vessels engaged in piracy, and they will in no case permit the ships or merchandise captured by such vessels to be introduced, deposited, or sold in any of their possessions.

*Article 6.* It is agreed that orders shall be given by the two governments to their officers and agents in the East, not to form any new settlement on any of the islands in the Eastern Seas, without previous authority from their respective governments in Europe.

*Article 7.* The Molucca islands, and especially Amboyna, Banda, Ternate, and their immediate dependencies, are excepted from the operation of the 1, 2, 3, and 4 Articles, until the Netherland government shall think fit to abandon the monopoly of spices; but if the said government shall at any time previous to such abandonment of the monopoly allow the subjects of any power other than a native Asiatic power to carry on any commercial intercourse with the said islands, the subjects of His Britannic Majesty shall be admitted to such intercourse upon a footing precisely similar.

*Article 8.* His Netherland Majesty cedes to His Britannic Majesty all his establishments on the continent of India; and renounces all privileges and exemptions enjoyed or claimed in virtue of those establishments.

*Article 9.* The factory of Fort Marlborough, and all the English possessions on the island of Sumatra, are hereby ceded to His Netherland Majesty: and His Britannic Majesty further engages that no British settlement shall be formed on that island, nor any treaty concluded by British authority with any native prince, chief, or state therein.

*Article 10.* The town and fort of Malacca, and its dependencies, are hereby ceded to His Britannic Majesty; and His Netherland Majesty engages for himself and his subjects never to form any establishment on any part of the peninsula of Malacca, or to conclude any treaty with any native prince, chief, or state therein.

*Article 11.* His Britannic Majesty withdraws the objections which have been made to the occupation of the island of Billiton and its dependencies by the agents of the Netherland government.

*Article 12.* His Netherland Majesty withdraws the objections which have been made to the occupation of the island of Singapore by the subjects of His Britannic Majesty.

His Britannic Majesty, however, engages that no British establishment shall be made on the Carimon Isles, or on the islands of Battam, Bintang, Lingin, or any of the other islands south of the Straits of Singapore, nor any treaty concluded by British authority with the chiefs of those islands.

*Article 13.* All the colonies, possessions, and establishments which are ceded by the preceding articles shall be delivered up to the officers of the respective sovereigns on the 1st of March, 1825. The fortifications shall remain in the state in which they shall be at the period of the notification of this treaty in India; but no claim shall be made on either side for ordnance, or stores of any description, either left or removed by the ceding power, nor for any arrears of revenue, or any charge of administration whatever.

*Article 14.* All the inhabitants of the territories hereby ceded shall enjoy, for a period of six years from the date of the ratification of the present treaty, the liberty of disposing as they please of their property, and of transporting themselves, without let or hindrance, to any country to which they wish to remove.

*Article 15.* The high contracting parties agree that none of the territories or establishments mentioned in Articles 8, 9, 10, 11, and 12, shall be, at any time, transferred to any other power. In case of any of the said possessions being abandoned by one of the present contracting parties, the right of occupation thereof shall immediately pass to the other.

*Article 16.* It is agreed that all accounts and reclamations arising out of the restoration of Java and other possessions to the officers of his Netherland Majesty in the East Indies,—as well those which were the subject of a Convention made at Java on the 24th of June, 1817, between the commissioners of the two nations, as all others, shall be finally and completely closed and satisfied on the payment of the sum of one hundred thousand pounds, sterling money, to be made in London, on the part of the Netherlands, before the expiration of the year 1825.

*Article 17.* The present treaty shall be ratified, and the ratifications exchanged at London within three months from the date hereof, or sooner if possible.

In witness whereof, the respective plenipotentiaries have signed the same, and affixed thereunto the seals of their arms.

Done at London, the seventeenth day of March, in the year of our Lord one thousand eight hundred and twenty-four.

George Canning.

Charles Watkin Williams Wynn.

### Note addressed by the British Plenipotentiaries to the Plenipotentiaries of the Netherlands.

London, March 17, 1824.

In proceeding to the signature of the Treaty which has been agreed upon, the Plenipotentiaries of His Britannic Majesty have great satisfaction in recording their Sense of the friendly and liberal spirit which has been evinced by their excellencies the plenipotentiaries of His Netherland Majesty; and their conviction that there is, on both sides, an equal disposition to carry into effect with sincerity and good faith, the stipulations of the treaty in the sense in which they have been negotiated.

The differences which gave rise to the present discussion are such as it is difficult to adjust by formal stipulation: consisting, in great part, of jealousies and suspicions, and arising out of the acts of subordinate agents, they can only be removed by a frank declaration of intention, and a mutual understanding as to principles between the governments themselves.

The disavowal of the proceedings whereby the execution of the Convention of August 1814 was retarded, must have satisfied their excellencies the Netherland plenipotentiaries of the scrupulous regard with which England always fulfils her engagements.

The British plenipotentiaries record, with sincere pleasure, the solemn disavowal on the part of the Netherland government, of any design to aim either at political supremacy or at commercial monopoly in the Eastern Archipelago. They willingly acknowledge the readiness with which the Netherland plenipotentiaries have entered into stipulations calculated to promote the most perfect freedom of trade between the subjects of the two crowns, and their respective dependencies in that part of the world.

The undersigned are authorised to express the full concurrence of His Britannic Majesty in the enlightened views of His Majesty the King of the Netherlands.

Aware of the difficulty of adapting, at once, to a long-established system of monopoly, the principles of commercial policy which are now laid down, the undersigned have been authorised to consent to the exception of the Molucca Islands from the general stipulation for freedom of trade-contained in the treaty. They trust, however, that as the necessity for this exception is occasioned solely by the difficulty of abrogating, at the present moment, the monopoly of spices, its operation will be strictly limited by that necessity.

The British plenipotentiaries understand the term Moluccas as applicable to that cluster of islands which has Celebes to the westward, New Guinea to the eastward, and Timor to the southward; but that these three islands are not comprehended in the exception; nor would it have included Ceram, if the situation of that island, in reference to the two principal spice isles, Amboyna and Banda, had not required a prohibition of intercourse with it so long as the monopoly of spices shall be maintained.

The territorial exchanges which have been thought expedient for avoiding a collision of interests render it incumbent upon the plenipotentiaries of His Britannic Majesty to make, and to require, some explanations with respect to the dependents and allies of England in the island from which she is about to withdraw.

A treaty concluded in the year 1819, by British agents, with the King of Acheen, is incompatible with the 3rd article of the present treaty. The British plenipotentiaries therefore undertake, that the treaty with Acheen shall, as soon as possible, be modified into a simple arrangement for the hospitable reception of British vessels and subjects in the port of Acheen.

But as some of the provisions of that treaty (which has been communicated to the Netherland plenipotentiaries) will be conducive to the general interests of Europeans established in the Eastern Seas, they trust that the Netherland government will take measures for securing the benefit of those provisions. And they express their confidence, that no measures hostile to the King of Acheen will be adopted by the new possessor of Fort Marlborough.

It is no less the duty of the British plenipotentiaries to recommend to the friendly and paternal protection of the Netherland government the interests of the natives and settlers subject to the ancient factory of England at Bencoolen.

This appeal is the more necessary, because, so lately as the year 1818, treaties were made with the native chiefs, by which their situation was much improved. The system of forced cultivation and delivery of pepper was abolished; encouragement was given to the cultivation of rice; the relations between the cultivating classes and the chiefs of the districts were adjusted; the property in the soil was recognised in those chiefs; and all interference in the detailed management of the interior was withdrawn, by removing the European residents from the out-stations, and substituting in their room native officers. All these measures were calculated greatly to promote the interests of the native inhabitants.

In recommending these interests to the care of the Netherland government, the undersigned request the plenipotentiaries of His Netherland Majesty to assure their government that a corresponding attention will be paid, on the part of the British authorities, to the inhabitants of Malacca and the other Netherland settlements which are transferred to Great Britain.

In conclusion, the plenipotentiaries of His Britannic Majesty congratulate their excellencies the Netherland plenipotentiaries upon the happy termination of their conferences. They feel assured that, under the arrangement which is now concluded, the commerce of both nations will flourish, and that the two allies will preserve inviolate in Asia, no less than in Europe, the friendship which has, from old times, subsisted between them. The disputes being now ended, which, during two centuries, have occasionally produced irritation, there will henceforward be no rivalry between the English and Dutch nations in the East, except for the more effectual establishment of those principles of liberal policy which both have this day asserted in the face of the world.

The undersigned request their excellencies the plenipotentiaries of His Netherland Majesty will accept the assurances of their distinguished consideration.

George Canning.
Charles Watkin
Williams Wynn.

London, March 17, 1824.

The undersigned, plenipotentiaries of His Majesty the King of the Netherlands, have found in the note which is just delivered to them by their excellencies the British plenipotentiaries, a faithful recapitulation of the communications which had taken place at the time when circumstances, independent of the will of the negotiators, caused a suspension of their conferences.

Summoned to resume a work, the completion of which has ever been desired with equal sincerity by both parties, the undersigned have not failed to recognise in their co-labourers in this work that spirit of equity and conciliation which facilitates the arrangement of the most complicated questions, and to which they cannot do justice at a time more fitting than that which is about to sanction, by the signature of a formal treaty, the resolutions, adopted after a most strict examination, as eminently useful for the maintenance of a good understanding even among the inferior agents of the contracting powers.

This essential aim and principal tendency of the treaty is evident to all who read its different articles with attention. What is therein expressly stipulated ought to suffice for the removal, by common consent, of all uncertainty which might present itself in the sequel. However, as the British plenipotentiaries have considered it necessary to enter into some further details, the undersigned, who, on their part, are sensible of the importance of leaving nothing doubtful in so important a matter, have no difficulty in following them through these details, and in supplying, by a concise display of their view of the subject, the answer which is due from them to the aforesaid note of their excellencies.

The 7th article contains an exception to the general principle of liberty of commerce. The necessity of that exception, already admitted by England in the conferences of 1820, rests upon the existence of the system which respects the exclusive trade in spice. Should the determinations of the government of the Netherlands lead to the abandonment of that system, the rights of free trade will be immediately restored, and the whole of that Archipelago, which has been very justly described as comprised between Celebes, Timor, and New Guinea, will be open to all lawful speculations, on the footing to be established by local ordinances, and, so far as particularly concerns the subjects of His Britannic Majesty, in conformity with the grounds

365

sanctioned by the treaty for all the Asiatic possessions of the two contracting powers.

On the other hand, so long as the exception in question remains in force, the ships which traverse the Moluccas must refrain from touching at any ports but those whereof the description has been officially communicated to the maritime powers some years back; except in cases of distress, in which it is superfluous to add, that they will find in all places where the flag of the Netherlands may be flying those good offices and succours which are due to suffering humanity.

If the government of Great Britain conceives it to be a real advantage, that by disengaging itself, according to the principles sanctioned by the treaty which is about to be signed, from the connexions which were formed by its agents four or five years ago in the kingdom of Acheen, it secures, by some new clause, the hospitable reception of British vessels and subjects in the ports of that kingdom; the undersigned hesitate not to declare, that, on their part, they do not see any difficulty in it, and conceive that they may assert, at the same time, that their government will apply itself, without delay, to regulate its relations with Acheen in such a manner, that that state, without losing anything of its independence, may offer both to the sailor and the merchant that constant security which can only be established by the moderate exercise of European influence.

In support of the information contained in the last note of the British plenipotentiaries, on the subject of Bencoolen, their excellencies have communicated to the undersigned the two conventions respectively signed on the 23rd of May and the 4th of July, 1818, by the lieutenant-governor of that establishment, on the one side, and by the chiefs of some neighbouring tribes, on the other. They have likewise communicated a despatch of the governor-general in council, dated Fort William, the 9th of May, 1823, and according to which the British government has abolished at Fort Marlborough the monopoly of pepper, encouraged the cultivation of rice, and placed on a firm and uniform footing the relations of the different classes of natives, as well among themselves as with their chiefs.

But inasmuch as the undersigned are not wrong in supposing that the object of these arrangements has been the security of the agricultural prosperity of the colony, and the removal of the vexations which often result from the immediate contact of the native population with the subordinate authorities of a foreign government, they experience great satisfaction in saying, that, far from having cause to dread retroactive measures, the individuals interested in the existing order of things may, on the contrary, cherish the hope that the new govern-, ment will respect their acquired rights and their welfare; and, what the undersigned are above all things desirous to guarantee, that it will cause the articles of the above-mentioned conventions to be observed, on the faith of which the inhabitants of Pasummah, Ulu Manna, and the other colonists in the interior, have recognised the authority, or accepted the protection, of the British East India Company; saving, however, the power of substituting, with the full consent of the parties interested, other analogous conditions, if circumstances should render a change necessary.

With respect to the equitable and benign intentions of the British government towards the inhabitants of Malacca, and the other Dutch establishments ceded by the treaty, the plenipotentiaries of His Majesty the King of the Netherlands accept the assurance thereof with unlimited confidence; and the same sentiment prevents them from insisting that the orders and instructions which shall be addressed to the English authorities in India, relative to the surrender of Fort Marlborough, and its dependencies, should be conceived in such clear, precise, and positive terms, that no cause of uncertainty, or any pretext for delay, may be discovered in them—being persuaded that the British plenipotentiaries, after having accomplished their labours with so much moderation and equity, will take care that the result of their common exertions be not compromised by any regard to subordinate interests and secondary considerations.

This result the British plenipotentiaries themselves have described in their last note; and it only remains for the undersigned to congratulate themselves on. having contributed thereto, and to unite their wishes with those of their excellencies, that their respective agents in their Asiatic possessions may ever shew themselves sensible of the duties which two friendly nations, animated with truly liberal views, have to fulfil, both with reference to each other, and also towards the natives whom the course of events or treaties have placed under their influence.

The undersigned avail themselves of this opportunity of renewing to their excellencies the British plenipotentiaries the assurance of their most distinguished consideration.

H. Fagel.
A. R. Falck.

# No. 2

*From the Resident Councillor at Singapore to the Honourable the Acting Governor of Prince of Wales Island, Singapore, and Malacca.*

Singapore, 17th February, 1843.

Sir,—I esteem it my duty to transmit a copy of a deposition taken by me relative to an act of piracy perpetrated near Poolow Tingie. There is no doubt whatever that, unless some protection is afforded to the trading boats from Cochin China, the loss of life and plunder of property will follow to the same extent, if not more so, than during the past season. On this important subject I have had occasion to write officially.

It is to be feared the Malays at Poolow Tingie are deeply implicated in the acts of piracy which are annually committed in that proximity.

I have, &c.

T. Church,
Resident Councillor.

Hoy, Nakodah of a Cochin China *tope*, of thirty-five *coyans*, left Cochin China eleven days since, bound for Singapore, with a cargo consisting of thirty-five *coyans* of rice, two *peculs* of raw silk, 600 mats, three pigs. Our crew consisted of fifteen hands. We had no arms of any kind on board. Six days after having left Cochin China we reached near Poolow Tingie, when we fell in with five sampans, having on board about thirty Malays; the Malays were armed with spears, *creeses*, swords, and muskets. We were boarded by them, and two of our number killed. They took the silk and a small part of the rice, and then scuttled our *prau*. Myself and twelve companions were taken by the pirates to Poolow Tingie, where they reside at this season of the year. We were then allowed to take to our *sampans*, with strict injunctions not to proceed to Singapore; we, however, were compelled to come here by the wind and current. We were five days without food and water .

S. Garling,
Acting Governor.

Before me,   T. Church,
Resident Councillor at Singapore,
17th February, 1843.

Admiralty, 13th October, 1843.

Sir,—Having laid before my Lords Commissioners of the Admiralty your letter of the 26th June, 1843, No. 164, with its enclosure from Captain the Honourable Henry Keppel, of the *Dido*, reporting the repulse of the attacks of certain piratical *praus*, on two occasions, by Lieut. F. W. Horton, and the officers and men employed under him, in three boats of the *Dido*, I am commanded to acquaint you that their Lordships are satisfied with the manner in which Lieutenant Horton, and the officers and men employed with him, repelled the attack made upon them.

John Barrow.

Vice-Admiral Sir Wm. Parker, G.C.B.
    Singapore.

Admiralty, 16th October, 1848.

Sir,—Having laid before my Lords Commissioners of the Admiralty your letter of the 13th of July, 1843, No. 183, with its enclosures, from Captain the Honourable Henry Keppel, of the Dido, reporting the spirited conduct of Lieutenant Hunt, and the officers, seamen, and marines of that ship, who accompanied him in a native-built boat, which was attacked by two piratical *praus*, off Cape Datu, in the island of Borneo; also detailing the proceedings of the boats of the Dido, with ninety-five officers and men, who were detached, under the command of Lieutenant Wilmot Horton, to the River Sarebus, where they effected the destruction of certain forts, and three settlements of pirates; I am commanded to acquaint you that their Lordships are pleased to express their approbation of the gallant and spirited conduct of the officers and men employed on these occasions in executing the judicious arrangements made by Captain Keppel.

John Barrow.

Vice Admiral Sir Wm. Parker, G.C.B.
    Singapore.

Cornwallis, in Madras Roads,
10th May, 1844.

Sir,—I have much pleasure in transmitting herewith the copies of two letters which I have received from the Secretary of the Admiralty, conveying their Lordships' approbation of the gallant and spirited conduct of the officers and men of the Dido, who were employed in the boats of that ship, on the coast and rivers of Borneo.

And I desire you will communicate the same to the officers and men accordingly.

I am, Sir, your very humble servant,
W. Parker, Vice-Admiral.

Captain the Hon. Henry Keppel,
Her Majesty's Ship *Dido*,

*From the Governor of Prince of Wales Island, Singapore, and Malacca, to Captain J. R. Scott, commanding the Hon. East India Company's steamer Phlegethon.*

Singapore, 13th September, 1844.

Sir,—I have the honour to acknowledge the receipt of your letter of this date, enclosing the copy of a communication to your address, from Captain the Honourable Henry Keppel, commander of Her Majesty's ship *Dido*, expressing the high sense he entertains of your zeal and attention, and the service rendered by the Honourable East India Company's steamer *Phlegethon* during the recent operations on the coast of Borneo, which I will not fail to submit to the supreme government.

That success would attend the expedition against the pirates on the n.w. coast of Borneo was to be anticipated, from the approved experience and acknowledged gallantry of your commander, Captain the Honourable Henry Keppel; but such an unprecedented result as the destruction of the main strongholds of men who have been the scourge of these seas for years past, and whose courage and cruelties are proverbial, could only have been effected by the most untiring zeal, energy, and enterprise from all concerned; more especially when it is remembered that these strongholds were situated between 50 and 100 miles up a difficult river, in which every obstacle was thrown, with a view of retarding your progress; and that the pirates were commanded by their chieftains, Seriff Sahib and Seriff Mulak.

It affords me the highest gratification to notice here what will be specially laid before the supreme government, the honourable testimony borne to the determined valour of Mr, Coverley, first officer, and Mr. Simson, second officer of the *Phlegethon*, by Captain the Honourable Henry Keppel, who observes, in his public despatch, when speaking of the gallant conduct of all engaged, and the creditable and efficient state of the *Phlegethon's* boats, that these officers were the two first on the heights of Undop, in leading to which the first lieutenant of the *Dido* was killed.

> I have the honour to be, Sir,
> Your most obedient servant,
> W. J. Butterworth,
> Governor of P. W. Island, Singapore, and Malacca.

Admiralty, February 28th, 1845

Sir,—I am commanded by my Lords Commissioners of the Admiralty to acquaint you, that they have received with much satisfaction your letter detailing the measures you had taken for the suppression of piracy on the coast of Borneo and up the Sakarran River. Their Lordships desire also to express their approbation at the gallantry and perseverance displayed by the officers, seamen, and marines under your orders, in overcoming the force and numbers opposed to them, and the many obstacles they had to contend with; and my Lords desire that you will, as far as may be in your power, convey to those employed under you in this enterprise the expression of their Lordships' satisfaction. My Lords, however, have to lament the loss on this occasion of a promising and gallant officer, Lieutenant Wade, R.N., and also that of Mr. Steward, who so generously lent his valuable services to the expedition; a loss, however, which their Lordships think might have been still more severe but for the discretion and the judicious conduct of those conducting the attack.

> W. A. B. Hamilton.

Captain the Hon. Henry Keppel.

## No. 3.

ADMIRAL SIR THOMAS COCHRANE'S DESPATCHES.

*From the London Gazette, Friday, Nov. 28th, 1845.*

Admiralty, Nov. 27th, 1845.

Despatches have been received at this office from Rear-Admiral Sir Thomas Cochrane, C.B., Commander-in-chief of Her Majesty's ships and vessels on the East India Station, of which the following are copies or extracts:—

*Agincourt,* off Pulo Laboan, coast of Borneo,
August 13th, 1845.

Sir,—I arrived off the River Bruné (Borneo Proper) on the 6th inst.

If their Lordships will be good enough to refer to a paragraph towards the conclusion of the memorandum addressed to me by Mr. Brooke, under date the 3rd of July, 1845, they will find a statement of two natives of India having been detained as slaves in the capital itself for two years, continuing under captivity in the presence of the British men-of-war, and from which slavery they made their escape on board the Hon. East India Company's steam-vessel *Phlegethon* on her last visit there, only a few weeks since.

Under such a glaring disregard of the understanding entered into with the *sultan* in respect of slavery, I felt, in conjunction with Mr. Brooke, that it would not be right to permit this transaction to pass without, in the first instance, holding the *sultan* responsible for it; and Pangeran Bedurudeen having stated that Pangeran Usop was the real offender, everything should be kept quiet until my arrival in the capital; on the following day I went with the steamers to visit this singular capital, or what is called city, being a miserable collection of bamboo-houses, elevated upon piles, surrounded by water, except at low tide, when under many of them you perceive the bare mud; the poverty of the buildings being singularly and inexplicably contrasted with the manners, dresses, and deportment of the higher orders.

I visited the *sultan* with all due ceremony, and, by previous understanding with the Rajah Muda Hassin and his brother Bedurudeen, the visit was entirely complimentary; but after my departure, on the same evening, and following morning, Mr. Brooke had several meetings with those persons. The *sultan* stated he was quite ready to punish Pangeran Usop if I would afford my assistance in accomplishing it. It appeared that Usop (I suppose from conscious guilt) concluded he was the object sought, and had, on the day of my visit, told the *sultan* that if called on to answer on the score of piracy, he would defend himself to the last.

In answer to my address to the *sultan*, I received the accompanying documents (Nos. 2 and 3), one calling for assistance, the other for personal protection; a subaltern's guard was accordingly sent to the *sultan's* residence; and it was settled, through Mr. Brooke, that the *sultan* should call on Usop to present himself before him, unarmed, to answer for his conduct, and if he did not do so, his residence was to be attacked.

The *sultan's* commands were accordingly conveyed to him, which not having been replied to within a given time, a shot was fired over his house, to which he promptly replied by a salvo from his battery, when a fire in earnest was opened upon him, and a few minutes sent him and all his adherents off to the woods, and the marines landed and took possession of his house, where, among other things, twenty handsome brass guns, of various calibre, were found, and 150 half-barrels of gunpowder.

The guns the *sultan* requested me to keep; but reserving two of the smallest, for the purpose of sale, to produce funds to remunerate the two natives (now serving on board the *Pluto*) for their four years' captivity, I sent the remainder to the *sultan*, with a message, through Mr, Brooke, to say, that we never accepted any remuneration for the protection of friends who were disposed faithfully to carry out the engagements they had entered into,

I learn from Mr. Brooke, who has been in communication with Muda Hassin and his brother since the flight of Usop and destruction of his property, that the occurrence has given great confidence to the well-disposed party, and that it will equally depress Usop's adherents in the town, of whom there were not a few; and I look for a double result from his punishment — namely, that while it assures the legitimate government of all proper support, they will equally perceive the rod that hangs over them, should they be found wanting in their own conduct,

I have, &c.

Thomas Cochrane,

Rear-Admiral and Commander-in-Chief.

To the Secretary of the Admiralty, London.

*Agincourt*, at Sea, in lat. 8° 14' N., long. 116° 4' E.

August 26th, 1845.

Sir,—Following out the intentions referred to in my despatch from Laboan (No. 142), of the 13th of August, I left that anchorage on the 15th instant, and reached the northern end of

Borneo on the 17th.

Having heard from various sources that Sheriff Osman had, for the last twelvemonth, been making preparations against a probable attack, that he had strongly fortified one of the branches of a river in Maloodoo Bay, and was of a character, and supported by resolute adherents, not likely to yield without a sharp struggle, I made corresponding arrangements for attack; and having anchored the *Agincourt* and frigates in a safe position, in the hitherto little-known fine bay of Maloodoo, I hoisted my flag on board the *Vixen* steam sloop, and, attended by the *Cruiser* and *Wolverine* brigs, and the Hon. East India Company's steam vessels *Pluto* and *Nemesis*, proceeded to the head of the bay, carrying deep water until within a couple of miles of the river's mouth, when the *Vixen* and brigs were obliged to anchor, and not far within them the *Pluto*, drawing only six feet, grounded on the bar.

It being hopeless to attempt to make a further progress in these small vessels, I directed Captain Talbot, assisted by Acting Captain Lyster, and Commanders Fanshawe and Clifford, to take command of the gun and other boats of the squadron, filled with as many marines and small-arm men as they could with propriety carry, and proceed up that branch of the Maloodoo stated by the pilots to be in the occupation of Sheriff Osman; and should their statements prove correct, to ascertain as far as possible the strength of his position and amount of force, either attacking the *sheriff* on his refusal to surrender, should he feel equal to the enterprise, or falling back to some suitable position, while he communicated with me in the event of his not considering his force sufficient to guarantee success.

The accompanying letter and report from Captain Talbot will convey to their Lordships a gratifying narration of his success, and prove the soundness of my judgment in selecting this officer for the important duty confided to him.

Their Lordships will not fail to unite with me in deep regret at the heavy loss we have incurred; but when the great strength of the position is referred to, and that the force was for one hour exposed to the steadily sustained fire of eleven heavy guns, within little more than 200 yards of our own position, it is rather astonishing than otherwise, and a source of thankfulness, that the casualties were not more numerous.

Their Lordships will not fail to notice the valorous conduct of Acting Captain Lyster, and those immediately under him, upon this occasion; who, undaunted by the fire with which they were assailed, steadily worked at a remarkably well-constructed boom for above an hour before he could effect an opening, and on the success of whose exertions mainly depended the advance of the force, who, in ignorance of any other manner of approaching the forts than by the river, could not be brought forward until this object was accomplished; and while I feel persuaded their Lordships will be fully alive to such meritorious conduct, I deeply lament that death has removed from their Lordships' power of reward that promising young officer, Mr. Leonard Gibbard, mate of the *Wolverine*, who bravely worked by Captain Lyster's side; the wound he received on that occasion having, unfortunately for his country and his friends, proved fatal on the following day.

I sent up the same evening a small detachment of gun-boats, under Commander Giffard, to burn such *prahues* and boats, and parts of the forts or town, as might have remained not completely destroyed, and to render unserviceable any iron guns, and to bring down with him any brass ordnance that might be there.

Two or three chiefs are known to have fallen on the present occasion, and there is every reason to believe that Sheriff Osman, so formidable to all the neighbouring country, and whose valour was worthy of a better cause, is among the number slain; at least I have certain information that he was carried off badly wounded; but whether dead or living, I consider his influence to be entirely annihilated, and his confederacy with various piratical chiefs in the Archipelago broken up; for his power as much depended upon his being the encourager of other piratical tribes, and their supplier with goods in exchange for slaves, as in the force naturally at his command. I may add that, among many other articles of European workmanship, a bell belonging to the ship *Guilhelm Ludwig*, of Bremen, was found in the town. This vessel was supposed to have been wrecked on the Garsi Isles, about October or November last, but nothing has been heard of the crew.    I have, &c.    Thomas Cochrane,
Rear-Admiral and Commander-in-Chief.
To the Secretary of the Admiralty, London.

Her Majesty's Steam-vessel *Vixen*, Maloodoo Bay,
August 20th, 1845.

Sir,—I have to report the proceedings of the expedition you did me the honour to place under my command.

Your Excellency's flag having been flying on board the *Vixen*, you are aware of its progress to the anchorage at the head of the Maloodoo Bay; I commence, therefore, the details from that period.

The force, consisting of 530 seamen and marines (the details of which I annex), conveyed in 24 boats, of which nine were gun-boats, left the *Vixen* at 3 o'clock p.m. on the 18th instant, and after some little difficulty on hitting on the channel, was anchored off the mouth of the Songybasar a little after sunset. Here we were joined by a boat from the *Pluto*, carrying *Agincourt's* field-piece.

The tide serving, about 11 o'clock p.m. weighed, and passing the bar, anchored within it. At daylight on the 19th we proceeded up the river in two divisions; after proceeding about two miles, I was informed by the *Bruné* pilots we were nearing the town. I therefore went ahead with Captain Lyster to reconnoitre. On coming to an abrupt turn in the river, about three miles higher, we found ourselves suddenly in front of the position, which consisted of two stockaded forts of eight and three guns each, commanding the reach.

About 200 yards below the forts was a boom across the river, apparently well constructed. The forts appeared to us to stand on a tongue of land, from which we were separated by the river, which at that point divided into two branches, and the pilots declared such to be the case; that turning to the right we observed was still further defended by a floating battery. There appeared, therefore, to be no means of carrying the position but by forcing the boom.

On rejoining the force, arrangements were made fear the gun-boats to advance to the boom, to cover the party appointed to cut through it, the remainder of the force to hold themselves in readiness to act when ordered. We had approached the boom to within one hundred yards, when a flag of truce was observed to be coming towards us. Conceiving the object of the enemy was merely to gain time, I sent back a message, 'that unless Sheriff Osman came to me in half an hour, I should open fire.'

This being conveyed to the fort, the flag returned with an offer to admit me with two boats, that I might visit the *sheriff*. I declined, and the flag retired; the moment it was clear of the line of fire the three-gun battery opened, and the cannonade became general on both sides.

The boom was composed of two large-sized trees, each supporting a chain cable, equal to 10 or 12 inches, firmly bolted and secured around the trunk of a tree on each bank; a cut in the right bank allowed a canoe to pass, but was impassable to any of our boats.

One hour nearly elapsed before we could in any way remove the obstacle, during which time the fire of the enemy was well sustained, all the guns being laid for the boom. I need hardly mention it was briskly returned from our side, both from guns and small arms; and some rockets well thrown by a party which had been landed on the right bank, appeared to produce considerable effect.

As soon as the passage was open for the smaller boats, they passed through rapidly, and embarked the marines from the large boats across the boom; ultimately the whole force passed through. The enemy immediately quitted their defences, and fled in every direction. The marines and small-arm men having cleared the town, the marines were formed as a covering party, and parties of seamen were pushed up both banks of the river, but met with no opposition; at the same time preparations were made for spiking the guns and destroying the stockades and town; in a short time these were completed, and the whole in flames, as well as three large *proas*, and several smaller ones.

Being anxious to save the tide, and conceiving that the object contemplated by your Excellency was accomplished, I ordered the force to be re-embarked, and proceeded down the river to the *Vixen*.

When your Excellency considers the strength of the enemy's position, and the obvious state of preparation in which we found him, you will be prepared to learn that this service has not been performed without considerable loss. I regret very much to state it at six killed and fifteen wounded. The loss on the part of the enemy was unquestionably very great; but the surrounding jungle afforded the enemy the means of carrying away their dead, according to their custom in such cases.

Nevertheless, some of those left on the field we recognised as persons of considerable influence.

Whilst I record my admiration of the gallantry and steadiness of the whole force under a galling fire, sustained for a long period, I must particularly mention Captain Lyster, who directed his attention to the boom, and by whose personal exertions that obstacle was overcome.

Mr. Gibbard, mate of Her Majesty's ship *Wolverine*, was, I grieve to say, mortally wounded by an early shot, when gallantly working at the boom with an axe.

I beg leave to point out to your Excellency the conduct of Mr. Williamson, Malay interpreter to Mr. Brooke; he was with me during the attack, and was exposed to the whole of the fire.

I have, &c,

Charles Talbot, Captain.

His Excellency Rear-Admiral Sir Thomas Cochrane, C.B.
Commander-in-Chief.

DETAIL OF THE NAVAL FORCE EMPLOYED IN THE ATTACK ON AND THE DESTRUCTION OF MALOODOO, UNDER THE COMMAND OF CAPTAIN CHARLES TALBOT, HER MAJESTY'S SHIP *VESTAL*, ON THE 19TH DAY OF AUGUST, 1845.

Her Majesty's ship *Agincourt's* gig, Captain Lyster; Mr. Creswell, midshipman; one petty officer, and five seamen.

Gun-boat (launch), Lieut. Lowther; Mr. Whepple, assistant-surgeon; Mr. Burnaby, midshipman; Mr. Barton, midshipman; 1 petty officer, and 18 seamen.

Gun-boat (barge), Lieut. Paynter; Mr. May, mate; Mr. Patrick, assistant-surgeon; 1 petty officer, and 14 seamen.

(*Pinnace*, with rockets), Mr. Reeve, mate; 3 petty officers, and 18 seamen.

(Cutter), Mr. Simcoe, midshipman; 11 seamen.

Gun-boat, manned from *Agincourt*, Hon. East India Company's steam-vessel *Nemesis*, with 1st company small-armed men (1st cutter), Lieut. Reid; Mr. Hathorn, mid-shipman; 1 petty officer, and 10 seamen.

Gun-boat (2nd cutter), Mr. Young, mate; 1 petty officer, and 10 seamen.

Gun-boat, with *Agincourt's* field-piece men, *Pluto's* (cutter), Lieut. Heard; 2 petty officers, and 15 men.

Her Majesty's ship *Vestal's* (barge), Lieut. Morritt, senior lieutenant; gun-boat, Mr. Pym, second master; 1 petty officer, and 13 seamen.

(*Pinnace*), Lieutenant Pasco; Mr. Ward, assistant-surgeon; Mr. Sanders, midshipman; 1 petty officer, and 13 men.

Her Majesty's ship *Vestal's* gun-boat (cutter), Mr. Durbin, mate; 11 seamen; (gig), Mr. Ecles, clerk, 5 seamen.

Her Majesty's ship *Daedalus*, gun-boat (launch), Mr. Wilkinson, second master; 1 petty officer, and 18 seamen; (barge), Lieut. Randolph, senior lieutenant; Mr. Huxham, midshipman; 2 petty officers, and 17 seamen; (*pinnace*), Mr. Nolloth, mate; Mr. Balcomb, midshipman; 1 petty officer, and 12 seamen; (cutter), Mr. Protheroe, midshipman; 1 petty officer, and 8 seamen.

Her Majesty's steam-vessel *Vixen's* gun-boat (*pinnace*), Lieut. Wilcox, senior lieutenant; Mr. Dent, mate; 1 petty officer, and IS men; (first cutter), Mr. W. Sainsbury, midshipman; 9 seamen; (second cutter), Lieut Bonham; 11 seamen.

Her Majesty's sloop *Cruiser's* gun-boat (*pinnace*), Lieut. Rodney, senior lieutenant; Mr. Cotter, midshipman; 1 petty officer, and 12 men; (gig), Commander Fanshawe; 1 petty officer, and 4 seamen; (cutter), Mr. Tuke, midshipman; 1 petty officer, and 8 seamen.

Her Majesty's sloop *Wolverine's* (*pinnace*), Lieut. Hillier, senior lieutenant; Mr. Johnson, midshipman; 1 petty officer, and 12 seamen; (gig), Commander Clifford; 1 petty officer, and 4 seamen; (cutter), Mr. Gibbard, mate; 1 petty officer, and 4 men.

### ABSTRACT OF THE FOREGOING DETAIL.

*Agincourt* officers, IS; petty officers, 10; seamen, 99. Total, 124.

*Vestal*—officers, 8; petty officers, 2; seamen, 42. Total, 52.

*Daedalus*—officers, 6; petty officers, 5; seamen, 55. Total, 66.

*Vixen*—officers, 4; petty officers, 1; seamen, 35. Total, 40.

*Cruiser*—officers, 4; petty officers, 3; seamen, 24. Total, 31.

*Wolverine* officers, 4; petty officers, 3; seamen, 24. Total, 81.

Grand total—officers, 41; petty officers, 24; seamen, 279. Total, 344.

### ROYAL MARINES EMPLOYED.

Captain Hawkins, Her Majesty's ship *Agincourt*.

Lieut. Hambly, Her Majesty's ship *Daedalus*.

Lieut. Dyer, Her Majesty's ship *Vestal*.

Lieut. Kennedy, Her Majesty's ship *Agincourt*.

Lieut. Mansell, Her Majesty's ship *Agincourt*.

Eight sergeants, 8 corporals, 3 fifers, 178 privates.

### ABSTRACT.

Captain, 1; lieutenants, 4; sergeants, 8; corporals, 8; fifers, 3; privates, 178. Total, 202.

Total number of seamen, 344; marines, 202.

Grand total, 546.

Charles Talbot,

Captain Her Majesty's ship *Vestal*.

# No. 4

## MEMOIR OF LIEUTENANT WADE.

Lieutenant Charles Francis Wade,[1] whose melancholy death is recorded in these pages, was the third son of the Rev. Thomas Wade of the county of Tipperary, and from an early period of life displayed a strong predilection for that profession in which Providence ordained that he should pass a short, yet honourable career. His family did not encourage this disposition, having no interest to ensure its successful enterprise; but the youth, when in London, having casually heard that the late Earl of Huntingdon was about to proceed to the West Indies, in command of H.M.S. *Valorous*, immediately waited upon his lordship, and volunteered his services. Though he had no previous acquaintance nor introduction, the frankness of his manners, and the good sense he exhibited at the boyish age of fourteen, so won upon the noble earl, that he at once became his patron and friend, and he was appointed to the *Valorous*, and sailed in her on her destination.

On her being ordered home, he was transferred to the *Barham*, flag-ship on the West India station; and by his good conduct strongly recommended himself to her commander, the Honourable Elphinstone Fleming, to whom, as well as to Lord Huntingdon, he expressed

---

1 The previous career of my lamented shipmate, Lieutenant Wade, was so full of honour, and so exemplary of the Nelson spirit—the glory and means of glory to the British navy, and of safety to the British nation—that I trust I may be excused in devoting a few pages of my book to his memory. My information is derived from officers under whom and companions with whom he served, and who admired and loved him: and had it pleased God to spare his life, and opportunity had been afforded him, he must have left the heroic name of a very distinguished man.—H. K.

his grateful attachment through life. At a later time, whilst he was serving as mate on board H.M.S. *Ocean* at Sheerness, it was suggested to him by several of his naval friends, that he might distinguish himself by joining the British Legion in Spain: he accordingly accepted the rank of captain of artillery in the British Legion under Colonel Colquhoun, R.A.

In 1837 he returned from this employment, after two years' gallant devotion to it, and memorialised the government for promotion in the navy as a reward for his services. In this he respectfully represented his meritorious actions in common with the navy at sea and the marines and other forces in the field, with both of which he had fought in several very sharp engagements; in honour of which he had received the Spanish crosses of St. Ferdinand and Isabella Catolica, and a gold medal for commanding the guns which breached the walls of the town of Iran, through which a party of troops entered, and under so heavy a fire, that he had two-thirds of his gun-detachment killed and wounded. In short, his conduct throughout was of the most gallant description, though a slight wound was the only mark he bore of having fought in almost every affair between the Legion and the Carlists during the period of his stay.

His preceding eight years in the West Indies, his having been afloat from 1824 to 1835, and his having passed his examination for a lieutenant in 1830, with a high character from every officer under whom he had served, were truly urged as a farther title to the favour he solicited. Lord Minto, then First Lord of the Admiralty, consequently appointed him to the *Rhadamanthus* in the Mediterranean; and in the June following, at the coronation of Her Majesty, he obtained his commission as lieutenant. In 1840 he joined H.M.S. *Curaçoa* in the Pacific; and here an incident occurred which may serve to shew the intrepid and chivalrous temper which formed so distinguished a feature in his character. Cruising not far from the southern tropic, and a few leagues from the meridian of the island that became the refuge of the descendants of Christian and his comrades, another island was seen, which was thought to be a discovery.

The nature of the shore and the sea that broke against it forbade any attempt at landing from a boat, but access to a swimmer seemed possible; and it being considered desirable that the newfound territory should be examined and possession of it taken, Lieutenant Wade volunteered to perform this service, and to swim on shore with the union-jack secured to him. He succeeded in landing, explored the island sufficiently to ascertain that it had neither inhabitants nor ship-wrecked mariners upon it, and that it had already been visited by a British ship of war. He then returned safely on board; but the consequences of the adventure were serious, for it was followed by a severe attack of rheumatic fever, occasioned by having remained so long in wet clothes; and finding there was no hope of regaining his health at sea, he quitted his ship, with regret, at San Blas, and returned through Mexico to England.

In December 1842, hardly recovered from the effects of the disease, but determined to deserve and to obtain promotion, he was appointed first lieutenant of the *Samarang*, then fitting for the survey of the Indian Seas. In March 1844 he joined for a short time H.M.S. *Driver*, and on the 5th June following was appointed first lieutenant of the *Dido*.

It is not easy to express in adequate language, says one who knew him intimately, the qualities by which poor Wade was distinguished, and how much he was beloved by all his acquaintance. Brave and enterprising, yet gentle, affectionate, and considerate of others; firm in principle, and exact in the performance of every duty, but unpretending, generous, and loyal; there seemed to be united in him all the properties which, joined to skill in his profession, would have ensured to him an eminent place in the brilliant annals of his service. But he was of those who fall in the front, and who die too soon for their own glory.

To his family and intimate friends his amiable, generous, and affectionate manners endear his memory; and although they must mourn his loss, yet they have the consolation of knowing that his whole conduct was influenced by a sincere Christian spirit, and that he was not less willing to devote his life to the service of his country than to manifest in his whole conduct the exalted principles by which he was ever influenced.

# No. 5

## MEMOIR OF MR. GEORGE STEWARD.

The late George Steward, who fell in August 1844, whilst fighting as a volunteer in the expedition against the pirates of Borneo, commanded by Captain Keppel, was the youngest of seven children of the late Timothy Steward, Esq. of Yarmouth. Having shewn an early predilection for the sea, a midshipman's berth was procured for him in the maritime service of the Honourable East India Company, in which he rose with as much rapidity as its regulations would admit;

but unfortunately for him, precisely at the period when he became eligible for, and had secured, the command of a first-class ship, the act of parliament was passed which abolished the mercantile privileges, and consequently extinguished the maritime service, of the Honourable East India Company, whose officers thereupon retired on pensions.

Not being disposed to continue at sea as a private adventurer, Mr. Steward remained unemployed for several years; but in 1842 his adventurous and daring spirit led him to embrace the proposition of his friend and brother-officer, Mr. Henry Wise, now connected with the East India and China trade, to undertake the charge of a commercial expedition to the infant settlement established at Sarawak under the auspices of Mr. Brooke. In the month of March 1843 he left England in the *Ariel*, a smart fast-sailing brig, purchased, fitted out, and armed by himself and Mr. Wise, in pursuance of the mercantile operation referred to, and for the additional security of Mr. Brooke.

The vessel arrived at Singapore in the following July. Here Mr. Steward was informed that the Borneo Seas were swarming with pirates; and the master of the brig having left her at that port, Mr. Steward assumed the command. On his arrival at Sarawak, he received from Mr. Brooke a welcome, the cordiality of which was enhanced by their recognising each other as schoolfellows. Of the enterprise, intelligence, liberal mind, and friendly disposition of Mr. Brooke, Mr. Steward has, in his correspondence, spoken with the utmost warmth, and to him he was at all times indebted for much valuable assistance and counsel. At Sarawak Mr. Steward remained until he unfortunately joined the expedition against the pirates, in which his life was sacrificed. In his last letter to England he spoke, fearlessly, of an expected descent of the pirates, of having fortified his iron house, and of the anticipated and much-desired visit of H.M.S. *Dido* to that settlement. The subsequent acts of his career are related by Captain Keppel.

# No. 6

### Extracts from the late Mr. Williamson's *Journal*.

In October 1845, Mr. Brooke commissioned some of the European gentlemen of his party to make a tour of inspection through the outlying Dyak tribes dependent on Sarawak, for the purpose of ascertaining their condition and prospects, and taking steps for the redress of any grievances of which they might have to complain. A few extracts from the rough journal kept on that occasion by Mr. Williamson may not be uninteresting to the reader, as shewing what a large measure of success had already attended Mr. Brooke's wise and earnest efforts to restore peace and plenty to the poor persecuted Dyaks; what incessant vigilance on his part was still requisite to check the inveterate propensity of the knavish Malays to plunder and oppress them; and with what well-directed activity he pursues his labours for the physical welfare and the moral regeneration of his subjects and neighbours.

"*Wednesday, Oct. 8th.*—At 11 a.m. arrived at Pankalum Bunting, where we found about thirty Dyaks in a small hut ready to welcome us, and carry our luggage up to the village. At one o'clock started for the Bakar village, about five miles from the landing place, at the foot of the Sadong hills. This tribe consists of one hundred families, occupying four villages. There are about twenty-five houses in Mungu Babi (*i. e.* Hog Hill), the village where we are at present, and five *padi* stores. It is very recently that the Dyaks have ventured to store their *padi* in houses. At 8 p.m. attended the feast given in our honour, where we saw the women dancing; they appeared very happy, and pleased to see us.

"*9th.*—This morning we had all the Orang Kayas of the four villages, who informed me they were very comfortable and happy. I told them the object of my mission, at which they all seemed pleased, and said that that if they were oppressed they would come to Sarawak and complain to the Tuan Besar, When I asked them about the Sadong Dyaks, they said I should hear all when I met them, as they will hide nothing from me.

"The only thing these Dyaks complain of is, that Nakodah Mahomed told them he had the *Tuan Besar's* chop, and gave them to understand that the powder, muskets, &c., in his possession, belonged to the *Tuan Besar;* in consequence of which they carried these goods for Nakodah Mahomed without receiving any payment for their labour. I told them that in future they need not carry goods for any man coming from Sarawak, or elsewhere, without due payment in ready money; and that should traders at any time leave their goods in the Dyak houses, they need not be alarmed, but bring the goods to the *Tuan Besar* and tell him how they were left behind. They further told me that the Siringi wish to claim their *siri* cave, where they get their birds-nests which is close to Kumpung, and has belonged to them as long as they can remember; that this cave is a whole day's journey from Siring—how, then, can it belong to the Siringi? I answered, that on my return the *Tuan Besar* would set the matter right, and give the cave to its proper owners.

"*Same day.*—Proceeded to Jinan, about eight miles distant. There are here fifteen houses, and the Dyaks are very comfortable, having plenty of grain, and being well off for sugar-cane, sweet potatoes, plantains, betel-nut, beside various other fruit-trees. The houses here, as at Mungu Babi, are very shabby.

"*10th.*—This morning met Orang Kaya Kusunan, who told me the Toup Dyaks were waiting half way to receive us. At 4 p.m. I had the Orang Kaya Tumangong of Toup, and the Orang Kaya of Kurran, Si Labi, Si Mabong, Daah, Bugu (Sadong tribes), and the Orang Kaya Pasunan, beside other Dyaks, the Bandar Cassim, with his Sadong Malays, and our own people, at the house where I was staying. I explained my mission to them, and made them understand that, at the *bandar's* express wish, the *Tuan Besar* had sent me to them to ascertain their condition. The *bandar* then told them it was his wish to institute the same laws and customs as at Sarawak; after which, I informed the Dyaks that there will be no more forcing of goods on them at exorbitant prices, and that for the future, should anyone '*serra*' them, they must complain to the *bandar*, and subsequently lay their case before Mr. Brooke. The conference, I am glad to say, ended to everyone's satisfaction.

"At 8 p.m. the Orang Kaya Rih and two others of the same tribe complained to me of their grievances, and told me that Si Tore, a Sadong man, had forced 10 pieces of iron, weighing 15 *catties*, on them about two years and a half ago, and that he now demanded 100 *pasus* of *padi* for it. (This is *serra* with a vengeance: 100 *pasus* are equal to 2½ tons weight!) They had paid 10 *pasus*; should they, they asked me, pay the rest? I told them I would settle the business at Bandar Cassim's village.

"*11th.*—The Dyaks gave us a feast last night; the women danced and the merriment was kept up till morning. At 11 started in boats with Bandar Cassim, and at 2 p.m. arrived at his village[1] called ————, where everything had been got ready for our reception; a house was well fitted with gay curtains and mats, and after a salute of three guns as we approached, we took up our residence and made ourselves very comfortable. At 7 in the evening we met all the respectable part of the community of this little Malay village. I told them what I was sent

---

1. The MS. having been under water in the wreck of the *Great Liverpool* steamer, this name and some others are illegible.

for, the *bandar* as usual giving way to our wishes, and repeating that Sarawak and Sadong, and Sadong and Sarawak, were as one country. I told Si Tore, Sebi Gani, and Sirdeen, that they must make no further demands on the Rih Dyaks, and that neither they nor anybody else could *serra* the Dyaks any longer—not even the *bandar* himself; for they must recollect that the Sadong Dyaks would take refuge in Sarawak if oppressed.

"After the *bandar* had left, the brother-in-law of the Orang Kaya of Sinkaru, together with the Orang Kaya of Si Nankau Kujang, and Orang Kaya Kurang, came to me. The former of these complained that Abang Tahar (the old *patingi's* son-in-law), about two years ago, forced a small *tatawak*[2] and one brass dish on them, for which he demanded three Dyaks as slaves, whom he seized at the time and took away, and that now he demanded another Dyak boy. I replied they were on no account to comply, that they must complain to the *bandar*, and if he took no notice of it, to go to Sarawak to the *Tuan Besar*.

"The Orang Kaya likewise told me that formerly there were twenty-five families in his tribe, but now they were reduced to fifteen, the rest having been seized and sold into slavery! (Here follow other complaints. The day's journal concludes thus:)—The Sinkaru Dyaks have not yet returned to their former *tumbawong*,[3] but are scattered about in the jungle and very poorly off. I told them to return to their former place of residence, and to collect the tribes there.

"*Sunday, 12th.*—Orang Kaya Si Rubin and Orang Kaya Signa Mantay, of Rubin, likewise came to me to say that they were scattered, some at ——— some at Bedope, and some at Rubin, and all badly off for grain. When collected, they have about thirty families; formerly they had about fifty. Those missing had mostly been seized and made slaves. At 11h. 30m. we started for ——— (part of Rubin tribe), where we arrived about half-past two. We found one house with five families in it, and a *pangah*[4] attached. Pa Rigan, the ——— of this tribe, told me that Abang Tahar, Abang Ally, Abang Bakar, &c. &c. (all of Gadong, under Patingi Müel), demand from the Dyaks old *serras*, which have been paid long ago. Dangon, a Sirkaru Dyak, told me that Abang Tahar, a short time since, demanded from his tribe a Dyak boy, and four Dyak boys from the En Singi Dyaks.

---

2. A sort of gong.
3. *Tumbawong* is a place they have deserted, or been forced to quit.
4. A head-house.

"Bandar Cassim put a stop to these demands at the time; but he has revived them since. The Malays of Sadong, whenever they go among the Dyaks, seize their fowls, eggs, rice, cocoa-nuts, and all sorts of property. The *bandar* tells me he never permits these people to go among the Dyaks, but that they do it by stealth over land, and that the *Tuan Besar* must do something to prevent them from oppressing and frightening the Dyaks. (Here follow other complaints against the Gadong people, after which the journal continues.)

"*13th.*—Girang, a Bedope Dyak of the Rubin tribe, told me how very much he is bullied and troubled by the Gadong people, who are constantly threatening to attack him. I advised him to collect the tribe at Rubin, their old *tumbawong*. At 7 started back for the *bandar's* village, where we arrived at 10 o'clock. After a bath and breakfast, the *bandar's* mother came to me with a present of two *sarongs*, one for the *Tuan Besar* and one for myself, and begged that I would urge the *Tuan Besar* to take care of the *bandar* as if he were his own son, and not to cast him off. I told her that Mr. Brooke would support the *bandar* as long as he conducted himself properly.

"The Orang Kaya Baga, Orang Kaya Sinching of Milikin, ——— of En Tayen, Orang Kaya Laja of Rahmone, Orang Kaya Rinjou of Sirkaru, Orang Kaya Mior Muntah, Pangara Lilli of Bunan, Orang Kaya Nijou of Mapuh, Orang Kaya Ganggong of En Kelas, and Pangara Achong of En Singi, all met me. I told them the object of my mission in presence of the *bandar* and several other Malays, and they were highly delighted. They asked me to allow the *bandar* to govern them, as they are much troubled by the Gadong people. Abang Tahar lately demanded four Dyak boys of Pangara Achong, and two from the Orang Kaya of Sirkaru; beside which, the Sadong people seize their property whenever they go among them. They are very poorly off for grain. They asked me for a letter which should prevent people from annoying them. I told them I should represent the matter to the Tuan Besar, and that no doubt he will give his chop to each tribe. They all speak well of Bandar Cassim; but his people are bad, and those at Gadong[5] are worse.

"*14th.*—At 6h. 30m. started up the River Kayan toward Tumma, having left Talip with nineteen men to return to Sarawak by way of Samarahan. At 8 we stopped at Mang-garut, where the Dyaks pre-

---

5. Gadong is a small Malay village on the Sadong, considerably nearer the sea than the *bandar's* village.

sented us with a deer they had caught. These Dyaks are badly off for grain, and it is the same tribe Bandar Cassim attacked in the Goa Siri (*siri* cave) some few years ago. Orang Kaya Pa Jampat told me, that on that occasion the *bandar* seized eight Dyaks and took them with him.[6] The river here begins to be narrow and shallow, with pebbly banks, and clear water. At noon we stopped at Muara Rubin, where we intended to stay a day to inquire for coal, which was stated to have been found in this neighbourhood; but as nobody knew the whereabout, and as the Hindoo remains (said to consist of one stone in the shape of a Malay hat) were five hours out of our way, we continued our route till evening, having parted company with the *bandar* at Muara Rubin, as I well knew the Tumma Dyaks would be afraid of his approach.

"*15th.*—At daylight started toward Tumma, and at 9 stopped below Muora Sangan, where we breakfasted, after which we pushed up again, and at 1 arrived at Si Sijack, where the Tumma are. Orang Kaya Pa Muany, the chief, told me they were very much bullied, as a Sarawak man, named Pakar, and Marrat, the father-in-law of Bandar Mulana of Sarawak, forced upon them a quantity of goods in the name of the *Tuan Besar* and the Bandar Mulana. (Here follows a list of things, such as gongs, *tatawaks*, jackets, handkerchiefs, and the like, with the most exorbitant prices affixed to them. The rice and *padi* had not, however, been paid for.)

"There are three villages of this tribe; two about 250 yards apart; one of which, containing about ten families, is ruled by the Orang Kaya Pa Muany, and the other, with about thirty families, by the Orang Kaya Mayo and the Orang Kaya Pa Balet. In the other village, about three reaches above, is the Orang Kaya Pa Magong, with ten families. They said they were very comfortable under the Patingi Ali (father of the present Bandar Mulana), but that since Bandar Mulana has succeeded, they have been oppressed. They told me they had run away from Sadong because they heard the *Tuan Besar* was a just and good *rajah*, and that all his Dyaks were comfortable, but now they are oppressed. Pakar told them that if they did not take his *tatawaks* they must not remain here, but run away!

"There are forty families of the Si Nangkan Soyar tribe, and thirteen families of the Tibader tribe. The Orang Kayas told me that, had I not arrived, the rice in payment of the goods forced on them would have been taken down, as Pakar was here hurrying them to carry

---

6. This occurred during Seriff Sahib's time; the Dyaks were frightfully oppressed.

it to Sanar; but that when he heard of my coming he could not be persuaded to wait and meet me. The following goods have just been returned by the Gregan Dyaks (here follows a long list of goods and prices). Pangara Achong of the En Singi tribe told me that he has one family of his tribe at Gregan, and he wanted them to return with him. I asked the *pangaran* of Gregan whether this family wished to return, but he did not know. I then told them no one could force them, but that they might do just as they pleased. The Orang Kaya Pa Jampat goes down with me to Kuching to lay before the *Tuan Besar* a claim made upon him by the Malay *Pangeran* of Samarahan. Beside which, I take down the Orang Kaya and Pangara of Tumma, Si Markan Singan and Tebadu, together with all the goods forced on them, that the case may be judged by the *Tuan Besar.*

"Bandar Cassim demands a debt of the Orang Kaya Pa Muany of Tumma; he originally sold them (*i. e.* forced on them, of course) a gong for 150 *pasus* of *padi*, 100 of which was paid; and the question is, whether they were to pay the rest. This was four years ago. I left it for the *Tuan Besar's* decision." (Here follows a list of goods forced on the Tebadu Dyaks.)[7]

# No. 7

*Proposed Exploring Expedition to the Asiatic Archipelago, by* James Brooke, Esq. 1838.

The voyage I made to China opened an entirely new scene, and showed me what I had never seen before, savage life and savage nature. I inquired, and I read, and I became more and more assured that there was a large field of discovery and adventure open to any man daring enough to enter upon it. Just take a map and trace a line over the Indian Archipelago, with its thousand unknown islands and tribes.

---

7. The goods brought down by Mr. Williamson were on a public trial confiscated, and the parties concerned fined. These Dyaks from their distance and timidity, were afraid to complain, but will in future not be imposed upon. It would be a hopeless task trying to prevent the Malays playing their tricks on the Dyaks; and the only chance of freeing the Dyaks from these exactions is by inspiring them with confidence. In Sarawak this has been done, and may easily be extended; for the Dyak, though greatly depressed by a course of persecution, I have always found ready to state his complaints whenever he has a hope of redress. The Orong Kaya Pa Jampat of Mang-garut was freed of the debt claimed by the Samarahan Pangara; and the other complaints referred to my decision have been either rectified, or steps taken to do justice, and to render the Dyak tribes of Sadong happy and easy.—*Note by Mr. Brooke.*

Cast your eye over the vast island of New Guinea, where the foot of European has scarcely, if ever, trod. Look at the northern coast of Australia, with its mysterious Gulf of Carpentaria; a survey of which, it is supposed, would solve the great geographical question respecting the rivers of the mimic continent. Place your finger on Japan, with its exclusive and civilized people; it lies an unknown lump on our earth, and an undefined line on our charts! Think of the northern coast of China, willing, as is reported, to open an intercourse and trade with Europeans, spite of their arbitrary government.

Stretch your pencil over the Pacific Ocean, which Cook himself declares a field of discovery for ages to come! Proceed to the coast of South America, from the region of gold-dust to the region of furs—the land ravaged by the cruel Spaniard and the no less cruel Buccaneer—the scene of the adventures of Drake and the descriptions of Dampier. The places I have enumerated are mere names, with no specific ideas attached to them: lands and seas where the boldest navigators gained a reputation, and where hundreds may yet do so, if they have the same courage and the same perseverance. Imagination whispers to ambition that there are yet lands unknown which might be discovered. Tell me, would not a man's life be well spent—tell me, would it not be well sacrificed, in an endeavour to explore these regions? When I think on dangers and death, I think of them only because they would remove me from such a field for ambition, for energy, and for knowledge.

Borneo, Celebes, Sooloo, the Moluccas, and the islands of the Straits of Sunda and Banka, compose what is called the Malayan group; and the Malays located on the sea-shores of these and other islands may with certainty be classed as belonging to one people. It is well known, however, that the interior of these countries is inhabited by various tribes, differing from the Malays and each other, and presenting numerous gradations of early civilization: the Dyaks of Borneo, the Papuans of New Guinea, and others, beside the black race scattered over the islands. Objects of traffic here as elsewhere present interesting subjects of inquiry; and while our acquaintance with every other portion of the globe, from the passage of the Pole to the navigation of the Euphrates, has greatly extended, it is matter of surprise that we know scarcely anything of these people beyond the bare fact of their existence, and remain altogether ignorant of the geographical features of the countries they inhabit.

Countries which present an extended field for Christianity and commerce, which none surpass in fertility, rich beyond the Americas in mineral productions, and unrivalled in natural beauty, continue unexplored to the present day; and, spite of the advantages which would probably result, have failed to attract the attention they so well deserve. The difficulty of the undertaking will scarcely account for its non-performance, if we consider the voluntary sacrifices made on the shrine of African research, or the energy displayed and the sufferings encountered by the explorers of the Polar regions: yet the necessity of prosecuting the voyage in an armed vessel, the wildness of the interior tribes, the lawless ferocity of the Malays, and other dangers, would prevent most individuals from fixing on this field for exertion, and points it out as one which could best and most fully be accomplished by Government or some influential body.

It is not my object to enter into any detail of the past history of the Malayan nations, but I may refer to the undoubted facts that they have been in a state of deterioration since we first became acquainted with them; and the records of our early voyagers, together with the remains of antiquity still visible in Java and Sumatra, prove that once flourishing nations have now ceased to exist, and that countries once teeming with human life are now tenantless and deserted. The causes of such lamentable change need only be alluded to; but it is fit to remark, that while the standard of education is unfurled, and dreams are propagated of the progressive advancement of the human race, a large part of the globe has been gradually relapsing and allowed to relapse into barbarism. Whether the early decay of the Malay states, and their consequent demoralization, arose from the introduction of Mahommedism, or resulted from the intrigues of European ambition, it were useless to discuss; but we are very certain that this "Eden of the Eastern wave" has been reduced to a state of anarchy and confusion, as repugnant to every dictate of humanity as it is to the prospect of commercial advantage.

Borneo and Celebes, and indeed the greater portion of the islands of the Malayan Archipelago, are still unknown, and the apathy of two centuries still reigns supreme with the enlightened people of England; while they willingly make the most expensive efforts favourable to science, commerce, or Christianity in other quarters, the locality which eminently combines these three objects is alone neglected and alone uncared for. It has unfortunately been the fate of our Indian possessions to have laboured under the prejudice and contempt of a large portion of the well-bred community. While the folly of fashion requires an acquaintance with the deserts of Africa, and a most ardent thirst for a knowledge of the usages of Timbuctoo, it at the same time justifies the most profound ignorance of all matters connected with the government and geography of our vast acquisitions in Hindoostan. The Indian Archipelago has fully shared this neglect; and even the tender philanthropy of the present day, which originates such multifarious schemes for the amelioration of doubtful evils, which shudders at the prolongation of apprenticeship for a single year in the West, is blind to the existence of slavery in its worst and most aggravated form in the East.

Not a single prospectus is spread abroad; not a single voice is upraised to relieve the darkness of Paganism, and the horrors of the Eastern slave-trade. While the trumpet-tongue of many an orator excites thousands to the rational and charitable objects of converting the Jews and reclaiming the Gipsys; while the admirable exertions of missionary enterprise in the Ausonian climes of the South Sea have invested them with worldly power as well as religious influence; while we admire the torrent of devotional and philosophical exertion, we cannot help deploring that the zeal and attention of the leaders of these charitable crusades have never been directed to the countries under consideration.

These unhappy countries have failed to rouse attention or excite commiseration; and as they sink lower and lower, they afford a striking proof how civilization may be dashed, and how the purest and richest lands under the sun may be degraded and brutalized by a continued course of oppression and misrule. It is under these circumstances that I have considered individual exertion may be usefully applied to rouse the zeal of slumbering philanthropy, and to lead the way to an increased knowledge of the Indian Archipelago. Such an exertion will be made at some cost and some sacrifice; and I shall here quit the general topic, and confine myself to the specific objects of my intended voyage.

It must be premised, however, that any plan previously decided on must always be subject during its execution to great modifications in countries where the population is always rude and often hostile, and where the influence of climate is sometimes so fatally opposed to the progress of inquiry. Local information, likewise, frequently renders such a change both advisable and advantageous; and circumstances, as they spring up, too often influence us beyond the power of foresight, more especially in my own case, where the utmost care would still leave the means very inadequate to the full accomplishment of the proposed undertaking. With a small vessel properly equipped, and provided with the necessary instruments for observation, and the means for collecting specimens in natural history, it is proposed in the first instance to proceed to Singapore, which may be considered as headquarters for the necessary intervals of refreshment and repose, and for keeping open a certain communication with Europe.

Here the best local information can be obtained, interpreters procured, the crew augmented for any particular service; and here, if needful, a small vessel of native construction may be added to the expedition, to facilitate the objects in view. An acquaintance may likewise be formed with the more respectable Bugis merchants, and their goodwill conciliated in the usual mode, *viz.*, by civility and presents, so as to remove any misconceived jealousy on the score of trading rivalry, and to induce a favourable report of our friendly intentions in their own country, and at the places where they may touch. The Royalist will probably reach Singapore in the month of March, 1839, at the latter end of the northwest, or rainy monsoon.

The delay consequent on effecting the objects above mentioned, beside gaining a general acquaintance with the natural history and trade of the settlement, and some knowledge of the Malay language, will usefully occupy the time until the setting in of the southeast, or dry monsoon. It may be incidentally mentioned, however, that in the vicinity of Singapore there are many islands imperfectly known, and which, during the intervals of the rainy season, will afford interesting occupation. I allude, more especially, to the space between the Straits of Rhio and those of Duryan, and likewise to the island called Bintang, which, although laid down as one large island, is probably composed of small ones, divided by navigable straits; a better acquaintance with which might facilitate the voyage from Singapore to the more eastern islands, by bringing to light other passages beside those of Rhio and Duryan; and, at any rate, would add something to our geographical knowledge in the immediate vicinity of our settlement.

On the commencement of the healthy season I propose sailing from Singapore, and proceeding without loss of time to Malludu Bay, at the north end of Borneo. This spot has been chosen for the first essay; and in a country every part of which is highly interesting, and almost unknown, the mere fact of its being a British possession gives it a prior claim to attention.

The objects in view may be briefly mentioned.

1. A general knowledge of the bay, and the correct position of

various points—more especially the two principal headlands at its entrance, so as to determine its outline. The westernmost of these headlands, called Sampanmange, will likewise determine the extreme north point of Borneo.

2. Inquiries for the settlement of Cochin Chinese, reported, on Earl's authority, to be fixed in the vicinity of Bankoka: an intercourse will, if possible, be opened with this settlement, if in existence.

3. The rivers which flow into the bay will be carefully and minutely explored, and an attempt will be made to penetrate into the interior as far as the lake of Kini Ballu.

4. For the same purpose, every endeavour will be used to open a communication with the aboriginal inhabitants of the country, and every means employed to conciliate their good opinion; and (if the ceremony exists in this part of the island) to enter into the bonds of fraternity (described by Mr. Dalton) with some of the chiefs.

I speak with great diffidence about penetrating into the interior of this country, for I am well aware of the insurmountable difficulties which the hard reality often presents, which are previously overlooked and easily overcome in the smoothness of paper, or the luxury of a drawing-room. The two points to be chiefly relied upon for this purpose are, a friendly intercourse with the natives, and the existence of navigable rivers. It is mentioned by Sir Stamford Raffles, on native authority, that a land communication, of not more than forty miles, exists between Malludu Bay and Lake Kini Ballu; but neither this computation, nor any other derived from the natives, however intelligent otherwise, can be relied on; for the inhabitants of these countries are generally ignorant of any measure for distance; and their reckoning by time is so vague, as to defy a moderately-certain conclusion.

The fact, however, of the vicinity of the lake to the bay may be concluded; and it follows, as a reasonable inference, that the river or rivers flowing into the bay communicate with the lake. The existence of such rivers, which were from the locality to have been expected, is vouched for by Captain Forrest. "Most of this north part of Borneo (he says), granted to the English East India Company by the Sooloos, is watered by noble rivers: those that discharge themselves into Malludu Bay are not barred." It is by one or other of these rivers that I should hope to penetrate as far as the lake and mountain of Kini Ballu, and into the country of the Idaan.

I have not been able to learn that any Malay towns of importance are situated in the bight of Malludu Bay, and their absence will render a friendly communication with the aborigines a matter of comparative ease. The advantages likely to result from such friendly relations are so evident, that I need not dwell upon them; though the mode of effecting such an intercourse must be left to the thousand contingencies which govern all, and act so capriciously on the tempers of the savage races. The utmost forbearance, and a liberality guided by prudence, so as not to excite too great a degree of cupidity, appear the fundamental rules for managing men in a low state of civilization.

The results of an amicable understanding are as uncertain as its commencement; for they depend on the enterprise of the individual, and the power of the native tribe into whose hands he may have fallen. I will not, therefore, enter into a visionary field of discovery; but it appears to me certain that, without the assistance of the natives, no small party can expect to penetrate far into a country populous by report, and in many parts thickly covered with wood. Without entertaining any exaggerated expectation, I trust that something may be added to our geographical knowledge of the sea-coast of this bay, its leading features, productions, rivers, anchorages, and inhabitants, the prospect of trade, and the means of navigation; and although my wishes lead me strongly to penetrate as far as the lake of Kini Ballu, yet the obstacles which may be found to exist to the fulfilment of this desire will induce me to rest satisfied with the more moderate and reasonable results.

It may not be superfluous to notice here, that a foregone conclusion appears to be spread abroad regarding the aboriginal (so called) inhabitants of Borneo, and that they are usually considered and mentioned under the somewhat vague appellation of Dyaks. They are likewise commonly pronounced as originating from the same stock as the Arafuras of Celebes and New Guinea, and radically identical with the Polynesian race. The conclusion is not in itself highly improbable, but certainly premature, as the facts upon which it is built are so scanty and doubtful as to authorize no such structure.

On an island of the vast size of Borneo, races radically distinct might exist; and at any rate, the opposite conclusion is hardly justifiable, from the specimens of language or the physical appearance of the tribes of the southern portion of the country. We have Malay authority for believing that there are many large tribes in the interior, differing greatly in their degree of civilization, though all alike removed from the vicinity of a superior people. We have the Dyaks of the south; the Idaan of the north; the Kagins; and a race little better than monkeys, who live in trees, eat without cooking, are hunted by the other tribes, and would seem to exist in the lowest conceivable grade of humanity.

If we may trust these accounts, these latter people resemble in many particulars the Orang Benua, or aborigines of the peninsula; but the Dyaks and Idaans are far superior, living in villages, cultivating the ground, and possessing cattle. Beside these, likewise, we have the names of several other tribes or people; and, in all probability, many exist in the interior with whom we are unacquainted.

There are strong reasons for believing that the Hindoo religion, which obtained so extensively in Java and Sumatra, and yet survives at Bali and Lombock, was likewise extended to Borneo; and some authors have conceived grounds for supposing a religion anterior even to this. If only a portion of these floating opinions should be true, and the truth can only be tested by inquiry, we may fairly look for the descendants of the Hindoo dynasty as well as an aboriginal people. It never seems to have occurred to anyone to compare the Dyaks with the people of Bali and Lombock. We know indeed but little of the former; but both races are fair, good-looking, and gentle. Again, respecting the concluded identity of the Dyaks and the Arafuras, it is clear we have a very limited knowledge indeed of the former; and, I may ask, what do we know of the Arafuras?

In short, I feel as reluctant to embrace any preconceived theory as I am to adopt the prevailing notion on this subject; for it requires a mass of facts, of which we are wholly deficient, to arrive at anything approaching a reasonable conclusion. To return, however, to the proceedings of the Royalist, I would remark, that it depends greatly on the time passed in Malludu Bay whether our next endeavour be prosecuted at Abai on the western, or Tusan Abai on the eastern coast. The object in visiting Abai would he chiefly to penetrate to the lake, which, on the authority of Dalrymple and Burton, is not far distant thence, by a water communication; but should any success have attended similar efforts from Malludu Bay, this project will be needless, as in that case the enterprise will have been prosecuted to the westward, and reach to the vicinity of Abai.

As Kaminis is the limit of the British territory to the westward, so Point Kaniungan, situated to the southward of the bay of Sandakan, forms the eastern boundary; and a line drawn from coast to coast between these points is represented as including our possessions. A reference to the chart will show the extent to be considerable; and the eastern coast from Malludu Bay to Point Kaniungan is so very little known, that it is highly desirable to become acquainted with its general features and conformation, and to seek thence the means of gaining an inlet into the interior, should it be denied at Malludu Bay.

The reported proximity of Kini Ballu to Malludu Bay, and likewise to Abai would (supposing it is anything like the size it is affirmed to be) lead us to expect that it cannot be far distant from the eastern coast; and it is but reasonable to conclude that some rivers or streams discharge themselves into the sea in the numerous indentations that abound on this shore. However this may be, the coast, with its bays and islands and bold headlands, is one of great interest, and almost unknown; and the careful inspection of it as far as Point Kaniungan will, I trust, add something to our knowledge. The longitude of Point Kaniungan and Point Unsang will likewise determine the eastern extremity of Borneo.

Much more might be added on this topic, especially of the reported communication by a line of lakes from Malludu Bay to Banjarmassim, which, if true, would in all probability place some of these lakes near particular points of the east coast, as the whole line, from the relative position of the two extremes, must be on the eastern side of the island. These reports, and the various surmises which arise from them, are rather matters for verification than discussion; and I will therefore only add that, tempted by success, I shall not devote less than a year and a half to this object; but, in case of finding a sickly climate, or meeting with a decidedly hostile population, I shall more easily abandon the field, and turn to others of not less interest, and perhaps of less risk.

Equal to Borneo in riches, and superior in picturesque beauty to any part of the Archipelago, is the large and eccentric country of the Bugis, called Celebes. So deep are the indentations of its coasts, that the island may be pronounced as being composed of a succession of peninsulas, nearly uniting in a common centre in the district of Palos; and thus, by the proximity of every part to the sea, offering great facilities for brief and decisive interior excursions. The Dutch are in possession of Makassar, and had formerly settlements on the northwest coast and in the bay of Sawa.

Their power appears, however, never to have been very extensively acknowledged; and at present I have not been able to meet with any account of the condition of their factories. This information will probably be gained at Singapore. Avoiding the Dutch settlements, I propose limiting my inquiries to the northern and northeastern portion of the island, more especially the great bay of Gunong Tella. It is impossible to state here the direction of these inquiries, or any definite object to which they should be turned, as I am acquainted with no author who speaks of the country, save in a general and vague manner. It is reported as rich, fertile, mountainous, strikingly beautiful, and possessed of rivers; abounding in birds, and inhabited, like Borneo, by wild tribes in the interior, and by the Bugis on the sea-shores and entrance of rivers.

The character of the Bugis, though so variously represented, gives me strong hopes of rendering them, by care and kindness, useful instruments in the prosecution of these researches; for all writers agree that they are active, hardy, enterprising, and commercial; and it is seldom that a people possessing such characteristics are deaf to the suggestions of self-interest or kindly feeling. The arrogance, and especially the indolence, of the Malays, counteracts the influence of these strong incentives; and the impulse which governs such rude tribes as the Dyaks and Arafuras is a dangerous weapon, which cuts all ways, and often when least anticipated. The Badjows, or sea-gipsys, are another race on whom some dependence may be placed. Mr. Earl, who had a personal acquaintance with this tribe, and could speak their language, always expressed to me a degree of confidence in their good faith, which must have had some grounds.

I may here conclude the first stage of the expedition, during the progress of which the headquarters will be fixed at Singapore. During some of the intervals I hope to see Manilla, and to acquire a cursory knowledge of the unexplored tract at the southern extremity of Celebes, called in Norie's general chart the Tiger Islands.

The time devoted to the objects above mentioned must, as I have before said, be regulated by the degree of fortune which attends them; for, cheered by success, I should not readily abandon the field; yet, if persecuted by climate, or other serious detriments, I shall frequently shift the ground, to remove myself beyond such evil influence. It is scarcely needful to continue a detail of projects so distant, having already carved out for myself a work which I should be proud to perform, and which is already as extended as the chances of human life and human resolves will warrant.

The continuation of the voyage would lead me to take the Royalist to Timor or Port Essington, thence making excursions to the Arru

Isles, Timor Laut, and the southern shores of New Guinea. That part of the coast contiguous to Torres Straits I am particularly desirous of visiting; as it has been suggested to me by Mr. Earl, and I think with reason, that a better channel than the one we are at present acquainted with may be found there. That such a channel exists, and will be discovered when the coast is surveyed, I entertain but little doubt; but the navigation is hazardous, and must, from the westward, be attempted with great caution.

My own proceedings must, of course, be regulated by the discoveries previously made by Captain Wickham or others; and as this gentleman has orders to survey Torres Straits, the field may be well trodden before I reach it. The rest of the voyage I shall consider as one merely of pleasure, combining such utility as circumstances will permit. It is probable that I shall visit our Australian settlements; glance at the islands of the Pacific; and return to Europe round Cape Horn. Before concluding, I may observe, that there are points of inquiry which may be useful to the studies of the learned, which (provided the process be moderately simple) I shall be willing to make, and I shall always be happy to receive any directions or suggestions regarding them. I allude to observations on the tides, to geology, to the branches of natural history, &c. &c., for the general inquirer often neglects or overlooks highly intersting facts, from his attention not having been called to them.

The specimens of natural history will be forwarded home on every visit to Singapore; and the information will be sent ot the Geographical Society, and may always, if it be of any value, be used as freely as it is communicated. In like manner, the objects of natural history will be open to any person who is at all interested in such pursuits. I cannot but express my regret, that from pecuniary considerations as well as the small size of the vessel, and the limited quantity of provision she carries, I am unable to take a naturalist and draughtsman; but I should always hail with pleasure any scientific person who joined me abroad, or who happened to be in the countries at the time; and I may venture to promise him every encouragement and facility in the prosecution of his pursuits.

I embark upon the expedition with great cheerfulness, with a stout vessel, a good crew, and the ingredients of success as far as the limited scale of the undertaking will permit; and I cast myself upon the waters—like Mr. Southey's little book—but whether the world will know me after many days, is a question which, hoping the best, I cannot answer with any positive degree of assurance.

# No. 8

## Sketch of Borneo, or Pulo Kalamantan, by J. Hunt, Esq.

*(Communicated, in 1812, to the Honourable Sir Thomas Stamford Raffles, late Lieutenant-Governor of Java.)*

The island of Borneo extends from 7° 7' north to 4° 12' south latitude, and from 108° 45' to 119° 25' east longitude; measuring at its extreme length nine hundred miles, at its greatest breadth seven hundred, and in circumference three thousand. It is bounded on the north by the Solo seas, on the east by the Straits of Macassar, on the south by the Java, and on the west by the China seas. Situated in the track of the most extensive and valuable commerce, intersected on all sides with deep and navigable rivers, indented with safe and capacious harbours, possessing one of the richest soils on the globe, abounding in all the necessaries of human life, and boasting commercial products that have in all ages excited the avarice and stimulated the desires of mankind,—with the exception of New Holland, it is the largest island known.

Of the existence of this extensive territory, so highly favoured by Providence, and enriched by the choicest productions of nature, there remains scarce a vestige in the geographical descriptions of the day; and its rich products and fertile shores, by one tacit and universal consent, appear abandoned by all the European nations of the present age, and handed over to the ravages of extensive hordes of piratical banditti, solely intent on plunder and desolation.

The natives and the Malays, formerly, and even at this day, call this large island by the exclusive name of Pulo Kalamantan, from a sour and indigenous fruit so called. Borneo was the name only of a city, the capital of one of the three distinct kingdoms on the island. When Magalhaens visited it in the year 1520, he saw a rich and populous city, a luxuriant and fertile country, a powerful prince, and a magnificent court: hence the Spaniards hastily concluded that the whole island not only belonged to this prince, but that it was likewise named Borneo. In this error they have been followed by all other European nations. The charts, however, mark this capital "Borneo Proper," or in other words, the only place properly Borneo: this is the only confession of this misnomer that I have met with among Europeans. The natives pronounce Borneo, Bruni, and say it is derived from the word Brani, courageous; the aboriginal natives within this district having ever remained unconquered.

The aborigines of Borneo, or Pulo Kalamantan, still exist in the interior in considerable numbers; there are various tribes of them, speaking different dialects. Some of them acknowledge Malay chiefs, as at Landa, Songo, Mantan, &c. Several communities of them still remain under independent chiefs of their own nation; and everywhere their origin, their language, their religion, their manners and customs, are totally distinct and apparent from those of the Islams, or Malays, who have settled on the island. About Pontiana and Sambas they are called Dayers; at Benjarmasing, Biajus; at Borneo Proper, Moruts; farther northward, Orang Idan. Their original history is as much enveloped in obscurity as that of the Monocaboes of Malaya, the Rejangs and Battas of Sumatra, or the Togals of the Philippines.

On a nearer acquaintance with their language, customs, traditions, &c., perhaps an affinity in origin may be discovered among all the original possessors of the Eastern isles. The Moruts and Orang Idan are much fairer and better featured than the Malays, of a more strong and robust frame, and have the credit of being a brave race of people. The Dayer is much darker, and approaches nearer in resemblance to the Malay. The Biajus I never saw. The few particulars which I have been able to collect of these people I shall briefly state: They live in miserable small huts; their sole dress consists of a slight wrapper round their waists, sometimes made of bark, at others from skins of animals, or perhaps of blue or white cloth; they eat rice or roots, and indeed any description of food, whether beast, reptile, or vermin: they are extremely filthy; this and bad food give them a cutaneous disorder, with which they are very generally afflicted. Several tribes of them smear themselves with oil and pigments, which gives them the appearance of being tattooed.

Whether this is intended to defend them against the bites of insects, to operate as a cure or prevention of this epidemic, or to adorn their persons, I cannot take upon me to decide. They believe, it is said, in a Supreme Being, and offer sacrifices of gratitude to a beneficent Deity. Polygamy is not allowed among them; no man has more than one wife; they burn their dead. They are said to shoot poisoned balls or arrows through hollow tubes; and whenever they kill a man, they preserve the skull to exhibit as a trophy to commemorate the achievement of their arms. They are said to have no mode of communicating their ideas by characters or writing, like the Battas. Driven from the sea-coast of Borneo into the mountains and fastnesses in the interior, they are more occupied in the chase and the pursuits of husbandry than in commerce.

They, however, barter their inland produce of camphor, gold, diamonds, birds-nests, wax, and cattle, for salt (which they hold in the highest degree of estimation, eating it with as much *gout* as we do sugar), china, porcelain, brass and iron cooking utensils, brass bracelets, coarse blue and white cloth, Java tobacco, arrack (which they also like), *parangs*, hardware, beads, &c. Some tribes of them are said to pull out their front teeth and substitute others of gold, and others adorn themselves with tigers' teeth. The greatest numbers and most considerable bodies of these men are found near Kiney Balu and about Borneo Proper.

The Malays represent them as the most savage and ferocious of men; but to be more savage or ferocious than a Malay is a thing utterly impossible. Their representations may be accounted for. These aborigines have always evinced a strong disposition and predilection for liberty and freedom; they have either resisted the yoke of the Malay, or have retired to their mountains to enjoy this greatest of all human blessings. The Malay, unable to conquer them, lays plans for kidnapping as many as he can fall in with. Every Dyak so taken is made a slave of, his children sold, and his women violated. The Malay, hence, is justly considered by them as the violator of every law, human and divine; and whenever any of these people meet with one, they satiate their vengeance, and destroy him as the enemy of their race, and as a monster of the human kind. The Portuguese missionaries found these people very tractable converts, and very large bodies of them are very easily governed by a single Malay chief, as at Landa, Songo, and Matan. I have seen very large bodies of them at Kimanis and Maludu, but none of them possessing the ferocity of a Malay.

The Islams, or Malayans, who now possess the sea-coasts of Borneo (as well as the sea-coasts of all the Eastern islands), are said to be colonies from Malacca, Johore, &c., planted in the fourteenth century; at this period, according to Mr. Poivre, "Malacca was a country well peopled, and was consequently well cultivated. This nation was once one of the greatest powers in the Eastern seas, and made a very considerable figure in the theatre of Asia; they colonized Borneo, Celebes, Macassar, Moluccas, &c." The Malays on Borneo are like the Malays everywhere else, the most atrocious race of beings on the earth; and from their general character, and imprudent institutions, both political and religious, are fast mouldering in self-decay, or mutual destruction.

From the earliest date that I have been able to trace, the island of Borneo was always divided into three distinct kingdoms. The kingdom of Borneo, properly so called, extended from Tanjong Dato, in latitude 3° 15' north, to Kanukungan point, in the Straits of Macassar, 1° 15' north, which included the whole north part of the island. The kingdom of Sukadana (from *suka*, happiness, and *dunia*, the world, or earthly paradise), extending from Tanjong Dato to Tanjong Sambar, which belonged to the King of Bantam (when or how acquired I have not learned): and the remainder of the island from Tanjong Sambar to Kanukungan Point aforesaid, to the kingdom of Benjarmasing (from *bendar*, a port of trade, and *masing*, usual, or the ordinary port of trade).

When the Portuguese first visited Borneo, in 1520, the whole island was in a most flourishing state. The numbers of Chinese that had settled on her shores were immense; the products of their industry, and an extensive commerce with China in junks, gave her land and cities a far different aspect from her dreary appearance at this day, and their princes and courts exhibited a splendour and displayed a magnificence which has long since vanished.

Pigofetta says there were twenty-five thousand houses in the city of Borneo Proper, and that it was rich and populous. Much later accounts describe the numbers of Chinese and Japanese junks frequenting her ports as great; but in 1809 there were not three thousand houses in the whole city, nor six thousand Chinese throughout that kingdom, and not a junk that had visited it for years. But the ports of Borneo have not dwindled away more than Acheen, Johore, Malacca, Bantam, Ternate, &c. All these places likewise cut a splendid figure in the eyes of our first navigators, and have since equally shared a proportionate obscurity.

Were the causes required which have eclipsed the prosperity of Borneo and the other great emporiums of Eastern trade that once existed, it might be readily answered—a decay of commerce. They have suffered the same vicissitudes as Tyre, Sidon, or Alexandria; and like Carthage—for ages the emporium of the wealth and commerce of the world, which now exhibits on its site a piratical race of descendants in the modern Tunisians and their neighbours the Algerines—the commercial ports of Borneo have become a nest of banditti, and the original inhabitants of both, from similar causes—the decay of commerce—have degenerated to the modern pirates of the present day.

In exact proportion as the intercourse of the Europeans with China has increased, in precise ratio has the decrease of their direct trade in junks become apparent. The Portuguese first, and subsequently the Dutch, mistress of the Eastern seas, exacted by treaties and other ways the Malay produce at their own rates, and were consequently enabled to undersell the junks in China. But these powers went further; by settling at ports on Borneo, or by their *guardas de costas,* they compelled the ports of Borneo to send their produce, calculated for the China market, to Malacca and Batavia, which at length completely cut up the direct trade by means of the Chinese junks.

The loss of their direct intercourse with China affected their prosperity in a variety of ways. First, by this circuitous direction of their trade, the gruff goods, as rattans, sago, cassia, pepper, ebony, wax, &c., became too expensive to fetch the value of this double carriage and the attendant charges, and in course of time were neglected; the loss of these extensive branches of industry must have thrown numbers out of employment. But the loss of the direct intercourse with China had more fatal effects; it prevented large bodies of annual emigrants from China settling upon her shores; it deprived them of an opportunity of visiting the Borneon ports, and exercising their mechanical arts and productive industry; and of thus keeping up the prosperity of the country in the tillage of the ground, as well as in the commerce of her ports.

The old Chinese settlers by degrees deserted these shores; and to fill up the chasms in their revenues by so fatal a change, the *rajah*s have been tempted to turn their views to predatory habits, and have permitted their lands to run to jungle, by dragging their wretched labourers from agricultural employments to maritime and piratical enterprises.

The first material alteration in the sovereignty of the territorial possession took place in the kingdom of Borneo Proper, when her *rajah* was obliged to call in the aid of the Solos to defend him against an insurrection of the Maruts and Chinese. In consideration of this important aid, the Rajah of Borneo Proper ceded to the Sultan of Solo all that portion of Borneo then belonging to him, from Kimanis, in latitude 5° 30' north, to Tapean-durian, in the Straits of Macassar, which includes the whole north of Borneo.

After this period, the power and fortunes of the Sultan of Solo rapidly declined. The Spaniards succeeded in conquering all their islands. Solo, the capital, was taken and fortified; the *sultan* and his court made prisoners. When the English captured Manilla, they found this *sultan* incarcerated. They agreed to relieve him from prison, and reinstate him on the *musnud* of his forefathers under the express stipulation that the whole of the aforesaid territory of Borneo, ceded to Solo by the *rajah* of that kingdom, should be transferred to the English East India Company, together with the south of Palawan, and the intermediate islands. These terms were joyfully acceded to by the Sultan of Solo, and signed, sealed, and delivered by him to the late Alexander Dalrymple, in the year 1763.

The kingdom of Sukadana was ceded by the Rajah of Bantam (in what year I know not) to the Dutch East India Company. Whether the kingdom of Benjarmasing was ever actually ceded to the Dutch or not, I have not been able to learn. But the occupancy of her capital, the military government of the country, by the erection of forts, and a permanent standing force, since transferred to the English arms, give to the East India Company, actually or virtually, the entire sovereignty and rule over the whole of this large island, with the exception of the piratical port of Borneo Proper, and the portion of territory yet annexed thereto.

The Portuguese, at a very early period, established themselves at Benjarmasing: at Borneo Proper there still remain two bastions and a curtain of a regular stone fort built by them: they had also one on the island of Laboan, since destroyed. They fixed themselves at old Sambas, from which they were driven by the Dutch in the year 1690, and nearly about this period from all their establishments on Borneo.

When, or from what causes, the Dutch were induced to evacuate Sambas, I know not, nor have I learned the period when they fortified themselves at Benjarmasing and Pasir, but believe it could not have taken place before the middle of the last century. They, however, settled at Pontiana in 1786, and built a fortified wall round the palace and factory, but were compelled to withdraw from it when the war broke out with the English in 1796. The ports at Benjarmasing, when evacuated, were sold by the Dutch to the sultan, and are since said to have been repurchased from him by the English.

The Dutch obtaining the cession of the kingdom of Sukadana from the Rajah of Bantam, and their subsequent measures in different parts of this territory, will show that they had extensive views of firmly establishing themselves on this island; and waking from an age of lethargy, at last began to see the great advantages and unbounded resources these rich possessions were capable of affording them, without any cost or expense whatever. The year they withdrew from Pontiana they had it in contemplation to take repossession of Sambas, and to unite all the ports, as well as the interior, under the Rajah of Pontiana, in trust for them. Some letters to this effect were written by the Dutch government to the late *rajah*.

That the English were not insensible to the value and importance of the once valuable commerce of Borneo may be inferred not only from the number of the Honourable Company's regular ships annually dispatched to her ports prior to the year 1760 (*vide Hardy's Shipping Register*), but from the efforts they have repeatedly made to establish themselves on her shores. There still exist the remains of a British factory at Borneo Proper. Before the year 1706, they had made two successive attempts to fortify themselves at Benjarmasing; twice they have attempted an establishment on the sickly island of Balambangan (lying north of Borneo, near Maludu); and in 1775, the Honourable Company's ship *Bridgewater* was sent to Pasir with similar views.

The failure of these British attempts, as well as the exclusion of all other powers from the ports of Borneo, may be principally attributed to the sordid desire of the Dutch of monopolizing the whole produce of the Eastern Archipelago, and their rooted jealousy in opposing the establishment of every other power in the vicinity of Java, or that of the Spice Islands.

These considerations and feelings have induced them to commit the most flagrant crimes, not only against the natives of these regions, but against every European power. Their infamous massacres at Amboyna, Banda, Bantam, &c., have been historically recorded to their eternal disgrace. By their intrigues at Benjarmasing, the British attempts at a settlement twice failed; and Forrest, in his Voyage to New Guinea, says, that the Solos were by Dutch instigation induced to cut off the infant establishment of Balambangan, in 1775. They frustrated the attempts of the Bridgewater at Pasir; and even the massacre of the garrison of Pulo Condore was effected by Javanese soldiers supplied by the governor of Batavia. The English, from their strong desire of having a port in the China Seas, hastily pitched upon the most unhealthy spots for that purpose, *viz.* Balambangan and Pulo Condore.

The father of the present Sultan of Pontiana was the descendant of an Arab, residing at Simpan, near Matan. By the advice and concurrence of the Dutch he was induced, about forty-two years ago, to settle on the unfrequented shores of the river Pontiana, or Quallo Londa, with promises of early co-operation and assistance, as well as of rendering it the mart of the trade and capital of all Sukadana. As soon as Abdul Ramman (the name of the first *sultan*) had succeeded in attracting around him several Chinese, Buguese, and Malay settlers, and in building a town, the Dutch (in 1786) came with two armed brigs and fifty troops to establish their factory. To make good their promises to Abdul Ramman (the treaty I have never seen), they immediately overthrew the chief of Mompava, and gave his country in trust to this ally: they shortly after invested the ancient city of Sukadana, burned it to the ground, transferred the inhabitants to Pontiana, or dispersed them and their chief into the interior.

The Dutch likewise placed the present *rajas* on the *musnuds* of Songo, Landa, &c., and kept up a force at the former, with the express stipulation that the whole of their produce should be sent from each of their respective districts to the Dutch factory of Pontiana. They had it in contemplation, in 1795, to take repossession of Sambas, and wrote to Abdul Ramman as to the preparatory measures requisite, when the English war, as before observed, obliged them to abandon Pontiana.

This Abdul Ramman, the first *sultan* or chief of Pontiana, reigned thirty-five years, and died in 1807, leaving his eldest son, the present Sultan Kasim, now forty-six years of age, his successor; who has a second brother, called Pangeran Marko, aged thirty-eight, and Pangeran Hosman, thirty-six years, beside four sisters, one of whom married the present Rajah of Matan, and about seventy half brothers and sisters, the natural children of his father, with an extensive sub-progeny. The present *sultan* has three sons (Abibuker, heir-apparent, twenty-one years old, Ali, and Abdul Ramman), and four daughters, lawfully begotten. None of the royal family make use of either opium, betel, or tobacco, in any shape whatever; and the present *sultan* has much the appearance of an Arab. The grandfather of the present *sultan* was from Arabia, a Sayed Suriff; one of his relations was fixed at Palimbang, whose name is unknown to me, and the other, Shad Fudyel, at Acheen, who has been long dead.

The wet season commences from September, and ends in April, when heavy rain, hard squalls, and much thunder and lightning are experienced. From April till September is called the dry season, but even in this portion of the year seldom a day elapses without a smart shower or two. The monsoons on the northerly shores of Borneo are found to correspond with those prevalent in the China seas, *viz.* from the N.E. from October to April, and from the S.W. the rest of the year. To the southward, about Benjarmasing, the monsoons are the same as in the Java seas, *i. e.* westerly from October to April, and easterly the rest of the year. Those parts of Borneo near or upon the equator have variable winds all the year, and land and sea breezes close in shore.

This country is by no means so warm as one would be led to imagine by its proximity everywhere to the line: this arises from the perpetual refreshing showers and the land and sea breezes, the former being wafted over innumerable rivers. In the month of November, the thermometer at Pontiana ranges from 78° to 82°.

During the wet season, the rivers swell and overflow the adjacent shores, and run down with such continued rapidity, that the water may be tasted fresh at sea at the distance of six or seven miles from the mouths: these overflowings fertilize the banks and adjacent country, and render the shores of Borneo, like the plains of Egypt, luxuriantly rich. Susceptible of the highest possible culture, particularly in wet grain, in the dry season the coast, from these overflowings, presents to the eye the richest enamelled fields of full grown grass for miles around. It is at this season that whole herds of wild cattle range down from the mountains in the interior to fatten on the plains, but during the wet season they ascend to their hills.

The whole of the north, the northwest, and the centre of Borneo is extremely mountainous. The greatest portion of the ancient kingdom of Borneo Proper is extremely elevated. That of Kiney Baulu, or St. Peter's Mount, in latitude 6° north, is perhaps one of the highest mountains known. The country about Sambas, Pontiana, and Sukadana is occasionally interspersed with a few ranges of hills, otherwise the land here might be deemed low. But to the southward, and more particularly to the east, in the Straits of Macassar, it is very low. The shore in these latter places is extremely moist and swampy, but the interior is said to be dry.

The common charts of Borneo will show the innumerable rivers that water this vast island in every possible direction; but it is worthy of remark, that all the principal rivers on this island have their main source in a large lake in the vicinity of that stupendous mountain before mentioned, Kiney Baulu. The River Benjarmasing takes its rise from thence, and after traversing in all its windings a distance of 1500 miles, intersecting the island into two parts, falls into the Java sea. Its rise and fall is said to be twelve feet, and it has only nine feet at low water on the bar. It is said to have numberless villages scattered on its banks; but I have obtained no particular accounts of them, or their produce.

The great river of Borneo Proper is certainly the finest on the island. It is a deep, navigable, and majestic stream; it has three fathoms upon the bar at low water; the rise and fall is, I believe, fifteen feet; there are docks here for Chinese junks of five or six hundred tons, and a first-rate ship of war might get up far above the town. The country, too, is populous, productive, and healthy. The southern branch of this river has been well surveyed, but the branch leading to the Marut country is little known; it has its source in Kiney Baulu.

In the ancient kingdom of Sukadana, the five principal rivers are the Sukadana, the Lava, the Pogore, the Pontiana, and the Sambas. The former rivers communicate inland, and their main source is in Kiney Baulu. The whole of these rivers are deep and navigable for seventy or eighty miles; but have all of them mud flats at their mouths, which would not admit of the entry of vessels exceeding fourteen feet at high water springs.

The third most considerable river on Borneo is the Kinabatangan, lying in the north of the island, and emptying itself into the Sulo seas. It is said to be deep and navigable much farther than the Benjarmasing River; it has several mouths, but it has never been surveyed. The rivers Kuran, Pasir, and a variety of others that fall into the Straits of Macassar, are said to be noble streams, navigable for vessels of large burthen; but I have no accurate information of them. The harbour of Sandakan is one of the finest in the world; a correct chart of the same is published. The harbour of Tambisan, near Cape Unsing, is equal to Pulo Pinang, and calculated for careening and building ships; a tolerable chart of these is also published. The harbours of Pulo Laut, Punangan, Maludu, and several others in the Straits of Macassar, afford good anchorage and complete shelter for shipping.

Situated as Borneo is, immediately under the equator, everything that can be produced in vegetation by the combined influence of heat and moisture is here displayed in the highest luxuriance and super-excellence. All the Oriental palms, as the cocoa-nut, the *area*, the sago, &c., abound here. The larger grasses, as the bamboo, the *canna*, the *nardus*, assume a stately growth, and thrive in peculiar luxuriance. Pepper is found wild everywhere, and largely cultivated about Benjarmasing and the districts of Borneo Proper. The *laurus cinnamomum* and *cassia odouriferata* are produced in abundance about Kimanis.

In no part of the world does the camphor-tree flourish in equal perfection as in the districts of Maludu and Payton, in the north of Borneo. The ebony, the *dammar*, the tree that yields the finest dragon's blood in the world, all abound here. The cotton and coffee trees are found in all parts of Borneo, though not much attended to. The chocolate nut of Sulo is preferred at Manilla to that from South America. The tree that yields the clove-bark, and the nutmeg, and clove, thrive luxuriantly, though never tried to any extent.

The woods about Pontiana for carpentry and joinery, are *kayu bulean, chena, mintangore, laban,* ebony, iron-wood, *dammar,* and *dammar laut,* &c. &c. The pine abounds in the bay of Maludu, teak at Sulo. The fruit-bearing trees which enrich and adorn the Indian continent, offer, on the Borneon shore, all their kindred varieties, nurtured by the bountiful hand of luxuriant nature. The *durian, mangustin, rambutan, proya, chabi, kachang, timon, jambu, kniban,* beside the *nanka* or jack, tamarind, *pomplemose,* orange, lemon, and citron, all the kindred varieties of the plantain, banana, melon, *annanas,* pomegranate, &c., are found on Borneo.

The garden-stuffs met with are onions, garlic, yams, pumpkins, *brinjals,* greens, beans, cucumbers; and turnips, cabbages, and potatoes would succeed, were there Europeans to attend to them.

The elephant was said to be seen about Cape Unsing, where several teeth are still found; but it is conceived this animal is extinct on the island. There are no dromedaries nor camels; nor are horses, asses, or mules met with on Borneo (the former are seen at Sulo). None of the larger breed of the feline species are found here, as the lion, tiger, leopard; nor the bear, the wolf, the fox, nor even a jackal, or dog, that I ever saw. The ourang-outang, or the man of the woods, is the most singular animal found in these regions. The rivers swarm with alligators, and the woods with every variety of the monkey tribe. The names of other animals on Borneo are the bodok or rhinoceros, *pelando* or rabbit, *rusa* or stag, *kijang* or doe, *minjagon, babi utan* or wild hog, *tingileng, bintangan,* &c. There are buffaloes, goats, bullocks, hogs, beside the rat and mouse species; a dog I never saw on Borneo.

There are few snakes on the sea-coast, owing to the moisture; plenty, however, are found in the interior. The mosquito, the fly, the frog, and the noisy beetle, with other insects and vermin found in Malay countries, abound here.

The coasts and rivers abound with excellent and wholesome fish in the greatest variety, and of the most delicious flavours; but such is the miserable state of society, that few Malays have either the inclination or the inducement to venture beyond the mouths of their rivers in quest of them; and even there they are more indebted to the

410

industry of the Chinese with their fishing-stakes than to their own labour for the supply of their markets. The names of their fish are, the *kakab, klabaw, jilawat, lai-is, pattain, udang* or prawn, shrimp, *talang, sinanging, bawan, rowan, taylaon, duri, bleda, tingairy, alu-alu, pako, jumpul, pari* or skait, *boli ayam, tamban* or shad, *belut* or eel, *iyu* or shark, *lida* or sole, *batu batu, kabab batu, klaoi, krang* or cockle, *tiram* or oyster, *tipy* and *lapis* pearl oysters, *cupang* or muscle, all the varieties of the turtle, with several other sorts.

The ornithology of Borneo is somewhat limited. There are the *bayan, nuri, dara, pepit* or sparrow, *tukukur* or turtle-dove, *berkey, kandang, kiridi, gogaw* or crow, *seyrindit, layang* or swallow, *kalilawan.* The Chinese rear ducks; the tame fowl abounds; but the turkey, goose, and peafowl are seldom met with.

The principal gold mines on Borneo are in the vicinity of Sambas. There is a mountain called Guning Pandan, about eighty miles inland; from this branch out three rivers—one leads to Mompava, one to Batu Bulat near Tanjong Mora, and one to Landa; the whole intermediate area between the above rivers is of a firm yellow argillaceous schistus, or ferruginous quartz, interspersed with horn and vitreous ores, of a remarkable dark reddish colour, abounding with the richest veins of gold, and equal if not superior to any mine extant. There are only fifty parets or mines now wrought in the whole kingdom of Sukadana, thirty of which are in the Sambas district, each mine having at least three hundred men, Chinese, employed in them. Their pay, one with another, is four dollars *per mensem.*

The mines are rented from the *rajah* at the rate of fifty *bunkals* of gold per mine *per annum,* beside a capitation tax of three dollars per head on every Chinaman. There are thirty thousand Chinese in the Sambas districts, and they feel themselves strong enough to oppose or evade this tax; it hence becomes a perpetual contest between greedy extortion on the one side, and avaricious chicane on the other; there are beside about twelve thousand Malays and Dayers.

The Laurat gold mines are situated to the eastward of the town of Sambas, and are particularly rich and productive. The mines of Siminis are one day's journey from Sambas, up a small creek leading from Sambas River, below the town; and the mines are abundant. Salako is up a river fifteen miles south of the Sambas River; it lies nearly forty miles up, but communicates with Sambas by another river: here the metal is found more abundant than anywhere else; and twenty thousand Chinese are found in this district. Mantrado is three days' journey up the Mompava River; it is under an independent Malay prince. Some accounts make the population of this district great, near fifty thousand Dayers, Malays, and Chinese; but perhaps half the number may be nearer the truth; these are chiefly employed on the gold mines, and in producing food for the miners; these mines, however, do not produce that quantity which they might under Chinese management.

Mandore is about a day's journey from Pontiana, and belongs to the sultan; it is reckoned a very rich mine, though but recently wrought. There are as yet only twelve *parets* of about two hundred men each, but it is capable of extension. Likewise are found in this district some very rich specimens of copper ore; it has not as yet been wrought, gold being deemed a much more productive article. The *sultan* wishes, however, he had some boring utensils and an experienced miner, to enable him to decide whether it would be worth working under the peculiar circumstances above mentioned. Numbers of Chinese are settled in this district, and the population is annually increasing.

About three days' journey up the Pongole River lies the district of Songo, with a population of twenty-five thousand souls, Dayers, and a few Chinese, under a Malay and an independent prince. The population is chiefly employed on the rich mines of gold in the neighbourhood, which is particularly pure and abundant; but the mines are not wrought with the same industry as those under Chinese management. The Dutch thought it of so much consequence as to keep a force at Songo, and to place the present *rajah* on that *musnud*. About two days' journey farther up lies another gold district, called Santam, the inhabitants of which are principally Dayers. Beyond Santam, and higher up on the same river, lies the town of Sukadow, abounding in gold, the inhabitants of which are also Dayers.

Matan belongs to the *rajah* of that name: he had the title of Rajah of Sukadana, until driven out of the latter place by the Dutch, seventeen years ago. There are ten thousand Dayers in this district, and a few Chinese and Malays. The mines of gold are abundant, and capable of becoming highly productive, as well as the mines of iron and unwrought tin; but the *sultan* is much addicted to the use of opium, and hence neglects a valuable country, capable, under better management, of becoming the most valuable district on all Borneo.

About three days' journey from Pontiana lies the celebrated mountain of Landa, which, after Golconda, is the most valuable diamond mine in the world. There are at least thirty thousand people, principally Dayers, employed on the mines and agriculture; it belongs to a Malay prince, raised to that *musnud* twenty-five years ago by the Dutch, through the agency of the present Sultan of Pontiana: here also much gold is produced; and much more might be had under proper management.

There is a very valuable gold mine in the north of Borneo, at a place called Tampasuk, situated in the district ceded to the English by the Sultan of Sulo; but having become the principal pirate port on the coast, the working of the mines has been discontinued.

The whole produce of the gold mines of Sukadana is said to be annually about twenty *piculs*, or a million of dollars, at twenty-five dollars a *bunkal*; but no calculation of this sort can possibly be correct. Living, as the Chinese do, under the rapacity of despotic and ferocious freebooters, who are actuated by no one principle of honour, justice, or good faith, it is their interest to conceal the riches they amass, not only to preserve themselves from the clutches of these tyrants, but as the most compact substance to transport to their native shores, to which they repair with the fruits of their industry, by the annual junks that arrive at Pontiana, leaving the mines to new settlers: from two to three hundred leave Pontiana every year.

The standard of Slakow gold at Pontiana is affixed at twenty-three Spanish dollars the bunkal, of two dollars weight. The Songo and Laurat is twenty-five dollars the said *bunkal*.

Not having had an opportunity to inspect any of the gold mines personally, I know not if the ores readily melt of themselves, or whether they require the aid of any fluxes before they yield the metal; but I believe the principal attention of the miners is directed to the rich veins of pure native gold, and that no operation is performed beyond that of pulverizing, and simple washing; all the gold about Pontiana being in dust, though some I have met with in Borneo Proper was run into bars. About Landa, where the diamonds are found, the whole of the stratum is observed to be a clay of a red burnt appearance, nearly to the same degree as that of burnt bricks, which gives to the rivers hereabouts a peculiar tinge. Whether this has been formed by the action of subterraneous fires, or is the effect of volcanoes or earthquakes, I cannot decide; the latter are said to be frequently felt at Pontiana and at Sambas; and the former are said to exist in the central mountains of Borneo.

From the slovenly manner in which the diamonds are sought for by the Dayers, they seldom collect them of a size exceeding three or four carats weight each. When rough, the Landa diamond has a white

413

or yellow hue; but none are found of that inky and flinty tinge, so valuable in some of the Golconda diamonds. But that Landa does produce them of a very considerable size, the extensive and valuable specimens in Java, as well as the quantities annually sent to Batavia, will evince. The King of Matan is at this instant in possession of a diamond weighing 367 carats: the value of which, according to the old mode of calculation, would be (367 x 367 x 2 = 269,378*l*.)

The Sultan of Pontiana says, however, that a much larger price was offered for it by the Dutch government of Java. He refused, it is said, twenty-five *laks* of dollars, two sloops of rice, fifty pieces of cannon, and a hundred muskets. Several from twenty to thirty carats have been dug up. At Mompava there are said to be very rich copper mines; but from want of population, a vigorous government, and scientific mineralogists, little is to be hoped from them at the present day. At Pulo Bongorong, near Borneo Proper, there is plenty of loadstone found.

About one degree north of Sambas there is a country called Sarawak, belonging to the Rajah of Borneo Proper; there is a vast district abounding in tin, in veins as rich and as plentiful as those wrought on Banca: but they have been neglected for a series of years; they were partially wrought before those of the latter were discovered, in the beginning of the last century. The tyranny of that government, the want of hands, and the contiguity of rich and valuable gold-mines, have together caused their utter neglect; and there is little probability of more favourable results, except under a change of government, and a happier order of things.

In the Matan districts there is an extensive and most valuable iron-mine, producing pure metal without any admixture of ore: it is fully equal in quality to the best Swedish iron. They run it into shot, and much of it is exported; but the gold-mines in its vicinity, and the want of a proper government, are obstacles to its further productiveness and utility. At Maday, on the northeast coast of Borneo, in the province of Mangidara, there is a very rich mine of gold. Pasir and Coti, in the Straits of Macassar, produce considerable quantities of gold; and gold and diamonds are brought down by the river to Benjarmasing. I have, however, no accurate information on the subject, and can simply note the general fact.

There are several fine specimens of crystal found at Kimanis and Sulo; they call them water diamonds. To give full effect to the mines in the kingdom of Sukadana, says the Sultan of Pontiana, and to raise the excess of food required for the additional hands, would together give employment to at least a million of Chinese. Under the British flag, he thinks thousands of new settlers will find their way in the annual junks.

All that extensive range, from Cape Unsing, passing by the Tawi Tawi islands and Sulo, as far as Baselan, is one vast continued bed of pearl-oysters, principally of the Behoren or mother-of-pearl-shell species; these are called by the natives *tipi*. There is likewise an extensive bed of the Ceylon oyster, called by the Malays *kapis*; the principal banks of the latter are found in Maludu Bay. The Sulo pearls have, from time immemorial, been the most celebrated, and praised as the most valuable of any in the known world. Pigofetta, the companion of Magalhaens, mentions having seen in 1520 two Sulo pearls in the possession of the Rajah of Borneo as large as pullet eggs.

Very large ones, from one to two hundred *chaw* weight, are at all times to be purchased at Sulo; and there are altogether sold here to the China junks, the Spaniards, &c. more than two *laks* of dollars worth annually. The quantity of mother-of-pearl-shell, *communibus annis*, sold there is two thousand *piculs*, at six dollars a *picul*. The fishery is partly carried on by the Malays, and partly by the Chinese; the large pearls they endeavour to conceal as much as possible, from a law that all pearls above a certain size of right belong to the *sultan*.

"The small narrow guts," says Dalrymple in his account of the Sulo seas, "about Tawi Tawi, are the most rich and valuable fishery in the world."

I have had an opportunity of inspecting the banks about Manar and Tutacoryn, as well as all the banks in the Sulo seas; but the former have not banks near as extensive, equalling in the quantity of oysters, in productiveness, size, or richness, the Sulo pearl, nor are they to be compared in any way to the Sulo beds. Still the Ceylon fishery has netted the British Government from one to two *laks* of *pagodas* for permitting it to be fished fourteen days annually. As this portion of Borneo belongs to the English, a much greater revenue might be drawn from these vast sources of wealth, under proper management.

As there are no people of sufficient opulence to contract for so vast a fishery, the Company might undertake it themselves; three or four gun-boats would be necessary to protect the fishermen; and a small fort should be erected at Tambisan or Tawi Tawi. But it is necessary to observe, the Sulo people do not practice diving at all, as is the case at Beharen and Ceylon, but only comprehend the slow method of dredging for the *tipy* with a thing like the fluke of a wooden anchor.

It would be a desirable thing, in the event of prosecuting this valuable fishery as a national concern, to obtain forty or fifty Arab divers from Beharen, and perhaps an equal number of Chulias from Nagore and Negapatam, from the number employed annually on the Ceylon fishery.

These men would teach the Malay the superiority of diving, which can, in fourteen days' fishing, bring into government a revenue of two *laks* of *pagodas*, pay the expenses of the fishery, and enrich all parties concerned; while the Malayan operose plan of dredging perhaps affords but a precarious subsistence. But had they divers, from the extent of the banks, instead of fourteen days in the year, they might, one after another, be fished the whole year round, and never be exhausted. The Chinese fishermen, though laborious, possess no enterprise, and can never be prevailed on to dive, from apprehension of the sharks. The Caffris from New Guinea and the Arroes would be superior to them.

The Sultan of Sulo, in 1810, proposed to me to bring over one hundred Chulia divers from Negapatam on our joint expense and profit: and the divers agreed to go over on receiving each twenty-five *rupees* advance, their victuals being found, and one-fourth of the produce of oysters allowed them, as at Ceylon. Circumstances, however, occurred to prevent an undertaking which I think must have turned out highly lucrative. They dredge the banks all the year round. The water on the Tahow, Maludu, and Tawi Tawi banks, is from seven to ten fathoms deep; in other places they fish in fifteen fathoms water.

The Malays of Borneo understand the art of cutting, polishing, and setting their diamonds. Gold and silver filigree works they excel in; gunpowder is manufactured at Pontiana; brass cannon is cast at Borneo Proper; iron-shot is run from their mine. They can manufacture and repair *krises*, and clean their arms. Their carpentry extends to the building and repairing of prows, and the erecting of a hut. Their industry is further exerted in collecting birds-nests and wax; in cutting rattan and felling timber; in the pearl and *tripan* fisheries; or as mariners in commercial or piratical pursuits. The tillage of the ground and the edible fisheries are often left to the more indefatigable industry of the Chinese. For the exercise of every other useful occupation also, the mechanical and scientific arts, and the labour of the mines, these indolent savages are indebted solely to the superior industry and civilization of the Chinamen.

The amusements of the Malays in other parts are unpractised on the shores of Borneo: the only ones I ever saw were flying the kite, swimming, and the songs of their women; this latter is confined to the *rajahs*.

Wherever a water-communication on Borneo presents, the indolence of the Malay will not permit him to think of the construction of a road. In the interior, however, there are pathways in all directions; about Mompava, where the river is narrow and shallow, they have constructed several roads. Being a people much occupied in maritime pursuits, they prefer, like the amphibious Dutch, travelling by rivers, or the innumerable cuts, canals, and creeks, which everywhere intersect the country: beside, their *prows* afford more protection from surprise, and they conceive their town as safer by being surrounded by a jungle and situated in a swamp; nor have they any conception beyond water-carriage.

Their laws neither depend upon the Koran nor any written code, human or divine, beyond the whim and caprice of the chief (assassin) and his gang of desperadoes. The Sultan of Pontiana has, however, established the following regulations:

Punishments for murder:—Life for life, except when the parties can commute the same by fine.

A proclamation is publicly affixed announcing the law, that if any person be found adulterating gold-dust, or uttering it, so depreciated, with a view to defraud, the perpetrator shall lose his right arm, and the adulterated gold shall be confiscated.

For theft:—Five dollars per head is given by the *sultan* to any one bringing in the head of a thief: if brought in alive, he is suspended by the heels and flogged as far as nature can bear short of death, and the punishment repeated *ad libitum*.

Prisoners taken from an enemy, whether found in arms or not, are made slaves of, or suffer death, at the option of the captor.

The Malay government is said to exhibit the feudal system in its most perfect form. The chief, or *rajah*, issues his orders to the *Pangerans*, or princes of the blood; to the *datus*, or nobles of royal descent; or to the Orang Kayas, or wealthy *vassals*. All these obey and follow him to war, free of expense, when the king is sufficiently powerful to enforce it; but whenever the *vassal* feels himself strong enough to throw off the yoke, and to assert his independence, he sets up for himself. These *vassals* exact the same obedience from their slaves or villains, who pay the like deference only so long as they are compelled to observe and obey them. The property acquired by a slave he is often allowed to enjoy unmolested during his lifetime; but at his death, his master administers to the estate as heir, executor, and sole legatee.

In fact, it is a government that inspires on all sides one universal distrust—that rules by precedents of oppression without a view to protection. The chiefs dread the power of their *vassals*, who, in return, apprehend everything from the rapacity of the governing power; while the bulk of the people, having no property to lose, are still compelled to appear abroad armed to defend their very persons from the outrage and violence of the next assassin they meet.

Where governments not only tolerate murder, rapine, thefts, piracies, conflagrations, with every outrage violating the happiness and safety of society, but are the first to set the example and to consecrate the atrocity—where the people are taught no one principle of morality or religion—where the arts and sciences are wholly unknown or despised—where the amusements and sociabilities of human life are totally disregarded—where the bounties and comforts of nature are rather dispensed with than enjoyed, and where the absolute necessaries to existence and the decorations of life are more scanty and wretched than yet discovered among the rudest set of barbarians extant; if, from the experience of the past, expectations of the future are to be formed, we may safely infer that every vestige of Malay government and dominion will be ingulfed in the vortex of self and mutual destruction. Such a system of society has in itself the seeds of dissolution, and is rapidly verging to an inherent decay and general oblivion, which it will doubtless meet, unless some beneficent power arrest its baneful impetus, and direct its feverish energies through channels calculated to promote the happiness and to consolidate the welfare of the inhabitants of these scattered regions.

Should so fortunate an occurrence ever fall to the lot of Borneo—should a strong and a wise government ever be established on her shores—a government that will religiously respect property and secure to industry the fruits of her labour—that will, by a wise system of laws, protect the peaceable and punish the violator of the laws of a well-organized society—that will direct their industry to useful purposes, and check their propensities to violence and plunder—such a government, in a short series of years, would behold, as if by magic, a paradise burst from her wilds, see cultivation smile upon her jungles, and hail a vast and increasing population, blessing the hand that awoke them to life, to happiness, and to prosperity. That so felicitous a change is not the mere reverie of a glowing imagination, or the sheer effusion of benevolence alone, is easily demonstrable.

Whoever has seen the Egyptian fertility of the soil, from the moistness of the climate, the numberless rivers meandering around and intersecting the country in all directions, with the mild temperature of the climate, from similar causes—whoever considers the vast extent and inexhaustible wealth of her innumerable mines of pure native gold, her block-tin, her copper, her iron, her diamonds, &c., her various valuable fisheries of pearl and *tripan*—whoever views her ports, her harbours, and her productive shores, at the threshold of the overteeming population of China, and at the same moment recollects that the country abounds in various valuable products in the highest possible estimation, and of increasing demand in the empire of China, must easily conceive what a tempting field and rich harvest this land of promise holds out to their industry and cupidity under such a system of laws and government as we have deemed a *sine qua non*.

If, under the present codes of tyranny, oppression, and general ferocity, where nothing is permanent but violence and desolation—if, under such a system of barbarism, a hundred thousand Chinese (which is the fact) have found inducements sufficiently strong to settle on her shores, what might we not hope and expect from the overburdened population of that vast empire under a happier order of things? The astonishing number of Chinese settled within a few years at Pulo Pinang, on a contracted soil, possessing no peculiar advantages but from a free trade and equitable laws impartially administered, is both a fact and an illustration; and what might not Borneo hope for from a happier soil, greater inducements, and other physical advantages? Java, under the despotism of the Dutch, with the character of a sickly climate, and the remembrance of the cruel massacre of sixty thousand innocent Chinese, could still boast a hundred thousand of these people at the period it fell to the British arms; and withal, let it be remembered that these shores were once blessed with the industry of these people to a far greater extent under a happier period of her history.

Whatever, indeed, might prove the work of ages in various other parts of the globe would, under the present circumstances of the Chinese Empire, be instantaneous on these shores; and their habits of industry and civilization, when once rooted to the soil, would soon spread their genial influence to the extensive population of the interior, unite them in the bonds of social life, cement them in the general prosperity, and render these extensive shores a valuable appendage and an increasing resource to the wealth and power that brought about so happy a revolution in their affairs.

For a considerable series of years past, the piratical ports of Borneo, &c., have been in the habit of committing depredations upon the commerce of British India, in the capture of her ships, the insulting of her flag, the offering of outrageous violence to the persons and lives of her mariners, merchants, &c., and this, too, with the most perfect impunity; no retribution having been exacted, no reprisals made, no remonstrance presented, and, in fact, no notice taken of their atrocious depredations. Hence these *desperadoes*, from inference and experience of the past, have been led to conclude, that whatever was practicable would be tolerated; that wherever they had the means or opportunity of overpowering, it was their duty, as it was to their advantage, to seize it to their own use, without any other apprehensions of the consequences than what might arise in the attempt.

Under this discouraging aspect of affairs, there was but little more left to the commercial community of India than either to abandon the valuable commerce of Borneo wholly; or, if allured to it by a prospect of gain, to proceed in armed vessels at an increased expense and high insurance, so as to cover the extraordinary risks. These enhanced prices either operated as a prohibition to the trade, or circumscribed it so much, that an occasional capture excited no surprise, and was frigidly dismissed as a matter of course.

But, from the prodigious accession of territorial possession, including the whole of the vast Dutch empire in the East, the communications between these and British India have necessarily increased a thousand fold; consequently, the recent alarming depredations upon our commerce, the serious obstacles to a safe communication, almost tantamount to a blockade of our Eastern ports by these pirates, imperiously call upon the British Government to adopt the most energetic means and decisive measures to crush their power and annihilate their resources, either by extirpating them wholly, or placing them and their possessions under such future control and checks, as shall prevent the possibility of a revival of a power capable of recurring to enormities that have so long outraged and disgraced the British flag in the Eastern seas.

The idea of extirpating whole hordes of piratical states, were it possible, must, from its cruelty, be incompatible with the liberal principles and humane policy of a British government. The simple burning down of a Malay town can prove no serious impediment to future piratical enterprises: constructed, as they are, of bamboos, mats, and *atap* leaves, a town is almost rebuilt in the same period of time as it takes to destroy it. The Dutch, who had centuries of dear-bought experience, knew there was no other mode of prevention and radical cure than building small redoubts at the principal towns, and keeping up an adequate force to check piratical enterprises, and to turn their restless minds to exertions of industry; satisfied if, with the attainment of these objects, they covered the expenses of the establishment. This is the true history of the innumerable little forts on Celebes, Borneo, Timor, and all the Eastern isles.

The principal piratical ports that still exist, beside those of Lingin, Rhio, and Billiton, are—1st, *Pangeran* Annam, at Sambas; 2nd, Port Borneo Proper, and four hundred prows at Tampasuk, both under the Rajah of Borneo Proper; 3rd, the Pasir pirates; 4th, the Sulo pirates; 5th, the Illano, or pirates on the Isle of Magindano.

I shall, from memory, cite such few of their depredations as I recollect.

In 1774, says Forrest, the British were expelled from their infant settlement of Balambangan by an insurrection of the Sulos, who, finding the garrison weak and sickly, unprepared and off their guard, murdered and plundered them, and set fire to their settlement:—this was in return for having released their *sultan* from prison, and re-established him on the *musnud* of his ancestors. In 1800, Captain Pavin and a boat's crew were cruelly murdered in the palace of the Sultan of Sulo while the commander was drinking a cup of chocolate: they fired upon the ship Ruby, but did not succeed in capturing her. In 1810, they plundered the wreck of the ship *Harrier* of a valuable cargo: several of her crew are still in slavery at Bagayan Sulo.

In 1788, the ship May of Calcutta, 450 tons burden, Captain Dixon, was cut off at Borneo Proper: they were invited up to the town with the ship, and while at dinner, the *sultan* and his people fell upon them, and murdered Captain Dixon, three officers, and ten Europeans; the lascars were retained in slavery, the valuable cargo plundered, and the ship burnt. In 1803 the ship *Susanna* of Calcutta, Captain Drysdale, was cut off near Pontiana by the Sambas and Borneo pirates; the Europeans were all massacred, and the vessel taken. In 1769, Captain Sadler, with his boat's crew, was murdered by the Sambas pirates off Mompava, having a prodigious quantity of gold-dust: they did not succeed in cutting off the ship.

In 1806, Mr. Hopkins and crew, of the *Commerce*, were murdered by the pirates of Borneo Proper; the ship was plundered by them and the Sambas pirates. In 1810, Captain Ross was cut off. In 1811, Captain Graves was cut off by the Pasir pirates with a rich cargo. In 1812, the enormities of Pangeran Annam have out-heroded Herod: these are too recent to require recapitulation. Independent of his depredations on the *Coromandel*, a Portuguese ship, &c., nine Europeans of the *Hecate* have been seized and made slaves; two have been since murdered; two have escaped; and five are hamstrung and otherwise maimed. Mrs. Ross and her son are still in slavery there.

The Tampasuk pirates, belonging to the Rajah of Borneo Proper, aiding and abetting Pangeran Annam against the English, are Datu Akop, Datu Aragut, and Datu Jumbarang, with ten large men-of-war prows: there is also there the Rajah Endut, a Siak chief.

Matan is under an independent *rajah*, who was formerly styled Sultan of Sukadana; but about seventeen years ago the Dutch burnt down his city. At length, by some pecuniary aid received from the late Sultan of Pontiana, he was enabled to re-establish his affairs as Rajah of Matan; and, in consideration of this aid, entered into a treaty of alliance, which stipulated, that on his daughter's marriage with the grandson of the late, and son of the present. Sultan of Pontiana, he would cede his kingdom and large diamond as a marriage-portion: the parties yet remain single. Under the head mineralogy we have pointed out how valuable a country this might become under better management. Iron, gold, tin, and diamonds abound here; also much wax, pepper, rattans, *garu*, and about two *piculs* of the finest birds-nests, which sell at twenty-eight dollars the *catty* at Pontiana. Most of the trade finds its way to Pontiana, Benjar, or Java, in prows. The population is about ten thousand Dayers, &c.

Sukadana, once the most celebrated city on Borneo, as the name implies, a terrestrial paradise, the capital of a kingdom and a great mart of trade, since burnt down and destroyed by the Dutch, exhibits nothing but ruins. There still remain numberless delicious fruit-trees, and a country still susceptible of general cultivation, being yet clear of jungle and morass. It is utterly abandoned: that it has not been rebuilt is owing to the Rajah of Pontiana, at whose suggestion it was destroyed, and whose interest it was to keep it down, having himself risen upon its ashes.

There are no towns of any importance between Matan and Pontiana. The rise of this dynasty of sultans has been noted in another place; it is, however, almost the only power that has been expressly raised, supported, and that still exists, by commerce. It is situated in latitude

4° north of the equator. The river has two mouths to it; the northern mouth is the deepest, the most direct, and of the greatest breadth; there are in this branch only two reaches up to the town. The city is no more than fifteen miles from the mouth of the rivers; its site is on the junction of the Matan and Landa Rivers. About two-thirds of the way up it is fortified; first, with a battery on piles in the centre of the stream, mounting five guns; on the left bank is another with wooden pales, mounting likewise five guns; on the opposite bank is a third, similar to the foregoing, with a like number of cannon; and, lastly, on the same bank is their grand battery, constructed of stone, mounting five eighteen-pounders, at the *batu*, or rock. Here the mausoleum of the royal family is erected, containing the tomb of the late *sultan*. The whole of this side of the river exhibits the marks of infant cultivation. The jungle has been, in part, cleared away, and here and there a solitary hut greets the eye. The *sultan's* palace has a battery of eleven guns of all sizes; none of these are calculated to make any serious resistance. So sensible is the *sultan* of this that he has commenced staking round with piles a low, swampy island, just detached from the palace. On this stands the grand *mosk*. He proposes throwing mud and stones within the ranges of piles, and planting upon them the heaviest-calibered cannon: it is a commanding site, and capable of being rendered formidable. There are no roads about Pontiana; the town is situated in the midst of a swamp, so low that the tide at high water overflows the lower parts of the houses, and this, with the addition of a country overrun with impenetrable jungle, renders it extremely unhealthy, and a most disagreeable residence.

The *campo* China contains about two thousand souls, and lies on the left bank of the Matan River, abreast of the palace; the *campo* Buguese, on the right bank of the Landa; and the *campo* Malayu adjoins the palace. The whole population is about seven thousand souls: no Dayers are found hereabout. The whole of the districts under Pontiana produce about three hundred *coyans* of rice, the average selling price of which is from fifty-five to seventy Spanish dollars the *coyan*. The king's revenue is forty thousand dollars *per annum*. The Chinese plead poverty, but some of the Buguese are pointed out as wealthy. The quantity of gold that finds its way to Pontiana is annually from three to four *piculs*. The imports there consist of opium, iron, steel, salt, rice, hardware, cutlery, blue and white *gurras, salampories,* Java cloths, gunpowder, beside China produce of all possible descriptions. They make their returns in gold, diamonds, birds-nests, wax, rattans, *garu*, ebony, *agar-*

*agar*, beside pepper, sago, camphor, *cassia*, *tripan*, &c. brought here by the prows: five Chinese *junks* annually visit Pontiana, bringing down produce amounting to about fifty thousand dollars. The depredations of the Pangeran Annam prevent an extension of this most useful of all trades to this country. One or two Siamese *junks* arrive annually. The Tringanu, Timbilan, Karimata, and Borneo Proper *prows* trade here; and before Java fell to the British arms, the Buguese from the eastward traded here to a considerable amount.

The stone walls built by the Dutch still encompass the palace. The piles on which their factory stood are yet discernible, but the buildings have been pulled down. Should the English hoist their flag here, a new factory must be erected; the most eligible situation for which would be where the *mosk* now stands, or the *mosk* itself might be converted into one, and another rebuilt elsewhere; but to this the *sultan* has insuperable objections. In an English fort, to think to have a *mosk* open to the ingress of a large body of Malays at all times is wholly incompatible with a certain reserve and security required from it.

Beside, as the island is small, and soldiers at times inconsiderate, they might profane or defile its holy precincts, and thus lay the foundation of perpetual disputes, or even a serious rupture. The fort and factory, if built at all at Pontiana, must hence be fixed in some detached place. The *sultan* is building a new palace and covering it with tiles; a novelty in this quarter. There is but a scanty supply of fowls and buffaloes, and the necessaries of life are scarce and dear. It is altogether the most uncouth and dreary spot under the sun, though the *sultan* prefers it to Sambas and Mompava.

Their naval force consists of two small ships, two brigs, fifty prows large and small, and about one thousand men. There is water on the bar to admit vessels drawing nine feet water. The roadstead, with seven fathoms water on it, lies seven miles from the river's mouth. Care must be taken not to mistake the Pongole River seen from the offing, and which lies ten miles farther southward. The only stock procurable here were hogs at ten dollars the *picul*, and water shipped off in China tank-boats at four and a half dollars the ton.

The next port is Mompava, about sixteen miles to the northward of Pontiana, and the second port belonging to the *sultan*. The river is shallow, narrow, extremely serpentine, and constantly running down with great rapidity. The country around is a paradise in comparison with Pontiana. It is upon an elevated site, and, wherever the eye reaches, it is clear of jungle, and of fine rich mould, susceptible of the highest culture. There is a walk up to the town about eight miles from the mouth of the river; here the fishing-stakes nearly extend across the river, beside two miserable forts, mounting each five or six pounders, to defend the river. The population is seven thousand men, Malays, Buguese, and Dayers, and about two thousand Chinese.

Formerly the territory of Mompava extended as far as 1° north latitude. This territory belonged to a chief or *rajah*, reduced by the Dutch twenty-five years ago, shortly after they settled at Pontiana; the territory thus conquered was delegated in trust to the Rajah of Pontiana. The Sambas *rajah* has forcibly taken possession of a part of it. Sultan Kassim, of Pontiana, governed this district during his father's lifetime. On his accession to the *musnud*, five years ago, he placed a half-brother there, a stupid fellow, about twenty-five years of age. This man, about eight months ago, was trying to establish his independence, which he found he could not maintain.

It has the same trade as Pontiana, but the regulations of the *sultan* do not admit of any vessel's touching here for that purpose. The palace is extensive, paled round with a sort of a fortification. The *campo* China, in October last, was in part burnt down by the people of Sambas, to the number of four hundred houses. There is a variety of roads hereabout; one leading to Sambas, one to Landa, one to Mintrada, &c. Groves of cocoanut-trees mark the site of ancient villages, since demolished; and indicate that it once enjoyed a superiority and pre-eminence, of which it has been despoiled. In point of susceptibility of cultivation, it is a full half century beforehand with Pontiana; it is capable of great improvement, and much grain might be raised with very little trouble.

There is a considerable mud-flat at the mouth of the Sambas River, extending four or five miles out, but no regular bar. Vessels drawing thirteen feet may get in at high water springs; nine feet is the least water, and there is thirteen at the flood. In the offing there is a rise and fall of seven feet. At the entrance of the river neither shore must be too closely hugged, having ledges of rocks near them. Twelve miles above the bar the river branches into two parts; the broad or northern branch is called the Borneo River, having its source in Kiney Baulu; the other, leading to the town of Sambas, is named the Landa River, having its source in the diamond mines; where these two unite below there was formerly a fort.

The Landa River is extremely serpentine, deep to the very bushes on both sides, and quite clear of danger up to the town, except near

Siminis Creek, about ten miles below the fort; here a reef of rocks runs across the stream, and as the fair way over them is somewhat intricate, the channel ought to be buoyed before attempted to be passed. The Barracouta, drawing thirteen feet, just scraped them at high water.

About five or six leagues up the Landa branch, and about thirteen from the sea, stands the town and palace of Sambas, on the confluence of the Landa and Salako Rivers. The fort on the right bank of the Landa is about a league below the town, built of two rows of large piles, the interstices being filled up with mud and stones, apparently mounting five guns, eighteens and twelves in the lower tier, and an equal number of smaller calibre on the ascend or more elevated range. A boom or dam of fishing-stakes was constructed across the river one-eighth of a mile below the fort, a large armed *prow* was moored in the centre of the river, mounting two long twelves, and a masked battery opposite to the right, the number of guns unknown. The reach which these forts command is a mile and a half. The land makes an elbow where these forts are, which obliged the Barracouta to haul athwart the river, to get her broadside to bear.

The whole of this Landa River is very narrow, but near the forts not one-third additional to her length. Both sides of this river toward the fort appear tolerably clear from the mast-head, interspersed with pleasant hills inhabited by the Chinese. The tides are pretty regular, six hours and six hours, running a knot and a half per hour. This river is too serpentine and narrow to admit sailing up; sweeps, towing, or tiding it up are the only modes that can be resorted to. The great branch of Borneo River, before mentioned, when up it twenty miles, divides into two; the branch running north being called Tampasan River, the other still retaining the name of Borneo. The Tampasan branch leads to old Sambas; it is from hence they get their supplies of rice and provisions, by the two cuts above the town of Sambas, which reunites the Landa and Borneo streams.

There are roads from the great branch leading to the town, fort, and palace. Since the Dutch abandoned Sambas, three *sultans* have reigned on this *musnud* (within fifty years, or thereabout). There are four *pangerans*, Annam being the most daring of the whole. His naval force consists of the Portuguese ship of 400 tons, one brig, and eight or ten large fighting prows, beside his allies from Borneo Proper, with ten large prows. The population amounts to twelve thousand Dayers and Malays, and thirty thousand Chinese.

Under the head mineralogy we have given a detailed account of the principal sources of its industry. Sambas produces, beside gold, ten *piculs* of birds-nests annually (of an inferior quality), much ebony, rattans, wax, &c. The trade here is much the same as at Pontiana, and susceptible of a tenfold increase: it is every way superior to the latter for the capital of a large mart.

The country is better cleared, and hence susceptible of more easy cultivation; the land more elevated and less swampy, consequently healthier; the river deeper and farther navigable; the population more dense, and, the land being clear of jungle, more capable of being increased. Beside, it is the vicinage of the most considerable gold-mines on all Borneo. The Sultan of Pontiana would make it his capital if desired; his apprehensions of the power of the Sambas princes lead him to give the preference to Pontiana.

The town of Calaca, belonging to the Rajah of Borneo Proper, lies north of Tanjong Datu; it is the principal port of trade south of the capital, and the mart of the Sedang country. Here much grain is produced, one hundred *piculs* of black birds-nests, two hundred *piculs* of wax, some gold, pepper, camphor, &c., but the tin-mines, before mentioned, are utterly neglected. There are several other towns upon each of the rivers along this coast; the principal ones are Salat, Bacalo, Pasir, and Baram. They produce nearly the same articles as the above, which are, however, sent on to the capital as fast as collected.

It is here necessary to observe, that all the rocks and shoals laid down on this coast do not exist at all; such as Volcano Island, the By-hors, Krenpel, the whole Slykenburgh, five Comadas, &c. Having beat up this coast twice, and carefully surveyed the whole, I can declare a finer and clearer coast does not anywhere exist. The old chart, published by A. Dalrymple, is much more correct than the recent ones. The numbers of immense drifts and floating isles hereabout must have given birth to all these imaginary dangers.

The town of Borneo Proper, the capital of the kingdom of the same name, lies in latitude 5° 7' north; it is situated fifteen miles up one of the finest rivers in the world, with three fathoms low water on the bar, and a rise and fall of fifteen feet. A correct plan of the river and town is published by Mr. Dalrymple. Here are mud docks for vessels of 500 or 600 tons. The town consists of about three thousand houses, built on stakes, in the middle of the river, with a population altogether of fifteen thousand souls, Chinese, Malays, Moruts, &c.

The palace is slightly fortified; but the Rajah of Pontiana says, the Rajah of Borneo Proper is preparing the means of defence, appre-

427

hending the resentment of the English in vindicating the rights of their flag, so frequently insulted by them with impunity; however, as there is sufficient water for a line-of-battle ship to the city, nothing need be apprehended from them. The remains of a stone fort up the river are still seen, but the one on Pulo Laboan is destroyed. Both banks of the river are planted with pepper, which formerly produced sixty thousand *piculs* annually; these are now running to decay from want of commerce.

The Chinese *junks*, for years past, have ceased touching here, from the numberless piratical depredations committed upon them; and the Portuguese from Macao have attempted to renew the trade from time to time, but at length, in 1808, their agent withdrew to Macao, a large ship having been cut off and the crew murdered the year preceding. They now have no other resource but piracy; and the produce, such as it is, finds its way in prows to Tringan, Sambas, Pontiana, Lingin, and Malacca. Very large quantities of the finest camphor in the world are procurable here; it comes down from the Morut country, by the great river; a great deal of wax, some gold, much birds-nests of an inferior quality, any quantity of sago, cassia, clove-bark, pepper, betel-nut, rattans, camphor-oil, &c., *tripan*, tortoise-shell, &c.

The hills hereabout are clear of jungle, and wear a beautiful appearance, and, without the aid of history, bear evident marks of a more extensive population and culture. There are plenty of black cattle, buffaloes, goats, fruits and vegetables of all kinds, abundance and variety of fish, turtle, &c. The articles best suited for this market are coarse China, white *cangyans*, brass plates, China crockery, brass wire, tea, sugar-candy, coarse China silks and satins, blue and white coarse *guras* and *salampories*, coarse *ventipallam* handkerchiefs, *arcot* chintzes, iron and steel, *quallies*, cooking utensils, and other articles suited to a Malay market—all coarse; no opium. The Borneo *catty* is two and a half lbs.

The English have been very desirous of a port in the China Seas for ages past, but have generally appeared to stumble on the most unhealthy and ill-adapted places possible, such as Balambangan, Pulo Condore, &c.; and even the principal object of Lord Macartney's embassy was the obtaining of a cession of this nature. But if a capital harbour, a navigable and majestic river, a productive country, a healthy site, population ready formed, and a commerce all sufficient to pay the expenses of an establishment (within one hundred miles of Balambangan) is required, the East India Company ought to have pitched upon Borneo Proper. It was once a most flourishing country, and a very short period under British auspices would render it the first mart in the East for China-Malayan commerce. There are large, populous towns of Moruts, and Orang Idan, who abhor the Malays, but who would be soon reconciled to a milder and less traitorous government.

Kimanis lies in latitude 5° 8' north; this is the first port on this coast ceded to the English by the Sultan of Sulo. The town lies ten miles up the river, at the foot of some of the most beautiful hills I ever saw, and is inhabited by thirty-five thousand Orang Idan. The river is small, and almost choked up at the mouth. This province has the following seaports in it, *viz.*, Kimanis, Benome, Papal, and Pangalat, each governed by Orang Kayas, which still continue to send their produce to Borneo Proper, consisting of ten *piculs* of birds-nests annually, two hundred *piculs* of wax, two *piculs* of camphor, and *cassia*, sago, betel-nut, and pepper, as much as required; *tripan*, camphor-oil, and rice; with fruit, fish, and provisions, of sorts which are cheap and plentiful. The articles mentioned as fit for Borneo answer here, only their produce is had about fifty per cent cheaper.

The province of Kiney Baulu has the following seaports:—Putatan, Mangatal, Innanam, Labatuan, Mangabong, Tawaran, Sulaman, Ambung, Abai, Tampasuk, and Padasan. The whole of this province is tremendously high. The stupendous mountain of Kiney is about fifteen miles from Tampasuk, which at present is the most considerable pirate-port in the Malay seas, and belongs to the Rajah of Borneo Proper. The pirates frequenting this place have committed such depredations hereabout as to have induced the English to call the north of Borneo Pirates' Point. These desperate *banditti* originally resided at Tawaran, but were compelled to leave it from the resentment of whole tribes of Orang Idan.

The whole of this province is very fertile; it is the source of all the great rivers on the island, and is more populous with the aborigines of the country than perhaps the rest of the island put together. The gold mines of Tampasuk have been mentioned; there are also mines of rock crystal. Tawaran and several other places abound in goats and cattle. Abai has a small harbour, and the whole of this coast is accurately laid down by Lieutenant James Burton, in the sloop *Endeavour*. There are produced in this province much wax, tortoise-shell, very fine camphor, sago, rattans, and a red birds-nest (which comes from Mantanane isle to Pandasan). They send their produce to Borneo Proper. The pirates are commanded by *datus* from Borneo Proper. The lake in the vicinity of Kiney Baulu is said to be delightful; it is many miles in circumference, well cultivated, populous, and productive. It is said to be very cold, from the extreme elevation, and the inhabitants are almost as fair as Europeans. There is a valuable coral-tree somewhere hereabout.

The Bay of Maludu, on the north of Borneo, is thirty miles in length, and from four to six in breadth, with numberless rivers flowing into it. There is no danger on the right-hand shore going up, but what is seen; on the larboard shore considerable coral-reefs are met with. Laurie and Whittle's chart of it is tolerably correct. The principal towns are, Sungy Bassar, nearly at the head of the bay, and Bankaka, on the left; the former, under Sheriff Mahomed, sends its produce to Sulo; the latter, under Orang Kayas, trades with Borneo Proper. The British, when last at Balambangan, threw up a small redoubt on the Bankaka side, with a view to supplies of rice and provisions; and this part is tranquil and a good roadstead, being sheltered from the swell brought in by the sea-breeze.

The rich and valuable fishery of *copis* or Ceylon oyster in this bay has been mentioned; it might be rendered of considerable value. The whole of the rivers for miles up abound in rattans; Mr. A. Dalrymple thinks four thousand tons might be easily cut down every year without exhausting it, and sent by *junks* to China. There are forests of beautiful pines of stately growth, well calculated for the largest masts, and in high esteem at China. There is no quarter of the world which abounds more in that species of the sea-turtle (called by the Malays *pakayan*) which yields the shell; any quantity may be had on all the shores and isles of this bay.

The interior abounds in camphor, which can be had in any quantities; so vastly abundant is it, and so little does the Orang Idan know of the extreme value of this commodity, that a bamboo of camphor may be procured in exchange for a bamboo of salt. The petty towns are Sandeck, Bowengun, Patasan, Pone, and Milawi. It produces in one year two hundred *piculs* of wax, fifty *piculs* of tortoise-shell, ten *piculs* of best camphor, and as much inferior; ten *piculs* of birds-nests, at ten dollars the *catty*; first camphor, twenty-five; rattans, one dollar per *picul*; tortoise-shell, one dollar the *catty*; wax, twenty the *picul*. Articles required are the same as at Borneo Proper. Rice, provisions, fish, and fruits are abundant and cheap; the sugar-cane also.

The province of Paytan is the principal district for camphor of any in the world. Whole forests for miles everywhere meet the eye, and the produce from them is the finest that can be conceived, large and transparent as Chin-chew sugar-candy. The principal towns are Pitan, Kinarubatan, Kulepan, and the famous town of Sugut. The coast is so full of coral-reefs, and has been so very indifferently surveyed, that it is only frequented by prows; there is a road from Sugut to Bankaka in Maludu Bay. Much wax, *tripan*, sago, &c., is produced here.

Labuk has the towns of Camburcan, Labuk, and Songsohi; its produce is somewhat similar to that of Paytan, with the addition of clove-bark and birds-nests.

Sandakan. This celebrated harbour has been already mentioned as one of the finest in the world. The towns within it are Towsam, Duyom, Lu, Bokean, Dom or Doung, Seagally-hood and Tong luly luku; all these are governed by Datus from Sulo, who have expressly settled here to collect the prodigious quantities of birds-nests abounding in this district. They are procured here at ten dollars the catty; and sent to Sulo, with *tripan*, wax, &c. The Sulos are very jealous of any ships going in here, and will leave no attempt untried in cutting off a vessel going in, although an English port.

In the province of Mangidora lies the great River Kinnabatingan, which is navigable a vast way up, with several towns of Orang Idan on its shores. The other towns are Salasany, Supabuscul, Tambesan, which forms also an elegant harbour, Laboan or Saboan, Tuncu, Salurong, Giong, and Maday, which has a gold-mine, before mentioned. The whole of this province, it is said, will produce above one hundred *piculs* of the finest birds-nests, much black *ditto*, some camphor, *tripan*, honey, wax, *dammer*, *Buru* mats, fine *spars*; sago and pepper were formerly largely cultivated here. The pearl-banks of Tawi Tawi have been mentioned.

Tirun. The sea-ports of this last mentioned and valuable province, ceded to the English by the Sulos, are chiefly inhabited by Buguese people. The towns are Sibuku, Sambakung, Leo or Ledong, Sikatak, Sabellar, Kuran or Barrow, Talysion Dumaung, Tapeandurian. The principal ports are Kuran and Sibuku; they produce a large quantity of very fine white birds-nests, a quantity of black *ditto*, much *dammer*, sago, *tripan*, wax, rattans, camphor, honey, *Buru* mats, gold, &c. The people of Tapeandurian are represented as very ferocious, and the sea-coast hereabout requires surveying.

The ports of Pasir and Coti originally belonged to the King of Benjarmasing; very fine birds-nests are procured here at twenty dollars the *catty*; much gold, *tripan*, wax, &c.

431

Were Borneo to be settled, I think the principal factory ought to be at Borneo Proper; the second at Sambas; the third at Benjarmasing; the fourth at Pasir; the fifth at Tabesan or Sandakan.

In looking over the map of the world, it is a melancholy reflection to view so large a portion of the habitable globe as all Borneo abandoned to barbarism and desolation; that, with all her productive wealth and advantages of physical situation, her valuable and interesting shores should have been overlooked by all Europeans; that neither the Dutch nor the Portuguese, with centuries of uncontrolled power in these seas, should have shed a ray of civilization on shores bordering upon their principal settlements; that her ports and rivers, instead of affording a shelter to the extensive commerce of China, should at this enlightened period of the world hold out only terror and dismay to the mariner; and that all that she should have acquired from the deadly vicinage and withering grasp of Dutch power and dominion has been the art of more speedily destroying each other, and rendering themselves obnoxious to the rest of mankind.

Now that her destinies are transferred to the enlightened heads and liberal hearts of Englishmen,—now that her fortunes are embarked under the administration of a wise and liberal government,—we may confidently hope that a happier order of things will, under the blessing of an all-ruling Providence, speedily restore these extensive shores to peace, to plenty, and to commerce; and we ardently trust that another age may not be suffered to pass away without exhibiting something consolatory to the statesman, the philosopher, and the philanthropist.

## No. 9

### This is the Epistle of Laputongei, Rajah of Waju, and Consort, to Mr. James Brooke,

#### and to the company of Merchants at Singapore.

The Prince Laduka bows, embraces, and kisses his (adopted?) father Mr. Brooke, and presents the compliments of the Queen Arutempih.

This is our statement. We have all conferred as to making Reuring Tuah the Arongmatuah, and did so after your departure. The people of Waju have also conferred with their *rajahs*, and have sent to Boni and Sopeng twice, but have not yet received an answer. Sopeng would have given an answer, but was afraid to do it before Boni. This is the reason why we have as yet received no answer.

We now let fly this writing to Singapore, under this our seal, both we and our people earnestly hoping to meet Mr. Brooke, as soon as may be, in the Bugis country, now in this monsoon. We make known to the Singapore merchants, that all our traders are in the habit of coming to us, declaring that they can in nowise endure the restraints of the Dutch, since once we could bring English goods to this and other countries; whereas now they utterly forbid us. How can we get a livelihood in this way? We now ask, we and our traders, what think ye? Is this right? To us it seems out of the question, if things go on so, that Singapore can ever be much of a place.

As a mere *sign* of our regard (for there is no *substance* to it), Laputongei sends to Mr. Brooke two pieces of Bugis cloth, and to Mr. Boustead a couple of bags of coffee.

Given in the country of Waju, on the 15th day of the month *Jumadal Akhir,* on Tuesday, 1257.

## No. 10

### Natural History.

*Mr. Brooke's Report on the Mias. (From the Transactions of the Zoological Society.)*

James Brooke, Esq., to Mr. Waterhouse.

My dear Sir:—Singapore, 25th March, 1841.

I am happy to announce the departure of five live ourang-outangs by the ship Martin Luther, Captain Swan; and I trust they will reach you alive. In case they die, I have directed Captain Swan to put them into spirits, that you may still have an opportunity of seeing them. The whole of the five are from Borneo: one large female adult from Sambas; two, with slight cheek-*callosities,* from Pontiana; a small male, without any sign of *callosities,* from Pontiana likewise; and the smallest of all, a very young male with *callosities,* from Sadung. I will shortly forward a fine collection of skulls and skeletons from the northwest coast of Borneo, either shot by myself or brought by the natives; and I beg you will do me the favour to present the live ourangs and this collection to the Zoological Society. I have made many inquiries and gained some information regarding these animals, and I can, beyond a doubt, prove the existence of two, if not three, distinct species in Borneo.

First, I will restate the native account: secondly, give you my own observations; and thirdly, enter into a brief detail of the specimens hereafter to be forwarded.

1st. The natives of the northwest coast of Borneo are all positive

433

as to the existence of two distinct species, which I formerly gave you by the names of the *Mias pappan* and *Mias rombi*; but I have since received information from a few natives of intelligence that there are three sorts, and what is vulgarly called the *Mias rombi* is in reality the *Mias kassar*, the *rombi* being a distinct and third species. The *Mias pappan* is the *Simia Wurmbii* of Mr. Owen, having *callosities* on the sides of the face: the natives treat with derision the idea of the *Mias kassar*, or *Simia morio*, being the female of the *Mias pappan* or *Simia Wurmbii*; and I consider the fact can be established so clearly that I will not trouble you with their statements: both Malays and Dyaks are positive that the female of the *Mias pappan* has cheek-*callosities* the same as the male; and if on inquiry it prove to be so, the existence of three distinct species in Borneo will be established. The existence of the *Mias rombi* is vouched by a few natives only, but they were men of intelligence, and well acquainted with the animals in the wild state. They represent the *Mias rombi* to be as tall as the *pappan*, or even taller, but not so stout, with longer hair, a smaller face, and no *callosities* either on the male or female; and they always insisted that it was not the female of the *pappan*.

The *Mias kassar* or *Simia morio* is of the same colour as the *Mias pappan*, but altogether smaller, and devoid of *callosities* either on the male or female adults.

By the native statements, therefore, we find three distinct species, *viz.* the *Mias pappan* or *Simia Wurmbii*, the *Mias kassar* or *Simia morio*, and the *Mias rombi*, which is either the *Simia Abelii*, or a fourth species. The existence of the Sumatran ourang in Borneo is by no means impossible; and I have already compared so many of the native statements, that I place more confidence in them than I did formerly, more especially as their account is in a great measure borne out by the skulls in my possession. I had an opportunity of seeing the *Mias pappan* and the *Mias kassar* in their native woods, and killing one of the former and several of the latter species. The distribution of these animals is worthy of notice, as they are found both at Pontiana and Sambas in considerable numbers, and at Sadung on the northwest coast, but are unknown in the intermediate country which includes the rivers of Sarawak and Samarahan.

I confess myself at a loss to account for their absence on the Sarawak and Samarahan Rivers, which abound with fruit, and have forests similar and contiguous to the Sadung, Linga, and other rivers. The distance from Samarahan to Sadung does not exceed twenty-five miles; and though pretty abundant on the latter, they are unknown on the former river. From Sadung, proceeding to the northward and eastward, they are found for about 100 miles, but beyond that distance do not inhabit the forests. The *Mias pappan* and *Mias kassar* inhabit the same woods, but I never met them on the same day; both species, according to the natives, are equally common, but from my own experience the *Mias kassar* is the most plentiful.

The *Mias rombi* is represented as unfrequent and rarely to be met with. The *pappan* is justly named *Satyrus*, from the ugly face and disgusting *callosities*. The adult male I killed was seated lazily on a tree, and when approached only took the trouble to interpose the trunk between us, peeping at me, and dodging as I dodged. I hit him on the wrist, and he was afterward dispatched. I send you his proportions, enormous relative to his height; and until I came to actual measurement my impression was that he was nearly six feet in stature. The following is an extract from my journal relating to him, noted down directly after he was killed:—

"Great was our triumph as we gazed on the huge animal dead at our feet, and proud were we of having shot the first ourang we had seen, and shot him in his native woods, in a Borneo forest, hitherto untrodden by European feet. The animal was adult, having four incisors, two canines, and ten molars in each jaw; but by his general appearance he was not old. We were struck by the length of his arms, the enormous neck, and the expanse of face, which altogether gave the impression of great height, whereas it was only great power. The hair was long, reddish, and thin; the face remarkably broad and fleshy, and on each side, in the place of a man's whiskers, were the *callosities* or rather fleshy protuberances, which I was so desirous to see, and which were nearly two inches in thickness. The ears were small and well shaped, the nose quite flat, mouth prominent, lips thick, teeth large and discoloured, eyes small and roundish, face and hands black, the latter being very powerful. The following are the dimensions:

|                                                    | Ft. | In.   |
| -------------------------------------------------- | --- | ----- |
| Height from head to heel                           | 4   | 1     |
| Length of foot                                     | 1   | 0     |
| Ditto hand                                         | 0   | 10½   |
| Length of arm from shoulder-blade to finger-end    | 3   | 5¾    |

| | | |
|---|---|---|
| Shoulder-blade to elbow | 1 | 6 |
| Elbow to wrist | 1 | 1½ |
| Hip to heel | 1 | 9 |
| Head to *os coccygia* | 2 | 5½ |
| Across the shoulders | 1 | 5½ |
| Circumference of neck | 2 | 4 |
| Ditto below the ribs | 3 | 3¼ |
| Ditto under the arms | 3 | 0 |
| From forehead to chin | 0 | 9¾ |
| Across the face, below the eyes, including *callosities* | 1 | 1 |
| From ear to ear across the top of the head | 0 | 9½ |
| From ear to ear behind the head | 0 | 9¾ |

The natives asserted the animal to be a small one; but I am sceptical of their ever attaining the growth of a tall man, though I bear in mind that full-grown animals will probably differ as much in height as man."

Some days after this, and about thirty miles distant, I was fortunate enough to kill two adult females (one with her young), and a male nearly adult, all the *Mias kassar*. The young male was not measured, owing to my having waded up to my neck in pursuit of him, and thereby destroyed my paper and lost my measure; but he certainly did not exceed 3 feet, while the two females were about 3 ft. 1 in. and 3 ft. 2 in. in height. The male was just cutting his two posterior molars: the colour of all resembled that of the *Mias pappan*, but the difference between the two animals was apparent even to our seamen.

The *kassar* has no *callosities* either on the male or female, whereas the young *pappans* dispatched by the Martin Luther (one of them not a year old, with two first molars) show them prominently. The great difference between the *kassar* and the *pappan* in size would prove at once the distinction of the two species; the *kassar* being a small, slight animal, by no means formidable in his appearance, with hands and feet proportioned to the body, and they do not approach the gigantic extremities of the *pappan* either in size or power; and, in short, a moderately strong man would readily overpower one, when he would not stand the shadow of a chance with the *pappan*. Beside these decisive differences may be mentioned the appearance of the face, which in the *Mias kassar* is more prominent in the lower part, and the eyes exteriorly larger, in proportion to the size of the animal, than in the *pappan*.

The colour of the skin in the adult *pappan* is black, while the *kassar*, in his face and hands, has the dirty colour common to the young of both species. If further evidence was wanted, the skulls will fully prove the distinction of species; for the skulls of two adult animals compared will show a difference in size alone which must preclude all supposition of their being one species. Mr. Owen's remarks are, however, so conclusive, that I need not dwell on this point; and with a suite of skulls, male and female, from the adult to the infant, of the *Mias kassar*, which I shall have the pleasure to forward, there can remain, I should think, little further room for discussion. I may mention, however, that two young animals I had in my possession alive, one a *kassar*, the other a *pappan*, fully bore out these remarks by their proportionate size. The *pappan*, with two molars, showed the *callosities* distinctly, and was as tall and far stouter than the *kassar* with three molars, while the *kassar* had no vestige of the *callosities*.

Their mode of progression likewise was different, as the *kassar* doubled his fists and dragged his hind quarters after him, while the *pappan* supported himself on the open hands sideways placed on the ground, and moved one leg before the other in the erect sitting attitude; but this was only observed in the two young ones, and cannot be considered as certainly applicable to all.

On the habits of the ourangs, as far as I have been able to observe them, I may remark, that they are as dull and as slothful as can well be conceived, and on no occasion when pursuing them did they move so fast as to preclude my keeping pace with them easily through a moderately clear forest; and even when obstructions below (such as wading up to the neck) allowed them to get way some distance, they were sure to stop and allow us to come up. I never observed the slightest attempt at defence; and the wood, which sometimes rattled about our ears, was broken by their weight, and not thrown, as some persons represent.

If pushed to extremity, however, the *pappan* could not be otherwise than formidable; and one unfortunate man, who with a party was trying to catch a large one alive, lost two of his fingers, beside being severely bitten on the face, while the animal finally beat off his pursuers and escaped. When they wish to catch an adult, they cut down a circle of trees round the one on which he is seated, and then fell that also, and close before he can recover himself, and endeavour to bind him.

In a small work entitled *The Menageries*, published in 1838, there is a good account of the Borneon ourang, with a brief extract from

Mr. Owen's valuable paper on the *Simia morio*; but, after dwelling on the lazy and apathetic disposition of the animal, it states in the same page that they can make their way amid the branches of the trees with surprising agility; whereas they are the slowest and least active of all the monkey tribe, and their motions are surprisingly awkward and uncouth. The natives on the northwest coast entertain no dread, and always represent the ourangs as harmless and inoffensive animals; and from what I saw, they would never attack a man unless brought to the ground.

The rude hut which they are stated to build in the trees would be more properly called a seat or nest, for it has no roof or cover of any sort. The facility with which they form this seat is curious, and I had an opportunity of seeing a wounded female weave the branches together, and seat herself within a minute; she afterward received our fire without moving, and expired in her lofty abode, whence it cost us much trouble to dislodge her. I have seen some individuals with nails on the posterior thumbs, but generally speaking, they are devoid of them: of the five animals sent home, two have the nails, and three are without them; one has the nail well formed, and in the other it is merely rudimentary.

The length of my letter precludes my dwelling on many particulars which, as I have not seen the recent publications on the subject, might be mere repetitions; and I will only mention, as briefly as I can, the skulls of these animals in my possession. From my late sad experience I am induced to this, that some brief record may be preserved from shipwreck. These skulls may be divided into three distinct sorts. The first presents two ridges, one rising from each frontal bone, which, joining on the top of the head, form an elevated crest, which runs backward to the cerebral portion of the skull.

The second variety is the *Simia morio*; and nothing need be added to Mr. Owen's account, save that it presents no ridge whatever beyond the frontal part of the head. No. 9 in the collection is the skull of an adult male: No. 2 the male, nearly adult, killed by myself: Nos. 11 and 3 adult females, killed by myself: No. 12 a young male, with three molars, killed by myself: No. 21 a young male, died aboard, with three molars: No. 19, young male, died aboard, with two molars. There are many other skulls of the *Simia morio* which exactly coincide with this suite, and this suite so remarkably coincides through the different stages of age, one with another, that no doubt can exist of the *Simia morio* being a distinct species. The different character of the skull, its small size and small teeth, put the matter beyond doubt, and completely establish Mr. Owen's acute and triumphant argument, drawn from a single specimen.

The third distinction of the skulls is, that the ridges rising from the frontal bones do not meet, but converge toward the top of the head, and again diverge toward the posterior portion of the skull. These ridges are less elevated than in the first-mentioned skulls, but the size of the adult skulls is equal, and both present specimens of aged animals. For a long time I was inclined to think the skulls with the double ridge were the females of the animals with the single and more prominent ridge; but No. 1 (already described as killed by myself) will show that the double ridge belongs to an adult and not young male animal, and that it belongs to the *Simia Wurmbii* with the huge *callosities*.

The distinction therefore cannot be a distinction of sex, unless we suppose the skulls with the greater development of the single ridge to belong to the female, which is improbable in the highest degree. The skulls with the double and less elevated ridges belong, as proved by No. 1, to the *Simia Wurmbii*; and I am of opinion the single and higher ridge must be referred to another and distinct species, unless we can account for this difference on the score of age. This, I conceive, will be found impossible, as Nos. 7 and 20 are specimens similar to No. 1, with the double and less elevated ridges decidedly old, and Nos. 4 and 5 are specimens of the single high ridge, likewise decidedly old.

These three characters in the skulls coincide with the native statements of there being three distinct species in Borneo, and this third Borneon species may probably be found to be the *Simia Abelii*, or Sumatran ourang. This probability is strengthened by the adult female on her way home: her colour is dark brown, with black face and hands; and in colour of hair, contour, and expression, she differs from the male ourangs with the *callosities* to a degree that makes me doubt her being the female of the same species.

I offer you these remarks for fear of accident; but should the specimens, living and dead, arrive in safety, they will give a fresh impetus to the inquiry, and on my next return to Borneo I shall, in all probability, be able to set the question at rest, whether there be two or three species in that country. Believe me, my dear sir, with best wishes, to remain,

Yours very truly,
J. Brooke.

Borneo, like Celebes, teems with Natural History unknown to European science; and Mr. Brooke has sent some remarkable specimens to England, though his own large collection was, unfortunately, wrecked on its voyage homeward. Every arrival, however, is now adding to the stores we already possess. The British Museum has been much enriched, even within the last year, with rare specimens of zoology and botany; and at the Entomological Society there have been exhibited and described many curious insects hitherto strange and unclassified.

## No. 11

### PHILOLOGY.

It was intended in this work to convey to the studious in philology,—upon which science, rationally investigated, so much depends on our ability to ascertain the origin and trace the earliest relations of mankind,—as copious a vocabulary of the Dyak language, with definitions of meaning and cognate references, as might be considered a useful contribution to that important branch of learning. But various considerations have induced us to forego the design; and not the least of them has been, not the difficulty, but the impossibility of reducing the whole collection to a system, or of laying down any certain rule of orthography in this Oriental confusion.

Nearly all the vowels, for example, have been found of equal value; and as they have but one general Malay name, so it happens that (for instance) the consonants *b d* might be pronounced with the intervening sound, *bad, bed, bid, bod, bud*, and sundry variations beside, unknown to the English tongue. This will in a great degree account for the universally vexatious, because puzzling, spelling, inflections, and pronunciation of Eastern names, which is so injurious to the literature and knowledge of those countries among Europeans.

The vowel-sounds adopted are:

*a*   like   *a* in *father*.

*e*   ,,   *a* in *fan*.

*i*   ,,   Italian *i*, or *ee* in *thee*.

*ĭ*   ,,   *i* in *pin*.

*o*   ,,   *o* in *spoke*.

*u*   ,,   *oo* in *cool*.

*ŭ*   ,,   *u* in *run*.

*ow (ou)* like *ow* in *cow.*

The final *k* in Malayan is frequently mute : thus Dyak is pronounced Dya*h*, with the slightest possible aspiration.

The acute accent is used to shew on what syllable the accent falls, and when necessary for the pronunciation the syllables are divided thus, *apī͡un͡dow.*

*gn* is a liquid sound.

I conceive it beyond question, that the whole of these dialects form links in the chain of that primitive language entitled by Marsden the Polynesian. Marsden in the introduction to the Grammar, remarks: "The doubts which have arisen respect only the third, or that original and essential part which, to the Malayan, stands in the same relation as the Saxon to the English, and which I have asserted to be one of the numerous dialects of the widely extended language found to prevail, with strong features of similarity, throughout the Archipelago on the hither side of New Guinea, and, with a less marked resemblance, amongst the islands of the Pacific Ocean or South Sea. This language, which, in its utmost range, embraces Madagascar also, to the westward, may be conveniently termed the Polynesian, and distinguished, as already suggested, into the Hither (frequently termed the East insular language) and the Further Polynesian."

It is an extraordinary confirmation of these just views to find the dialects of the wildest and rudest tribes in Borneo—tribes far removed, and holding no communication one with another—forming links of the chain which extends so far over the insular portion of the globe, and is as yet untraced to either continent. Good vocabularies of the language of some of the South Sea islands, New Zealand, and Madagascar, might even at the present day throw farther light on our knovidedge of these dialects, which at the time that Marsden wrote was far inferior to what has subsequently been attained.

The *Orang Laut*, or the *Orang de bower angin*—for they disown the term of Malay—inhabiting the various rivers on the n.w. coast, all speak dialects of their own. Bruni, the capital, is stated to have been peopled by the Orang Laut from Johore; Sarawak from Java; Sadong, probably the same; Samarahan *from Pegu!* Linga from the island and kingdom of that name, corruptly called Lingin; Sarebus from Menangkabau in Sumatra: and all these may be called *patois* of the Malay language, mixed and corrupted by the Dyak dialects of the neighbourhood.

LEONAUR

# ALSO FROM LEONAUR

**AVAILABLE IN SOFTCOVER OR HARDCOVER WITH DUST JACKET**

**THE 9TH—THE KING'S (LIVERPOOL REGIMENT) IN THE GREAT WAR 1914 - 1918** *by Enos H. G. Roberts*—Mersey to mud—war and Liverpool men.

**THE GAMBARDIER** *by Mark Severn*—The experiences of a battery of Heavy artillery on the Western Front during the First World War.

**FROM MESSINES TO THIRD YPRES** *by Thomas Floyd*—A personal account of the First World War on the Western front by a 2/5th Lancashire Fusilier.

**THE IRISH GUARDS IN THE GREAT WAR - VOLUME 1** *by Rudyard Kipling*—Edited and Compiled from Their Diaries and Papers—The First Battalion.

**THE IRISH GUARDS IN THE GREAT WAR - VOLUME 1** *by Rudyard Kipling*—Edited and Compiled from Their Diaries and Papers—The Second Battalion.

**ARMOURED CARS IN EDEN** *by K. Roosevelt*—An American President's son serving in Rolls Royce armoured cars with the British in Mesopatamia & with the American Artillery in France during the First World War.

**CHASSEUR OF 1914** *by Marcel Dupont*—Experiences of the twilight of the French Light Cavalry by a young officer during the early battles of the great war in Europe.

**TROOP HORSE & TRENCH** *by R.A. Lloyd*—The experiences of a British Lifeguardsman of the household cavalry fighting on the western front during the First World War 1914-18.

**THE EAST AFRICAN MOUNTED RIFLES** *by C.J. Wilson*—Experiences of the campaign in the East African bush during the First World War.

**THE LONG PATROL** *by George Berrie*—A Novel of Light Horsemen from Gallipoli to the Palestine campaign of the First World War.

**THE FIGHTING CAMELIERS** *by Frank Reid*—The exploits of the Imperial Camel Corps in the desert and Palestine campaigns of the First World War.

**STEEL CHARIOTS IN THE DESERT** *by S. C. Rolls*—The first world war experiences of a Rolls Royce armoured car driver with the Duke of Westminster in Libya and in Arabia with T.E. Lawrence.

**WITH THE IMPERIAL CAMEL CORPS IN THE GREAT WAR** *by Geoffrey Inchbald*—The story of a serving officer with the British 2nd battalion against the Senussi and during the Palestine campaign.

Lightning Source UK Ltd.
Milton Keynes UK
UKOW042028201112

202509UK00001B/145/P